The Genealogist's Internet

To the memory of

Douglas Godfrey Christian

1923–1974

The Genealogist's Internet

4TH EDITION

Peter Christian

The National Archives

First published in 2009 by

The National Archives
Kew, Richmond
Surrey, TW9 4DU, UK

www.nationalarchives.gov.uk

The National Archives brings together the Public Record Office,
Historical Manuscripts Commission, Office of Public Sector
Information and Her Majesty's Stationery Office.

A catalogue card for this book is available
from the British Library.

ISBN 978 1 905615 39 1

Cover illustrations from back left to front right: the Countess of Dudley, 1891
(© Hayman Seleg Mendelsohn, COPY 1/409); George Knight, 1963; Annie
Christian nee Manning, the author's great-grandmother, c. 1928; John North,
1891 (© John Edward Shaw; COPY 1/409); Newhaven fishwife, 1895
(© Alexander Adam Inglis, COPY 1/419); The Reverend Lawson Gyre, 1895
(© Walter Mudford; COPY 1/420); Alex Lyons, from Pentonville's photograph
albums, 1879–83 (PCOM 2/103); Charlotte McCurry, the author's mother, c. 1947;
Frederick Marshall, the author's great-grandfather, c. 1915; source unknown;
Lily Hanbury, 1891 (© Elliott & Fry; COPY 1/409); John Isaac Cameron,
Waterloo veteran, 1890 (© Sidney Sutton Miller, COPY 1/400).
Document references are to National Archives' holdings.

Design by Goldust Design
Printed in the UK by
TJ International, Padstow, Cornwall

CONTENTS

PREFACE x
Citing internet addresses x
Disappearing resources xi
What's new in this edition xii
Acknowledgements.. xiii

1   INTRODUCTION 1
Genealogy and the internet 1
Offline genealogy 2
History 3

2   FIRST STEPS 6
Tutorials 6
Getting help 12
Genealogical terms and abbreviations 13

3   ONLINE STARTING POINTS 15
The British Isles 16
General genealogy gateways 21
Web directories 26

4   USING ONLINE SOURCES 28
Approaches to digitization................................ 28
Paying for records.. 30
Indexes, transcriptions and images 32
Indexing issues 33
Payment systems... 38
Major commercial data services 39
Document services 50
Image formats and viewers 52
Which data service? 57
Common problems.. 57

5   **CIVIL REGISTRATION** 60
      England and Wales 60
      Scotland 72
      Ireland 74
      Offshore 77
      Certificate exchanges 77
      Overseas 78

6   **CENSUS** 80
      General information 80
      Free census indexes 81
      The commercial services 84
      The 1911 census 88
      Comparison 91
      Ireland 95
      Overseas 98

7   **CHURCH RECORDS** 99
      Parish churches 100
      FamilySearch 101
      FreeReg 106
      Local resources 106
      Commercial data services 108
      Scotland 109
      Ireland 109
      The Roman Catholic Church 110
      Nonconformist churches 111
      Monumental inscriptions 113

8   **PROPERTY, TAXATION AND CRIME** 115
      Wills 116
      Land and taxation 120
      Crime 125

9   **OCCUPATIONS** 128
      Occupational terms 128
      General information 129
      Individual occupations 131
      The learned professions 134
      Company records 140
      Trade unions 141

10 THE ARMED FORCES 142

General information 142

The Royal Navy and merchant navy 144

The Army 148

The Royal Air Force 151

Medals 152

Commemoration 153

11 MIGRATION AND COLONIES 158

Passenger lists 161

The Americas 162

Australasia 164

Africa and the Caribbean 166

India 169

European immigration 171

12 PRINT SOURCES 175

Books 175

Directories 179

Newspapers 184

13 ARCHIVES AND LIBRARIES 192

Gateways to archives 193

The National Register of Archives 195

National archives 196

The national libraries 202

County record offices 203

Public libraries 203

University libraries 204

Family History Centers 205

The Society of Genealogists 208

Beyond the British Isles 208

14 SURNAMES, PEDIGREES AND FAMILIES 209

Surname interests 209

Pedigree databases 215

Genetics and DNA testing 224

Royal and notable families 226

Locating living people 232

15 GEOGRAPHY 237
  Gazetteers. 237
  Modern maps 245
  Historical maps 248
  Map collections 257
  Finding maps. 258
  Interactive mapping 258

16 HISTORY 260
  General resources 260
  Local history 261
  Social history. 264
  Names. 266
  Understanding old documents 270

17 PHOTOGRAPHS 279
  National collections 279
  Local collections 281
  Personal sites 284
  Commercial photographs 284
  Professional photographers. 285
  Portraits 286
  Dating, preservation, restoration 287
  Photo sharing 289

18 DISCUSSION FORUMS 293
  Mailing lists 293
  Newsgroups. 302
  Web forums 303
  Netiquette. 306
  Starting your own discussion group. 308
  Which discussion group?. 308

19 SEARCH ENGINES 310
  Using a search engine. 312
  Formulating your search 313
  Refining your search. 320
  Search tips 320
  Searching for files 321
  Sites and domains. 323
  Limitations. 324
  The 'invisible web'. 325

Choosing a search engine 326
Using multiple search engines. 329
Genealogy search tools. 330
Further information 331

20   PUBLISHING YOUR FAMILY HISTORY ONLINE 333
Publishing options 333
Family trees for the web. 335
Web publishing basics 338
Software 343
Website design. 352
Uploading your website 355
Publicity. 356
Preserving your family history 358
Help and advice. 358

21   THE WORLD OF FAMILY HISTORY 360
Societies and organizations 360
Events 361
Courses. 362
Magazines and journals 363
News. 366
Podcasting 370
Software 371
Online shops 373
Professional researchers. 376
Lookup services. 377

22   ISSUES FOR ONLINE GENEALOGISTS 379
Good practice 379
Using online information. 380
Copyright. 382
Privacy 383
Quality concerns. 385
Finding material 386
Longevity 387
Outlook 388

Internet Glossary. 390
Bibliography. 393
Index. 394

PREFACE

The statistics tell us that a large majority of the UK population have internet access at home,[1] and many others no doubt have access from work or a local library, so this book assumes a reader who has at least basic familiarity with the internet, using email and a web browser. However, I have not assumed any experience of other internet facilities, nor any technical knowledge, so even the absolute internet novice should not be unduly baffled. The book is about what you can do online rather than on the technology behind it. All the same, there are one or two areas where it's useful to have some understanding of how things work (and why they sometimes don't), so there is detailed discussion of search engines, mailing lists, and web publishing in the later chapters. The professional internet user will probably want to skip some of this, but the queries and problems which are raised in online discussion forums suggest that even quite seasoned internet users do not always exploit these resources as fully as they could.

This book also does not assume you are already an expert in genealogy, but it can't pretend to be a general introduction to researching your family tree, nor provide guidance in how to organize your research. The basics of family history are covered briefly in Chapter 2, 'First Steps', along with some recommended internet resources for the beginner, and the chapters relating to records explain briefly why you might want to look at those records. But if you are completely, or fairly, new to family history you'll need a good book on offline genealogy as well (see p. 6 for recommendations).

Citing internet addresses

In this book URLs (Uniform Resource Locators) for internet resources have been placed between angled brackets. According to strict citation

---

1   At the end of 2007, according to research from Ofcom, 67 per cent of UK adults had internet access at home, and 58 per cent a broadband connection (see <**www.ofcom.org. uk/research/cm/cmr08/**> – these statistics are taken from Figure 5.66 in the full report). In the March 2007 *Genealogists' Magazine* the Society of Genealogists published survey results which showed 77 per cent of its UK members with home internet access, and another 9 per cent accessing the internet in libraries.

standards, every internet resource should begin with a specification of its type: the National Archives home page on the World Wide Web should be cited as <http://www.nationalarchives.gov.uk/> rather than simply as <www.nationalarchives.gov.uk>. However, since web browsers manage perfectly well without the 'http//:' I have allowed myself to omit these. The URLs were pasted into the text of the book directly from the web browser. Sometimes, where an address starts with **www** you can actually omit this and it won't make any difference (as with <nationalarchives.gov.uk>, for example), but sometimes it will, and there's no way to work out in advance which.

Any hyphen within a URL is an essential part of the reference, not a piece of ad hoc hyphenation. Some of the longer URLs in this text have been broken over two lines for typographical reasons, but the URL should be read as an unbroken sequence of characters – there are *never* spaces or line breaks in internet addresses.

Addresses for web pages are *partially* case sensitive. Anything up to the first / is not case sensitive; anything after that usually *must* be in the correct case. In practice, URLs are mostly all lower case, but note that Genuki in particular uses upper case for county abbreviations (e.g. LAN in all the Lancashire pages) and often has the first letter after a / in upper case.

In general, titles of websites have been indicated solely by initial capitals, while individual pages are between inverted commas. However, the distinction between a site and page is not always easy to make, and I wouldn't claim to have been thoroughly consistent in this respect.

Occasionally, a URL has been so long that I have given instructions on how to get to the page rather than give the full URL. Unfortunately, this tendency for long URLs seems to be increasing, as more and more sites deliver their pages from a database or content management system. The longest URL for a resource mentioned in the book is a 187-character address for a page on the Customs and Excise site:

<customs.hmrc.gov.uk/channelsPortalWebApp/channelsPortalWebApp.
portal?_nfpb=true&_pageLabel=pageLibrary_PublicNoticesAndInfo
Sheets&propertyType=document&columns=1&id=HMCE_CL_000157>

County record offices seem to have a particular propensity for unwieldy URLs. In such cases the direct link is available on the website for this book at <www.spub.co.uk/tgi4/>.

Disappearing resources

Internet resources are in a constant state of flux. Each revision of this book finds around 20 per cent of the links in the previous edition no longer work or, even worse, take you to quite different material. All of the URLs will have been checked just before the book goes for printing, and if you're reading this as a newly published book you will find, with any luck, that none of the URLs have gone out of date while it was at the printers. As time goes by, you're certain to find *some* dead links; at some point one of the major sites will undergo a complete overhaul and two dozen links will expire overnight.

Of course, we should be grateful when out-of-date material is removed from public view, and it is only to be expected that personal sites will move or vanish without warning as people change internet service provider or decide they no longer have the time to maintain them. In a number of cases, valuable material is preserved only in the Internet Archive at <**www. archive.org**>.

Official and commercial sites are less likely to disappear as a whole, but are regularly being improved by redesign and reorganization, as one would wish. But unfortunately, their consideration for users does not always extend to redirecting you from the old pages to the new. Too often they simply tell you the old page is not there – actually not even that, they simply say there is no such page and don't indicate whether they've moved the page or you've mistyped the URL. They then expect you to use their search engine to see if the material is still anywhere on the site. To those responsible for such sites: sorry folks, I know that maintaining a large website is hard work, but this is bad practice, and doesn't do much for your image!

For print, this instability raises insurmountable problems, and it is something all internet books have to live with. But one of the advantages of the web is that links can be kept up to date, so on the website for this book at <**www.spub.co.uk/tgi4/**> there are links to all the resources mentioned in the text, and the aim is to keep those links current or, if necessary, to flag the material as no longer available.

What's new in this edition

The many resources that have moved or disappeared since the previous edition of this book are one good reason for revision. Some of the most important sites have undergone major reorganizations: the National Archives, the National Archives of Ireland, the Society of Genealogists, and the BBC Family History sites all have completely redesigned websites. Another change is that all RootsWeb's pages, long hosted by Ancestry, have been 'moved' to the Ancestry website.

But there are also some more positive reasons. For a start, we are now in a position where every publicly available census is available online, and this means a much more definitive and complete chapter on the census, including the newly-released 1911 census for England and Wales.

There have also been major changes in the commercial data services.

Rather surprisingly, there are now *fewer* of these than there were in the last edition of this book. In 2006, the National Archivist was taken over by Findmypast (renamed from 1837online), which in its turn became part of Brightsolid, the company behind ScotlandsPeople. FamilyHistoryOnline, the online data service of the Federation of Family History Societies, has announced a partnership with Findmypast and its imminent closure. (For that reason, although it is still online as this book goes to press, it has not been covered in this edition.) Stepping Stones has been bought up by TheGenealogist; the 1901 census has been purchased from QinetiQ by Genes Reunited. The Irish data service Otherdays seems to have vanished without trace, with another company using its domain name.

Many of the projects promised or in progress in the last edition, such as the Digital Library of Historical Directories (see p. 179) have now been launched or completed, though not, alas, the one we most need, the digitization of civil registration records, the postponement of which is discussed in Chapter 5. The most important new development, and one still in its early stages, is the new FamilySearch Record Search (p. 104) which will see millions of microfilms re-indexed and matched to digitized images.

But there have also been more general online developments which affect the genealogist. The major book digitization projects described in Chapter 12 have seen many older printed works, available in perhaps only a few specialist libraries, becoming freely available online. The spread of blogging, still something of a novelty amongst genealogists in the last edition, means that Google now finds over 200,000 genealogy blogs. Podcasting, too much of a novelty to make it into the previous edition, now has a firm place in the world of family history.

Thankfully, the National Archives have given me some extra pages to cope, in part, with this expansion. However, there are still many useful websites that simply could not be fitted in. This applies particularly to the material in Chapters 8 to 11 and to resources that are of purely local interest – here, the text will alert you to the sort of things that are available and highlight some of the best examples, but you will need to see for yourself whether there is equivalent material for a particular village, regiment, church, etc., that is relevant to your own family's history. Nonetheless, you will find further recommendations and some new post-publication discoveries among my public bookmarks at <**delicious.com/petex**>.

Acknowledgements

Many of the new sites covered in this edition are here because someone drew them to my attention. While I can't thank everyone who has ever mentioned a site to me, there are some who have been a regular source of new material: John Fuller's announcements of new mailing lists (p. 294),

Dick Eastman's online newsletter (p. 366), and the Cyndi's List mailing list (p. 21) have all been invaluable. In the five years of writing my monthly internet news column for *Ancestors*, I have often been alerted to new resources by the editor, Simon Fowler. Indeed, coverage of internet resources in the family history magazines has increased significantly in the last two years, and this has been useful in keeping up to date. The increasing number of genealogy news blogs (see p. 367) have also been helpful (Figure 21-5 will show you which ones I have relied on).

Again, I have to thank John Dawson for suggesting a number of improvements over the previous edition. The collaboration with David Annal, my co-author on *Census: The Expert Guide*, published to coincide with the online release of the 1911 census, has helped me to make a number of improvements to the census coverage.

Finally, since things are changing at such a rapid rate, I am grateful to the commercial data services for providing advance information on forthcoming developments on their sites. Particular thanks are due to Elaine Collins of Findmypast for giving me pre-launch access to the 1911 census of England and Wales (see p. 88) and answering many questions on the project.

Peter Christian

Stop Press

Ancestry have made an important addition to their civil registration data at <www.ancestry.co.uk>, described on pp. 67–68. The site now offers the GRO birth indexes for England and Wales 1916–2005 in the form of a searchable database with links to images of the pages of the index volumes. Information about this dataset will be found at <www.ancestry.co.uk/search/db.aspx?dbid=8782>.

Also, the National Archives of Scotland has launched the Scottish Register of Tartans at <www.tartanregister.gov.uk>. This is the official national repository of information on tartans, and the register includes the tartans of both clans (see p. 230) and army regiments (see p. 149).

1

INTRODUCTION

Genealogy and the internet

The steady growth in the number of people interested in family history may have its roots in greater leisure time, and it is no doubt a reaction to social and geographical mobility. Recent television series devoted to family history, and the use of DNA testing to trace migration patterns, have certainly contributed to a surge of interest. But above all this is closely related to the growth of the internet and the fact that the majority of the population now have internet access. While the internet has not changed the fundamental principles of genealogical research, it has changed the way in which much of that research is done and made a huge difference in what the individual genealogist can do with ease.

Indexes to primary records, in many cases linked to a digitized image of the original document, are now widely available online. Even where records themselves are not online, the ability to check the holdings of record offices and libraries via the web means that a visit can be better prepared and more productive. Those who have previously made little progress with their family tree for lack of time or mobility to visit archives can pursue their researches much more conveniently, with access to many records from their desktop. Likewise, those who live on the other side of the world from the repositories which hold records of their ancestors' lives can make progress without having to employ a researcher. Online data is a boon, too, for anyone who has difficulty reading from microfilm or original records.

Archives have realized that the internet is also a remedy for some of their pressing concerns: lack of space on their premises, the need to make their collections available while preserving them from damage, not to mention the pressure from government to provide wider access. In addition, there is the obvious commercial potential: online record transcriptions can attract distant and, particularly, overseas users in large numbers, while even those living less far away will use a charged service which saves them time and travel costs.

Genealogists also benefit from the ease with which messages and electronic documents can be exchanged around the world at effectively no cost. It is easier than ever to contact people with similar research interests, and even to find distant cousins. It is easier than ever, away from a good genealogy library or bookshop, to find expertise or help with some genealogical problem. And if you need to refer to a book, there are genealogy bookshops with online catalogues and secure ordering, and for older books you may even find the whole text online.

Any information stored digitally, whether text or image, can be published on the web easily and more or less free of cost to both publisher and user. This has revolutionized the publishing of pedigrees and other family history information. It has allowed individuals to publish small transcriptions from individual records, material which it would otherwise be difficult to make widely available. Individual family historians can publicize their interests and publish the fruits of their researches to millions of others.

The internet has enhanced cooperation by making it possible for widely separated people to communicate easily as a group. While collaborative genealogy projects did not start with the internet, email and the web make the coordination of vast numbers of geographically distributed volunteers, such as the 10,000 or so involved in FreeBMD (see p. 62), much easier.

Offline genealogy

Over the last few years the internet has matured as a resource for family historians. There is now hardly any aspect of the subject which is not catered for online. In some cases, such as census records, the online facilities have made their offline predecessors more or less redundant. I'm sure it is now the case that anyone starting out on their family history assumes that most of their research will be carried out online. Inevitably, however, this has given rise to unrealistic expectations in some quarters. Stories of messages posted to mailing lists asking, 'Where will I find my family tree online?' are not apocryphal.[2]

The fact is that if you are only beginning your family tree, you will have plenty to do offline before you can take full advantage of what is online. For a start, because of privacy concerns, you won't find much online information about any ancestors born less than a century ago. Scotland has some more recent records online for marriages and deaths (see p. 72), but for England and Wales there are so far only *indexes* to twentieth-century birth, marriage and death records online. This means that in tracing the most recent generations most of the work must be done offline, though for living people you may well be able to find addresses, phone numbers and perhaps websites.

---

2 See 'Internet Genealogy' at <**www.cyndislist.com/internet-gen.htm**> for a look at some of the common misconceptions about what the internet can do for the genealogist.

But even if recent primary records are not online, you can still expect to make contact with other genealogists who share your interests. To do this effectively, however, you will need to have established a family tree for the last three or more generations. The reason for this is as follows: you presumably know or knew your grandparents and their siblings (your great aunts and uncles), so you know or are at least aware of your first and second cousins. On the whole, then, any new relatives discovered via the internet will be no closer to you than third cousins, descended from your great-great-grandparents, who were born perhaps 100 or so years before you. Unless you know the names of your great-great-grandparents and where they came from, you will probably not be in a position to establish that you are in fact related to someone who has posted their pedigree online.

Of course, if your surname is unusual, and particularly if your family has not been geographically mobile in recent generations, you may be able to make contact with someone researching your surname and be reasonably certain that you are related. Or you may be lucky enough to find that someone is doing a one-name study of your surname. In this case, they may already have extracted some or all of the relevant entries in the civil registration records, and indeed may have already been able to link up many of the individuals recorded.

But, in general, you will need to do work offline before you can expect to find primary source material online and before you have enough information to start establishing contact with distant relatives.

However, one thing that is useful to every family historian is the wealth of general genealogical information and the huge range of expertise embodied in the online community. For the absolute beginner, the internet is useful not so much because there is lots of data online, but because there are many places to turn to for help and advice. And this is particularly important for those who live a long way away from their family's ancestral home.

All the same, it is important to remember that, whatever and whoever you discover online, there are many other sources for family history which aren't on the web. If you restrict yourself to online sources you may be able to construct a basic pedigree back to the nineteenth century, but you won't be able, reliably, to get much further, and you will be seeing only the outline of your family's history. On the other hand, if you are one of those who refuses on principle to use the internet (and who is presumably reading this by accident, or to confirm their worst fears), you are just making your research into your family history much harder than it need be.

History

We now take the ready availability of genealogical records and information on the World Wide Web for granted. But most of the sites we rely on are of relatively recent origin. Before 2002, there were *no* UK censuses online, for example; before 2003, no civil registration indexes. Indeed, only a handful of genealogy sites can trace their history back to the twentieth century: FamilySearch was launched in 1999, Cyndi's List in 1996, Genuki in 1995. But in fact the web is only the latest electronic medium for genealogy resources, and 'online genealogy' has a longer history that those statements suggest.

On the internet itself, before the web had been invented, online genealogy started in 1983 with the newsgroup net.roots and with the ROOTS-L mailing list. Net.roots became soc.roots, and eventually spawned all the genealogy newsgroups discussed in Chapter 18; ROOTS-L gave rise to RootsWeb <**www.rootsweb.ancestry.com**>, the oldest online genealogy co-operative, now hosted by Ancestry.[3]

But in the 1980s internet access was still largely confined to academia and the computer industry, so for many people online genealogy meant bulletin boards run by volunteers from their home computers and accessible via a modem and phone line. A system called FidoNet allowed messages and files to be transferred around the world, albeit slowly, as each bulletin board called up its neighbour to pass messages on. The only commercial forums were the growing online services which originally targeted computer professionals and those in business, but which gradually attracted a more disparate membership. Of these, CompuServe, with its Roots forum, was the most important. One significant feature of these commercial services was the ability to access them from all over the world, in many cases with only a local call. Even so, to keep costs down, people would make sure they kept their time online to a minimum.

These systems had the basis of what genealogists now use the internet for: conversing with other genealogists and accessing centrally stored files. But the amount of data available was tiny and discussion was the main motivation. Part of this was down to technical limitations: with modem speeds something like five hundred times slower than a modern broadband connection, transferring large amounts of data was unrealistic or at best painfully slow, except for the few with deep pockets or an internet connection at work. No government agencies or family history societies had even contemplated an online presence, though genealogical computer groups were starting to spring up by the end of the 1980s.

What changed this was the World Wide Web, created in 1991 (though it was 1995 before it started to dominate the internet), and the growth of

---

3   For a history of the newsgroups, see Margaret J. Olson, 'Historical Reflections of the Genealogy Newsgroups' at <**homepages.rootsweb.ancestry.com/~socgen/Newshist.htm**>. For the history of ROOTS-L and RootsWeb, see <**www.rootsweb.ancestry.com/ roots-l/**>.

commercial internet services. The innovation of the web made it possible for a large collection of material to remain navigable, even for the technologically illiterate, while at the same time the explosion in public use of the internet was providing the impetus for it to become more user-friendly.

The result of these developments is that the internet is now driving developments in access to genealogical information – just as computers had done in the 1980s, and microfilm before that. This in turn is drawing more people to start researching their family tree, which increases the chance of encountering distant cousins online, and motivates data holders to make their material available on the web.

We are also seeing a change in online culture brought about by a new wave of changes, often referred to as 'Web 2.0'. Until recently, the internet was treated by most people as a combination of library and postal service – you used the web to retrieve information and email to correspond with friends and family. A relatively small number of family historians actually used the web to publish their own family trees. But the last few years have seen the development of a much greater level of interactivity, whether it is in social networking sites like Facebook and YouTube, in the ability to run a blog which people can comment on, or in the move towards online software to replace the applications on the computer desktop. The combination of these developments and the rise of the always-on broadband connection means that the internet is less a special place to go and get information, more just a natural part of the research environment of anyone tracing their family tree.

The Genuki Timeline at <**homepages.gold.ac.uk/genuki/timeline/**> identifies some of the more significant online developments for UK family historians and gives starting dates for key websites and online facilities.

2

FIRST STEPS

Your first online steps in genealogy will depend on how much research you have already done on your family tree, and what your aim is. If you are just beginning your family history, you will be able to use the internet to help you get started, but you shouldn't expect to find much primary source material online, i.e. original records, until you get back to the early twentieth century.

The box on the next page shows a simplified outline of the process of constructing a family tree, which is the foundation on which your family history will be built. For the first two steps, you will find indexes to certificates online (see Chapter 5), but not the certificates themselves, and online materials won't help you work out which is going to be the certificate you need. This stage is mostly about interpreting information from family members and trying to verify it. It's only once you get to step 4 that you will find a significant amount of source material online. In the initial stages, the internet will probably be more important as a source of information, help and advice. The material in the 'Tutorials' and 'Getting help' sections below should help you get going.

If you are not new to family history, but have just started to use the internet, your needs will be rather different. You will already be familiar with civil registration and census records, and know what is involved in researching your family tree, so your initial questions will not be about constructing a family tree but: what's online and how do I find it? Who else is working on my family?

▌ Tutorials

One area where the internet resources still have a great deal of catching up to do is in tutorial material for the new family historian. It will be some time before you can start your family tree without a good reference book. If you are a relative beginner, you might start with Anthony Adolph's *Collins Tracing Your Family History*, or Nick Barrett's *'Who Do You Think You Are?' Encyclopedia of Genealogy*. If you have already made some progress, Mark Herber's *Ancestral Trails* should be on your bookshelf.

1. Interview your elderly relatives and collect as much first- or second-hand information as you can (and continue doing so, as you find out more in subsequent steps).
2. Get marriage and birth certificates for the most recently deceased ancestors.
3. From these, work back to the marriages and then births of the parents of those ancestors.
4. Keep repeating this process until you get back to the beginning of General Registration (1837 for England and Wales, later for Scotland and Ireland).
5. Once you have names and either places or actual addresses for a date in the nineteenth or early twentieth century, you should refer to the censuses to see
   (a) whole family groups
   (b) birth places
   (c) ages, from which you can calculate approximate birth years.
6. Once you have found a census entry for an adult ancestor who was born before General Registration, use the birth place and age information in the census to locate a baptism in parish registers.
7. From this, work back to the marriages, and then baptisms, of the parents of that ancestor in the parish registers.
8. Repeat for each line of your ancestry until you hit a brick wall (at which point you will need to consider other approaches and other sources).

Nonetheless, while individual web resources cannot compare in scope to these printed works, there is a great deal of helpful, if more basic and concise, material online covering the essentials of genealogical research in the British Isles.

One important source for such materials is Genuki (described more fully in Chapter 3, p. 18), which has a page devoted to 'Getting Started in Genealogy and Family History' at <**www.genuki.org.uk/gs/**>. There are individual pages on major topics, such as that for 'Civil Registration in England and Wales' at <**www.genuki.org.uk/big/eng/civreg/**>. Roy Stockdill's concise but comprehensive 'Newbies' Guide to Genealogy and Family History' is available on Genuki at <**www.genuki.org.uk/gs/Newbie.html**>.

The FamilyRecords portal (see p. 16) has a guide for beginners at <**www. familyrecords.gov.uk/guides/beginners.htm**>, while the National Archives has extensive introductory material on its website. Its 'In-depth learning guides' include material on family history, local history, and palaeography.

The family history section is at <**www.nationalarchives.gov.uk/family history/guide**>.

The Society of Genealogists (SoG) has a number of introductory leaflets online at <**www.sog.org.uk/leaflets.html**>. Though they are not designed as a coherent introduction to family history, they include 'Starting genealogy' and 'Note taking and keeping for genealogists'. The Federation of Family History Societies (FFHS) has 'Research Tips. First Steps in Family History' at <**www.ffhs.org.uk/tips/first.php**>. GenDocs has a substantial page for those 'New To Family History' at <**homepage.ntlworld.com/hitch/ gendocs/newbie.html**>.

The BBC has long had an excellent family history site, and, with the popularity of *Who Do You Think You Are?*, it has been much expanded. At the time of writing, a revised site is under development at <**www.bbc.co. uk/familyhistory/**> (Figure 2-1). It's not yet clear what the full range of material will be (and the addresses of some pages will no doubt change), but there are two main tutorial sections linked from the current home page, 'The Basics' and 'Next Steps'. There are pages devoted to many aspects of

Figure 2-1 The BBC's Family History site

family history including surnames, genetics, and military records. There are also useful links to local BBC sites which have relevant material, message boards, and photos submitted by users. BBC Wales has its own family history site at <**www.bbc.co.uk/wales/history/sites/themes/family. shtml**> with some material specifically relating to Welsh family history.

The *Guardian* has an online version of a printed guide from 14 April 2007 edition of the paper at <**lifeandhealth.guardian.co.uk/guides/ familyhistory/0,,2053687,00.html**> (yes, that's two consecutive commas), with a wide range of material including a step-by-step guide and articles on topics such as Caribbean family history, dating photographs, etc.

For an introduction which focuses on web resources, see the online history magazine *History in Focus* (see p. 365) which has a 'Family History on the Internet' guide in its launch issue at <**www.history.ac.uk/ihr/Focus/ Victorians/family.html**>.

StudyAncestors is a fairly new site at <**www.studyancestors.com**> with detailed sections devoted to certificates, census records and graves. The 'Advanced Genealogy' pages tackle subjects like adoption, wills, and passenger lists, though some of these are still fairly brief.

Probably the most comprehensive set of guides to British and Irish family history are the material on the FamilySearch website of the Church of Jesus Christ of Latter-day Saints (LDS). From the home page at <**www. familysearch.org**> select 'Guidance' from the 'Research Helps' menu. There are separate 'Search Strategy' pages for England, Wales, Scotland and Ireland. Each of these has links to material on looking for births, marriages and deaths in the three main periods for genealogical research: general registration, parish registers, and before parish registers. Clicking on the 'For Beginners' tab will take you to general material on:

- organizing your paper files
- how to find the name of the place where your ancestor lived
- how to find information about the place where your ancestor lived
- how to find maps
- how to find compiled sources

One important limitation of this material, though, is that it tends to point you to books or microfilms in the Family History Library (see p. 206) and often makes no mention of online sources. For example, the 'England: Newspapers' page does not even hint at the newspaper material online, described under 'Newspapers' on p. 184ff.

If you select 'Articles' from the 'Research Helps' menu at FamilySearch, you get a list of documents, sorted by place. There are a number of guides for each of England, Wales, Scotland and Ireland. The 'Research Outline' is

CIVIL REGISTRATION: DEATH
1855 to the Present

Use Death Certificates To:
- Find your ancestor's death information.
- Establish a time and place of residence.
- Find the names of your ancestor's parents.

Tips
- Always note the informant. He or she may be a family member, and his or her address may suggest another locality to search for information.
- The certificate often indicates whether or not the parents of the deceased person are living.

CONTENT	1855	1856–1860	1861–1966	1967–present
Full name and occupation	X	X	X	X
Date, time, and place of death	X	X	X	X
Age	X	X	X	X
Marital status	X	X	X	X
Usual residence if different than place of death	X	X	X	X
Parents' names (including mother's former names) and whether deceased	X	X	X	X
Cause of death and name of medical attendant	X	X	X	X
Burial place and undertaker's name	X	X	X	X
Name of spouse	X	X		
Names of children and their ages (or, if deceased, their age at death)	X			
Informant's name, signature, and relationship (if any)	X	X	X	X
Date of birth				X

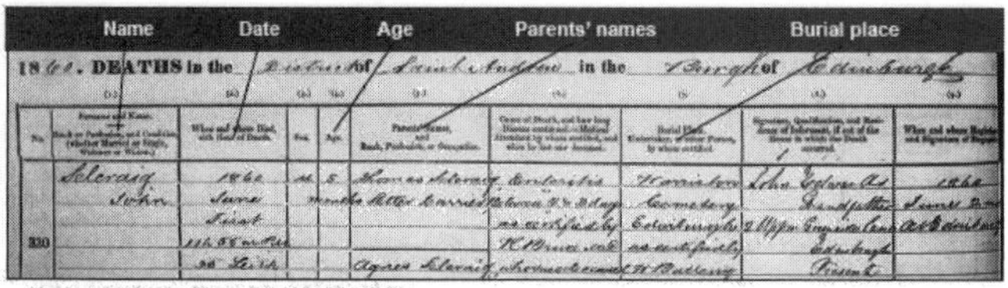

Name	Date	Age	Parents' names	Burial place

186*. DEATHS in the ... of ... in the ... of ...

1860 death certificate of Thomas Selcraig's brother John

Searching Death Certificates

Before searching this record, you must know:
- Your ancestor's name.
- The date or approximate date of death.
- The place or approximate place of death.

Knowing the spouse's name can also be helpful.

This record is located at:
www.scotlandspeople.gov.uk

Search by your ancestor's name.

Figure 2-2 A page from Finding Records of your Ancestors Scotland at FamilySearch

a set of web pages covering all the major records. For England and Scotland there are substantial guides in PDF format called 'Finding Records of your Ancestors' which cover all the basics for the start of your research. Figure 2-2 shows the page on Scottish death certificates. Each guide covers only the period from the start of civil registration to the 1901 census, but they are ideal once you start to get back beyond the living generations.

There are also class materials for those beginning research into English genealogy>. From the 'Education' page at <**www.familysearch.org/eng/library/Education/frameset_education.asp**> (or select 'Education' from the 'Library' menu) the link to 'Family History Library Research Series Online' leads to videos and class outlines for five lessons in the basics of English genealogy.

As you will see, the site has material for many other countries (and for individual US states), making it a good place to start for ancestors from outside the British Isles.

Other introductory material specific to Scottish research includes the 'Getting Started' section of ScotlandsPeople – go to <**www.scotlandspeople. gov.uk**>, select 'Help & Other Resources', then 'Getting Started' – and the Scottish Archive Network's family history pages at <**www.scan.org.uk/ familyhistory/**>. Genuki has an 'Introduction to Scottish Family History' at <**www.genuki.org.uk/big/sct/intro.html**>.

For Ireland, the Irish Ancestors site has an excellent range of introductory material at <**www.irishtimes.com/ancestor/browse/**>, including information on the counties and emigration (see Chapter 11) and good pages on the various Irish genealogical records. This is based largely on John Grenham's book *Tracing your Irish Ancestors*. Also by John Grenham is the 'Irish Roots' section of Moving Here (see p. 158) at <**www.moving here.org.uk/galleries/roots/irish/irish.htm**>. The Irish Genealogy Toolkit at <**www.irish-genealogy-toolkit.com**> offers guidance on getting started in Irish family history.

On Cyndi's List (see p. 21) you will find a comprehensive 'Beginners' page at <**www.cyndislist.com/beginner.htm**>, and a collection of links on 'Researching: Localities & Ethnic Groups' which will be useful if you need to start looking for ancestors outside the UK and Ireland. Cyndi's 'How to: tutorials and guides' page at <**www.cyndislist.com/howtotut.htm**> provides an outline of all the introductory materials on seven major genealogy sites. These sites are US-based, so much of the material on specific records will not be of use unless you are tracing American ancestors. However, this page should help you find some of the more general information buried in these sites.

About.com has a large collection of introductory articles at <**genealogy. about.com**>. The best way to find material on particular topics is to go to the list of articles by category at <**genealogy.about.com/blresourceindex. htm**>. Although, again, many of the articles on specific records are intended for those researching American ancestry, there is useful material on general topics, such as 'Top Ten Genealogy Mistakes to Avoid' at <**genealogy. about.com/od/basics/ss/mistakes.htm**>, and links to articles on the British Isles will be found at <**genealogy.about.com/od/british_isles/**>.

Wikipedia's 'Genealogy' page at <**en.wikipedia.org/wiki/Genealogy**> has links to articles on the major types of record used in genealogy and a number of other introductory topics. The material is not specific to any one country.

If you are trying to research British or Irish ancestry from overseas, Genuki's 'Researching From Abroad' page at <**www.genuki.org.uk/ab/**>

will be useful. The SoG has a leaflet 'Notes for Americans on tracing their British ancestry' online at <**www.sog.org.uk/leaflets/americans.pdf**>.

If you are unfamiliar with the administrative subdivision of Britain into counties and parishes, you should consult Jim Fisher's page 'British Counties, Parishes, etc. for Genealogists' at <**homepages.nildram.co. uk/~jimella/counties.htm**>. This also explains the meaning of names for regions such as the Peak District or the Wirral, which are not those of administrative divisions and are not necessarily well-defined. Genuki's pages on 'Administrative Regions of the British Isles' at <**www.genuki.org. uk/big/Regions/index.html**> is worth consulting. See also the section on 'Counties and towns' on p. 242.

Getting help

Even with these tutorial materials, you may still have a question you can't find an answer to. One solution is to use a search engine to find pages devoted to a particular topic (see Chapter 19). However, this can be a time-consuming task, since you may end up following quite a few links that turn out to be useless before you find what you are looking for. Also, if you are new to family history, it may not be easy to establish how authoritative or comprehensive the material is.

The various discussion forums discussed in Chapter 18 are ideal places for getting help and advice. Before posting a query to one of these, though, make sure you read the FAQ (Frequently Asked Questions) – see p. 306. This will give the answers to the most common questions. The FAQ for the main mailing list for British genealogy, GENBRIT, will be found at <**www. genealogy-britain.org.uk**>.

There are a number of mailing lists for beginners, notably GEN-NEWBIE-L 'where people who are new to computers and genealogy may interact'. Information on how to join this list will be found at <**www. rootsweb.ancestry.com/~newbie/**>, and past messages are archived at <**archiver.rootsweb.ancestry.com/th/index/GEN-NEWBIE**>. UK-GENEALOGY-NEWBIES is a similar list with a specifically UK focus – details at <**lists.rootsweb.ancestry.com/index/intl/UK/UK-GENEALOGY-NEWBIES.html**> – but it seems rather quiet, with only 16 message for the whole of 2008, so it may not be very helpful. If you are already a member of a family history society, it may have a mailing list where you can turn to other members for assistance. Another place to look is the archive of newsgroup messages (see p. 303) on Google Groups at <**groups.google.com**>.

Enquire is a 'UK collaborative [*sic*] of over 80 public libraries throughout England and Scotland staffing the service', and part of the People's Network. It replaces the earlier 'Ask-a-Librarian' service. Unfortunately it has a really unhelpful URL: <**www.questionpoint.org/crs/servlet/org.oclc.home.TFS Redirect?virtcategory=10836**>. You can email a question and you will get a reply within two working days. Alternatively, you may get an immediate response via the online chat facility during the working day. As you would expect, the service is basically a library reference service, so don't expect them to search original records on your behalf to find your great-grandparents' marriage.

Genealogical terms and abbreviations

Whatever your level of experience in family history, you're very likely at some point to come across unfamiliar terms and, especially, abbreviations. Internet resources for legal terms are covered in Chapter 16 (p. 275) while words for obsolete occupations are covered in Chapter 9 (p. 128). But genealogy as a discipline has its own specialist terms, which may baffle at first.

GenealogyPro has a Glossary of Genealogy Terms at <**genealogypro. com/details/glossary.html**> with around 130 entries, while Sam Behling has a page of about 400 terms at <**homepages.rootsweb.ancestry. com/~sam/terms.html**>. Gareth Hicks' page on Technical Words/ Expressions at <**home.clara.net/tirbach/hicks3.html**> is arranged under a number of key topic headings, which is useful if you're not sure of the distinction between a vicar, rector and parson, for example. This provides quite detailed explanations of historical terms, and is more or less an encyclopedia. Dr Ashton Emery's 'A-Z Of British Genealogical Research' at <**www.genuki.org.uk/big/EmeryPaper.html**> covers about 100 important terms presented as a dictionary rather than a connected account. As this has not been updated in the last ten years, references to organizations will often be out of date, but the other material remains useful.

In the long run, the most comprehensive online reference work of this type will probably be the collaborative online Encyclopedia of Genealogy at <**www.eogen.com**>, started by Dick Eastman in 2004, which has articles on a wide range of topics, entries for abbreviations, and acronyms for genealogy organizations. The advantage of this project is that it allows users to comment on and correct the entries, as well as submitting new entries of their own.

If you have to read documents written in a language other than English then FamilySearch has wordlists of key genealogical words in 15 European languages at <**www.familysearch.org/Eng/Search/rg/research/type/Word_ List.asp**>. These lists are not comprehensive but should at least help you identify key words like 'husband', 'parish' and 'baptism'. Web resources for Latin are discussed in more detail on p. 273.

One frequent question from those getting started is about the meaning of phrases like 'second cousin once removed'. To help you with this,

About.com has a Genealogy Relationship Chart at <**genealogy.about.com/ library/nrelationshipchart.htm**>. Genealogy.com's article 'What is a First Cousin, Twice Removed?' at <**www.genealogy.com/genealogy/16_cousn. html**> explains all. Irritatingly, if you try and access this page via a UK ISP you will get an intervening page which asks whether you want to remain on Genealogy.com or go to the Ancestry UK site – select Genealogy.com, otherwise you will end up at the Ancestry UK home page.

For making sense of abbreviations and acronyms, there are a number of sites to help you. Most of the glossaries mentioned earlier include many abbreviations. Mark Howells has a page devoted to 'Common Acronyms & Jargon' found in UK genealogy at <**www.oz.net/~markhow/acronym-uk. htm**>, and RootsWeb has a more general list of abbreviations used in genealogy at <**www.rootsweb.ancestry.com/roots-l/abbrevs.html**>. But by far the most comprehensive is GenDocs' 'Genealogical Abbreviations and Acronyms' page at <**homepage.ntlworld.com/hitch/gendocs/abbr.html**> with over 2,000 entries.

For links to other online dictionaries and lists of abbreviations, look at the page on Cyndi's List devoted to 'Dictionaries & Glossaries' at <**www. cyndislist.com/diction.htm**>. The *Oxford English Dictionary* is discussed on p. 178, and dictionaries for other language on p. 273ff.

3

ONLINE STARTING POINTS

Subsequent chapters in this book are devoted to particular types of genealogical resource or internet tools. This one looks at some of the online starting points for genealogy on the web, sites which provide links to other resources. These go under various names: directory, gateway or portal. Although these terms are often used interchangeably, there are in principle distinctions to be made:

- An internet directory is the electronic equivalent of the Yellow Pages, a list of resources categorized under a number of subject headings.
- A gateway is a directory devoted to a single subject area, and may also offer knowledgeable annotation of the links provided as well as additional background information. A gateway is not just a directory; it can be more like a handbook.
- A portal is a site which aims to provide a single jumping-off point on the internet for a particular audience, bringing together all the resources they might be interested in. Like a gateway, a portal may provide information as well as links.

In genealogy, since the audience is defined by its interest in a particular subject, it is not always possible to maintain a clear distinction between gateways and portals. 'Portal' tends to be the preferred term in the case of a site which has some official status or which aims to be definitive. Both gateways and portals are selective and only include links to recommended resources, whereas directories tend to be less scrupulous. (The term 'gateway' is also used in a quite different sense, see p. 302.)

Directories, gateways and portals are not the only way to find information on the internet: general-purpose search engines such as Google <**www.google.com**>, discussed in Chapter 19, can also be used to find genealogical material online. The differences between directories, gateways and portals on the one hand and search engines on the other are summarized in Table 19-1 on p. 311. The most important is that directories, etc. provide lists of web*sites* while search engines locate individual web *pages*, so the former are better for locating significant resources on a particular topic rather than mere mentions of a subject. This makes them preferable for initial exploration. The fact that the entries are selected, and perhaps helpfully annotated, makes them even more useful. However, there are certain things they are poor for, notably information published on the personal websites of individual family historians, and material relating to individual surnames.

The British Isles

There are two online starting points which are essential for British genealogy: the FamilyRecords portal, which is the government's gateway to official websites for family historians; and Genuki, which aims to be comprehensive in its coverage of sites relating to genealogy in the British Isles. In addition, there are a number of other official and unofficial sites which provide starting points for exploring specifically British and Irish internet material. Sites linking to more general resources are discussed later in this chapter (p. 26ff.).

FamilyRecords

The FamilyRecords portal at <**www.familyrecords.gov.uk**> (Figure 3-1) is run by a consortium made up of the National Archives, Public Record Office of Northern Ireland, National Archives of Scotland, National Library of Wales, General Register Office, General Register Office for Scotland, and British Library India Office. The site provides basic information about the major national repositories, including contact details and links to their websites – this is in the 'Partners' area of the site at <**www.familyrecords.**

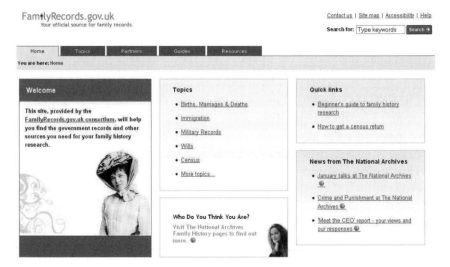

Figure 3-1 The FamilyRecords portal

gov.uk/partners.htm>. In the 'Topics' area at <www.familyrecords.gov.uk/
topics.htm> are brief descriptions of the main types of public record, with
links to the bodies that hold them. Although deliberately limited in scope,
it provides a good way of locating specific material on the official websites.
The websites of the individual bodies linked to the FamilyRecords portal
are discussed under 'Civil registration', Chapter 5, and under 'National
Archives' in Chapter 13 (p. 196ff.). If you're an experienced family historian
you'll probably find little on this site beyond what you already know, but
it's an excellent starting point for the relative novice because it's concise,
authoritative and well focused on your initial needs.

Directgov

While the FamilyRecords portal is restricted to genealogical coverage, there
is also a general-purpose government gateway called Directgov at <www.
direct.gov.uk>. This site provides access to *all* official information online,
with links to all branches of local and national government. It therefore
covers local authorities, who are responsible for county record offices and
public libraries (whose sites are not linked from FamilyRecords). The
easiest way to find these is via the 'Find your local authority' link from the
home page. There is a search facility as well as alphabetical indexes of
national and local government services. Library and record office websites
are covered in Chapter 13.

Ireland

There is, as you'd expect, no link from FamilyRecords to official bodies in
the Republic of Ireland, but the official website of the Irish government will
be found at <www.irlgov.ie>, and this has links to sites of government
departments and state organizations.

The National Archives of Ireland at <www.nationalarchives.ie> has a
genealogy page at <www.nationalarchives.ie/genealogy/> with links to
information on Irish sources and other useful websites.

Genuki, described in the next section, has a comprehensive collection
of links to Irish material online at <www.genuki.org.uk/big/irl/>. The
Irish Ancestors site has links to the major Irish bodies with genealogical
material at <www.irishtimes.com/ancestor/browse/links/>, with sub-pages
devoted to libraries, societies and individual counties, as well as to
passenger lists and emigration resources. Irish libraries and archives
are covered in Chapter 13, while Irish civil registration is covered in
Chapter 5.

Genuki

The most comprehensive collection of online information about family history for the British Isles, with an unrivalled collection of links, is Genuki, the 'UK & Ireland Genealogical Service' at <**www.genuki.org.uk**>. Genuki describes itself as 'a virtual reference library of genealogical information that is of particular relevance to the UK & Ireland'. As a reference source, the material it contains 'relates to primary historical material, rather than material resulting from genealogists' ongoing research'. This means it is effectively a handbook of British and Irish genealogy online. But Genuki also functions as a gateway, simply because it has links to an enormous number of online resources for the UK and Ireland, including every genea-logical organization with a website.

Genuki has its origins in the efforts of a group of volunteers, centred on Brian Randell at the University of Newcastle and Phil Stringer at the University of Manchester, to set up a website for genealogical information in 1995, when the World Wide Web was still very young. Genuki has always been an entirely non-commercial and volunteer-run organization. All the pages are maintained by a group of about 50 volunteers on many different websites, mostly at UK universities or on the personal sites of the volun-teers. Many other individuals have provided information and transcripts of primary data. Genuki started as an entirely informal group, but is now a charitable trust.

There are two distinct parts to Genuki. First, there are a number of pages devoted to general information about family history in the British Isles:

- 'Frequently Asked Questions' (FAQs) – typical queries asked by Genuki users
- getting started – a range of beginners' guides or links to them (see 'Tutorials' on p. 6)
- pages devoted to individual general topics, such as 'Military Records' or 'Immigration and Emigration', all linked from <**www.genuki.org.uk/big/**> (many of these are mentioned in later chapters)
- researching from abroad – useful links for those who dwell outside the UK, especially in North America
- world genealogy – a small collection of links for those researching non-British ancestry
- genealogical events relating to UK and Ireland ancestry (see p. 361)
- information on Genuki itself – how it is run, the principles on which it is structured

Second, it provides information on and links to online resources for all the constituent parts of the British Isles, with pages for:

England   Contents   Information relating to all of Sussex   Sussex Towns & Parishes

SUSSEX

Sussex, maritime County in SE. of England, bounded N. and NE. by Surrey and Kent, SE. and S. by the English Channel, and W. and NW. by Hants; greatest length, N. and S., 27 miles; greatest breadth, E. and W., 76 miles; area, 933,269 acres, population 490,505. From the Hants border, near Petersfield, to Beachy Head, the county is traversed by the South Downs; to the N. of this range of chalk hills is the valley of the Weald, rising into the Forest Ridge on the NE., and sinking on the SE., towards the sea, into wide marshes. The rivers are not important; they are the Arun, Adur, Ouse, and Rother, all flowing S. to the English Channel. ...more

[Transcribed from *Bartholomew's Gazetteer of the British Isles*, 1887.]

- Archives and Libraries
- Bibliography
- Census
- Church History
- Church Records
- Civil Registration
- Court Records
- Description and Travel
- Directories
- Genealogy
- History
- Language

- Maps
- Memorial Inscriptions
- Military History
- Names, Geographical
- Newspapers
- Occupations
- Poorhouses, Poor Law, etc.
- Probate Records
- Societies
- Taxation
- Voting Registers

Information Relating to All of Sussex

Archives & Libraries

- The East Sussex Record Office is located in Lewes. It holds material for the Archdeaconry of Lewes, present-day East Sussex, and therefore generally holds historical material only for East Sussex parishes.
  - An on-line catalogue for some of the collections held by the ESRO is available under the Access to Archives (A2A) project.
- The West Sussex Record Office is located in Chichester. Because it hold the records of the Diocese of Chichester, which covers the whole of Sussex, it has church records relating to both parts of Sussex.
  - An on-line catalogue for some of the collections held by the WSRO is available under the Access to Archives (A2A) project.

Figure 3-2 A Genuki county page

- England, Wales, Scotland, Ireland, the Isle of Man, and the Channel Islands
- every individual county in these areas
- many individual towns and parishes

The county pages (see Figure 3-2) in turn provide links to the websites of:

- county record offices and other repositories of interest to family historians (see Chapter 13)
- local family history societies (see Chapter 21)
- county and other local mailing lists (see Chapter 18)
- county surname lists (see Chapter 14)
- any online data collections for the county
- other online resources relating to genealogy in the county

Each county page (Sussex is shown in Figure 3-2) has a link to a list of individual towns and parishes, and many of these have their own pages with local information and links.

Most material on Genuki will be found on these geographical pages, which are organized hierarchically. Figure 3-3 shows a diagram of the hierarchy.

Genuki also has central listings of:

- national genealogical organizations and local family history societies at <**www.genuki.org.uk/Societies/**>
- all mailing lists relevant to British and Irish genealogy at <**www.genuki. org.uk/indexes/MailingLists.html**>
- all county and other surname lists at <**www.genuki.org.uk/indexes/ SurnamesLists.html**>

Because of the enormous amount of material on Genuki – there are almost 90,000 pages – it is well worth taking the time to look at the 'Guidance for First-Time Users of These Pages' at <**www.genuki.org.uk/org/**>, which

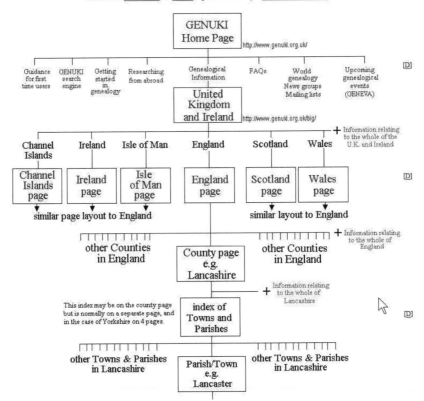

Figure 3-3 How Genuki is organized

gives an outline of what Genuki is. There is a more detailed online user guide 'How the information on this server is presented to the user' at <**www.genuki.org.uk/org/user.html**>.

A particular virtue of Genuki is that it uses well-defined subject categories, which are based on those used in the LDS Church's library catalogue and have therefore been designed by genealogically literate librarians. Its coherent coverage of every county, with a long-term aim of covering every parish, is the other feature which makes it useful. The list of categories used on Genuki is shown in Table 3-1.

Some of these categories – Handwriting or Politics and Government, for example – will be relevant only at the top, national levels, but topics such as church records, local records and maps should be represented on every county page. Since the list of subject headings pre-dates the internet, there are no specific categories for internet-related subjects such as surname lists and mailing lists, so Genuki places these under the Genealogy heading.

Genuki also has a search facility at <**www.genuki.org.uk/search/**>, discussed on p. 331.

Because Genuki is very comprehensive, it can be easy to overlook the fact that there are things it does not do. First, it has deliberate restrictions in its linking policy: it does not link to sites which provide information only on an individual family, pedigree or surname; its links are strictly confined to sites which are relevant to UK and Ireland genealogy. However, as long as what you are looking for is available online and falls within Genuki's scope, you should expect to find it listed.

Another service Genuki does not provide is answering genealogical queries from individuals. There is a Genuki email address, but this is intended only for reporting errors on the site or drawing attention to new resources not listed on Genuki. See 'Getting help' on p. 12 and Chapter 18 for places to post genealogical queries.

General genealogy gateways

If you have ancestors who lived outside the British Isles you will need to look at some of the general genealogy directories and gateways. And even if all your ancestors were British or Irish, there are good reasons to use other gateways and directories. Since FamilyRecords and Genuki take a strictly geographical approach, you need to look elsewhere for genealogical resources, such as computer software, which are not tied to a particular country or region.

Cyndi's List

The most comprehensive genealogy gateway is Cyndi's List at <**www.cyndislist.com**>, maintained by Cyndi Howells. You can get an idea of the

Table 3-1 Genuki subject headings

Almanacs	Merchant Marine
Archives and Libraries	Migration, Internal
Bibliography	Military History
Biography	Military Records
Business and Commerce Records	Minorities
Cemeteries	(Monumental Inscriptions – see
Census	Cemeteries)
Chronology	Names, Geographical
Church Directories	Names, Personal
Church History	Naturalization and Citizenship
Church Records	Newspapers
Civil Registration	Nobility
Colonization	Obituaries
Correctional Institutions	Occupations
Court Records	Officials and Employees
Description and Travel	Orphans and Orphanages
Directories	(Parish Registers – see Church
Dwellings	Records)
Emigration and Immigration	Pensions
Encyclopedias and Dictionaries	Periodicals
Ethnology	Politics and Government
Folklore	Poorhouses, Poor Law, etc.
Gazetteers	Population
Genealogy	Postal and Shipping Guides
Guardianship	Probate Records
Handwriting	Public Records
Heraldry	Religion and Religious Life
Historical Geography	Schools
History	Social Life and Customs
Inventories, Registers, Catalogues	Societies
Jewish History	Statistics
Jewish Records	Taxation
Land and Property	Town Records
Language and Languages	Visitations, Heraldic
Law and Legislation	(Vital Records – see Civil
Manors	Registration)
Maps	Voting Registers
Medical Records	Yearbooks

scope of the list, which has over 250,000 links, from the 180 or so main categories on the home page.

Unlike Genuki (p. 18) or Yahoo (p. 26), Cyndi's List has a fairly flat structure: most subject headings lead to a single page, while a few act as indexes to a whole group of pages on their subject (these have the word 'index' in their title). So, for example, the main UK page at <**www.cyndislist.com/ uksites.htm**> acts simply as an index to the sub-pages devoted to the various parts of the British Isles, to general UK sites and to British military sites. The advantage of this flat structure is that you don't have to go deep into a hierarchy to find what you're looking for; the disadvantage is that the individual pages tend to be quite large.

Alongside the main home page, Cyndi provides other, quicker ways to get to where you want once you are familiar with the site. There are four other 'home pages':

- The 'No Frills' index is essentially the home page, but with just the headings, no descriptions or update information, and no cross-references.
- The 'Alphabetical Category' index is a complete list of all pages and subpages in alphabetical order, with cross-references.
- The 'Topical Category' index lists all categories under 11 main headings (Localities, Ethnic Groups and People, Religions, Records, Research Tools and Reference Materials, Help from Others, Marketplace, History, Military, Internet Tools for Genealogy, Miscellaneous).
- The 'Text Only Category' index.

There are links to these from a box in the left-hand column of the home page and it is worth bookmarking the one you prefer. Particularly if you are using a dialup rather than broadband connection, these may be preferable home pages as they are quicker to load than the main home page.

Even if your genealogical interests are confined to the British Isles, a number of categories and topics on Cyndi's List are worth noting. The pages devoted to individual religious groups will be useful if you have Catholic, nonconformist or Jewish ancestors (covered in Chapter 11). The 'Software & Computers' page <**www.cyndislist.com/software.htm**> has a very useful collection of links for genealogy software. The 'Personal Home Pages' section at <**www.cyndislist.com/personal.htm**> lists several thousand websites of individuals, while the 'Surnames' pages linked from <**www. cyndislist.com/surnames.htm**> has thousands of sites for individual surnames.

Cyndi's List also has a very comprehensive page of 'Handy Online Starting Points' at <**www.cyndislist.com/handy.htm**>, with about 100 sites which provide general genealogy links.

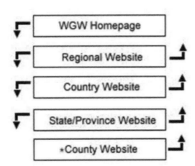

* Not all countries have counties.
The term county is used here in the general sense and
refers to the most common political or administrative district
in a country. Other names include shires, parish, townlands,
states, prefects, rajones, etc.

Figure 3-4 How WorldGenWeb is organized

GenWeb

For ancestors from outside the British Isles, you will find a wide coverage of countries and regions on Cyndi's List. But there is also a purely geographical gateway with worldwide coverage in the GenWeb projects. In GenWeb, the world is split into a number of regional projects, each of which has its own website, and a separate volunteer is responsible for each individual country or island in the region. Apart from USGenWeb at <**www.usgenweb. org**> and CanadaGenWeb at <**www.rootsweb.ancestry.com/~canwgw/**>, which are independent, the remainder are coordinated under the WorldGenWeb project at <**worldgenweb.org**>.

In all, there are around 100 countries, islands or island groups for which there are actively-maintained websites, grouped as follows:

- Africa
- Asia
- British Isles, including the Falkland Islands, Gibraltar, St Helena
- Canada
- Central Europe (actually Northern Europe would be a more accurate description)
- Caribbean
- Eastern Europe
- Mediterranean (actually more like Southern Europe, since it excludes African and Middle Eastern states, though it includes Turkey)
- Middle East
- North America (actually Central America, since it excludes Canada and the USA)

- Pacific, including Australasia
- South America
- United States

Most of the links to UK and Irish material at <**www.britishislesgenweb. org**> will in fact be found on Genuki, whose county pages are generally more comprehensive. So the real strength of the GenWeb sites, from the point of view of British and Irish family historians, lies in the material relating to former British colonies and those countries from which immigrants came to the UK (see Chapter 11). The Caribbean GenWeb at <**www. rootsweb.ancestry.com/~caribgw/**>, for example, is an essential starting point for West Indian ancestry.

There is huge variation in the amount of material available: for some countries there is a single page, while for others there are individual pages for administrative subdivisions, for example French *départements*. In general, the level of detail does not go down to the equivalent of individual parishes, though for each US state there are pages for the constituent counties. The structure of GenWeb, taken from <**worldgenweb.org/policy. html**>, is shown in Figure 3-4.

While most of the pages are in English, quite a few are maintained by natives of the countries concerned and are in the local language. Some, notably the Caribbean and South American pages, are available in more than one language.

On the WorldGenWeb projects, the topics on each page are sorted under the following headings:

- History
- Resource Addresses (libraries, archives)
- Society Addresses
- Maps
- Geography
- Culture and Religious History
- Query Board
- Mail List
- Reference Materials (census, deeds, biographies)

Beyond this, the pages do not necessarily have the same layout or look. A useful feature to note is that every GenWeb page has a Query Board where readers can post queries. Such a board is often available for countries which have no maintained web page.

Other gateways

While Cyndi's List may be the most widely used general genealogy directory, and Genuki is certainly the pre-eminent gateway for UK material, there are many others. Each has its own particular strengths, though many are US-based and are therefore naturally stronger in US resources. There is not enough space here to list them all, let alone describe them in detail. The following represent a small selection:

- The Genealogy Gateway at <**www.gengateway.com**>
- Genealogy Links at <**www.genealogylinks.net**>
- I Found It! at <**www.gensource.com/ifoundit/**>

Many others are listed on the 'Handy Online Starting Points' on Cyndi's List at <**www.cyndislist.com/handy.htm**>.

The sites discussed in this chapter are general genealogy gateways with some pretension to be comprehensive, but there are also gateways which are devoted to particular aspects of genealogy or which, although not primarily aimed at genealogists, are useful for family history.

Intute, the publicly-funded education and research gateway at <**www. intute.ac.uk**>, is probably the most generally useful of these. It has a highly selective and well-annotated database of links on all academic subjects. It does not have a 'genealogy' or 'family history' subject heading, but the general search can be used to find relevant entries. It incorporates the National Maritime Museum's old Port gateway, with its material on naval history and naval service (see Chapter 10), and the 'History' category includes many resources useful to family historians, as is discussed in more detail on p. 260).

Other relevant gateways are mentioned in the appropriate chapter.

Web directories

In addition to the genealogy gateways discussed so far, the general directories of the Web also provide genealogical links. On the whole, anyone who is sufficiently interested in genealogy to be reading this book will probably find them less useful than the dedicated sites already mentioned, not least since they do not seem to be edited and maintained by people with expertise in the subject, and cannot aim to be comprehensive.

Yahoo

The best known and most widely used directory is Yahoo <**dir.yahoo.com**>. This organizes subjects in a hierarchical structure, and the main Genealogy area comes under History, itself a subsection of Humanities. However, companies that sell genealogy products will be found under the Business heading, and genealogy resources for individual countries will be found under the relevant country heading. The main general page for genealogy is <**dir.yahoo.com/arts/humanities/history/genealogy/**>, and there is UK-specific material at <**uk.dir.yahoo.com/Regional/Countries/United_ Kingdom/Arts_and_Humanities/Humanities/History/Genealogy/**> . You can get a complete list of relevant Yahoo subject pages by doing a search on *genealogy*, as there are many other areas of Yahoo which will have material of interest to a family historian.

Although Yahoo, like other directories and gateways, is selective, its basis of selection is not entirely satisfactory since it depends in part on submissions from websites that want to be listed. For example, only a handful of UK family history societies are listed; the National Archives and the FamilyRecords sites are not listed at all! To be honest, Yahoo's genealogy pages might just be useful for someone who is wondering what genealogy is, but any other site in this chapter will be a much better general starting point.

The Open Directory Project

The Open Directory Project at <**dmoz.org**> is a non-commercial web directory, entirely maintained by volunteers. (Yahoo does not, of course, charge users, but it does carry advertising and give prominence on some pages to sponsored links.) Genealogy comes under the heading 'Society' at <**dmoz.org/Society/Genealogy/**>.

There is no UK version, and so the links for some of the categories have a US bias – 'Immigration', for example, means immigration into the USA – but many of the other topics such as 'Heraldry' or 'Software' (under 'Products and Services') are of general relevance. Specifically UK material will be found at <**dmoz.org/Regional/Europe/United_Kingdom/**>. A particular strength of the Open Directory is its collection of genealogy links for ethnic groups (on <**www.dmoz.org/Society/Genealogy/By_ Ethnic_Group/**>) and the links on the main genealogy page to equivalent pages for other languages.

4

USING ONLINE SOURCES

The core of any family history research in the British Isles is the information drawn from the registrations of births, marriages and deaths over the last 170 years, and from the records of christenings, marriages and burials in parish registers starting in the sixteenth century. Linking these two sources are the census records, which enable an address from the period of civil registration to lead to a place and approximate year of birth in the time before registration.

Chapters 5 to 7 examine online sources for each of these sets of records in turn. The aim of this chapter is to look at some of the general issues of using the internet for genealogical data and the major data services which provide access to these records online.

Approaches to digitization

While the internet is the ideal way of making all this material widely available, particularly to those who are distant from the relevant repositories and major genealogical libraries, the fact is that a huge amount of work is involved in publishing such material on the web. For example, there may have been as many as 100 million births, marriages and deaths registered between 1837 and 1900; between them, the censuses of England and Wales from 1841 to 1911 include details of 200 million individuals. Nonetheless, there has been enormous progress over the past few years in putting genealogical data online.

There are a number of ways in which genealogical data projects can be funded. Volunteer-run projects tend to rely entirely on goodwill and occasional sponsorship, while a number of projects have public funding, usually from the Heritage Lottery Fund or from academic funding sources. In such cases, access to the data is normally free. Other data holders have taken three main routes to making their records available online commercially:

- setting up an inhouse data service
- partnership with a commercial firm for a combined data service (e.g. ScotlandsPeople)

- licensing of data to third parties

The first of these was the route taken by the National Archives for its document service DocumentsOnline (see p. 51). The Federation of Family History Services took the same route to provide a consolidated service for indexes created by individual local family societies with its FamilyHistoryOnline site. In this case, the digital data was already available. However, the technical and administrative infrastructure required to run such a service is quite considerable for a relatively small charitable organization, and so it is perhaps not surprising that FamilyHistoryOnline is closing as an independent data service and has announced a partnership with Findmypast.

The most notable example of the second option is ScotlandsPeople, which hosts all the Scottish civil registration, census and parish register records for Scotland from the General Register Office for Scotland. The link here is so close that operational details of the service, such as the charges, have to be approved by the Scottish Parliament. This approach also seems to be the one chosen by the GRO for its stalled project to digitize civil registration records for England and Wales (p. 71).

However, this option does also raise questions: it's one thing for a charity like the Society of Genealogists to sign an exclusive deal with a particular commercial provider for indexes it has itself created. It's quite another for a government agency to grant a monopoly to a single company for public records that are being digitized from scratch. One result of this can be seen in ScotlandsPeople: for all the site's merits, the quality of the images is quite poor by contemporary standards, and in the absence of competition there is no incentive to improve them. On the other hand, the various commercial sites offering census data for England and Wales have been regularly improving the images they provide, so as not to lose subscribers. Also, given that all indexes have a significant level of error, the presence of a monopoly index means that the records of some individuals, in the absence of an alternative index with *different* errors, are essentially unfindable. As it happens, Ancestry UK have gone ahead and created their own Scottish census indexes without the agreement of GROS (and apparently without any legal repercussions), but have been refused permission to offer digitized images, so one still needs to go to ScotlandsPeople to verify the information.

In the case of the 1901 census for England and Wales, although the digitization started out as an exclusive arrangement between the National Archives and QinetiQ, the films were ultimately made available for wider licensing. The result was that Ancestry launched its own 1901 census index in April 2004, with other companies following, so that the original index now has three competitors. For the 1911 census, even though the initial digitization contract involves an exclusive deal with Brightsolid/Findmypast, once the entire census has been online for six months, the images will be available for other companies to licence and create their own indexes for. This seems a good solution to the issue of how to fund the initial digitization (which is *very* expensive) while giving scope for alternative indexes.

In fact, there are signs that the regime in Scotland will be changing. According to the 'GROS Strategic Corporate, General and Key Business Objectives for 2007–08' at <**www.gro-scotland.gov.uk/files1/about-us/gros-corporate-general-key-business-objectives/j878603.htm**>, GROS aims in the future to 'offer licences to other providers to further improve the availability of on-line family history information to customers'. Though there has been no firm news of developments on this front at the time of writing (January 2009), GROS has clarified that they anticipate two possibilities: 'a licence to enable a company to use digital images and indexes already created by GROS; and a licence that would enable a company to make digital images and indexes of the original records'. The major data services described later in this chapter will presumably go for the latter.

All this suggests that licensing is going to be the dominant option for the foreseeable future, where substantial collections of records are concerned (though for local sources an inhouse service no doubt remains preferable and practicable). Indeed, from the present perspective, it is hard to see how it can be otherwise. Now that there are several well-established data services, each with a substantial customer base and the ability to undertake new large-scale digitizations, it would seem to be problematic, in spite of competitive tendering, for government agencies to have long-term exclusive deals with one company for sets of national records. But the close association of record providers and digitizers seen in some of these projects is nonetheless beneficial, since those providing the records will be aware of many of the problems in the original documents, and their involvement can help to ensure a better quality of digitization.

The civil registration records may occupy a special place, because the digitization is not primarily aimed at genealogists. Rather, the main aim is to ensure that accurate birth, death and marriage data is available to all arms of government. Still, it's difficult to imagine that there won't be pressure for these records, too, to be available under licence, though it would be reasonable for this only to apply to the older records.

Paying for records

All this takes for granted that genealogists *should* be paying to access digitized public records. But prior to the release of the 1901 census in January 2002, there was considerable debate within the genealogical community about the appropriateness of government agencies, already funded by the taxpayer, seeking income by charging for online access to public records. There was a feeling that the limited offline availability of the 1901 census on microfiche, which cynics viewed as a move to safeguard online income, took insufficient account of the many people who had no internet access.

Of course, that particular argument has now lost any validity it might have had at the time. Anyone who has difficulty finding a place with internet access nowadays will surely find it even harder to get to the National Archives or a record office! For almost everyone, the costs of using a commercial data service are significantly less than the costs in time and travel of visiting a repository, not to mention the fact that the money goes to the data providers rather than to transport or oil companies. In fact, if you *can* get to the National Archives in Kew, you can indeed enjoy free access to much of the data for England and Wales.

But in fact, now that internet access is so widely available whether in the home or from public libraries, providing a service primarily online is not the contentious issue it once was. Indeed, with the government promoting the use of the internet for the delivery of all sorts of services, it is now very hard for a public body to publish *any* records or data without being obliged to make it available on the web.

Also, it shouldn't be forgotten that traditional modes of access to records are also heavily biased against quite large groups of people: anyone who is not mobile, lives far from repositories they need to consult, or has no free time during the working day has always found it hard to make progress with their family history. One of the reasons for the growth of genealogy in recent years is that the internet has made it realistic for these people to devote time to family history research.

Leaving aside the matter of principle, however, the fact is that progress on digitizing the nation's historical records would have been very much slower if it had to be done from existing funds or rely on Lottery funding. Look at FreeBMD: even with 10,000 volunteers and good infrastructure it has taken 10 years to transcribe 160 million very brief records, many of which are in printed form (see p. 62). Since the creation of large digital resources is immensely expensive at a time when public funding for repositories is decreasing, charging really is the only option unless we are prepared to wait quite a long time.

And one mustn't overlook the argument of the non-genealogists: unless you're prepared to start contributing to their football season tickets or yoga classes, why should they be subsidizing your hobby?

Although one still comes across complaints in the online discussion forums about having to pay for access to public records, nowadays this argument has little merit and certainly no realistic hope of succeeding.

Indexes, transcriptions and images

There are three main ways in which any historical textual source can be represented digitally:

- as an image – the original document is scanned
- in a transcription – the full text of a document is held in a file
- as an index – a list of names, with or without other details, directs you to the relevant place in a transcription or to the relevant scanned image, or provides you with the full reference to an original document

Ideally, an online index would lead to a full transcription of the relevant document, which could then be compared to an image of the original. But for material of any size this represents a very substantial investment in time and resources, and very little of the primary genealogical data is so well served, and nor is it likely to be in the foreseeable future.

The reason for this is the very great disparity between the amount of data involved in making text and images available online. In spite of advances in information technology, images require significantly more resources from the website which hosts them, both in terms of disk space to store them and the bandwidth to download them to the user. Even disregarding any costs for creating the digital images of source documents, for a large project this can mean enormous differences in financial practicability between a text-only data collection and one which includes digitized documents.

Images can be supplied economically for census records because they are central to family history and are universally needed, which means that costs can be covered. This has also been done in a number of lottery-funded projects for less widely-used material, such as the Old Bailey Proceedings (see p. 125), where costs do not have to be recouped at all. It has been done for wills, where a transcription of the entire document would be commercially impracticable, but where a higher charge can be made for a complete digitized document. Certainly for non-commercial projects images of records are the exception – the only major examples that spring to mind are FreeBMD (p. 62) and the new FamilySearch Indexing Project (p. 104).

However, there are many more images than transcriptions. For a document containing running text, a transcription takes much more time to prepare than an index, and except for particularly difficult documents (e.g. a seventeenth-century will) is not really necessary, as long as there is good indexing. A project like the Old Bailey Proceedings, which has document images with an indexed transcription, is in fact very exceptional. On the other hand, it is certainly true that with some sources, such as the censuses, comprehensive indexing can sometimes approach a full transcription.

Most online data, then, comes in the form of indexes linked to images, or, more often, just plain indexes. And this has important implications for how you use the internet for your research: you simply cannot do it all online. Except where you have access to scans of the original documents, all information derived from indexes or transcriptions will have to be checked against the original source. This might not be apparent to you if you are just starting out, since the first online sources you use, the GRO indexes and census records, are available as images, but you will find a very different story once you get back beyond 1837. Older printed sources will have been scanned, but there are as yet very few earlier manuscript sources which have been digitized.

Indexing issues

The perfect index would be made by trained palaeographers, familiar with the names and places referred to and thoroughly at home with the hand-writing of the period, working with original documents. Their work would be independently checked against the original, and where there was uncertainty as to the correct reading this would be clearly indicated.

Needless to say, very little of the genealogical material on the web has been transcribed in this way. The material online has been created either in large-scale projects or by individual genealogists, and often working from microfilms, or digitized images of them, not original records. On large-scale projects the data are input at best by knowledgeable amateurs such as family history society members, but more often by clerical workers. In the latter case, there will always be a question about the quality of data entry. It is self-evident that adequate levels of accuracy can only be achieved where there are good palaeographical skills, and knowledge of local place names and surnames.

Even so, one must recognize that our manuscript historical records are sometimes very hard to read, never mind transcribe with absolute certainty. Although I am quite critical of the quality of online indexes, one cannot escape the fact some of the errors are completely understandable, and one cannot really expect a commercial index to a census of say 20 million individuals to allow transcribers five minutes to stare at every difficult surname. When compiling the error statistics for the online censuses, reported on p. 94, I spent many hours poring over the pages for a single small enumeration district and was still left with an average of perhaps one surname every other page I could not be absolutely sure of. It would be unfair to expect non-expert clerks working to commercial targets to do better. To see the sort of thing a transcriber has to cope with, look at the scans for a servant in the household of Sarah Maskell in the 1871 census for Peckham

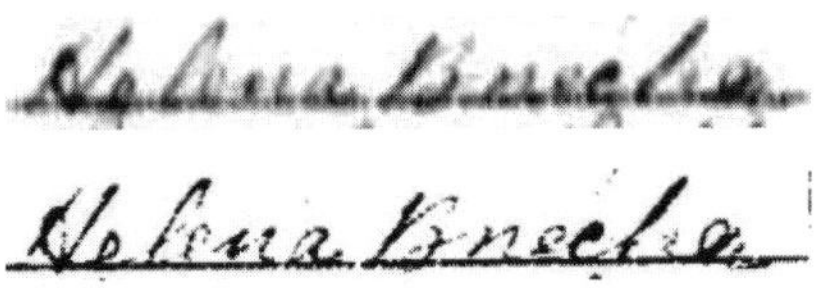

Figure 4-1 Could you transcribe this name with confidence?

(RG 10/734, fol. 64, p. 54) shown in Figure 4-1. At the top is the greyscale image from Ancestry, below it the black and white scan from Origins. The latter seems slightly easier to read, but I would be surprised at anyone claiming to identify the surname with 100 per cent confidence from either of them.

The only area where one can expect a lower error rate is in the transcription of printed sources such as trade directories, where problems of identifying names or individual letters are less great. On the other hand, printed sources lend themselves to optical character recognition (OCR), but this is a mixed blessing – although OCR is less much labour-intensive than manual transcription, it can produce spectacularly inaccurate results where the original documents are poorly printed, and therefore requires laborious proof-reading.

Nonetheless, there are some types of error which really are easily avoidable: those which are the result of poor data validation. Validation is an essential component of any data entry project – it means checking that everything entered is, if not demonstrably correct, at least plausible. Of course, it's one thing to do this with, say a modern postcode, where it's a simple matter to check that it is present in a list of valid postcodes or that it at least has the correct structure for a postcode. It is much harder to do the same with handwritten historical sources, particularly where surnames are involved. Even so, there have been some notable and entirely avoidable failures in major genealogical projects, which have reduced the reliability and usefulness.

Perhaps the most notorious of these was in the original release of the 1901 Census, which had individuals with biologically implausible ages over 200. You'd have thought those entering the data might have had second thoughts about these themselves, but even so, given that data entry errors are inevitable, why was there no mechanism in place to spot data which cannot possibly be correct?

In other cases, there are things that *might* be right, but are statistically so anomalous that they need individual checking. For example, all the census indexes have significant numbers of people indexed with a gender which does not seem to match with their forename. Ancestry, for example, has 407 female Johns in its 1901 census index, and 772 female Williams (I've taken figures from Ancestry's index here because it allows a search on just forename and gender, which other sites do not). One or two of these Johns are genuine (I noticed a *Marion St John Adcock*), but almost all the ones I have checked are very clearly transcription errors, usually a misreading of a female forename, sometimes an error in reading the relationship field. It's easy for a transcriber to get a name wrong in a census, whether by misreading or miskeying, but some of the errors will be self-evident, because of gender differences in naming – it is a trivial matter to query a database for gender errors with common forenames, to flag entries that need checking.

Sometimes a lookup table will suffice to trap errors: there are some strange misspellings of place names in the census indexes (e.g. *Harimersmith* for *Hammersmith*), or some strange combinations (*Somerset, London*?). Ancestry has the Sarah Maskell, whose servant was Helena from Figure 4-1, born in *Syrian Arab Republic, Hange Common*, instead of the admittedly hard-to-read *Surrey, Ham Common* on the original. But one doesn't need to see the originals to know that these transcriptions simply must be wrong. Couldn't they have been checked against a gazetteer? Even if it was not possible to fix them immediately, could they not have been flagged as doubtful, for later investigation?

Even with forenames, one ought to be pretty suspicious of a name that is not in the forename dictionary. I suppose it's possible that England in 1861 had bearers of the forenames *Gluyabeth* or *Iomnic*, but even without seeing the original, I bet you can guess that the first ought to be *Elizabeth* (in fact the ascender from the letter on the line below has made the *E* look, at first sight, like a G) and the second either *Dominic* or *Jonnie* (actually the latter). It's an obvious enough principle: even if a name is hard to make out, it's much more likely to be a badly-written common name than a badly written name with no other recorded instances. You would have to be absolutely sure there was no alternative other than *Gluyabeth* to put that down as your transcription.

But given there will always be genuinely hard-to-read entries, the question is how they are treated. Techniques for editing manuscript documents to indicate uncertainties of reading were available long before the advent of computers and much work has been done by those who edit historical manuscripts on ways of indicating variants and unreadable text in electronic editions. So why do genealogical projects not take account of this? As far as I can see, the major transcriptions used by genealogists rarely use any mechanism (and certainly nothing more sophisticated than a question mark) for indicating that an individual character or a word is not unambiguously decipherable, in spite of the fact that it is a common enough experience for every genealogist. The transcriber simply puts their best guess, a solution which is utterly inadequate and entirely unhelpful to the user. For example, the barely legible surname in Figure 4-1 is transcribed by Ancestry as *Boucha* and by Origins as *Bnecker*. Neither is obviously right, and both seem reasonable attempts in the circumstances. But surely neither of the transcribers in this instance can have been sure that their reading was correct. It would be much more helpful for a data provider to admit that there cannot be a definitive reading here and recognize that someone looking for *Bnecker* or *Boucha*, or a range of similar names, should be shown this entry as a possible match.

Why don't the electronic transcriptions do this? Because, to be fair, it's actually quite difficult to do. Having complicated ways of indicating doubtful characters is all very well, but it has two unwelcome repercussions. For a start you would have to teach your transcribers how to use them and check that they were doing so correctly and consistently. Then you would have to modify your search engine to retrieve these entries when something close enough was entered. The real solution, then, is to have good techniques for identifying loose matches, and all the data services give you the option of choosing an exact or a loose match.

But all this points to another issue which underlies much of the difficulty of finding people in online genealogical databases – they do not distinguish clearly between a transcription and an index. The job of a transcriber is to reproduce exactly the letters that can be identified on the original page, that of the indexer to make things findable. The problem with *Gluyabeth* only arises in a transcription. With a proper *index* the answer is simple: you link this entry to both *Elizabeth* and *Gluyabeth*. An index is a finding aid, and it is much better for it to give occasional false positives than for it to regularly ignore obvious, not to mention more likely, alternative readings.

This question also arises very noticeably in the representation of place names, and *Guildford* in Surrey is a good example. There are two obvious alternative spellings one might expect to find: *Guilford* and *Gilford*, and both do in fact occur in records. The question is: how should these be treated. The transcription approach is the simplest – just record what is written. But the problem with this is that the user has to try all the alternatives. The index approach is more complex: either the spelling can be normalized or there can be multiple index entries. Either way, in a search for someone born in *Guilford*, Surrey, you should also find those whose birthplaces are recorded as *Guilford*, Surrey or *Gilford* Surrey. Normalization can be risky, though: there is actually a *Guilford* (in Pembrokeshire) and a *Gilford* (in County Down). It can sometimes be misguided. In The Genealogist's index for the 1871 census, there is an enumeration district (RG12/166, folios 35-43) with some odd birthplaces: Birmingham London; Liverpool, London; Somerset, London. What seems to have happened here is that, because no county is given, the transcriber or the compiler has carefully given every town which has not already got a county specification, the county the enumeration district is in. But they have not taken account of the fact that the original enumerator was inconsistent.

But if normalizing can be problematic, multiple index entries can be hard work – is it reasonable to expect all alternative spellings to be caught when searching for a place name? In fact, it depends: in the case of county names, it really shouldn't be a challenge. There are only 53 historic counties in England and Wales. We know what they are, we know their recognized alternative names (*Shropshire* and *Salop*, for example), and likely spelling variants are easily guessed (*Surrey* and *Surry*). There is no reason why county names should not be normalized or the variants correctly matched. In fact some sites go further: they don't even run the risk that users might get the spelling wrong, but offer a drop down list for you to select from. In fact the real problem is not that the various sites take different approaches, but that they don't give you any indication which approach they take.

So how good should we expect the online indexes to be? When the GRO placed the tender for the DOVE project (p. 71) it specified a maximum error rate of 0.5 per cent. This sounds quite small, but in a large project it would mean a *lot* of records with errors. If this error rate requires that 99.5 per cent of *records* should be completely correct, that would still mean one million civil registration records with an error in one field or another. More likely, it means 99.5 per cent of *fields* should be error-free, which would result in around one million wrong surnames, another million wrong fore-names, etc. You may think, therefore, that 99.5 per cent sets the bar too low, and that, indeed, was the genealogical community's reaction to this figure. On the other hand, I understand that at least one company did not bid for the contract because they thought that threshold was unachievable. We will, of course, find out whether that assessment is correct, though perhaps not for some years. The fact is that for the censuses at least, where some comparative statistics have been compiled (see p. 94), none of the commer-cially available indexes gets near this figure, though the official 1911 Census Blog at <**blog.1911census.co.uk**> reported, in a posting on 21st January 2009, an initial accuracy level of better than 98.5 per cent. For the GRO's digi-tizers to hit their target will be a genuine cause for congratulation.

On the whole, my view is that there are relatively simple error checking and quality control measures which could be implemented with only a bit more trouble. Genuine indexes rather than searchable transcriptions would solve many problems about uncertain readings, but might bring additional complications. And of course, we have to accept that there will always be an irreducible core of illegible words – there are many cases where the ink is too faint to give any certain letters at all – and we simply have to live with these and find ways around them.

On a more positive note, though, it is worth remembering that although all indexes are subject to error, the great virtue of online indexes is that mistakes can be corrected – most of the systematic errors in the 1901 census have now been dealt with, for example. Ancestry may have 407 female Johns for 1901, but the last edition of this book credited them with 3,000. In printed or CD-ROM publications this sort of error removal can only be undertaken if and when a subsequent edition is produced.

Also, one must be pragmatic: as long as an error does not prevent you actually locating an individual, then checking against the digitized image or the original record will provide the correct information. That means errors in gender or occupation may not be very significant – as long as you don't specify these in a search, that is. On the other hand, large errors in ages and misspellings of surnames and birthplaces may well make someone effectively unfindable. As with any transcription or index, a failure to locate an individual in an online index does not permit you to draw negative inferences.

Payment systems

There are some major data collections such as FreeBMD (see p. 62) and FamilySearch (p. 101) which do not charge for access to their material, and there are smaller free collections which are maintained by volunteer efforts or have some source of public funding. But generally there is a charge for access to larger datasets. There are three basic methods that sites use to levy their charges: subscription, pay-per-view and online shop.

Initially sites tended to be pay-per-view, and Ancestry UK was the sole data service with a subscription-only system. This was almost certainly because sites tended to start with just a small number of datasets – Findmypast, for example, initially had only the BMD indexes. Also, I suspect they were unsure whether the UK's notoriously stingy genealogists would be prepared to commit themselves to an annual charge. But for heavier users a subscription is much more economical, and as the sites have added more and more data, this option has become more attractive both for the companies and for the users.

Now things are much more mixed. Of the major data services discussed later in this chapter, only ScotlandsPeople, which has a monopoly on Scottish data, and two sites specifically targeted at the less experienced and perhaps less committed family historian, Genes Reunited and RootsUK, are exclusively pay-per-view. In fact, the Scottish data will almost certainly become available by subscription also, as a result of Brightsolid's purchase of Findmypast (see p. 46). One of the reasons for this shift is that the data services have started offering things like scanned trade directories where it makes no sense to charge users for each page viewed. Origins has in fact gone over completely to subscription, while Ancestry, as a requirement of its census licences from the National Archives, has introduced a pay-per-view option.

In pay-per-view systems you pay, in principle, for each item of data viewed. However, it is problematic to collect small amounts of money via credit and debit cards, not to mention tedious for users to complete a new financial transaction for each individual record they want to view. Therefore, all such systems require you to purchase a block of 'units' or 'credits' in advance, which are then used up as you view data. Sometimes these are only available in discrete amounts, and work with either real or virtual vouchers for round sums of money; sometimes you must pay a minimum charge up-front, and at the end of your session a higher charge is made if you have viewed more data than is covered by the minimum. There is usually a time limit, which means you could have units unused at the end of your session. You won't be able to claim a refund, but in some cases you can carry forward unused portions of a payment to a subsequent session.

In an online shop, whether it's for genealogical data or for physical products, you add items to a virtual 'shopping basket' until you have everything you want, and pay for all of them in a single transaction at a virtual 'checkout'. Only then can you download the data you have paid for. Such a procedure would make little sense for individual data entries, but is a good way of delivering entire electronic documents, so it is ideal for the wills available from DocumentsOnline or ScotlandsPeople (see Chapter 8). It also allows items to be priced individually, though these two services in fact charge at a flat rate.

An overview of the current charging systems for the major commercial data services in the UK is shown in Table 4-1.

▌ Major commercial data services

The following chapters cover the various types of record and look at sites relevant for each. But there are a number of major commercial sites which have datasets drawn from a variety of different records, and these are discussed here for convenience. All the sites mentioned are constantly adding to their data, sometimes on a monthly basis, so you will almost certainly find there is a wider range of data than mentioned here. Prices, on the other hand, have tended to be very stable, and are not likely to be much higher than those quoted.

The sites described here are all mature services and most offer facilities beyond their data collections which space does not permit coverage of here. In particular, they are starting to offer 'community' facilities like discussion forums and shareable family trees. It should be easy to discover what additional features the sites offer, and they can sometimes be used without payment, though you may have to complete some form of registration.

Table 4-1a Commercial data services: subscriptions

Site/subscription	Duration	Cost	Datasets
Ancestry Essentials	1 month	£10.95	UK BMD + census
	1 year	£83.40	
Ancestry Premium	1 month	£12.95	UK + Ireland records
	1 year	£107.40	
Ancestry Worldwide	1 month	£18.95	All records
	1 year	£155.40	
Familyrelatives	1 year	£35.00	All records
Findmypast Voyager	30 days	£14.95	Passenger lists
Findmypast Explorer	6 months	£54.95	All records
	12 months	£89.95	
British Origins	72 hours	£6.50	UK records
	1 month	£8.95	
Irish Origins	72 hours	£4.50	Ireland records
	1 month	£8.95	
Origins Total Access	72 hours	£7.50	All records
	1 month	£10.50	
	1 year	£47.00	
The Genealogist Personal Premium	6 months	£39.95	All records
	1 year	£68.95	

Table 4-1b Commercial data services: pay-per-view

Site/scheme	No. credits	Duration	Cost	Cost per credit	Charged item	Cost in credits
Ancestry	12	14 days	£6.95	57.9p	Record view	1
Ancestry voucher	10	14 days	£5.75	57.5p		
Findmypast	60	90 days	£6.95	11.6p	BMD index image	1
	280	365 days	£24.95	8.9p	Census household	3
					Census image	3
1911 Census	50	3 months	£6.95	13.9p	Census household	10
	280	1 year	£24.95	8.9p	Census image	30
	600	1 year	£49.95	8.3p		
Familyrelatives	60	90 days	£6.00	10p	Search results	2
	150	90 days	£12.00	8p	Image	1
The Genealogist Personal Plus	800	1 year	£55.92	7p	BMD index image	1
	175	1 quarter	£24.95	14.2p	Census search	1
	75	1 quarter	£14.95	19.9p	Census image	3
The Genealogist Pay-as-you-go	100	90 days	£9.95	10p	As Personal Plus, but single database only	
	200	1 year	£19.95	10p		
Roots UK	100	3 years +	£5.00	5p	BMD index image	2
	400	3 years +	£14.95	3.7p	Census advanced search	5
					Census image	5
Genes Reunited	50	7 days	£5.00	10p	BMD index image	1
					Census person	5
					Census household	5
					Census image	5
1901 Census Online	500	7 days	£5.00	1p	BMD index image	10
					Census person	50
					Census household	50
					Census image	75
ScotlandsPeople	30	90 days	£6.00	20p	Search results per page	1
					Image	5

Figure 4-2 Origins

Origins

Origins was the first UK genealogy data service, and its website at <**www. origins.net**> comprises three sub-sites: British Origins, Irish Origins, and Scots Origins. The first two of these are online data services.

British Origins at <**www.britishorigins.com**> went live at the end of 2000 (under the name English Origins) with data from the collections of the SoG, but now includes a wide range of other material including census indexes.

The main categories of data are:

- census records for 1841, 1861 and 1871
- marriage records from parish registers and previously published indexes
- wills from London, Yorkshire, Canterbury and Surrey
- apprenticeship records
- a number of London datasets

The records on British Origins will mostly be of use to those who have already got some way with their pedigree, as, apart from the censuses, many of the datasets only go up to the mid-nineteenth century. The range of London records makes this site invaluable to those with ancestors from the City. Further will collections are due to be added in 2009.

Irish Origins at <**www.irishorigins.com**> currently includes the following datasets:

- Griffith's Valuation 1847–1864
- Index of Irish wills 1484–1858
- Militia Attestations Index 1872–1915
- a number of local census indexes and extracts
- Passenger Lists: Irish ports to USA 1890

There are also collections of maps, plans and photographs.

Origins was originally a pay-per-view service but it moved to a subscription system in July 2004. There are a variety of subscriptions: 72 hours or one month for the individual Origins services, with an additional annual option for the 'Total Access' subscription. The prices are given in Table 4-1, and more detailed information is on the site at <**www.originsnetwork. com/signup-info.aspx**>. If you just want to try the site, the 72-hour subscriptions are relatively expensive, and the one-month option is only a third more for much longer access. Members of the SoG have one free 72-hour session on British Origins per quarter, giving access to the 10 SoG-supplied datasets.

There are, broadly speaking, three different types of result you may get from a search on Origins. In the case of indexes, you will probably get all the available information. For other records, Origins has a scan of the original document, which you will be able to view. Finally, for some of the records from the SoG and the Borthwick Institute, you get a document reference and can either visit the relevant library or place an online order for a copy of the document to be made and posted to you. There is a separate charge for this, as the copies are made by the supplying organization, not Origins itself.

ScotlandsPeople

The Scottish civil registration indexes were the first genealogical records in the UK to be put online by a government agency, when Scots Origins opened its electronic doors in 1998 to provide the data on behalf of GROS. In 2002, the contract for the online service was awarded to Scotland Online, who now provide it on the ScotlandsPeople site at <**www.scotlandspeople. gov.uk**>. In 2008 Scotland Online took over Findmypast (see below) and changed its name to Brightsolid.

The site was initially designed just to supply the civil registration, census and parish records, but has now expanded its brief to cover all national records, including those previously on the National Archives of Scotland's ScottishDocuments site (see p. 199), which has therefore ceased to carry records itself.

The site offers the following Scottish records:

- baptisms and marriages from the old parish registers, 1553–1854
- birth, marriage and deaths from 1855
- all censuses, 1841–1901
- wills and testaments, 1513–1901
- coats of arms

A more detailed description of what material is available for each of these classes of record will be found in the sections on civil registration (p. 72), census (p. 87), parish registers (p. 109), and wills (p. 118). Work on these data collections is ongoing. Civil registration material is complete, with indexes and images. The 1911 census will not be available until at least April 2011. There is no indication that the obvious missing records, the parish register burials, are to be added to the site (see p. 109).

This is a pay-per-view system and you purchase access in blocks of 30 credits for £6. An initial search is free of charge, but this only tells you how many hits your search produces. Each page of search results costs you one unit and includes a maximum of 25 entries. In addition to viewing the scanned registers online, you can order a copy of the relevant certificate for £10. This is paid for separately and does not come out of your pre-paid units. There is no subscription option, though it is likely that the data will be available via subscription options of Findmypast (see below) in due course.

The site keeps a record of all search result pages and certificates that you

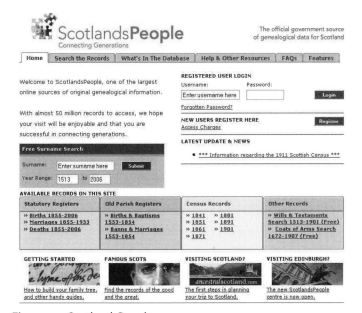

Figure 4-3 ScotlandsPeople

have paid to view, and these can be retrieved at any time, not just during the session in which they were first accessed. You therefore don't need to pay to return to the site to review material you have already paid for, even if you have run out of valid units.

The images are delivered as TIFF format files. These are displayed in a special viewer plug-in, which requires Java to be installed on your computer (see p. 58). Images can be enlarged or printed direct from the viewer, and you can save them to your hard disk. TIFF is a standard graphics format, so you should be able to display, manipulate and print the files with any graphics program. Note that the images are black and white, not greyscale like photographs, and for some of the poorer quality originals can be hard to read, particularly as they are scanned at only 200 dots per inch.

The wills and coats of arms are not part of the pay-per-view system but are sold via an online shop (see p. 118).

The Help & Other Resources option links to material to help you get the most from the site, and includes glossaries of occupations and other terms.

Ancestry

The Ancestry.com website <**www.ancestry.com**> is the largest commercial collection of genealogical data. It holds over 25,000 separate datasets, many of them derived from printed materials which may be more or less difficult to find outside a major genealogical library. Ancestry is a long-established US company, and started to host UK data in 2002 with the launch of Ancestry UK at <**www.ancestry.co.uk**> offering a subscription covering the UK data only. At the start of 2009, the UK data amounts to some 800 datasets. For Americans with UK ancestors, there is a subscription option at the main site which includes both US and UK records.

Among the records for the British Isles are:

- census indexes linked to images for 1841–1901
- GRO indexes for marriages and deaths, 1984–2002
- parish and/or probate register extracts for all counties
- Pallot's Baptism and Marriage Indexes
- military records
- passenger lists and migration records
- a number of historic books and newspapers

To view the list of datasets available on Ancestry, click on the link beside 'Browse our collections on the Ancestry UK home page', then on the 'Ancestry card Catalogue' page, use the filter options in the left-hand column to see what is available for a particular county or type of record.

Figure 4-4 Ancestry

Ancestry has traditionally been a subscription service, and a quarterly or annual payment provides unlimited access to *all* databases included in the particular subscription package. There are three levels of subscription:

- Essentials membership: civil registration, census records, WW1 military records for the UK; no parish registers or Irish records
- Premium membership: all UK and Ireland records
- Worldwide membership: all Ancestry datasets

With the introduction of the UK censuses in partnership with the National Archives, a pay-per-view option was introduced, with a payment of £6.95 permitting 12 page views within a 14-day period. This covers not just the census , but all datasets on the site. If you use the pay-per-view option, you can extend it to a quarterly or annual subscription by paying the difference.

The main Ancestry site at <**www.ancestry.com**> has a 14-day free trial offer, but if you sign up for this you should be aware that a full subscription will be charged to your credit card if you do not cancel before the end of the trial period. Free access to Ancestry's UK data is available from many libraries, from the Society of Genealogists and from the public computer facilities at the National Archives.

Although Ancestry is a commercial service, some of the material is free of charge. For example, FreeBMD's GRO index data is available here as well as on FreeBMD's own website (see p. 62).

A useful blog is the Ancestry Insider at <**ancestryinsider.blogspot. com**>, which offers an 'unofficial, unauthorized view' of Ancestry.

Findmypast

Findmypast at <www.findmypast.com> went live in April 2003, under the name 1837online, offering the GRO indexes. Since then, the company has expanded its material considerably, and now offers:

- civil registration indexes
- censuses 1841–1901 (the 1851 and 1901 censuses to be completed by summer 2009)
- migration records (including passenger lists and passport applications)
- a range of military records
- occupational records

In 2008 it was taken over by Brightsolid (see above) and became involved in the project to digitize the 1911 census, hence the fact that this site, although at a different address <www.1911census.co.uk>, has Findmypast's branding. This census is discussed separately on p. 88.

The site operates both subscription and a pay-per-view (they call it 'PayAsYouGo') systems, and the prices are given in Tables 4-1a and 4-1b. The different subscription options give access to different datasets:

- Voyager: passenger lists only
- Explorer: all records

Figure 4-5 Findmypast

At the time of writing there is also a Discovery subscription, but this is being phased out. An additional enhanced Explorer subscription is to be introduced, which will include the 1911 census.

In the case of the pay-per-view option, it is worth noting that credits purchased on the Findmypast site will also appear as credits on the 1911 Census site, so you do not need to buy credits on both systems. The 1911 data will be available at Findmypast itself in due course.

The Genealogist

The Genealogist at <www.thegenealogist.co.uk> is a data service run by well-known software retailer S&N Genealogy Supplies. It provides a wide range of resources, including:

- civil registration indexes
- census
- parish registers, both transcripts and scans of published indexes
- directories
- military records

Figure 4-6 The Genealogist

Figure 4-7 RootsUK

The payment options are quite complex and comprise:

- 'All-inclusive' subscription, with unlimited access to all databases
- 'Personal Plus' subscription, a halfway house between subscription and pay-per-view, with access to all the datasets but a limit on how many searches you can carry out
- 'Pay-as-you-go' option, a type of pay-per-view system, except that you get access to a single county for a single census year with 150 searches and 50 image views

The choice is therefore between credit-free access, credit-based access to all databases, and credit-based access to a single database. Full details are available from <**www.thegenealogist.co.uk/nameindex/products.php**>. The 'Pay-as-you-go' option, however, is very limited as it gives access to census records for one county for one census year.

The civil registration records are also made available on S&N's BMDindex site at <**www.bmdindex.co.uk**>, which is discussed on p. 65.

The same data is available on S&N's RootsUK site at <**www.rootsuk. com**>. This site is targeted more at the relative newcomer and offers only the data that those starting their family history will need, along with much simpler search facilities. This makes the site ideal for the relative novice but probably too limited for the experienced genealogist. The data available comprises:

- civil registration
- census records
- electoral rolls

All indexes and images are identical to those on TheGenealogist, but the site offers only pay-per-view access – see Tables 4-1a and 4-1b for prices.

FamilyRelatives

FamilyRelatives was launched at the end of 2004 at <**www.familyrelatives. com**>. The site offers a pay-per-view system only and has no subscriptions. It started off with just the civil registration indexes, but now has a much wider range of material. An unusual feature of the civil registration records is that it offers not just images of the original index books, but transcription of the entries for the period 1866–1920. The site's datasets include:

- civil registration indexes
- trade and professional directories
- scans of printed parish register transcriptions
- military records
- Irish wills and other Irish records

In January 2009 the site started to add census data (see p. 87).

Figure 4-8 Familyrelatives

Genes Reunited

With its pedigree database and contact service, Genes Reunited at <www. genesreunited.co.uk> is best known as a social networking site. However, it also offers genealogical data on a pay-per-view basis. In 2006, it purchased the 1901 Census from QinetiQ (see p. 80) and therefore also runs the 1901 census site at <www.1901censusonline.com>. Both sites offer the same data, though the search facilities differ:

- census records 1841–1901
- civil registration 1837–2004
- WWI and WWII deaths

In spite of the fact that the data is identical on the two sites, the payment regimes are subtly different (see Table 4-1). One issue with these sites compared to those discussed above is that the validity of the units is *very* short, a mere seven days.

Other sites

The sites discussed above are, at the start of 2009, the most important commercial data services for UK genealogy, but they are not the only ones, and a number of local or specialized collections are mentioned in later chapters.

Other sites that have a range of records include AncestryIreland, run by the Ulster Historical Foundation, at <www.ancestryireland.com>. It has birth, death and marriage records for County Antrim and County Down available on a pay-per-view basis, with free searches but a rather expensive charge of £4 to view a record. There are many other types of record available to members of the Ulster Genealogical and Historical Guild, subscription to which costs £30 per annum.

The only real competitor to Ancestry in terms of worldwide coverage is the US-based World Vital Records at <www.worldvitalrecords.com>. While there is a US-only subscription, access to the UK datasets requires a World Collection Membership at $119.40. Unlike the other data services, it does not seem to create its own datasets but licences data from other companies. So among its UK data are military records and passenger lists from British Origins and the England and Wales censuses from Findmypast. It is probably not worth considering if you only have ancestors from the British Isles, but for an American family with some roots in Britain or Ireland, it could be very useful.

▌ Document services

The data services discussed above offer individual entries from much larger sets of records, but an alternative way of making records available is to offer

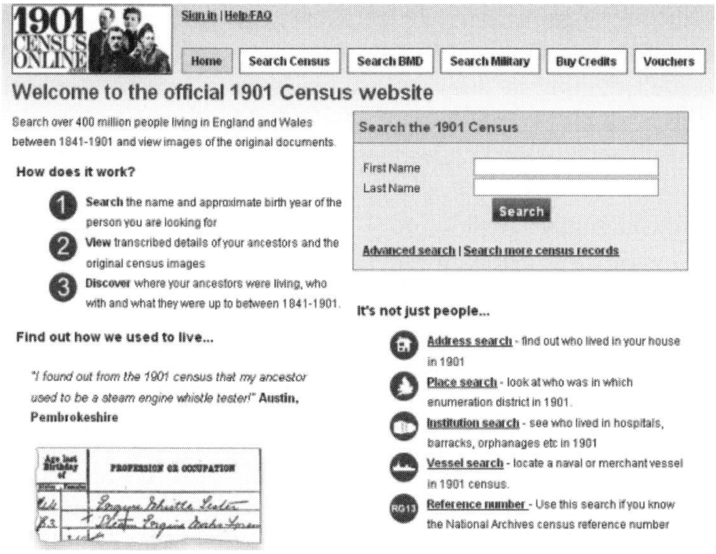

Figure 4-9 1901 Census Online

a scan of a whole document for a one-off payment, via an online shop rather than by subscription or pay per view.

ScotlandsPeople in fact offers this alongside its pay-per-view service. For the Scottish wills and coats of arms, you pay a flat rate for a digital scan. In these cases, there is no transcription, just an index to help you identify the correct document. Once paid for, you can download a PDF file with scans of all the pages in the original combined in a single document.

While the National Archives does not run its own data service, and instead licences its records to commercial data services, it does have its own electronic documents services on its own website. DocumentsOnline at <**www.nationalarchives.gov.uk/documentsonline**> (Figure 4-10) is not aimed solely at genealogists but at all those who need to consult its records. It therefore includes things like cabinet papers and Ministry of Defence UFO reports. The categories of document of most interest to family historians include:

- a range of army records, particularly relating to medals, but including WAAC service records
- navy records, including many service records
- wills and death duties, including Prerogative Court of Canterbury wills 1384–1858
- aliens registration cards

Most documents cost £3.50 to download, but medal cards are £2.00.

A commercial document service is The Original Record at <**www.the**

originalrecord.com>, which has a very sizeable collection of indexed scans of printed records. Many of them are lists which you are very unlikely to find elsewhere on the web. The site does not offer a master listing, you can only find out what is available by selecting one of the decades between 1000 and 1950 to see what it contains. But, for example, the decade 1900–1909 includes:

- Boys entering Sherborne School (1904)
- Associate Members of the Institution of Civil Engineers (1904)
- Outstanding soldiers of the 10th (The Prince of Wales' Own Royal) Hussars (1881–1901)
- Missing Next-of-Kin and Heirs-at-Law (1900)
- Nottingham borough officers and officials (1836–1900)

Unfortunately, there are two things which make the site less useful than it first appears. First, the search facility permits search on surname and date range only, so it is impossible to be sure a match is the person you are looking for, and you may therefore end up paying for many more documents than you actually need. Second, given that uncertainty, the price per document of £4 or more seems rather high.

Image formats and viewers

One issue that faces anyone using online services that provide images of original records is the file format of the image and the viewer needed to view them. You might think that you don't want to and indeed don't need to worry about this. But it is in fact one of the main sources of problems in the data services. Even if you can see the image without problems in your browser, are you sure that when you save it to your hard disk you have software on your machine that can display the image? Will you be able to crop or enhance it in order to suit your own particular requirements?

It would be easy to fill twenty pages with discussion of the online services' image facilities and how to make the most of them. Here, I will just look at the four main image formats and some of the issues with the image viewers required by the genealogical data services. This is based on the much more comprehensive material in *Census: The Expert Guide* which examines in detail the census images on each of the data services.

Adobe Acrobat (PDF)

Adobe Acrobat is, at first sight, a pretty unproblematic format. It is not in fact an image format at all, rather a *document* format which can incorporate images. It is often referred to as 'PDF', which stands for 'portable document format', and Acrobat files always end in the extension *.pdf*. Its particular advantage for genealogical records is that it can combine many

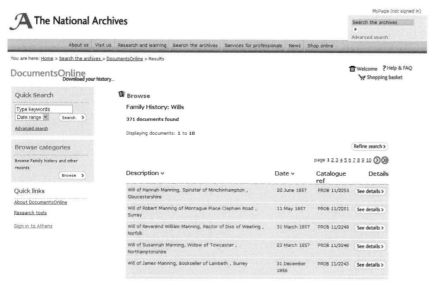

Figure 4-10 A will search in DocumentsOnline

images in a single file, each on its own page. This makes it ideal for multi-page documents like a will, which can be downloaded in one file containing a separate image of each page.

To view Acrobat files you need the Adobe Acrobat Reader. Acrobat files are so widely used on the web that unless you are an internet novice using a newish computer, you will almost certainly have the software installed already. If not, it can be downloaded free of charge from Adobe's home page at <**www.adobe.com**>. When you install it, your browser will automatically be configured so that it knows to use the reader when it comes across an Acrobat file, and it will display the document within the browser window.

Sites that provide images in PDF format are:

- The Genealogist
- RootsUK
- Genes Reunited
- 1901 Census Online
- DocumentsOnline
- National Archives of Ireland Census of Ireland 1911 (p. 96)

Once you have downloaded a PDF file (click on the 'Save a copy' icon at the top left of the reader window), you can view it again by clicking on its icon— this will automatically start the Acrobat Reader.

The problem with Acrobat files comes when you want to manipulate the images. You might think you won't want to do this, but at some point you will certainly want to extract from a page just the bit you need; or you may want to adjust the contrast or brightness to see if you can read something that looks illegible. But since PDF is not a graphics format, you cannot simply load it into a graphics program to carry out these tasks. And the Acrobat Reader cannot save a file in any other format.

The way around the problem is:

1. click on the snapshot tool in the toolbar at the top of the Acrobat Reader window
2. click with the cursor on any corner of the area you want to extract
3. drag the cursor until the highlighted rectangle encloses the area you want
4. release the mouse button

At this point an image of the selected area has been saved on the Clipboard, and you should be able to paste it into your graphics editor.

JPG

JPG or JPEG is probably the most widely used graphics file format on the web. Browsers can display JPG images without additional software, and any graphics editor can be used to edit them.

The following data services provide images in JPG format:

- Ancestry
- FamilySearch Pilot (p. 104)
- ScotlandsPeople (wills)

In each of these sites the JPG is not displayed on its own but is loaded into a special window which has a range of controls at the top for things like zoom, rotate image, and save.

Ancestry in fact has two different viewers, though both use the same graphics format. The basic viewer is perfectly adequate, but the Enhanced Viewer is preferable because of its additional options and facilities. However, it only works on Windows computers using Internet Explorer 5.5 and later, or Firefox 3, and some browser settings will prevent it installing. If you have difficulties, the site's help section has comprehensive details on getting it installed: click on 'Help' at the top of the screen and look for 'Why the Enhanced Image Viewer may not install'.

TIFF

The TIFF format is a very common image format for professional graphics work, but is not that common on the web, and browsers cannot display

TIFF images without special software. The two sites that use TIFF images are:

- Origins
- ScotlandsPeople

Origins recommends that you install a free viewer called AlternaTIFF, and the 'can't view image?' link at the bottom of every image display page brings up information about this and how to install it. In fact, even if your browser already has a plug-in which displays TIFF images, it may be worth installing AlternaTIFF since it offers several useful tools for viewing: zooming, panning, printing and saving are all catered for. It can be downloaded free of charge from <**www.alternatiff.com**>. There are two different versions, one for Internet Explorer and one for other browsers.

If you are using a Mac, you should find that the image is displayed automatically using Apple's QuickTime plug-in. However, this does not offer any image controls to zoom or print the page. Origins' help page on image viewing at <**www.originsnetwork.com/help/popup-helpbo-images.htm**> offers some alternative suggestions for Mac users.

On ScotlandsPeople, you have a choice between three different image viewers:

- direct download
- Java Applet
- ActiveX viewer

Direct download will work with any browser – it simply downloads the image to your hard disk. ActiveX is a feature of Internet Explorer and is not available with other browsers. The Java Applet option will work if your computer has Java installed and your browser has Java enabled. ScotlandsPeople recommend Internet Explorer users to use the ActiveX option as the image will appear more quickly.

A link from the account page allows you to test the various options and see whether they work with your browser. If the Java Applet does not work, you can install Java from <**java.com**>, which also has an option to test whether Java is installed on your computer. If it is already installed but not working in your browser, then your browser may not have Java enabled (this is sometimes done for security reasons). See your browser's help for how to rectify this.

There is further information about the image viewing options in the help section of the site: click on the 'Help & Other Resources' tab, select 'Technical Information', then 'Viewing Images'. It is well worth reading this before you start searching, to make sure you will be able to see the image the first time you select one for viewing.

Any graphics editor should be able to deal with TIFF files.

Flash and DjVu

These two file formats are used by Findmypast, and DjVu is also used by FamilyRelatives.

Flash is a file format that is very widely used on the web for animation, and you may well have the 'player' installed already. If not it can be downloaded free of charge from Adobe's home page at <**www.adobe.com**>, just like the Acrobat Reader. When you save an image from the Flash player, it is saved in JPG format (see above).

DjVu (pronounced like *déja vu*) is a fairly exotic graphics format and you may well never have encountered it before, which means that before you can view the images, you will need to install the DjVu viewer. Familyrelatives uses it for all images; on Findmypast it is the Enhanced Viewer and brings a number of advantages over Flash, most notably much improved download speed.

There is no need to repeat here the instructions on how to install this, which will be found on the two sites (at <**www.findmypast.com/help advice/faqs/djVu-viewer/**> and <**www.familyrelatives.com/information/ info_detail.php?id=40**>). But you need to be aware that there are potential installation difficulties, depending on your browser and its configuration, so it really is a good idea to refer to the relevant help page first, and not just after you encounter a problem.

The DjVu viewer does have one significant problem: very few graphics editors can deal with images in this format, so you may be unable to edit the images with the graphics software you normally use. There are two solutions:

1. Ignore the 'Save Image' button and instead right-click on the image, then select 'Export to File'. From the drop-down file-type list, ignore DjVu and select BMP. This is the standard Windows Bitmap format, which any graphics program should be able to deal with.
2. Find a graphics program which supports the DjVu image format. For example, you can download the IrfanView graphics viewer for Windows, free from <**www.irfanview.com**>, and this has a DjVu plug-in which can also be downloaded.

You don't need to worry about this unless you want to edit a DjVu image; you will still be able to view the saved images – clicking on the file name in an Explorer window will load the image in a standalone version of the DjVu viewer.

▌ Which data service?

It would be nice to make a firm recommendation as to the best of the data services discussed on the previous pages, or give them comparative scores. However, it would be very difficult to justify doing so.

For a start, it will depend on your genealogical needs and your budget. If you are on a tight budget, then you will probably want to stick to the sites with pay-per-view options rather than subscriptions. If you are already quite advanced with your family tree, you will probably want to avoid the more basic services and go for a site with a wider range of records and more sophisticated searching. All of these sites have their fans and their critics. Often people simply prefer the search facilities or the interface on one site rather than another. Many of the sites offer additional facilities, particularly the ability to maintain an online family tree, which might sway you one way or another.

The other problem is that even if you are reading this book very soon after it comes off the press, one or more of the sites will have improved facilities and additional datasets which may increase its usefulness to you.

One thing that is certainly impossible is to say much about the quality of the data. Chapter 6 discusses some objective comparative data on the various census indexes, but this cannot necessarily be extrapolated to the quality of a site's data as a whole. Some of these sites draw their data from a range of different sources, so the quality of one set of records is no guide to the quality of another.

The three sites that suit both beginners and advanced users are Ancestry, Findmypast and The Genealogist. Origins is recommended if you want to move beyond the obvious records, and if you are an SoG member you will want to use your free access allocation. If you're a relative beginner and don't need anything beyond civil registration and census records, then RootsUK and Genes Reunited are worth looking at. Origins and FamilyRelatives probably have the best collections of Irish data. Ancestry has the largest number of datasets overall. Perhaps the only thing that can be said with certainty, for the moment at least, is that if you are researching Scottish ancestors, you have no choice but to use ScotlandsPeople.

▌ Common problems

It is not uncommon for users to experience problems with commercial genealogy sites, as indeed with all e-commerce sites. This is nothing to do with the security concerns people have about online payments (these are addressed in Chapter 21), but relate to the web browser and how it is configured. While it is not possible here to cover every eventuality, most of these problems arise from a readily identifiable set of facilities used by commercial websites, and are more or less straightforward to solve. Sites that use such facilities usually provide information on what is required – see, for example, the National Archives' 'Technical settings' page for DocumentsOnline at <**www.nationalarchives.gov.uk/documentsonline/ help/help-technical.asp**> – and you should normally see a warning if some required facility is absent from your configuration.

The main features which cause problems are:

Cookies

A 'cookie' is a piece of information a website stores on your hard disk for its own future use. This is how a site can 'remember' who you are from one visit to the next – even if you are using a different ISP – or even during a single session.[4] However, browsers can be configured to reject cookies, and some people do this to preserve their internet privacy. This will make pay-per-view sites and online shops unusable – in fact any site that requires some sort of login will only work with cookies enabled. If you are concerned about cookies, you can configure your browser to accept only those sites you specify. The online help for your browser should tell you how to check whether cookies are enabled. Most sites that require cookies will also give instructions.

JavaScript

This is a scripting language which, among other things, makes it possible for a web page to validate what the user enters in an online form (checking, for example, that you haven't left some crucial field blank) before the information is submitted to the server. You will be unable to use sites that require this if JavaScript is disabled. The online help for your browser should tell you how to check whether JavaScript is enabled, and how to ensure it is. Most sites that require it will also give instructions.

Java

Java is a programming language which allows programs (called 'applets', i.e. small applications) to run on any type of computer as long as it has software installed which can understand the language. This allows for programmable websites. Java facilities (referred to as a 'Java virtual machine') are normally installed and enabled automatically when you install a new browser, but can be disabled. Individual websites download their own applets to your machine – you will often see a grey box saying

---

4 It may appear to you to be a single session, but it is not like a phone call where a line is allocated exclusively to you for the duration of your call. On the web, each page requested from the server is a competely separate transaction, and cookies are the main way of identifying continuity.

'loading' in the browser window while an applet is being downloaded. The online help for your browser should tell you how to check whether Java is enabled, and how to ensure it is.

Plug-ins

A 'plug-in' is a small utility program which a web browser uses to display material which it can't handle with its own built-in facilities. A number of plug-ins are fairly standard (for example, Flash, QuickTime, and Shockwave) and may well be on your machine already. But some commercial sites have their own plug-ins for viewing images of documents – this is the case for the 1901 Census site, ScotlandsPeople and Findmypast. A plug-in needs to be downloaded before it can be run. This will usually take significantly longer than a normal web page to download, but once the plug-in is installed you won't need to repeat the process. The National Archives' site has a useful page on plug-ins at <**www.nationalarchives.gov. uk/help/technical-plugins.htm**>, with links so you can download some of the most common.

Compatibility

Although the web is based on open standards, browsers do not all implement these as fully and consistently as they might. Also, some website designers insist on using features that only work properly on a particular browser (usually Internet Explorer, as that is the most popular). The only way around problems from this source is to have a recent version of your preferred browser and, if that is not Internet Explorer, a copy of that too. Since all the main browsers can be downloaded free, there's no real reason not to have the latest version, unless your computer is running an old operating system or has limited memory or disk space. However, the latest version of Internet Explorer (7.0) is more standards-compliant than previous versions and the major sites that were flagged as problematic in the last edition of this book have improved their browser compatibility, so this issue is now less likely to affect your use of the web.

If you have any difficulties with online data services, there will always be a variety of help available. Sites selling data should always have a help page, and perhaps a separate technical help page which spells out hardware and/ or software requirements. You are very likely to find a FAQ ('Frequently Asked Questions') page. As a last resort there should always be an email address to contact for assistance, and there may also be a telephone helpline.

Incidentally, for a commercial, official, or major volunteer-run site, it is a good idea to mail the webmaster if you find pages that don't display properly in your browser.

5

CIVIL REGISTRATION

Birth, marriage and death certificates are generally the first official documents the family historian encounters. In an ideal world – for the genealogist at least – all of them would be online. But privacy concerns make it unlikely that full certificate details for 'recent' events will be easily accessible on the web, and so far only a small percentage of the 'historical' certificates, those from Scotland, are available online.

But even where certificates are not online, there is much information about birth, marriage and death records on the web to help you identify and order paper certificates, including a wide range of sites with civil registration indexes.

England and Wales

Civil registration of births, marriages and deaths started in England and Wales on 1 July 1837, and the original certificates are held in duplicate by the original local register office and by the General Register Office (GRO), which is part of the Home Office's Identity and Passport Service. The original certificates cannot be seen and are not yet available online, but copies can be ordered from the GRO via the web, by post or phone. The indexes to the certificates can be all be consulted online on free or commercial sites.

The FamilyRecords portal has basic information on birth, marriage and death certificates at <**www.familyrecords.gov.uk/topics/bmd.htm**>: it explains how to get certificates and what information is on each of them. The GRO website at <**www.gro.gov.uk**> has comprehensive information about ordering certificates. There is also information about adoptions and overseas records.

The GRO does not yet have a data service – the planned project for making certificates available online has been substantially delayed, and this is discussed on p. 71. However, there is an online service for ordering certificates at <**www.gro.gov.uk/gro/content/certificates/**> (covering England and Wales). In order to use the online ordering system you need to log in, and if you register (rather than using a one-off guest login) your details will be stored for future use and will not have to be re-entered for subsequent orders. If you do not already know the GRO index reference for the event, you will need to give quite detailed information including the exact date and place of the event. This is fine if it's your own birth certificate, but for deceased ancestors you are unlikely to have the complete and accurate information required for this, so before ordering a certificate you will need to refer to one of the services discussed in the next section to establish the index reference for a particular registration.

Beyond these sites, there are a number of unofficial sources of information on general registration which will be helpful for initial orientation. Genuki has a page devoted to civil registration in England and Wales at <**www.genuki.org.uk/big/eng/civreg/**>. Barbara Dixon's Registration Certificate Tutorials site at <**home.clara.net/dixons/Certificates/indexbd. htm**> describes how to order certificates and gives a detailed description of the fields on the three types of certificate. Another useful guide is Kimberley Powell's 'Civil Registration in England and Wales. How to Get Birth, Death & Marriage Certificates' at <**genealogy.about.com/od/england/a/bmd.htm**>.

GRO indexes

In 1998, in the absence of any official programme to digitize either the original certificates or the GRO indexes, a volunteer project called FreeBMD secured permission from the ONS to transcribe the indexes over 100 years old for free online access. In 2003, the GRO announced a completely open policy – any organization which has purchased the microfiche indexes is now free to transcribe or digitize the original pages and make them available online, free or charged, with no cut-off in years of coverage.[5] This has provided impetus for a number of online services offering digitized images of the original indexes.

While the older indexes are contained in physical books, scans of which are available online, the material from 1984 onwards is rather different: the GRO has electronic records from this date, held in a number of databases. It has permitted these, too, to be made available online. The advantage of the databases over the older material is that entries can be searched for individually – rather than having to look at a series of pages in the hope of identifying the correct entry, you can search the whole range of years at once. The GRO ceased to supply indexes to third parties after 2005.

5   The announcement was posted (unofficially) to the soc.genealogy.britain newsgroup on 13th February 2003 under the heading 'GRO Indexes – England & Wales', and can be found in the archive of the GENBRIT mailing list at <**archiver.rootsweb.ancestry.com/th/ index/GENBRIT/2003-02**> or on Google groups at <**groups.google.com**>.

FreeBMD

FreeBMD is one of the most successful collaborative projects the genealogy world has seen. It has a massive group of over 10,000 volunteers, who either transcribe the indexes from digital images in planned extractions or simply submit entries from their own extractions along with the surrounding entries. It has two sites: <**www.freebmd.org.uk**> is the home site and there is also a mirror on RootsWeb at <**freebmd.rootsweb.com**>, which can be useful in periods when the main site is busy and therefore slow to respond to searches.

By the end of 2008, the project's database had reached 160 million distinct records. The original plan was to capture all the nineteenth-century entries and this has more or less been achieved. The data is in fact largely complete up to 1929, with a small number of entries for later years so far. Up-to-date information on the percentage of coverage for each year and each type of event will be found at <**www.freebmd.org.uk/progress.shtml**>, and it is a good idea to check this before carrying out a search, particularly for the twentieth century.

All the entries so far transcribed can be searched online. A comprehensive search page (Figure 5-1) allows you to search for a specific person in a chosen place and date range, or to extract all the entries for a particular surname.

Figure 5-1 shows a search for all events for the surname Marshall in the Brighton registration district between 1837 and 1850. Figure 5-2 shows the

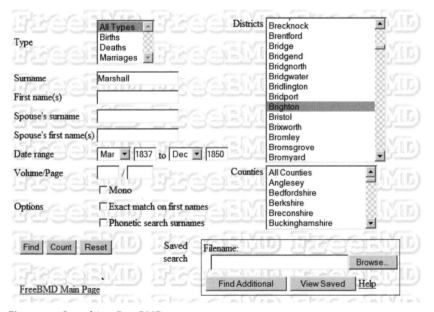

Figure 5-1 Searching FreeBMD

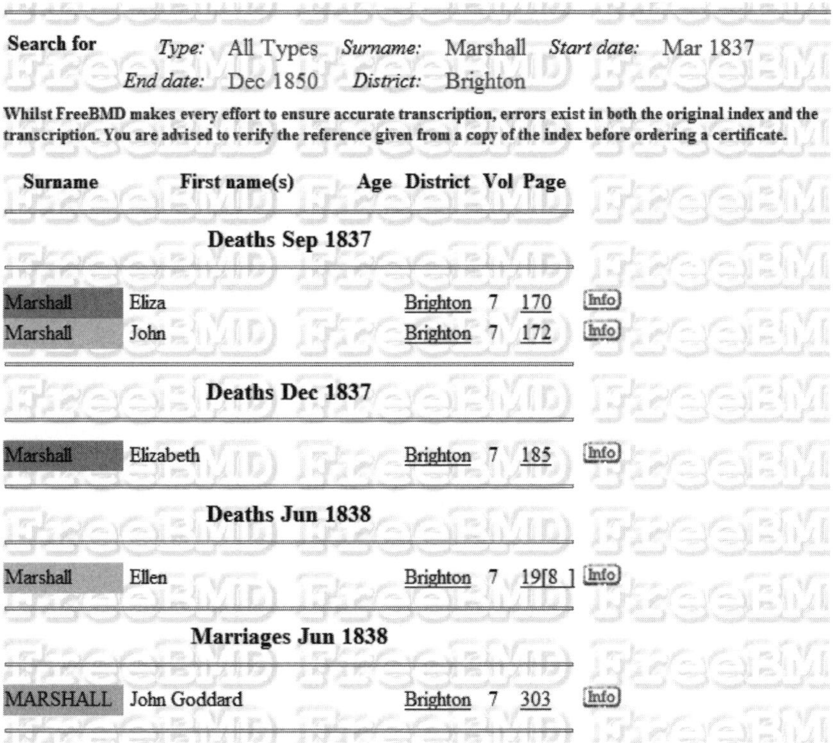

| Search for | Type: All Types Surname: Marshall Start date: Mar 1837 |
| | End date: Dec 1850 District: Brighton |

Whilst FreeBMD makes every effort to ensure accurate transcription, errors exist in both the original index and the transcription. You are advised to verify the reference given from a copy of the index before ordering a certificate.

Surname	First name(s)	Age	District	Vol	Page	

Deaths Sep 1837

| Marshall | Eliza | | Brighton | 7 | 170 | Info |
| Marshall | John | | Brighton | 7 | 172 | Info |

Deaths Dec 1837

| Marshall | Elizabeth | | Brighton | 7 | 185 | Info |

Deaths Jun 1838

| Marshall | Ellen | | Brighton | 7 | 19[8] | Info |

Marriages Jun 1838

| MARSHALL | John Goddard | | Brighton | 7 | 303 | Info |

Figure 5-2 FreeBMD search results

results of this search. Clicking on the links in the district column will take you to information on the registration district, while following the link in the page column brings up a list of all the events on that page in the original register (*not* the index). Note that the contributor's contact details are provided only for error reporting, and you cannot expect to contact the contributor for full details of the event, since he or she has only looked at the index, not the original certificates. You will need to order any certificate yourself.

A very useful feature is the ability to save a search and re-run it at any time. When you repeat a saved search, you see only new records that have been added since you saved.

Although the main focus of the project is the transcription of indexes, FreeBMD also makes digitized images of the original index pages free of charge. There is no search facility for this – once you have selected the type of event, the year and quarter, and the initial letter of the surname, it is up to you to judge where in the pages for that letter your surname occurs. In some cases, therefore, you may need to view several images to get the right one. The site gives you several image formats to choose from: PDF, GIF,

JPG and TIFF. Of these, the JPG is the largest and should be avoided if you have only a dialup connection as the files are around 3Mb in size. The GIFs are around 450Mb and the other formats around half that. At present only the index pages up to 1935 are available on the site.

FreeBMD is always looking for new volunteers, and details of what is involved can be found on the website. You can keep up to date with the progress of the project by joining the FreeBMD-News-L mailing list – subscription information will be found at <**lists.rootsweb.ancestry. com/index/intl/UK/FreeBMD-News.html**>.

Commercial indexes
Findmypast
Findmypast at <**www.findmypast.com**>, described on p. 46, offers all the GRO indexes. For the period to 1983, the site provides not a database of individual entries but simply digital images of the original paper documents, and you will need to identify which page holds the entry you are seeking.

The site offers two ways of finding the correct page. First, you can browse by selecting an event, year, quarter and then the appropriate place in the alphabetical listing of names. This is a good option if you are fairly sure when the event was registered, but it is less convenient for looking through a whole range of years and quarters. For this purpose, the search option is preferable – the results list all the matching pages for a whole period. Findmypast supplies the first and last name on each page, with both

Figure 5-3 Initial search at Findmypast

Figure 5-4 A page from the GRO indexes at Findmypast

surname and forename (see Figure 5-3), so you should be able to locate precisely the right page without too much trouble. If you are accessing the site on a pay-per-view basis, each index page view costs one credit (under 10p).

Findmypast offers the post-1983 indexes in a searchable database, and you use a search form to locate an individual entry rather than an index page. The search results give the full name, month, year and place of registration, so even with a common name it should normally be straightforward to identify the right entry. These records also cost one credit to view.

BMDindex

BMDindex is the BMD site of The Genealogist (see p. 47) at <**www. bmdindex.co.uk**>, and the same data is available at <**www.thegenealogist. co.uk**>. Like Findmypast, the site offers images of the original paper GRO indexes for the period up to 1983 and a searchable database for 1984–2005. The BMD data is also included in The Genealogist's 'all-inclusive' subscription – see p. 46.

A search for a name and a year range brings up links to the images for the relevant index page in each quarter. The search itself is not charged, but each image you look at costs one credit. Images are provided in Adobe Acrobat format (PDF). As long as you already have the PDF viewer installed in your browser, you will not need to download any plug-in, and this viewer has built in zoom, save and print facilities.

The search has two additional options which are very useful: when searching for a death, you can specify a birth year, so that the age at death can be used to identify the correct person; in the post-1983 birth records you can search for children based just on surname and mother's maiden surname, and thus find all children of a particular couple.

In addition to the GRO indexes, the site also offers births, marriages and deaths from Nonconformist records in the National Archives. These are discussed under 'Nonconformist churches' on p. 111.

Familyrelatives

Familyrelatives at <**www.familyrelatives.com**> (see p. 49) also offers GRO index images, but differs from the other services in that for the period 1866–1920 the indexes have, in addition, been transcribed. It looks as if the transcriptions have been created by optical character recognition, and without conducting some tests it is impossible to say how accurately this

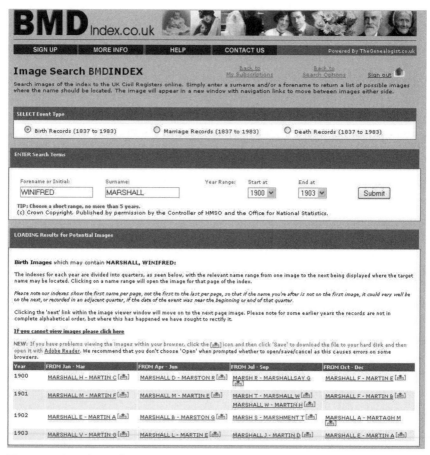

Figure 5-5 Search results in BMDindex

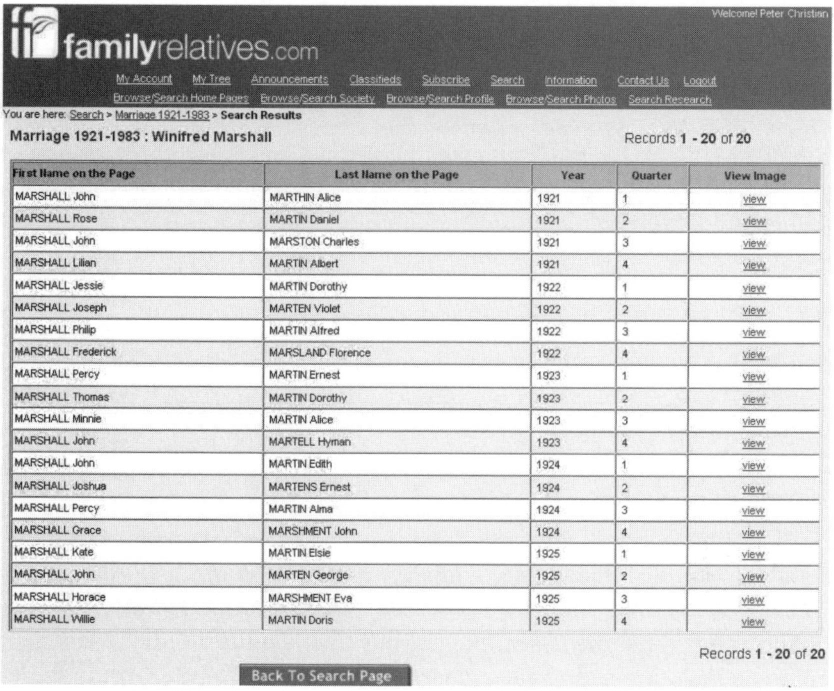

First Name on the Page	Last Name on the Page	Year	Quarter	View Image
MARSHALL John	MARTHIN Alice	1921	1	view
MARSHALL Rose	MARTIN Daniel	1921	2	view
MARSHALL John	MARSTON Charles	1921	3	view
MARSHALL Lilian	MARTIN Albert	1921	4	view
MARSHALL Jessie	MARTIN Dorothy	1922	1	view
MARSHALL Joseph	MARTEN Violet	1922	2	view
MARSHALL Philip	MARTIN Alfred	1922	3	view
MARSHALL Frederick	MARSLAND Florence	1922	4	view
MARSHALL Percy	MARTIN Ernest	1923	1	view
MARSHALL Thomas	MARTIN Dorothy	1923	2	view
MARSHALL Minnie	MARTIN Alice	1923	3	view
MARSHALL John	MARTELL Hyman	1923	4	view
MARSHALL John	MARTIN Edith	1924	1	view
MARSHALL Joshua	MARTENS Ernest	1924	2	view
MARSHALL Percy	MARTIN Alma	1924	3	view
MARSHALL Grace	MARSHMENT John	1924	4	view
MARSHALL Kate	MARTIN Elsie	1925	1	view
MARSHALL John	MARTEN George	1925	2	view
MARSHALL Horace	MARSHMENT Eva	1925	3	view
MARSHALL Willie	MARTIN Doris	1925	4	view

Figure 5-6 Search results in Familyrelatives

has been done, though I have not found any errors in the individuals I have searched for.

If you are using the site's pay-per-view rather than subscription option, costs vary according to the material available. Each page of search results costs two units, viewing a page image costs one unit. Looked at per entry, this is a more expensive service than the others, but the ability to search a database of individual entries means that, for the 1866–1920 period, you should be able to identify the relevant record with much less trial and error, so overall the costs may well not be any greater.

Ancestry

As mentioned on p. 62, Ancestry UK at <**www.ancestry.co.uk**> hosts a mirror of the FreeBMD index. This can be used on the site free of charge without a subscription, though it does require (free) registration. In addition, it offers as part of all its UK subscriptions access to the same material as the three sites discussed above: images of the index pages 1837–1983 and a database of registrations 1984–2005. You can in fact carry out a search of the latter without a subscription and the results give the full names and the county of registration, but to see the full details requires a subscription (Figure 5-7).

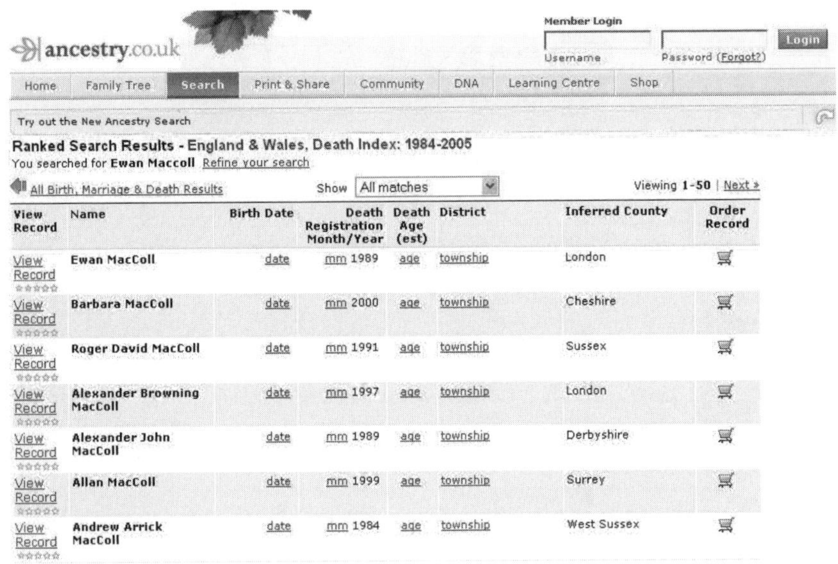

View Record	Name	Birth Date	Death Registration Month/Year	Death Age (est)	District	Inferred County	Order Record
View Record	Ewan MacColl	date	mm 1989	age	township	London	
View Record	Barbara MacColl	date	mm 2000	age	township	Cheshire	
View Record	Roger David MacColl	date	mm 1991	age	township	Sussex	
View Record	Alexander Browning MacColl	date	mm 1997	age	township	London	
View Record	Alexander John MacColl	date	mm 1989	age	township	Derbyshire	
View Record	Allan MacColl	date	mm 1999	age	township	Surrey	
View Record	Andrew Arrick MacColl	date	mm 1984	age	township	West Sussex	

Figure 5-7 Non-subscription search results for deaths at Ancestry

You can browse the index images, but this is quite a tedious business: once you have selected a year, a quarter and an initial letter, you are shown the first page of the index for that letter and then have to guess which page in the volume to jump to in order to find the name you are looking for. Also, the first few surnames for a letter may be found on the last page of the index for the previous letter.

Ancestry provides several different ways to get to the BMD indexes, but the easiest is just to go straight to the BMD home page at <**www.ancestry.co.uk/search/rectype/vital/freebmd/bmd.aspx**>.

Local BMD projects

While all the sites mentioned so far are national in coverage, there are a number of projects centred on local register offices. These go under the generic name UKBMD, and links to all local BMD projects will be found on Ian Hartas's UKBMD site at <**www.ukbmd.org.uk**>.

It's not just that these sites supplement the national datasets. An important difference between these and all the national sites mentioned above is that they work from the original local registration records and so will be largely free of the errors that dog the GRO indexes. (The latter were made from copies of the original registrations, putting them at two removes from the originals.) If your family comes from one of the parts of the country covered, these should be used in preference to the services mentioned in the previous sections.

The first of these projects was CheshireBMD at <**cheshirebmd.org.uk**>,

Cheshire BMD

Births, Marriages and Deaths on the Internet

In the results below, the reference number will be a link. Clicking on this link will add your choice to a summary list on a new page. From this summary page you will be able to review all your search results and you will find links to printable application forms which can be used to order the certificate for the index entry. Full details of the charges and the Register Office address can be found on the form.

	Cheshire Birth indexes for the years: 1933 to 1935				
Surname	Forename(s)	Sub-District	Registers At	Mother's Maiden Name	Reference
WOOD	Alan Williams	Dukinfield	Tameside		DUK/21A/33
WOOD	Alan	Ashton Town	Tameside		AST/217/15
WOOD	Alan	Bollington	Cheshire East		BOL/48/1
WOOD	Alan	Bredbury	Stockport	WILSON	BRE/10/33
WOOD	Alan	Congleton	Cheshire East		CO/93/65
WOOD	Alec	Mossley	Tameside		MOS/36/100
WOOD	Alice	Bredbury	Stockport	STEVENSON	BRE/11/16
WOOD	Alice	Stockport Second	Stockport		ST2/45/2
WOOD	Allan Collins	Stalybridge	Tameside		STB/25A/12
WOOD	Allan	Macclesfield	Cheshire East		MAC/31/68
WOOD	Allen	Newton & Godley	Tameside	DAWES	NEW/50/63
WOOD	Anne	Wrenbury	Cheshire Central		WR/6A/121
WOOD	Anne	Wrenbury	Cheshire Central		WR/6B/121
WOOD	Annie Joyce	Eastham	Cheshire West		EAS/71/8
WOOD	Annie	Mossley	Tameside		MOS/37/24
WOOD	Arnold	Ashton Town	Tameside		AST/215/34

Figure 5-8 CheshireBMD search results

a collaboration between Cheshire County Council, Wirral Metropolitan Borough, and the Family History Society of Cheshire.

Cheshire aims to have all index entries for births, marriages and deaths online for the period 1837–1950. The site has detailed information on the coverage so far for each registration district, and makes the ordering of certificates very straightforward – a link from each search result brings up a form for printing off, with the certificate reference (though not the other details) already filled in (Figure 5-8). The site already has over 5 million entries available for searching.

So far seven similar projects have taken a lead from the example of Cheshire, and use the same website design and software:

- BathBMD at <www.bathbmd.org.uk> has just over 1 million entries.
- LancashireBMD at <www.lancashirebmd.org.uk> contains just over 9 million records.
- NorthWalesBMD at <www.northwalesbmd.org.uk> has around 1.5 million records.
- StaffordshireBMD at <www.bmsgh.org/staffsbmd/> has almost 2 million records.
- WestMidlandsBMD at <www.bmsgh.org/wmbmd/> has around 2.3 million records.

- WiltshireBMD at <www.wiltshirebmd.org.uk> has around 220,000 records.
- YorkshireBMD at <www.YorkshireBMD.org.uk> has around 4.5 million entries to date.

Quite a number of other local authorities are developing indexes on similar lines, sometimes with the help of local family history societies:

- Barnsley
- Cambridgeshire County Council
- Darlington
- Durham County Council
- Gateshead
- Hertfordshire
- Isle of Wight
- Kent
- Kingston upon Thames
- Newcastle
- North Lincolnshire
- Rotherham
- Sheffield
- South Tyneside
- Stockton-on-Tees
- Tees Valley (covers the former county of Cleveland, now replaced by Middlesbrough, Hartlepool, Stockton-on-Tees, and Redcar & Cleveland)
- Warwickshire
- Wrexham

Links to all these will be found on UKBMD by clicking on the 'Local BMD' button on the left of the page. There is also a link to UKBMD's 'multi-region search'. NortheastBMD at <www.northeastbmd.org.uk> provides a gateway to all projects covering the north east of England.

There is wide variation in the coverage of these various services – some are complete or nearly so, others do not cover all events or the full period since 1837 – so it is a good idea to check the details of coverage before searching for an entry.

Register offices and registration districts
While the LocalBMD projects are very useful, they will not be much help if you do not know where an event was registered. Also, if you want to order a certificate from a local registrar, you will need to know which office to

approach. For both these reasons knowledge of registration districts is valuable, and there is extensive information available online.

For historical information about registration districts (up to 1930), Genuki has a set of pages prepared by Brett Langston at <**www.ukbmd.org. uk/genuki/reg/**> which provide comprehensive details about registration districts in England and Wales, giving:

- name of the district
- date of creation
- date of abolition (if before 1930)
- names of the sub-districts
- the GRO volume number used for the district in the national indexes of births, marriages and deaths
- an alphabetical listing of the parishes, townships and hamlets included within its boundaries (if a district covered parts of two or more counties, the areas in each county are listed separately)
- the name(s) of the district(s) which currently hold the records

If two or more offices are listed, the one which holds most records is named first, and the one with least is given last. There is an alphabetical list of districts at <**www.ukbmd.org.uk/genuki/reg/districts/**>, with links to lists for individual counties, and if you are not sure what registration district a particular place is in, consult <**www.ukbmd.org.uk/genuki/places/**>.

Genuki also has tables matching the GRO volume numbers to registration districts at <**www.genuki.org.uk/big/eng/civreg/GROIndexes.html**>.

The names and current contact details of individual register offices will also be found on Genuki, at <**www.ukbmd.org.uk/genuki/reg/regoff. html**>. This list does not link to the websites of register offices which have an online presence, but it does provide email addresses and links to any LocalBMD sites which include that registration district.

The GRO's home page at <**www.gro.gov.uk**> has a search box to find local register offices for a particular postcode or place. The search results provide a link to the relevant local authority web page.

Digitization of certificates

While Scotland, as described later in this chapter, has had most of its civil registration records online for some years, the story for England and Wales has been a different one. The process has been a long and tortuous one, with plenty of controversy and still no firm end in sight.

As early as January 2002, a Government white paper *Civil Registration: Vital Change* proposed moving to an online certificate service. After the initial proposals ran into objections, both genealogical and parliamentary

– you can see a brief outline at <**www.gro.gov.uk/gro/content/aboutus/ lookingahead/**> – in 2005 the GRO eventually launched the DOVE (Digitisation of Vital Events) project. This aimed to digitize all birth, marriage, and death indexes up to 2006, and the contract for the project was awarded to Siemens. Meanwhile the closure of the Family Records Centre in Islington went ahead, partly justified by the claim that, with all the records imminently online, there was no need for GRO indexes to have a physical home.

However, in July 2008, the GRO announced that, with roughly half the work done, the contract with Siemens had expired and was not being renewed. The situation in January 2009 is that the GRO is now *reviewing* the whole matter, and future progress will apparently depend on whether 'the business case confirms that sufficient benefits will result from digitisation'. If so, the project will restart later in 2009. If they prioritize making the already digitized records available, we might, I suppose, see something online by 2010, but otherwise it looks unlikely that we will see any results from the original proposal before its tenth anniversary in 2012.

Needless to say, throughout this process the GRO's proposals and actions have received close scrutiny from the genealogical world, the lead being taken by the Society of Genealogists and the Federation of Family History Societies.

You can keep up to date with the official announcements at <**www.gro. gov.uk/gro/content/aboutus/lookingahead/Digitisation_Project.asp**>, and new developments (or the lack of them) are widely discussed on genealogy blogs (see p. 367) and discussion forums (Chapter 18).

Scotland

In Scotland, general registration dates from 1 January 1855. The website of the General Register Office for Scotland (GROS) at <**www.gro-scotland. gov.uk**> is the official online source of information about these records.

Genuki's 'Introduction to Scottish Family History' at <**www.genuki.org. uk/big/sct/intro.html**> has information on civil registration in Scotland, and GROS has a page 'How can GROS help me research my Scottish ancestors?' at <**www.gro-scotland.gov.uk/famrec/hlpsrch/**>. GROS provides a list of local register offices with contact details at <**www.gro-scotland.gov. uk/files1/registration/reglist.pdf**>. Links to websites are not provided in this listing, but the domain name given in the email address (the part after the @) prefixed with *www.* will probably get you to the local authority website which hosts the pages for the local registration service. GROS also has a list of parish and registration districts available in PDF or Excel spreadsheet format from <**www.gro-scotland.gov.uk/famrec/hlpsrch/list-of-parishes-registration-districts.html**>.

The situation with the Scottish general registration records is much better than that for England and Wales. The indexes to births, marriages and deaths are available, along with images of the older records, via the pay-per-view system at ScotlandsPeople (described in detail on p. 42). The site currently offers the following registration records:

- birth indexes and images of certificates 1855–1908; indexes only 1909–2006
- marriage indexes 1855–1933
- death indexes and images of certificates 1855–1958, indexes only 1959–2006

Each year, coverage is extended by a further year, with the new data normally added in January. Not all certificates can be viewed or ordered online, and for those that cannot, the GROS website provides ordering information at <**www.gro-scotland.gov.uk/famrec/bdm.html**>.

As reported on p. 30, there seems to be the possibility that some time in the not too distant future, the Scottish civil registration records will also be available on other commercial sites.

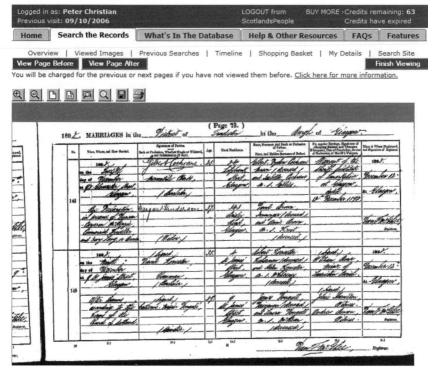

Figure 5-9 A marriage register image at ScotlandsPeople

The University of Glasgow has an extensive and informative website devoted to the history of general registration in Scotland in The Scottish Way of Birth and Death at <**www.gla.ac.uk/departments/scottishwayof birthanddeath/**>.

Ireland

In Ireland, registration of Protestant marriages dates from 1 April 1845, while full registration began on 1 January 1864. The records for the whole of Ireland up to 31 December 1921 are held by the Registrar General in Dublin, who also holds those for the Republic of Ireland from that date. The equivalent records for Northern Ireland are held by the General Register Office (Northern Ireland), GRONI. The relevant websites are at <**www.groireland. ie**> and <**www.groni.gov.uk**> respectively.

While Scotland had already solved the issues of online access to historical civil registration records by 2002, it seems as if the Irish authorities, North and South, are a long way behind, and there is no official civil registration data for Ireland currently available on the web. In the Republic, a consultation document *Bringing Civil Registration into the 21st Century* at <**www.groireland.ie/images/consultation.pdf**>) was published by the government in May 2001. In October 2003 they announced the official launch of the 'government approved modernisation of the civil registration service', with the promise that 'Further developments within the modernised Civil Registration Service will include the introduction of automated genealogy/family research facilities and the provision of a range of services over the Internet'. But there have been few outward signs of progress and we do not seem to be any closer to online civil registration records for the Republic than we were at the time of the first edition of this book back in 2001. Ireland's Civil Registration Bill 2003 (<**www.irlgov.ie/bills28/ bills/2003/3503/b35c03d.pdf**>) makes no mention of online access to historical records in its 68 pages; it merely empowers the Registrar to consider the use of 'electronic or other information technology' where appropriate. GRO Ireland has links to relevant documents relating to the 'Civil Registration Service Modernisation Programme' at <**www.groireland. ie/groproject.htm**>, but there is no information more recent than October 2003.

The Genealogical Society of Ireland's page (on its old website) devoted to civil registration proposals at <**www.dun-laoghaire.com/genealogy/ civreg.html**> provides a highly critical account, both of the detail of the proposals and of the failure to make progress. The Council of Irish Genealogical Organisations reports on its own campaign to secure improvements to civil registration and access to the records in the Republic at <**www.cigo.ie/campaigns_gro.html**>.

Sean Murphy's very useful Guide to the General Register Office of Ireland at <**homepage.tinet.ie/~seanjmurphy/gro/**> covers all aspects of civil registration in Ireland, though it has not been updated since 2002 and is therefore not the place to look for latest developments.

No firm plans to place records or indexes online have been announced by GRONI either. However, a consultation document *Civil Registration in the 21st century*, published in October 2003, reveals that all the indexes have been electronically indexed. Digitization is envisaged as being complete 'several years from now' and the paper offers no firm view on what material should be available online. I can find nothing on the GRONI website to indicate any progress since the previous edition of this book in 2005.

However, while nothing has been happening on the official front, there has been a major development elsewhere. In January 2009, FamilySearch announced the addition of the Irish civil registration records up to 1958 (i.e. those over 50 years old) on its pilot Record Search site at <**pilot.family search.org**> (see p. 104). There is a searchable index, with links to images of the original manuscript and printed indexes. While the information on the site carries no indication that this material is incomplete, I found that a great many entries I had previously extracted from the microfilm indexes were missing from the online index. Whether this is an unpublished limitation in the data or a technical teething problem with the index – this is, after all, a pilot site – is impossible to say, but no doubt this will be solved in due course (at the time of writing the material had been available for only three days). In any case, even without the full index, it is possible to use it to locate the relevant index images, just as we are used to doing on the civil registration index sites for England and Wales – searching for a name and a specific year, will lead you to the images of that year's index volume, which you can then page through. (In fact, the IGI at <**www. familysearch.org**> (see p.101) also has some Irish civil registration data: the births for the first five years of registration in Ireland, 1864–68, and some early Protestant marriage registrations.)

Of course, FamilySearch provides only the indexes, so we are still a long way from the situation in Scotland. All in all, it is difficult to see how any complete civil registration records for Ireland could be available on the web, officially, for some years. At least in the case of GRONI, though, there seems to be no reason to doubt that it will happen, even if the timescale is uncertain. In fact GRONI has already taken the first step in that certificates can be ordered online via a secure e-commerce system, or you can print off blank forms in PDF format.

A list of Irish registration districts, which are based on Poor Law Unions, is provided by Sean Murphy at <**homepage.eircom.net/~seanjmurphy/**

gro/plus.htm> and by ConnorsGenealogy <**www.connorsgenealogy.com/ districts.htm**>, which includes the volume numbers and links to a map of registration districts at <**www.connorsgenealogy.com/RegDist.htm**>.

From-Ireland has a page devoted to Civil Registration at <**www.from-ireland.net/gene/civilregistration.htm**>, which links to some small extracts for a wide range of registration districts at <**www.from-ireland.net/gene/ district.htm**>.

Local transcripts

In the absence of any national programme of digitization for Irish registration records, there are nonetheless a few local and partial transcription projects.

The only coherent project I am aware of is Waterford County Library's online index to local death registrations, with full transcriptions of the original certificates, at <**www.waterfordcountylibrary.ie/en/familyhistory/ deathregisters/**> as part of its electronic catalogue (Figure 5-10).

The following have small collections of registration data transcribed:

- Margaret Grogan has a range of transcriptions for County Cork, mostly for individual places, at <**myhome.ispdr.net.au/~mgrogan/cork/a_civil. htm**>, compiled from submissions to the Cork mailing list. You need to check each one as there is no overall search facility.

Figure 5-10 An entry from Waterford County Library's death register database

- The Ireland CMC Genealogy Record Project at <**www.cmcrp.net**> has user-submitted data which includes some civil registration records, though these are mostly individual entries rather than systematic extractions. There are separate pages for Clare, Cork, Dublin, Kerry, Limerick, Mayo, Tipperary, Waterford, Wicklow, and a single page for all other counties. Once on a county page, there are links at the top of the page to the various groups of records.

Offshore

The Isle of Man, and the individual Channel Islands (Jersey, Guernsey, Alderney and Sark) have their own civil registration starting from various dates.

The Isle of Man Civil Registry has a website at <**www.gov.im/registries/ general/civilregistry/**>, though it is mainly devoted to new registrations. The 'Contacts' button at the top of the page, though, will lead you to contact details, including an email address, enabling you to make your own enquiries. The Family History Library catalogue (see p. 206) has details of microfilmed civil registration records for the island available in Family History Centers.

Alex Glendinning has a 'Research in the Channel Islands FAQ' at <**user. itl.net/~glen/genukici.html**> with information on civil registration (on the pages for the individual islands), but there is no civil registration data online for these islands.

The Superintendent Registrar for Jersey has web pages at <**www.gov.je/ HomeAffairs/Registrar/**>, though there is no information about accessing records. The States of Guernsey website at <**www.gov.gg**> appears to have no information about civil registration at all.

The Priaulx Library on Guernsey has a list of 'Chanel Islands Civil Records on Microfilm' at <**www.priaulxlibrary.co.uk/images/library/ CHANNEL-ISLAND-CIVIL-RECORDS.pdf**>.

John Fuller's 'Channel Islands Genealogy' page at <**www.rootsweb. ancestry.com/~jfuller/ci/volunteers.html**> mentions some volunteers prepared to do look-ups in the Guernsey death registers.

Certificate exchanges

Although current GRO rules specifically forbid family historians from putting scanned certificates online,[6] the UK BDM Exchange at <**www.ukbdm.org. uk**> has a service allowing people to exchange information on certificates. The site has an index of some 90,000 certificates and gives an email address

---

6 'Guidance on the Copying of Birth, Death and Marriage Certificates', HMSO Guidance Note No. 7, online at <**www.hmso.gov.uk/copyright/guidance/gn_07.htm**>.

so that you can contact the certificate holder for more details. The listing also indicates those cases where a certificate is no longer needed by the owner. There are also some baptisms, marriages and burials from parish registers. Search results include full names as well as date and place. Clicking on the small number in the left-hand column brings up a screen with contact details for the owner of the certificate. The site requires registration and payment of £5 per year, though you can start with a one-month free trial, which can be extended by entering information from your own certificates.

A much smaller free site is BMD Certificate Exchange at <**bmd-cert-exch-site.ourwardfamily.com**> with around 2,500 certificates.

For Scotland, there is the Scotland BDM Exchange at <**www.sctbdm.com**>, which has almost 40,000 entries, though this includes some entries from parish registers. The site is free. A much more limited facility for Ireland, with under 1,000 certificates, will be found at <**www.thauvin.net/chance/ireland/bmd/**>.

Overseas

Some events registered overseas form part of the UK's records and are held by the GRO, notably consular records and those for the armed forces. Findmypast (see p. 46) has a wide range of these at <**www.findmypast.com**>. The only way to see a full list is from the search page for the overseas records, but they include:

- Natal and South African Forces deaths 1899–1902
- WW1 marriages (behind British Lines) and deaths
- WW2 deaths
- WW2 deaths Indian Services
- Consular & UK High Commission births, marriages and deaths
- Army births, marriages and deaths
- Service Department marriages and deaths
- Regimental Birth Indexes
- Chaplains births, marriages and deaths
- Air births
- Air deaths and missing persons
- Marine births and deaths
- Ionian Islands births, marriages and deaths

The Genealogist at <**www.thegenealogist.co.uk**> (see p. 47) also offers many British overseas records from the GRO:

- Overseas BMDs (from Army, Consular, Ionian Island, and Regimental records)

- Overseas Marine Deaths
- World War 1 Deaths
- Wold War 2 Deaths

If you have ancestors who were immigrants or emigrants, you may need access to other countries' civil registration services. There is no single way of getting this information for every country, but there are two good places to look for links. GenWeb (see p. 24) has sites for over 100 different countries, and the index of countries at <**www.worldgenweb.org/countryindex. html**> will take you to the relevant regional GenWeb site. Even if there is no civil registration information, there will often be a message board where you can ask. It also makes sense to check the relevant country or regional page on Cyndi's List at <**www.cyndislist.com**>. Sections devoted to individual countries will also be found on the pages for:

- Births & Baptisms <**www.cyndislist.com/births.htm**>
- Deaths <**www.cyndislist.com/deaths.htm**>
- Marriages <**www.cyndislist.com/marriage.htm**>

The Research Guidance leaflets for individual countries at FamilySearch (see p. 9) should also contain information on civil registration records.

Don't expect other countries to be as far on the road to complete digital records as Scotland is, but you may be lucky. Some states in English-speaking parts of the world have indexes online. For example, New South Wales has an online index to historical registration records at <**www.bdm. nsw.gov.au/familyHistory/searchHistoricalRecords.htm**>, and British Columbia has a similar service at <**www.bcarchives.gov.bc.ca/textual/ governmt/vstats/v_events.htm**>. For births, both of these sites list only events over 100 years ago, but more recent marriages and deaths are included. For the USA, Cyndi's List has detailed information for each state (under the heading 'Records'), at <**www.cyndislist.com/usvital. htm#States**>.

6

CENSUS

A census has been taken every 10 years since 1801, except in 1941, and names of individuals are recorded from the 1841 census onwards. The significance of these records for genealogists is that they provide snapshots of family groups at 10-year intervals. More importantly, from 1851 onwards they give a place of birth, which is essential information for individuals born before the start of general registration. Since an approximate date of birth can be calculated from the person's age, this makes it possible to trace the line back to the parish registers.

While we seem doomed to an interminable wait for civil registration records to go online, there has been enormous progress in digitizing census records. The 1901 census for England and Wales, digitized by the National Archives and defence contractor QinetiQ, went online in January 2002. While the immense demand initially caused the site to crash, this at least showed the huge potential interest, and the result was that by April 2006, all the censuses for England, Wales and Scotland from 1841 to 1901 were available online. Indeed all the data is now available on more than one data service.

The 1911 census for England and Wales started to go online in January 2009 and should be complete by the middle of the year. Even Ireland, the laggard in getting genealogical records online, has started to release the 1911 census in digital form.

The censuses are probably the most complex genealogical records to go online, and with so many sites offering large amounts of census data, this chapter can only aim to give an overview and comparison of the main sites. *Census: The Expert Guide* gives much more detail, including a step-by-step guide to each of the commercial services; here the most detailed coverage is for the 1911 Census.

▌ General information

There are a number of starting points for official information on the census. The FamilyRecords Portal 'Census' page at <**www.familyrecords.gov.uk/ topics/census.htm**> has basic details and links to other official websites with census information and data.

If you are not familiar with census records and the way they are referred to, the British-Genealogy site explains piece numbers, folio numbers, and schedules at <**www.british-genealogy.com/resources/census/**>.

Genuki has pages on the census for:

- England and Wales <**www.genuki.org.uk/big/eng/CensusR.html**>
- Scotland <**www.genuki.org.uk/big/sct/Census.html**>
- Ireland <**www.genuki.org.uk/big/irl/#Census**>

It also has a searchable database of places in the 1891 census at <**www. genuki.org.uk/big/census_place.html**>, which gives the county, registration district, registration sub-district, National Archives piece number and LDS film number (see p. 206) for any place in England, Wales and the Isle of Man. The GenDocs site shows exactly what information was recorded for each census from 1841 to 1901 at <**homepage.ntlworld.com/hitch/ gendocs/census.html**>, and gives the date on which each census was taken. Talking Scot's pages devoted to the Scottish census at <**www.talkingscot. com/censuses/census-intro.htm**> do the same for Scotland.

All census records for England and Wales are catalogued in the National Archives' catalogue at <**www.catalogue.nationalarchives.gov.uk**>. Even if you are using an online census index this may be useful, as it provides a way of establishing the piece number(s) for a particular place in each census.

Histpop at <**www.histpop.org**> is a site devoted to the history of the British population, and holds an enormous number of official documents relating to the censuses, including the population abstracts and the final census reports. For the population of individual counties and towns, see A Vision of Britain Through Time at <**www.visionofbritain.org.uk**> (p. 238), which has graphs of population change between 1801 and 2001. This also holds many census reports and a 1977 official *Guide to the Census Reports*, which 'outlines the history of the census and describes how coverage of various topics has developed'.

▮ Free census indexes

While you will need to use the commercial services as the only ones which provide images of the original records – you will need to consult these to check the index entries – there are four major projects which provide census indexes free of charge, and many local census indexes.

The 1881 Census Index

The 1881 Census Index for England and Wales was a joint indexing project between the Genealogical Society of Utah (GSU) and the Federation of Family History Societies, which gave rise first to an index on microfiche and then, with Scotland, on CD-ROM. In October 2002, the data for England and Wales was made available on the FamilySearch site at <**www.familysearch.org**>. It is automatically included in any search on 'All Resources', when you select 'Advanced Search' from the 'Search Records' but there is also the possibility of searching only this dataset, by selecting 'Census' instead. Unlike the index issued on CD-ROM, the online version excludes the index for Scotland, which is available online only on the ScotlandsPeople site.

FamilySearch Record Search

In July 2008, FamilySearch launched a very new type of census project on its pilot Record Search site at <**pilot.familysearch.org**>. Until this point, there had been a clear distinction between commercial and non-commercial databases. The innovation of the new service was to create a hybrid service, with a free index linked to commercial images. FamilySearch offers a free index to the 1841 and 1861 censuses but linked to the census images at Findmypast and Origins. FamilySearch does not itself make a charge for access to the images but you need to purchase Findmypast credits (p. 46) to view them. The search facility works in a very similar way to the parish register search on the pilot site described on p. 104, so there is no need to give an example here.

This is still a very new service running on a pilot site. The main limitation is that, so far, the search options are quite restricted, certainly compared to what is available on Findmypast. If you are already using Findmypast or Origins, this site does not bring any benefits. The big advantage of this service, however, is for those on a tight budget: access to the images is free if you are using a computer in a Family History Center.

The indexes themselves are from Findmypast and Origins and therefore do not represent an alternative to what is already available on those sites.

FreeCen

FreeCEN at <**freecen.rootsweb.com**> is a comprehensive volunteer project which aims to provide a free index to all English and Welsh censuses from 1841 to 1891. Work so far has concentrated on the 1891 census, and there is still a very long way to go. However, some counties are complete or nearly complete for individual census years: Aberdeenshire, Banff for 1841; East Lothian for 1841 and 1851; Bedfordshire, Cornwall, Devon for 1891. By January 2009, the site had transcribed almost 14 million records. Usefully, the site gives details of exactly which piece numbers are covered, and there is a status page for each county currently being transcribed, linked from <**freecen.rootsweb.com/project.htm**>.

FHS Online

Until recently the major online source for the many local census indexes prepared by family history societies had been FamilyHistoryOnline, the data service run by the FFHS. Some of these indexes are being added to Findmypast, notably the material for 1851, but S&N genealogy has launched a new site, FHS Online at <**www.fhs-online.co.uk**>, to help FHSs publish their data. The site currently hosts 49 free county census indexes, though they generally do not cover the whole county for a particular census year.

Access is free, though you need to complete a registration in order to carry out searches. Search facilities are very basic – just name and age – and the results give only the area and the National Archives' census reference, not the address (Figure 6-1). However, once you have found an individual, you can get a complete listing of the household.

Local indexes

There are countless other small indexes to census material on the web. You will find much census material on sites for individual villages or parishes, and even on some FHS sites. The Workhouses site at <**www.workhouses. org.uk**> has census extracts for many workhouses.

Census Finder has probably the most comprehensive set of links to local transcriptions on its UK page at <**www.censusfinder.com/united_kingdom.**

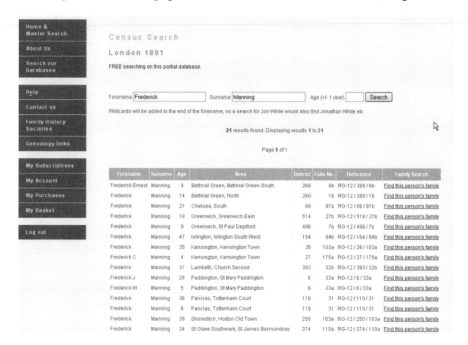

Figure 6-1 Search results at FHS Online

htm>, organized by county. The Genuki county and parish pages will also have links to local census indexes.

▍ The commercial services

By the beginning of 2009, all the commercial data services listed on p. 39ff. were offering census material on a subscription or pay-per-view basis (prices are given in Tables 4-1a and 4-1b). In general, they either already offer or aim to offer by the end of 2009 a complete run of census indexes 1841–1901 for England and Wales, with a few exceptions:

- ScotlandsPeople has exclusively the indexes and images for the Scottish 1841–1901 censuses
- The 1911 census site is, initially, the only site with the 1911 census for England and Wales
- Ancestry is the only site apart from ScotlandsPeople to provide census indexes (not images) for Scotland
- British Origins has only the 1841, 1861 and 1871 censuses
- Familyrelatives has a very new service offering census images without indexes

Although there are many different commercial sites offering censuses data, the number of distinct sets of census indexes is in reality much smaller. For a start, The Genealogist and RootsUK are both run by S&N Genealogy with identical data but different facilities. Second, Genes Reunited and 1901 Census Online are both run by Genes Reunited. Also, apart from the 1901 census index, which is that from the original 1901 Census project, all the indexes on these two sites are licensed from S&N and are therefore identical to what is available at The Genealogist and RootsUK. Third, Findmypast and Origins have cross-licensed some of their indexes, so that all those available at Origins are identical to those at Findmypast. Finally, all the 1881 censuses for England and Wales take the free FamilySearch index (p. 81) as their basis. Broadly speaking, then, there are only three groups of indexes for England and Wales:

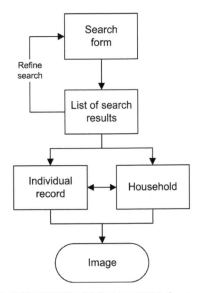

Figure 6-2 Typical census search process

- Ancestry
- Findmypast and Origins
- TheGenealogist (also used on RootsUK, Genes Reunited, 1901 Census Online)

This is important because, if you can't find someone in the census index on one site and want to try another, there is no point in using one with an identical index. However, the 1901 census index on Genes Reunited and 1901 Census Online is the National Archives' original 1901 census index and is not shared with The Genealogist.

The general process of census searching one of the commercial services is generally quite similar on all these sites and the flowchart in Figure 6-2 gives an overview of the typical process. The search options of the individual sites are shown in Table 6-1. Only ScotlandsPeople differs very significantly from the others: you have to pay to see each page of search results, and it does not offer a transcription of an individual record or household, but goes straight from the list of search results to the page image.

The image formats and viewers used by the various sites are discussed on p. 52ff.

Each of the commercial services is described briefly below, followed by a more detailed look at the 1911 Census, and a comparison of the various sites.

Findmypast

Since Findmypast has been heavily involved with the 1911 Census project, it's no surprise that their own census indexes are very similar in features and appearance (see below).

The range of search facilities is very comprehensive, with all fields searchable, including address and census reference. If you are using the pay-per-view facility, it is worth noting that the search results lead straight to a household listing, so you do not need to pay for both an individual and household details. However, there is a limitation in their search results: because only name, age, district and county are given, and not birthplace, it can sometimes be hard to identify the right individual immediately, which is a concern to pay-per-view customers.

Findmypast's images are among the best available, though their use of the DjVu image format (p. 56) inevitably causes difficulties for some users.

Ancestry

Although Ancestry has a pay-per-view system, this is a fairly recent addition, and it is at heart a subscription service. It has extremely flexible search facilities, and a striking feature is that searching does not require a surname. This can be very useful if looking for a woman under an earlier or later married name, or if you have simply failed to find the right person searching on the expected surname. While you can choose exact or loose search, with the latter, the site orders results by its own ranking system, which is far from transparent. A useful feature for the local historian or anyone with a need to look at the whole of a street, is that you can browse through the individual enumeration districts. From the listing of any household, you can also get a list of all the people on the same page of the census schedule.

Ancestry's image quality is generally good and its image viewer has a range of useful options. The site has suffered from some notable lapses in data validation (see p. 34), but the flexibility of the search does help to compensate for errors.

At the time of writing, Ancestry is the only site apart from ScotlandsPeople to offer indexes to the Scottish censuses, though it has not been permitted to add the images.

Origins

Origins has only three censuses available. Since it licensed its 1841 and 1871 to, and has licensed the 1861 census from, Findmypast, the main advantage of Origins lies in its other records, particularly those from before 1837.

Nontheless, the census data will be useful to those who are mainly interested in those other datasets, or who need access only to the earlier censuses. While the number of search fields is more limited than Findmypast or Ancestry, they will certainly be enough for most purposes. The site uses the NameX surname matching system (see p. 268), which has the useful feature than you can select how close a match needs to be. Images are a mixture of black and white and greyscale. The site's indexes have a good reputation for accuracy.

The Genealogist and RootsUK

The Genealogist and Roots UK are run by the same company, S&N Genealogy Supplies, and therefore have the same census indexes and images. However, they differ significantly in their charging systems, since RootsUK is pay-per-view only and The Genealogist has three different types of access. RootsUK is ideal if you are on a tight budget or have only limited needs, but The Genealogist's much more sophisticated range of search facilites – there are more different types of search, and each is very flexible – make it the better site for the serious genealogist.

One limitation with these two sites is that in some cases they are still using relatively low-resolution black-and-white images. However, these older images are gradually being replaced by greyscale so this is becoming steadily less of an issue.

Genes Reunited and 1901 Census Online

Genes Reunited purchased the original 1901 Census data and website, and has added to it indexes and images for earlier years, licensed from The Genealogist (this is apparent from a number of shared errors – see <**www. spub.co.uk/census/tables.php**>). The 1901 Census site retains its own identity, but the material is also accessible directly from the main Genes Reunited site. The two sets of data have not really been integrated and the charging regimes are subtly different, but the main issue is that the 1901 census has very good search facilities, while those for the remaining census years are very limited. Another issue is that any credits purchased are valid for a mere seven days, well short of the 90 days that is the norm elsewhere.

In view of these limitations, and the fact that, for the most part, the same indexes and images are available at The Genealogist with far superior search facilities and more flexible charging, the only real reasons to use this site are loyalty to Genes Reunited or a wish to access the original 1901 Census index.

ScotlandsPeople

As of January 2009, ScotlandsPeople is the only site offering indexes and images for all the Scottish censuses. For the present, then, its merits and limitations are somewhat moot. Even if you use Ancestry's indexes to the Scottish censuses, you will need to use ScotlandsPeople to view the page images. Unfortunately the quality of the images is rather poor by the standards of some of the other data services discussed here, though the fact that you have a range of different viewers available is very welcome. A very useful feature is the record the site keeps of all your searched and viewed inages, so that you can return to these at any time. The absence of a subscription option is an issue for heavy users of the site, especially since you have to pay for each page of search results.

Familyrelatives

During 2009, Familyrelatives will be adding census data to its subscription site. At the time of writing, there had been no official announcement about the availability of this data, but a small amount was had been posted on the site for the 1841 and 1861 censuses. Since the material had not been officially launched, and some aspects were clearly still undergoing development, the following observations should be treated as provisional.

This site differs from the other census data services in that, so far, it offers census images only, not indexes. These are browsable by county and place – selecting a place brings up the first page of the relevant enumeration book, which can then be scrolled through. Unusually, you can download the entire set of pages for an enumeration book in a single file, a very useful feature for the local historian.

The 1911 census

The 1911 census is different in a number of respects from the earlier censuses. Most notably, the individual household schedules, written by the head of household him- or herself, have been preserved. Also, the form contains fertility information: for each couple, the number of years married, the total number of children born, and the number still living. Finally, in addition to the household schedule, there are a number of other forms showing details of the dwelling and of other buildings in the street. The 1911 census, therefore, gives you much more information about your ancestors than earlier censuses.

The 1911 census for England and Wales was expected to be available to the public from January 2012. The fact that it has been published in advance of that date is the result of a request from Guy Etchells under the Freedom of Information Act. The National Archives' initial refusal of earlier access was appealed to the Information Commissioner, who ruled in December 2006 that, as long as certain sensitive items of information were concealed, there was no reason why the information could not be made available. Although the initial request was for access to the record for a single household, the National Archives decided more or less immediately that it would digitize the whole 1911 for release in 2009. In 2007 the contract for the project was awarded to Scotland Online (now called Brightsolid), the company behind ScotlandsPeople (see p. 42). With the subsequent takeover of Findmypast by Brightsolid in 2008, Findmypast became involved in the project, and on 13th January the first batch of data went online at <www.1911census.co.uk>, with Findmypast's branding.

The site runs a pay-per-view system, though it is more expensive than the other pay-per-view census sites: the household listing costs 10 credits (i.e. £1), and the census image 30 credits (i.e. £3). The justification for the higher costs is that the amount of material to be transcribed is much greater and instead of a single page to view, you get a whole bunch of them, photographed in colour, not just digitized from microfilm.

This initial release covers all English counties except Cumberland, Durham, Northumberland, Westmorland, Yorkshire (East Riding and North Riding). These counties, along with Wales, Isle of Man, Channel Islands, Royal Navy ships at sea and military establishments overseas are due to be added by the summer of 2009. In the first release only the household schedules are available, but for any household where you have paid to see the household schedule, you will subsequently be able to view the additional pages without further charge.

You can sign up to a mailing list to be kept informed of developments (notably the addition of the remaining counties), and there is an official blog at <**blog.1911census.co.uk**>.

Using the 1911 Census

The basic search on the home page allows you to specify only first and last names, place of residence and year of birth, but the full person search, shown in Figure 6-3, has additional fields and should be used in preference unless you have a very unusual name to search for, or have little information.

Clicking on the 'Show advanced fields' button brings up a whole range of additional options, including relationship to head of household, occupation and a census reference. You need to be careful with the year of birth, as the index contains a calculated year of birth which will often be out by one year, so it is best not to chose the 'Exact' option. The results for the search in Figure 6-3 – for my great-grandfather, Frederick Marshall, born in 1859 – are shown in Figure 6-4.

From here, you can either view a transcript or view the page image. Alternatively, if you don't want to waste credits on looking at the wrong entry – these two differ only in year of birth – it may be worth refining the search and entering the name of his wife or one of the children. In fact, since Frederick Marshall was born on 21st December, it's easy to guess that his age is correctly given at 51, and the household transcript is shown in Figure 6-5. If you don't see a likely individual in this initial listing, you will

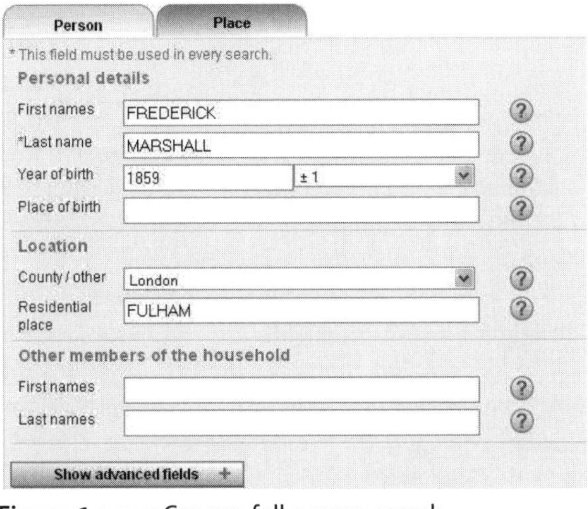

Figure 6-3 1911 Census: full person search

1911 census: person search results

2 results found. You searched for:	
First names	FREDERICK
First names Algorithm	Exact
Last names	MARSHALL
Last names Algorithm	Exact
Birth Year	1859
Birth Year	+/- 1 years
County	London
Residence	FULHAM

Schedule type	Last names	First names	Sex	Birth year	Age in 1911	District / other	County / other	Transcript	Original page
HOUSEHOLD	MARSHALL	FREDERICK	M	1860	51	Fulham	London	View Transcript	View Original Page
HOUSEHOLD	MARSHALL	FREDERICK	M	1858	53	Fulham	London	View Transcript	View Original Page

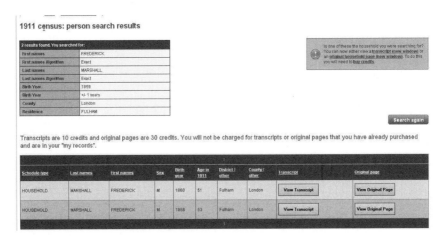

Figure 6-4 1911 Census: search results

1911 Census Household Transcript

Name:	Relationship to head:	Marital Status:	Years married:	Sex:	Age in 1911:	Occupation:	Where born:	Report error	View Original Page
MARSHALL, FREDERICK	HEAD	MARRIED		M	51	CYCLE MAKER DEALER	LONDON WESTMINSTER	Report error	View Original Page
MARSHALL, HARRIET ANN	WIFE	MARRIED	23	F	50		SURREY WEST HORSLEY	Report error	View Original Page
MARSHALL, FREDERICK	SON	SINGLE		M	20	CYCLE MAKER	LONDON KNIGHTSBRIDGE	Report error	View Original Page
MARSHALL, ELLA	DAUGHTER	SINGLE		F	15	AT HOME	LONDON KNIGHTSBRIDGE	Report error	View Original Page
MARSHALL, WINIFRED	DAUGHTER			F	8		LONDON FULHAM	Report error	View Original Page

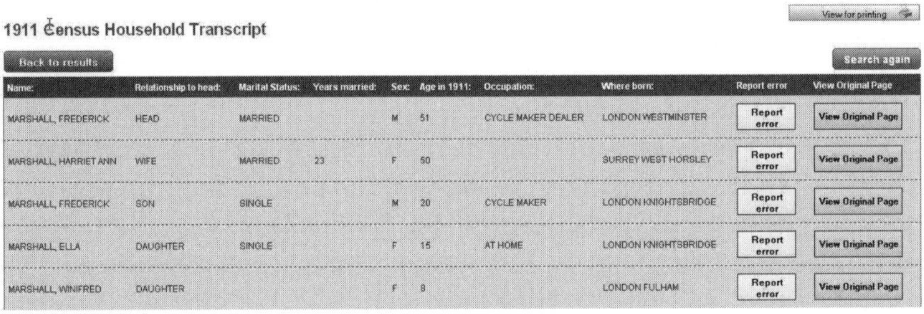

Figure 6-5 1911 Census: household transcript

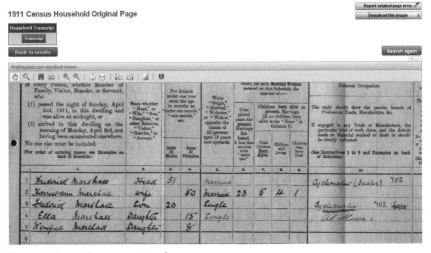

Figure 6-6 1911 Census: original page

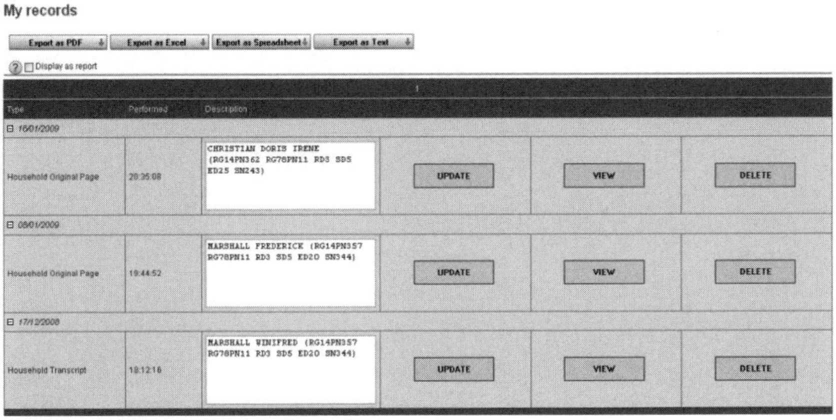

My records

Figure 6-7 1911 Census: my records

need to refine your search terms – normally leaving information out is a good idea, since you could easily be wrong about something, or there could be an error in the transcription.

On the household transcript page, clicking on the 'View Original Page' button will bring up an image of the original schedule in the viewer window (Figure 6-6).

In the centre here, you can see the fertility information: five children born, four living, one died. At the bottom right of the page, you would be able to see the original signature. The icons at the top of the viewer window allow zooming, rotation, printing and saving.

A useful feature of the site is that it keeps a record of what you have paid to view, and a 'my records' button at the top of the screen brings up a table of what you have viewed, so you can see them again (Figure 6-7).

▌ Comparison

With so many different places to turn for census indexes and images, for England and Wales at least, the obvious question is which to use. It is complicated by the fact that all the sites apart from the 1911 Census offer many additional datasets, and that will obviously play a role in your decision. The general comments about choosing an online service made on p. 57 will be relevant.

There are five main criteria which could be used to make this decision: coverage, cost, search facilities, image quality and index quality. Coverage is perhaps the least important of these – we are very close to the situation where all the main sites have all census years, apart from 1911. (It will perhaps be 2010 before we see the 1911 census available beyond the original site and Findmypast.) Costs are listed in Table 4-1 in Chapter 4. If you can get free access at the National Archives, the SoG or your public library (or perhaps

	Ancestry	Findmypast	1911 Census	The Genealogist	RootsUK	Genes Reunited	1901 census	1841–91 standard	Origins	Scotlands People	Ireland	1881
Search type	Advanced	Advanced	Advanced	Advanced	Advanced	Standard	1901 advanced	1841–91 standard	Standard	Standard	Standard	Standard
Name fields	2	3	3	2	2	2	3	2	2	2	2	2
Name variants	Custom	NameX	In development	Custom	Custom	Wildcards only	Wildcards only	Wildcards only	NameX	Soundex		Custom
Age	Year	Year	Year	Age	Age or year	Year	Year	Year	Age range	Age range	Age	Year
Birthplace	✓	✓	✓	County		Place keywords	✓		County/country			County
Residence	1 field, more addable	8 fields	County, district, place	County, district, address	County		10 fields	Keywords	County, parish	County or city, district	County, district, street	Country, county, town
Occupation	✓	✓	✓	✓	✓							
Gender	✓	✓	✓	✓		✓	✓			✓	✓	
Marital status		✓	Year of marriage									
Relation to head		✓	✓	✓								
Family members	4 fields	1 member	List first and last names	Separate family forename search						1 additional forename		Head
Keyword	✓		✓	Separate keyword search								
Address search	Yes – by leaving name field blank	Separate address search	Separate address search	Separate address search			Separate address search	Separate address search (beta)			Browse	
Reference		Separate ref. search	✓									

Table 6-1 Census search facilities compared

a Christmas present of a subscription), these won't necessarily be a factor.

Searching

Table 6-1 provides a comparison of the search facilities of the sites discussed. While the simple searches are very appealing, they can be extremely limiting if you are mistaken about some of your information, or an error in the index makes your ancestor initially unfindable. On the other hand, if in the advanced searches you enter many different items of information, then the chances that one of them does not match what is in the index only increase. But one of the most useful options is the ability to give names of other family members. This greatly increases your chances of identifying the right family, particularly with a common name.

As a general principle, more sophisticated search facilities can, to some extent, compensate for failures in index quality.

Image quality

It is hard to state any categorical preference in terms of image quality, since the individual microfilm frames which have been digitized vary quite significantly. Also, many of the sites are gradually replacing older, lower-quality images with better ones.

However, there are two main ways to evaluate it. The first is resolution. The 'Resolution' column in Table 6-2 shows the number of dots per inch in a sample page image from each site. Other things being equal, the higher this figure, the clearer the image. Lower resolution will tend to make the handwriting look blockier, and fine lines may be lost.

	Colour depth	**Typical resolution (estimated)**
Ancestry	Greyscale	200dpi
Findmypast	Greyscale	300dpi
The Genealogist	Older black and white Newer greyscale	200dpi
Genes Reunited	1841, 1851 greyscale Others black and white	200dpi
Origins	Mostly greyscale	300dpi
ScotlandsPeople	Black and white	200dpi

Table 6-2 Census image quality

Another issue is colour depth. Before the 1911 census project, which was digitally photographed in colour, all the census images came from digitizing microfilm. Therefore the only options are greyscale (as in a 'black and white' photograph, or the screenshots in this book), or monochrome (true black and white, as in the printed text in this book). Other things being equal, greyscale is preferable because it shows more detail. With monochrome every spot on the image becomes either black or white, with no intermediate shades. Monochrome can have the benefit of enhancing detail, especially where contrast is low, but some detail will be lost entirely – any mark on the paper lighter than some threshold value will end up white.

You can get an idea of the difference from Figure 4-1 on p. 34 the black and white image is arguably clearer in this case, but it is obviously missing some of the details of the writing, which is preserved in the fuzzier-looking greyscale image.

Index quality

Probably the most important issue is the accuracy of the indexing. The issues with online indexes and transcriptions have been discussed in some detail in Chapter 4 (see p. 33). The question is: can we decide which is the best site in terms of census index quality? Unfortunately, while there are plenty of anecdotal accounts of particular errors or types of error, it would be an impossible task to check a large enough sample in all the sites to come to any reliable conclusion. Also, of course, all the sites are making efforts to get rid of both systematic errors and the individual errors reported by users. All we can do here is look at a very small sample for three of the major data services.

Table 6-3 shows some comparative error levels for two sample enumeration districts. The 1861 example was the enumeration district for Pevensey in Sussex (RG 9/566) with 385 individuals. The 1891 sample was an enumeration district of 496 individuals in Islington (RG 12/166). The first was a fairly clearly written enumeration book, the second more difficult to read, hence the consistent difference in the number of errors. The choice of these was not entirely random: I chose two small enumeration districts so it would be a manageable task; I chose areas I was familiar with; I looked for one book with better and one with worse handwriting.

The data were compiled in July 2008 and are published in full at < **www. spub.co.uk/cenus/tables**>. I have excluded from the error count any entries I considered to be genuinely problematic (if not plain unreadable), so the error levels represent the number of entries the transcriber *should have* got right but didn't. The error levels do not represent purely the skill of the transcriber, but also reflect differences in the quality of the digitized images from which the transcriptions were made.

% errors	Forename		Surname		Birthplace	
	1861	1891	1861	1891	1861	1891
Ancestry	0.3%	9.3%	3.6%	43.5%	5.4%	17.9%
Findmypast	2.9%	1.4%	10.9%	12.1%	9.6%	2.4%
The Genealogist	3.4%	4.0%	8.8%	28.4%	19.0%	10.1%

Table 6-3 Census indexing errors

Analysis of the individual errors suggests some general conclusions:

- Transcribers were often ignorant of the names of surrounding parishes or districts and failed to recognized them – The Genealogist, for example, often misidentifies Wartling and Hooe, neighbouring parishes to Pevensey, as Worthing and Hove, both over 25 miles away.
- Transcribers seemed very ready to transcribe something completely implausible when there was a much more obvious alternative – Findmypast has *Daud* for *David*, *Stabel* for *Isabel*; a transcriber sometimes could not even recognize the name of the enumeration district when it turned up as a birthplace!
- Transcribers did not sufficiently take account of the writing habits of the original enumerator – Victorian capital letters may be florid, but they are normally consistent in any one hand.
- Transcribers were not always properly trained or supervised – Ancestry's transcriber for 1891 treated all dittos as meaning ' the same as the head of the household', even if there was a different name in-between (which accounts for the staggering percentage of surname errors in this transcription).

This is obviously a very small sample and one should we wary of drawing too firm conclusions from it, but at the very least it clearly sets a minimum level of errors to be expected: whichever service you choose, there will probably be at the very least about 3 per cent of fields mistranscribed. You therefore need to be imaginative in your searching if your initial search fails.

Ireland

The situation with the Irish censuses has been very different from that else-where in the British Isles. Until December 2007, there was no official or commercial site offering images of census records, and the only indexes were those made for individual counties or towns by volunteers. Of course, the situation with the records themselves is also very different – almost no

Irish census records survive for the nineteenth century. On the other hand, the 1901 and 1911 censuses have been publicly accessible in Ireland for over 30 years, so the irrelevance of the privacy issues that have controlled the timing of their digitization in England, Wales and Scotland ought to have seen them digitized sooner rather than later, one would have thought.

The National Archives of Ireland have a brief page of information at <www.nationalarchives.ie/genealogy/censusrtns.html>, as has the PRONI at <www.proni.gov.uk/your_family_tree_series_-_02_-_1901_census.pdf>. A good guide to the Irish censuses, detailing what is missing and what has survived, is available on the Fianna site at <www.rootsweb.ancestry.com/~fianna/guide/census.html>.

The next Irish census due for release is that for 1926, the first one conducted by the newly formed Irish Free State. As in England, there is a movement to reduce the closure period for the next census from 100 years to 75, which would make it immediately available. A petition to the Irish government is being promoted by the Council of Irish Genealogical Organisations (CIGO), which has information on their campaign at <www.cigo.ie/campaigns_1926.html>. The petition itself is at <www.petitionspot.com/petitions/1926C>, though in its first six months it has gathered fewer than 2,000 signatures.

The 1911 Census of Ireland

In December 2005 the National Archives of Ireland and Library and Archives Canada announced a joint project to digitize the two surviving Irish censuses, and in December 2007 the first fruits of this collaboration, the 1911 Census for Dublin, went online at <**census.nationalarchives.ie**>. It was expected that the remainder of the 1911 census would be online by the end of 2008, with the 1901 census to follow. However, this schedule has proved too ambitious: no further counties were added until in December 2008 material for Counties Antrim, Down and Kerry came online. Presumably the full complement of counties won't be available till the end of 2009 at best, and when the 1901 census will be complete seems very hard to guess.

However, it's difficult to complain very much about this delay, since the index and images are all available free of charge, making it the only census site with free images.

The search allows you to specficy name, age in 1911, the townland or street, and, if you know it, the enumeration district. The initial search results listing (Figure 6-8) shows name, address, age and gender, but the absence of birthplace in this listing may mean you cannot immediately identify the correct individual. However, since it costs nothing to check all the likely entries, this hardly matters.

Clicking on the name takes you to a page listing the entire household,

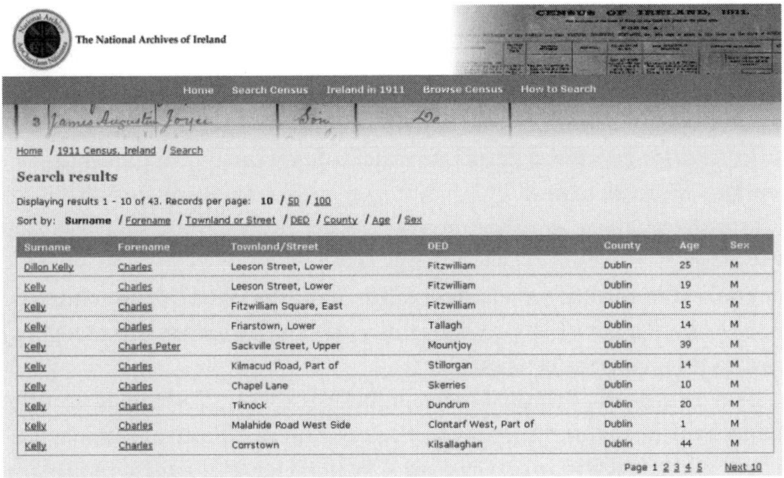

Figure 6-8 Ireland 1911 census: search results

and this has links to the images. Alongside the image of the household
return, the site provides all the other forms (enumerator's abstract, house
and building return, out-office and farm-steading return) in PDF format, one
file per return, and the images open in the Acrobat viewer (see p. 52).

Where those in the household are Irish speakers, the household return
will be in Irish, using the Irish script, and with the Irish forms of names
(e.g. *Seán* for *John*). However, the head of household's name, anglicized,
will be in the index as this occurs on the reverse of the household return.
See p. 274 for resources to help with the Irish language.

Local indexes

There are a number of sites with census data for individual counties. In the
Republic of Ireland some data from the 1901 census is online at <**www.
leitrim-roscommon.com/1901census/**>. Available data covers all or part of
the following six counties: Roscommon, Leitrim, Mayo, Sligo, Wexford,
Westmeath and Galway. Data for Leitrim and Roscommon is essentially
complete, but for the others, only small amounts of material are present. A
table gives detailed information about which individual parishes are wholly
or partly covered.

Census Finder has links to many local transcriptions for Ireland at
<www.censusfinder.com/ireland.htm>. These include some surviving frag-
ments of nineteenth-century censuses, but are mainly for the 1901 census
with some material for 1911.

Because of the amount of Irish census material destroyed, the so-called
'census substitutes' are important. One of the most important census substitutes, Griffith's Valuation, is discussed in Chapter 8, p. 124. Fianna has a

useful guide to these at <**www.rootsweb.ancestry.com/~fianna/guide/cen2. html**>, while the National Archives of Ireland has a briefer description at <**www.nationalarchives.ie/genealogy/valuation.html**>. The PRONI has similar information leaflets on valuation records and tithe applotment books linked from <**www.proni.gov.uk/index/family_history/family_ history_key_sources.htm**>.

Overseas

It is not possible to deal here with census data for countries outside the British Isles, but Cyndi's List provides links to census sites around the world at <**www.cyndislist.com/census2.htm**> .

The census data on FamilySearch includes the 1880 US census and the 1881 Canadian census, and there is a large amount of US census data online at Ancestry.com <**www.ancestry.com**>, which, for UK users, requires a worldwide subscription (see p. 44).

Census Links at <**www.censuslinks.com**> has links to census transcriptions for a number of countries.

7

CHURCH RECORDS

Before the introduction of General Registration in 1837, church records of baptisms, marriages and burials are the primary source for the major events in our ancestors' lives. Unfortunately, there is very much less data online for parish registers than for the civil registration and census records covered in the previous chapters, and there are good reasons why this should be so.

The national records are centrally held and recorded on forms which ensure that the structure of the data is consistent and very obvious. They all date at the earliest from the 1830s, and they have generally been kept in fairly good conditions. All this makes digitizing and indexing them a manageable, if mammoth, task.

But for parish registers, there is much more variety. First, in England and Wales at least, they are not held centrally, so no one body can be approached to put them online. Second, there is a huge variation in their format and preservation, the more so because they cover the whole period since the sixteenth century. And, third, while most genealogists can become accurate readers of nineteenth-century handwriting, the same cannot be said of the writing in some of the eighteenth-century registers, never mind those from the sixteenth century. Although many parish registers have been transcribed and published in print or typescript, getting the requisite permissions simply to digitize and index these from the hundreds of individuals and groups concerned would be a substantial task. Indeed, the right to transcribe and publish parish register material seems to be legally unclear, with some dioceses refusing to allow transcription. All this conspires to make the prospect of a comprehensive collection of online parish registers for England and Wales much more distant than it is for civil registration and census records. Nevertheless, a considerable amount of data is available in online indexes, as well as information that will help you to identify what parish registers remain. However, there are as yet no digital images of parish registers available, so recourse to the originals, or microfilms of them, in record offices remains essential.

If you are unfamiliar with parish register material, British-Genealogy has some useful pages on English Parish Registers at <**www.british-**

genealogy.com/resources/registers/indexf.htm>. These describe the information given for baptism, marriage and burial entries at different periods and have some examples of original documents. The tutorials discussed in Chapter 2 will also have information on using parish registers. For help with the handwriting found in older registers, refer to the material on p. 271ff.

John Fuller has a page for mailing lists relating to individual churches and denominations at <**www.rootsweb.ancestry.com/~jfuller/gen_mail_ religions.html**>.

Parish churches

The most important church records, in earlier times even for Roman Catholic or Nonconformist families, are those of the established Church. The easiest way to identify which church is most likely to have baptized, married or buried your ancestors, is Genuki's Church Database at <**www. genuki.org.uk/big/churchdb/search.html**> described on p. 239. The Church of England's A Church Near You site at <**www.achurchnearyou. com**> will find the nearest CofE churches to a given location, shown in Figure 7-1 . Clicking on the map marker leads you to current information about the church.

The UK Church directory at <**www.findachurch.co.uk**> provides similar facilities for the whole of the British Isles (including the Republic of Ireland)

Figure 7-1 A Church Near You

and includes other denominations, though the information about some of the churches is minimal.

The official websites for the Anglican churches of the British Isles also have details of their churches, though naturally they are orientated towards the present-day parishes. The relevant sites are:

- Church of England <**www.cofe.anglican.org**>
- Church in Wales <**www.churchinwales.org.uk**>
- Church of Ireland <**www.ireland.anglican.org**>
- Church of Scotland <**www.churchofscotland.org.uk**>
- Scottish Episcopal Church <**www.scotland.anglican.org**>

Many individuals have placed pictures of parish churches online, and these are discussed under 'Photographs' in Chapter 14, on page 284.

FamilySearch

The major online resource for all parish records is the LDS Church's FamilySearch site at <**www.familysearch.org**>. The material on this site is drawn from a number of sources, and it is important to note that not all of it is from transcriptions of parish registers ('controlled extractions', as the LDS calls them). Two of the data collections on the site, Ancestral File and Pedigree Resource File, consist of entirely unverified material submitted by individual genealogists, which is therefore secondary material and of

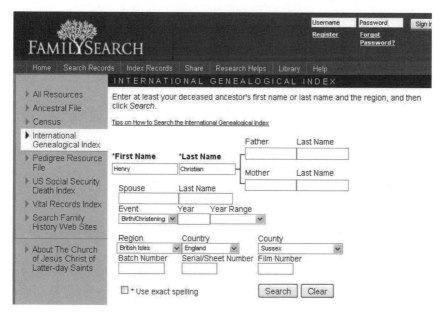

Figure 7-2 IGI search page on FamilySearch

ariable reliability – these datasets are discussed in Chapter 14. The collection that contains British parish register extractions is the International Genealogical Index (IGI), originally published on microfiche and then on CD-ROM. A further collection, the Vital Records Index (VRI), has been published on CD-ROM and is available on the FamilySearch Pilot site (see p. 104). There is a listing of the parishes covered at <**www.genoot.com/downloads/BVRI2/**> – the site has two PDF files for each county, detailing marriage and birth coverage.

The IGI is a substantial collection of parish register records for England and Wales online, with many millions of entries, and as such is one of the essential tools for UK genealogy on the web. There is also much material for other countries. The majority of the IGI material is for baptisms and marriages, though with some births and a few deaths and burials.

While you can use the search form on the FamilySearch home page, this will search *all* the records on the site, which include US and Canadian census records. To search the IGI specifically, you need to select 'Advanced Search' from the 'Search Records' menu, and then click on 'International Genealogical Index' in the left-hand column (Figure 7-2). Since you are likely to use this site quite frequently, it is worth bookmarking the URL at this point.

As well as entering names in the relevant fields, you will also need to select 'British Isles' from the 'Region' drop-down list, and you will probably then want to select a country from the 'Country' list. You can search on all records for a country, but once you have selected one, you then get the option of selecting an individual county. Among the other options, you can also choose to look for all events or for just, say, marriages; you can leave the year blank, or give a precise year or a range of years. If you are looking for a specific individual, you can also enter the name of the father and/or mother. There are some options you can't combine. It's difficult to see any overall pattern in these, but if you try an unpermitted combination, you will get a message telling you which fields need to be filled in or left blank.

When the search has been completed, you are presented with a list of search results (see Figure 7-3), with sufficient detail to identify the most plausible matches, and you can then click on the name to get the full details of the record (Figure 7-4).

You can select an individual record or a group of records to download in GEDCOM format (see p. 335), ready to be imported into your genealogy database. Of course, you can also simply save the web page for individual records or the list of search results, though these will have to be saved in text or HTML formats and the data will have to be added to your database manually.

Figure 7-3 FamilySearch search results for the search shown in Figure 7-2

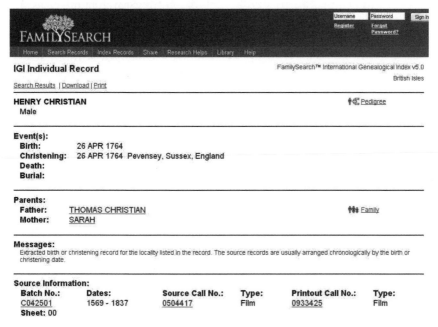

Figure 7-4 An individual record in FamilySearch

If you are not just looking for a single individual but want to look at a surname in a whole parish, then the information at the bottom of the screen in Figure 7-4 will be useful. This identifies the particular transcription from which this record comes by its 'batch number'. You can take the batch number, and enter it in the batch number field on the search form (Figure 7-2) to restrict the search to a particular source document. In the example in Figure 7-4 'C042501' indicates the parish registers for Pevensey in Sussex (the link from the 'Source Call No.' in the individual record takes you to this information). Clicking on the number will automatically return you to the initial search form with this number entered in the relevant field. If you search just on a batch number, you can get all entries for a surname in a particular set of records, and you can even leave the name field blank and get a listing of all the entries in a particular set of records.

The batch number is also important because it indicates whether a record comes from controlled extractions – in general, batches that start with a digit are from submissions by individual Church members, while those starting with a letter are from controlled extractions (and are on the whole less likely to be incorrect). You should always make sure you identify the source of any entries you are going to use as a basis of further research.

Of course, it would be useful to be able to select the parish straight off without having to run a preliminary search and decode an individual record. You can do this by doing a 'Place Search' in the Family History Library Catalogue, as explained on p. 206. Genuki has detailed instructions on how to find out batch numbers by this method at <**www.genuki.org. uk/big/FindingBatchNos.html**>. The Global Gazette has a detailed article by Fawne Stratford-Devai, 'The LDS FamilySearch Website: Using The Batch Numbers', at <**globalgenealogy.com/globalgazette/gazfd/gazfd36. htm**>, which explains what the batch numbers are and how to use them.

Also, there are a number of sites that list batch numbers for particular counties. The most extensive, at <**freepages.genealogy.rootsweb.ancestry. com/~hughwallis/IGIBatchNumbers.htm**>, has a comprehensive listing based on trying out each possible number. Others can be found by looking under the 'Church records' heading on the Genuki county pages. The Global Gazette page mentioned above has links to batch number information for a number of counties. Bear in mind that these listings are unofficial, and should not be regarded as authoritative. Also note that for many parishes there will be more than one batch number.

FamilySearch Indexing

While the IGI has always been a very valuable resource, it is far from perfect as a source of data. In particular the decision to mix controlled extractions and unchecked personal submissions in the same dataset means the overall reliability is less than it might be. Also, of course, the need to check IGI data against the original parish registers has always meant that you still need to visit the relevant record office, or, armed with the film number at the bottom of the individual record, go to a Family History Center to consult the microfilm.

However, FamilySearch recently launched a new project, FamilySearch Indexing, which led to a much improved collection of parish register data on the site. In September 2005, the LDS Church announced that they would be re-indexing all the records they had microfilmed and linking the index entries to digitized images of the original records. This is a massive project, since there are over two million rolls of microfilm, and the scope is much wider than just UK parish registers.

A presentation given at the announcement can be found in the education section of FamilySearch at <**www.familysearch.org/eng/Library/ Education/sneak_peak_David_E_Rencher.pdf**>. It is particularly interesting in showing exactly how a major digitization project is done.

In 2008, the first fruits of this project came online, albeit on a pilot site, Record Search, at <**pilot.familysearch.org**> which is not always available (since it is being regularly modified and improved). At the time of writing, there are already a small number of records available for the UK, the most significant of which is a complete set of baptisms, marriages and burials for Cheshire 1538–1907. To search these records, select a region from the home page (either by clicking on the map, or by selecting from the drop-down list), and then select the records you want to search. Figure 7-5 shows a page of search results.

While the search facilities on the initial search form are much more basic than those for the main FamilySearch site, once you have a set of search results there are sophisticated options for narrowing down your search, which you can see at the top of Figure 7-5.

From here you can click on the name to see the full details of a record, or click on the icon to the left to see the image of the original record (Figure 7-6). The image viewer does not require an plug-in and has facilities for zooming, panning, and rotating the image. You can also print or save the

Figure 7-5 FamilySearch Pilot: search results

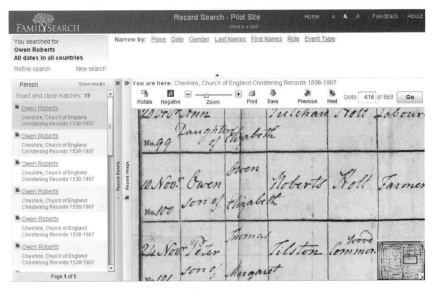

Figure 7-6 FamilySearch Pilot: record image

image – the image is saved in JPG format and the filename includes details of the records the image comes from. The images are greyscale and at quite high resolution.

Obviously, this will be a very valuable resource when it is complete and a huge improvement over the existing IGI.

As mentioned above, the British Vital Records Index is also available online for the first time on the site, though there are no images.

FreeReg

FreeReg at <**freereg.rootsweb.com**> is another volunteer project, like FreeBMD and FreeCEN, which aims to put UK genealogy data online 'to provide free internet searches of baptism, marriage, and burial records, which have been transcribed from parish and Nonconformist church registers in the UK'. At the beginning of 2009, the project had around six-and-a-half million records, over half of which are marriages. Of course, this is only a tiny percentage of the likely total number of records, but even so it will be worth checking. The 'Counties and Parishes' page shows the date of the earliest registers for each parish and the years which have been covered.

Local resources

Many local family history societies have created indexes to parish records for their own county or area, and a number of these have been available on FamilyHistoryOnline. With the closure of FHO, it is not clear what the fate of these will be, though some of them will certainly be made available on

FindMyPast (see p. 46). Because these indexes are also sold on CD-ROM, they are not likely to be available free of charge on FHS websites.

Since family history societies have been heavily involved in parish register indexing, county record offices seem to have concentrated their digitization efforts on other records – see, for example, the various CRO will digitization projects discussed in the following chapter. However, the FHSs do not have the resources to create digital images of the records, with the result that, apart from the FamilySearch Pilot discussed above, there are almost no images of records online, apart from the Scottish material on ScotlandsPeople (p. 109). The only local authority that has digitized parish registers, as far as I am aware, is Medway, whose CityArk project includes images of parish registers from the Diocese of Rochester. The CityArk home page is at <**cityark.medway.gov.uk**>, the link to 'Parish Registers Online' will take you the records. There is no single link to the image database; instead, at the bottom of this long page, is a list of parishes with a link for each. Unlike other online image databases, this one has no index of names – you just page through the collection of images in search of the entry you want, exactly as you would do with microfilm. The images themselves are rather large and you may want to use your browser's zoom-out facility (Figure 7-7).

In view of FamilySearch's plans to digitize its microfilm holdings, we should probably not expect many other projects of this nature.

Figure 7-7 Medway's CityArk: a page from a burial register

Commercial data services

Although the commercial data services are better known for their national datasets, all have some material for parish registers.

The Genealogist (see p. 47) has parish register transcriptions for Cornwall, Kent, Nottinghamshire, Suffolk, Wiltshire, Worcestershire and Yorkshire, and marriage indexes for 27 English counties derived from printed books. A very useful feature of the transcription database is that from a baptism you can get a listing of other children of the same parents, and from a marriage you get a list of potential children extracted from the baptisms for the same parish.

Findmypast (see p. 46) has a parish records collection based mainly on indexes created by family history societies. In particular, it has the National Burial Index, the index of over 13 million burial records transcribed by local family history societies under the coordination of the FFHS. Details of the county coverage will be found at <**www.ffhs.org.uk/projects/nbi/ nbi-coverage.php**> – the list on this page links to a detailed list of individual parishes. In addition to the NBI, Findmypast has:

- parish records for various parishes and counties 1538–2005
- City of London burials 1742–1904
- overseas marriage parish records 1690–1997
- London docklands baptism records 1712–1933

The British Origins site at <**www.britishorigins.com**>, described on p. 41, has a number of important parish record indexes available online:

- Boyd's Marriage Index 1538–1837 (over seven million names)
- Boyd's London Burials (300,000 names)
- Marriage Licence Allegations Index 1694–1850 (670,000 names)
- London Burials Index 1538–1853 (300,000 names)

Ancestry at <**www.ancestry.co.uk**> (see p. 44) has parish register material in the Parish and Probate Record collection available on Ancestry UK. Details of the coverage will be found in the list of UK databases at <**www. ancestry.co.uk/search/locality/dbpage.aspx?tp=3257**> under the 'Birth, Marriage and Death' heading. The site generally does not give precise source information for this material, only the general statement 'Electronic databases created from various publications of parish and probate records'. However, it seems likely that many of these records are taken from printed parish register indexes. Two important indexes available on Ancestry are Pallot's baptism and marriage indexes for England, covering the period

1780–1837, the originals of which are held by the Institute of Heraldic and Genealogical Studies. These have 200,000 baptisms and one-and-a-half million marriages, mainly from Middlesex and the City of London, but with some material from other counties.

Familyrelatives at <www.familyrelatives.com> (see p. 49) has online indexes to material from Phillimore's Marriage Registers, published around the start of the twentieth century. The site has coverage of 26 English counties.

Scotland

Unlike England and Wales, Scotland has collected most of its parish registers in one place, the GROS. The GROS website has information on Scottish parish registers at <www.gro-scotland.gov.uk/famrec/hlpsrch/opr.html>, and this page has links to a 'List of the Old Parochial Registers' which in turn links to a number of files in PDF format covering individual counties or groups of counties.

All the births/baptisms and banns/marriages dating from 1553 to 1854 (the start of general registration) are available online at ScotlandsPeople <www.scotlandspeople.gov.uk>, described on p. 42). Indexes and images of the original register pages are available on the site.

There are no deaths or burials from the OPRs at ScotlandsPeople and the site gives no indication whether or when they might be included. A Scottish National Death and Burial Index, aiming to index all recorded pre-1855 deaths and burials in Scotland, is being created by the Scottish Association of Family History Societies in conjunction with its member societies and the GROS. A small amount of material is available on CD-ROM, but it is not clear whether it will ever be made available online. Some very basic information on the project is available at <www.gwsfhs.org.uk/content/projects.aspx>. One can understand GROS's reluctance to tread on the toes of the country's family history societies, but in view of the incredibly slow progress of this project, it is very regrettable that ScotlandsPeople seems to have no plans to add the burials to its collection.

The Anglo-Scottish Family History Society has compiled a Scottish Strays Marriage Index, i.e. an index of marriages that took place outside Scotland, where at least one of the partners was born in Scotland. The index, which has around 6,000 entries, is available free of charge as a series of PDF files at <www.mlfhs.org.uk/AngloScots/>.

Ireland

Ireland differs from the other parts of the British Isles in that the relative importance of the established church, the Church of Ireland, is much less.

The National Archives of Ireland has information about Irish church records at <**www.nationalarchives.ie/genealogy/church.html**> and PRONI has a guide to Northern Ireland church records at <**www.proni.gov.uk/ your_family_tree_series_-_03_-_church_records.pdf**>, covering all denominations. The National Library of Ireland has guides to Roman Catholic Parish Registers at <**www.nli.ie/en/parish-register.aspx**> (irritatingly, these PDF documents do not display in your browser window but get downloaded to your hard disk).

There is useful information online about the location of church records. IrelandGenWeb at <**www.irelandgenweb.com**> and NorthernIrelandGenWeb at <**www.rootsweb.ancestry.com/~nirwgw/**> have county pages which often include details of the parishes whose registers have been filmed by the LDS. Fianna has a convenient list of LDS microfilm numbers for Irish parishes at <**www.rootsweb.ancestry.com/~fianna/county/ldspars.html**>, though of course this information can also be gleaned from the Family History Library catalogue (see p. 205).

There is very little Irish parish register material online apart from a small amount at FamilySearch. However, there are a number of places to look for the little other material that is available:

- The Irish Ancestors site has links to online resources for individual counties at <**www.irishtimes.com/ancestor/browse/links/counties/**>, which includes some parish register material.
- The Genuki county pages for Ireland, linked from <**www.genuki.org. uk/big/irl/**>, have sections devoted to Church Records.
- RootsWeb has a small number of user-submitted databases with Irish parish register material listed at <**userdb.rootsweb.ancestry.com/ regional.html**> – note there are two sections for Ireland, one of which is under 'United Kingdom'. Some of these are *very* limited in scope and just cover particular surnames.
- The Ulster Historical Foundation has around one-and-a-half million records for County Antrim and County Down on its pay-per-view service at <**www.ancestryireland.com/database.php**>, though at £4 per record it is rather expensive. The site does not give any indication of the denominations and parishes covered.

The Roman Catholic Church

The official websites for the Roman Catholic Church in the British Isles are:

- England and Wales <**www.catholic-ew.org.uk**>
- Scotland <**www.bpsconfscot.com/**>
- Ireland <**www.catholicireland.net**>

The National Archives has a Research Guide on 'Catholic Recusants' at <**www.nationalarchives.gov.uk/catalogue/RdLeaflet.asp?sLeafletID=112**>, which gives a guide to the relevant official records. The Catholic Record Society at <**www.catholic-history.org.uk/crs/**> is the main publishing body for Catholic records, while the Catholic National Library has a guide to its collections at <**www.catholic-library.org.uk**>. The Catholic Archives Society has a website at <**www.catholic-history.org.uk/catharch/**>.

Information about the Catholic Family History Society will be found at <**www.catholic-history.org.uk/cfhs/**>, and the Catholic History site at <**www.catholic-history.org.uk**> also hosts three regional Catholic FHS websites. (At the time of writing, the home page of this site was corrupted and clearly had been for some time, though in fact all the links work correctly.)

The Local Catholic Church History and Genealogy Research Guide and Worldwide Directory at <**home.att.net/~Local_Catholic/**> is a comprehensive research guide to Catholic records. It has details of individual churches and links to online information, with very thorough pages for the UK and Ireland. The Fianna website has a guide to Roman Catholic records in Ireland at <**www.rootsweb.ancestry.com/~fianna/county/parishes. html**> taken from Brian Mitchell's *A Guide to Irish Parish Registers*.

Useful links for the British Isles will be found on the Catholic Genealogy site at <**www.amateur-genealogist.com/catholic_genealogy.htm**>, which also offers discussion groups for (paid) subscribers. Cyndi's List has over 200 links to Catholic resources at <**www.cyndislist.com/catholic.htm**>.

The websites of the libraries and archives discussed in Chapter 13 are worth checking for information about local Catholic records.

▌ Nonconformist churches

The British Isles are home to many Protestant denominations outside the established Church. The Spartacus Internet Encyclopaedia has a brief history of the most important religious groups at <**www.spartacus. schoolnet.co.uk/religion.htm**>, with links to details of individual reformers and reform movements. Wikipedia at <**en.wikipedia.org**> has substantial articles on the main groups both worldwide and in Britain.

Cyndi's List has individual pages devoted to Baptist, Huguenot, Methodist, Presbyterian and Quaker materials, and links to many other relevant resources on the 'Religion and Churches' page at <**www.cyndislist. com/religion.htm**>. Many of the denominational mailing lists at <**www. rootsweb.ancestry.com/~jfuller/gen_mail_religions.html**> are for dissenting groups. (Huguenot immigration is covered on p. 173).

For details of the records, consult the FamilyRecords portal's factsheet on 'Nonconformist Registers' at <**www.familyrecords.gov.uk/frc/pdfs/**

nonconformist_registers.pdf>. For Scotland and Ireland, look at Sherry Irvine's article 'Protestant Nonconformity in Scotland' at <**www.genuki. org.uk/big/sct/noncon1.html**>, while Fianna has guides to Baptist, Methodist, Presbyterian and Quaker records in Ireland linked from <**www. rootsweb.ancestry.com/~fianna/county/churches.html**>.

GenDocs has lists of London churches for a number of Nonconformist denominations on its 'Victorian London Churches' page at <**homepage. ntlworld.com/hitch/gendocs/churches.html**>.

Societies which are relevant for those with Nonconformist ancestors are:

- The Quaker Family History Society <**www.rootsweb.ancestry.com/~ engqfhs/**>, which has details of Quaker records and their location, with a page for each county
- The Baptist Historical Society at <**www.baptisthistory.org.uk**>, which has no general genealogical material but does have information on Baptist ministers

There are a number of libraries which specialize in Nonconformist material. The John Rylands University Library in Manchester has a strong Nonconformist collection, particularly for the Methodist Church. A description of the main resources will be found at <**www.library. manchester.ac.uk/specialcollections/collections/guide/subjectgroups/ theology/**>, and the home page of the Methodist Archives and Research Centre is at <**www.library.manchester.ac.uk/specialcollections/ collections/methodist/**>.

Dr Williams's Library is an essential repository for those researching English Nonconformist ancestors. Its website at <**www.dwlib.co.uk**> has information about the library and its holdings, as well as a family history area with a brief introduction to Nonconformist records and an explanation of which denominations are and are not covered by the library. The ARCHON Directory at <**www.nationalarchives.gov.uk/archon/**> (see p. 193) has an entry for the Library with links to the materials catalogued in the National Register of Archives, including papers relating to around 200 clergymen.

The official Quaker website has information about the collections in the library at Friends House at <**www.quaker.org.uk/library/**>, which includes a guide to the library's genealogical sources.

Until recently, there were no significant Nonconformist records online, but in 2008 TheGenealogist (see p. 47) launched an online database of non-parochial records taken from the documents in the National Archives series RG4–RG8, which include:

- Dr Williams's Library, 1742–1865
- Presbyterian, Independent and Baptist Registry, 1742–1837
- Wesleyan Methodist Metropolitan Registry, 1818–1838
- Protestant Dissenters' Registry
- Society of Friends' Registers, Notes and Certificates of Births, Marriages and Burials 1578–1841

Further details are given on the site, and complete information is available for each series in the National Archives catalogue (see p. 196).

Monumental inscriptions

While monumental inscriptions (MIs) are not official records, their close connection with the deceased means that they can provide family information not given by a death certificate, and can make up for a missing entry in a burial register. Similar information can come from obituaries, which are covered on p. 191.

The best starting point for cemeteries and MIs is Guy Etchells's Tombstones & Monumental Inscriptions site at <**www.framland.pwp. blueyonder.co.uk**>. This aims to 'provide a photographic record of the various churches, churchyards and cemeteries for the benefit of those genealogists who live some distance away', but it also has a comprehensive collection of links to related sites for the UK and other English-speaking countries, as well as links for war memorials. Cyndi's List has a 'Cemeteries & Funeral Homes' page at <**www.cyndislist.com/cemetery.htm**> with a number of links for UK sites and many general resources for cemeteries.

Examples of other county-based projects are:

- Dyfed FHS's list of Burial Grounds in Cardiganshire, Carmarthenshire and Pembrokeshire, with links to a number of MI transcriptions at <**www.dyfedfhs.org.uk/register/burials.htm**>
- Cornish Cemeteries at <**freepages.genealogy.rootsweb.ancestry. com/~chrisu/cemeteries.htm**>, with material for around a dozen cemeteries and churchyards in Cornwall
- The National Archives of Memorial Inscription at <**www.memorial inscriptions.org.uk**>, a pay-per-view site with around 170,000 names from Bedfordshire and Norfolk (searching is free)

There is quite a lot of material for London. GenDocs has a list of Victorian London Cemeteries at <**homepage.ntlworld.com/hitch/gendocs/cem. html**>, with addresses and dates. The London Burial Grounds site at <**www. londonburials.co.uk**> has details of many London burial grounds.

There are also countless small volunteer transcriptions. For example, the

England Tombstone Project at <www.rootsweb.ancestry.com/~engcemet/>
has transcriptions for a number of cemeteries including four from London.
Interment.net at <www.interment.net> has collections of MI transcriptions for some UK cemeteries. These are individual user-submitted records,
and only some of the materials represent complete transcriptions for a
cemetery or churchyard.

Apart from the general resources mentioned above, good ways to see if
there is anything for a particular place or church is to look at the relevant
Genuki parish page if there is one, or simply use a search engine to find
pages with the place name and the phrase 'monumental inscriptions'.

British-Genealogy has pages on recording and publishing memorial
inscriptions at <www.british-genealogy.com/resources/graves/>. For help
with Latin inscriptions, see p. 273.

The British Association for Cemeteries in South Asia cares for and
records European cemeteries wherever the East India Company set foot. Its
website at <www.bacsa.org.uk> gives details of the published records.

There are many mailing lists relating to cemeteries and monumental
inscriptions. Those most relevant to the British Isles are:

- UK-CEMETERIES, subscription details at <lists.rootsweb.ancestry.
  com/index/intl/UK/UK-CEMETERIES.html>
- MI-ENGLAND at <lists.rootsweb.ancestry.com/index/intl/ENG/MI-
  ENGLAND.html>
- SCOTLAND-CEMETERIES at <lists.rootsweb.ancestry.com/index/
  intl/SCT/SCOTLAND-CEMETERIES.html>
- SCT-TOMBSTONE-INSCRIPTIONS at <lists.rootsweb.ancestry.com/
  index/intl/SCT/SCT-TOMBSTONE-INSCRIPTIONS.html>
- IRELAND-CEMETERIES at <lists.rootsweb.ancestry.com/index/intl/
  IRL/IRELAND-CEMETERIES.html>
- IRL-TOMBSTONE-INSCRIPTIONS at <lists.rootsweb.ancestry.com/
  index/intl/IRL/IRL-TOMBSTONE-INSCRIPTIONS.html>

War memorials are discussed in Chapter 10.

8

PROPERTY, TAXATION AND CRIME

The foregoing chapters have looked at the three core types of genealogical record, the ones which, in principle at least, provide a record for every person who has lived in the British Isles for the last 450 years. But there are, of course, many other types of record of interest to the family historian, and these are covered in this and the following four chapters.

One problem when you start to look at other types of record is that you cannot be sure in advance whether there will actually *be* any records pertaining to a particular ancestor. Not everyone served in the military, made a will, or was convicted of a crime; many occupations left little or no documentation. In particular, in the female line there may be very few records of this sort before the twentieth century.

But the particular advantage where these records have been digitized is that they can be checked very quickly. You might not be able to justify spending a day in a record office going through a whole sheaf of documents in the uncertain hope that an ancestor might be mentioned. But there's no reason not to check these records if there is an online index.

These chapters look at the most useful sites for the most important types of record, but there is much more than can be covered here. The commercial data services have significant collections of material from sources other than civil registration, census and parish registers, as indicated in the sections devoted to each site in Chapter 4. Where there are official records, the websites of the national or local repositories will give details of any large-scale plans for digitization (see p. 196ff.). But even where there are no such plans, many individuals and groups are publishing small collections of data from other records online. These tend to be piecemeal indexes and transcriptions, rather than the publication of complete national datasets, and some are discussed under 'Local history' and 'social history' in Chapter 16.

In addition, the archives and libraries discussed in Chapter 13 have details of other records which may or may not have been digitized.

Wills

Wills are an important source for family historians and there has been a considerable increase in the number of wills available online in the last few years. Wills have been proved in many different places, and locating the right source for the potential will of a particular ancestor can sometimes be difficult, so it is important to look at the general information about probate records before looking for a specific will.

Although wills and probate records are specifically property records – they record what the testator intended to happen to his or her property after death – their importance extends beyond this. Because they indicate an approximate death date, they provide a substitute for a missing burial record, and they can be valuable for clarifying family relationships. Indeed, apart from rare personal diaries and letters, they are the only major documentary source likely to give information about the personal relations between our ancestors and their families.

Basic information about wills in all parts of the British Isles can be found on the FamilyRecords gateway at <**www.familyrecords.gov.uk/topics/wills.htm**> and in the National Archives' family history guide at <**www.nationalarchives.gov.uk/familyhistory/guide/people/wills.htm**>.

England and Wales

The best starting points for information about wills in England and Wales are the National Archives' three research guides on the topic:

- Probate Records <**www.nationalarchives.gov.uk/catalogue/RdLeaflet.asp?sLeafletID=168**>
- Wills before 1858: where to start <**www.nationalarchives.gov.uk/catalogue/RdLeaflet.asp?sLeafletID=220**>
- Wills and Death Duty Records after 1858 <**www.nationalarchives.gov.uk/catalogue/RdLeaflet.asp?sLeafletID=219**>

Probate records since 1858 are under the jurisdiction of the Probate Service, which has pages on the Court Service website at <**www.hmcourts-service.gov.uk**>. There is a page on 'Probate Records and Family History' at <**www.hmcourts-service.gov.uk/cms/1183.htm**> and a 'Guide to obtaining probate records' at <**www.hmcourts-service.gov.uk/cms/1176.htm**>. A 2004 review of probate business by the Court Service (<**www.hmcourts-service.gov.uk/cms/files/rop-final-report.pdf**>) concluded that the full Probate Calendar from 1858 should be online by April 2006, but this has failed to materialize.

FamilySearch also has useful material relating to English probate jurisdictions. The search facility at <**www.familysearch.org/eng/Library/ FHL/probate.asp**> will tell you which courts had jurisdiction for a particular place, though so far it covers only London and Essex. There are also probate jurisdictions maps for these two counties linked from <**www. familysearch.org/eng/Library/FHL/frameset_library.asp?PAGE=english_ probate_jurisdictions.asp**>. The same page has links to two older guides for Cambridgeshire and Kent.

For pre-1858 wills, the most important site is the National Archives' DocumentsOnline service at <**www.documentsonline.nationalarchives. gov.uk**>. This offers images of over one million wills from the Prerogative Court of Canterbury, the largest probate court for England and Wales, for the period 1384–1858. Detailed information on coverage is given at <**www. nationalarchives.gov.uk/documentsonline/wills.asp**>. Each will costs £3 to download, regardless of length.

Another source of wills for England and Wales is British Origins at <**www.britishorigins.com**> (see p. 41), which has the following will indexes currently available:

- Bank of England Will Extracts Index 1717–1845 (61,000 names)
- Archdeaconry Court of London Wills Index 1750–1800 (5,000 names)
- Prerogative Court of Canterbury Wills 1750–1800 (208,000 records)
- York Medieval Probate Index 1267–1500 (over 10,000 wills)
- York Peculiars Probate Index 1383–1883 (over 25,000 wills)
- Prerogative & Exchequer Courts of York Probate Index 1842–1858 (over 50,000 names)
- Surrey Will Abstracts 1470–1856 (over 500,000 names)

The first three are from the Society of Genealogists, and the Yorkshire records from the Borthwick Institute. There is a page with information on each of these collections, which should enable you to see whether they will be worth checking in a particular instance. In some cases, there is an online facility for ordering copies of the original documents. The Bank of England and Surrey indexes are notable in that the content of the will is summarized.

Most pre-1858 wills were proved in local diocesan courts, whose records are now in county record offices. It is, therefore, a good idea to check the website of a likely CRO for information on the relevant court or courts for parishes in the county. There are several CRO-based projects to digitize wills, including:

- Cheshire's Wills Database Online at <**www.cheshire.gov.uk/Recordoffice/ Wills/Home.htm**>

- the Wiltshire Wills project at <**history.wiltshire.gov.uk/heritage/index. php**>
- Gloucestershire's Genealogical Database Search, which is at <**ww3. gloucestershire.gov.uk/genealogy/Search.aspx**>, includes an index of wills and inventories.
- the Guildhall Library has indexes to the probate inventories of the Peculiar Court of the Dean and Chapter of St Paul's Cathedral <**www. history.ac.uk/gh/invent.htm**>.
- North East Inheritance at <**familyrecords.dur.ac.uk/nei/**> has lottery funding to digitize Durham and Northumberland probate records, 1527–1857, and the material is expected to go online during 2009.

Beyond the CROs there are a number of smaller volunteer-based sources. For example, Maureen Rawson has many Kent will transcripts and some inventory indexes at <**freepages.genealogy.rootsweb.ancestry.com/ ~mrawson/probate.html**>, and the Norfolk Family History Society has an index of around 600 Norfolk wills at <**www.norfolkfhs.org.uk/resources/ wills/willstranscripts.asp**>.

The commercial data services offer online indexes to two related resources:

- Index to Death Duty Registers 1796–1903, available at Findmypast <**www. findmypast.com**> (see p. 46)
- the Inheritance Disputes Index 1574–1714, with over 26,000 lawsuits, on British Origins at <**www.britishorigins.com**> (see p. 41)

Caryl Williams maintains an England Wills Exchange Database at <**members.tripod.com/~Caryl_Williams/ewills.html**>, which has a number of will transcriptions from around the country.

Scotland
The National Archives of Scotland has a guide to wills and testaments at <**www.nas.gov.uk/guides/wills.asp**>

The official source for Scottish wills is ScotlandsPeople (see p. 42). The site offers an index of over half a million entries to the testaments (wills) of Scots recorded in the Registers of Testaments from 1500 to 1901. Unlike the other material on ScotlandsPeople, the wills are not part of the pay-per-view system, but scans can be purchased at £5 each via an online shop (all wills cost the same, regardless of length). Searching the indexes is free, and the index entries themselves give quite detailed information about testators.

The site also has some examples of wills from each 50-year period

X Close window

Testament Dative and Inventory of Robert Burns
CC5/6/18 pp 74-75

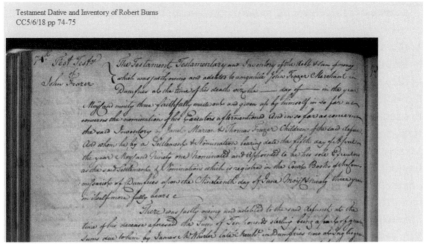

Figure 8-1 Will of Robert Burns at ScotlandsPeople

covered by the index – click on 'What's in the Database', then 'Record Types & Examples.' A selection of wills of famous Scots can be viewed free of charge in the Features section of the site (Figure 8-1 shows the will of Robert Burns). For those unfamiliar with Scottish probate records and terminology, the FAQ pages at <**www.scotlandspeople.gov.uk/content/ faqs/**> provide a comprehensive introduction to all aspects of the records under the heading 'Property & Inheritance'. There is also an explanation of the various Scottish courts with a role in probate. Further help is available in the 'Research Tools' area (under 'Help & Other Resources'), which includes material on handwriting, abbreviations found in wills and occupations.

Ireland

A good overview of wills and probate in Ireland will be found on the Irish Ancestors' site at <**www.irishtimes.com/ancestor/browse/records/wills/**>. Ancestry has a two-part article on Irish wills by Sherry Irvine at <**www. ancestry.com/learn/library/article.aspx?article=2515**> and PRONI has a useful set of pages on wills in Northern Ireland at <**www.proni.gov.uk/ index/search_the_archives/will_calendars/about_wills.htm**>.

There are three national indexes to Irish wills:

- Irish Origins at <**www.irishorigins.com**> has an index to pre-1858 wills held at the National Archives of Ireland.
- Ancestry UK has indexes to Irish Wills taken from published indexes –

details at <www.ancestry.co.uk/search/db.aspx?dbid=7287>.

- PRONI has a Will Calendar Search for counties of Northern Ireland at <www.proni.gov.uk/index/search_the_archives/will_calendars/wills_search.htm>, which includes a concise abstract of each will.

You can also expect to find local transcriptions done by volunteers. For example, there is an index to wills for the Diocese of Raphoe, Donegal at <freepages.genealogy.rootsweb.ancestry.com/~donegal/wills.htm>, while Ginni Swanton has scanned images of the published index to Irish Wills for the Dioceses of Cork and Ross at <www.ginnisw.com/Indexes%20to%20Irish%20Wills/Thumb/Thumbs1.htm>. Other sites with Irish wills can be found from the 'Locality Specific' section on the 'Wills and Probate' page of Cyndi's List at <www.cyndislist.com/wills.htm>, or by using a search engine.

Land and taxation

Property records are important in showing a place of residence before the start of the census or where, as in Ireland, census records are missing. Even those too poor to own property may be recorded as occupiers, though of course only a head of household will be given. However, most older property records are not strictly property records at all. Rather they are generally records of tax assessments *based on* land ownership and occupation, which was the norm before the permanent introduction of income tax in 1842. They therefore do not necessarily give much information about the property held other than its acreage or rateable value. The 1911 census (see p. 88) is the only general national source to give much information about the properties occupied by our ancestors.

It is not possible here to look at all classes of property and taxation records, only to draw attention to some of the most useful resources available online.

The National Archives' 'In depth guide to family history' has information on the main records under the heading 'Recording the people', and various research guides linked from <www.nationalarchives.gov.uk/catalogue/researchguidesindex.asp> provide more detailed information about Hearth Tax, Land Tax, Tithe Records, and a general guide to Taxation Records Before 1689.

The E179 Database at <www.nationalarchives.gov.uk/e179/> is a catalogue of taxation records. It does not contain any information about individuals, its sole function being to identify the relevant documents for a particular place, tax and period.

The National Archives of Scotland has a guide to Scottish taxation records at <www.nas.gov.uk/guides/taxation.asp>.

Many property and taxation records are held at local level, so it is worth checking the relevant county record office website for information. There are few national projects in this area, but many small transcriptions for individual parishes. Also, many of these records have been published in book form by the various record societies, so a search of the digital book archives described in Chapter 12 is recommended.

Tithes

Tithe records and in particular the nineteenth-century tithe maps are important sources for both owners and occupiers of land. A very thorough discussion of tithe records will be found in the National Archives' research guide 'Tithe Records: A Detailed Examination' at <**www.catalogue.nationalarchives.gov.uk/Leaflets/ri2148.htm**>. The National Library of Wales also has comprehensive pages on this topic at <**www.llgc.org.uk/index. php?id=549**>. County record office websites often give information about tithe maps and schedules in their collections, and these are obvious candidates for digitization. Devon and Worcester have projects to index their tithe maps – these both have mammoth URLs of 100 or so characters, so follow the links on the site for this book or search from the county council home pages at <**www.devon.gov.uk**> and <**www.worcestershire.gov.uk**> respectively. Cornwall Record Office has a Tithe Project in development, though this still has some way to go and there are no materials online as yet. Details will be found at <**www.cornwall.gov.uk/index.cfm?articleid =4090**>.

A major tithe records project is the University of Portsmouth's Tithe Survey of England and Wales at <**tiger.iso.port.ac.uk:7785/www/web. html?p=tithe_intro**>, which also offers data for 15 parishes.

There are many individual transcriptions of tithe schedules. For example:

- Tithe Titles for Kelsall, Cheshire <**www.the-dicksons.org/Kelsall/kelsall/ tithespg.htm**>
- Tithe Book of Bolton with Goldthorpe, 1839 <**www.genuki.org.uk/big/ eng/YKS/Misc/Transcriptions/WRY/BoltonGoldthorpeTitheBookInd ex.html**>

The best way to find them is probably to search on the word 'tithes' or the phrase 'tithe map' and the relevant place name.

Taxation

There have been many property-based taxes levied on the population since the Middle Ages. It is not possible to aim at any sort of comprehensive list of online resources, as there seem to be no national resources devoted to these taxes, but rather many small transcriptions and indexes for particular localities.

Genuki Devon at <genuki.cs.ncl.ac.uk/DEV/> has a number of transcriptions of land tax records for Devon parishes, while Genuki Pembrokeshire has many extractions from tax records, mainly land tax, for the parish of Monkton at <www.genuki.org.uk/big/wal/PEM/Pemtax1.html>.

The Sussex Record Society at <www.sussexrecordsociety.org.uk/> has transcriptions of the Lay Subsidy Rolls for the county of Sussex 1524–1525 and the 1747 Window Tax.

The 1662 Hearth Tax Returns for Ploughley Hundred in Oxfordshire are indexed at <www.whipple.org/oxford/ploughley_100_hearth_tax_1662.html>.

The English Surnames Survey has a number of local datasets at <www.le.ac.uk/el/pot/intro/intro3a.html>, including Lay Subsidy transcriptions for Lincolnshire (1332) and Rutland (1296/7), and some Poll Tax records.

Land ownership and occupation

The 1873 Returns of Owners of Land list all those who owned more than an acre of land. A complete set of scans of the printed records for England, Wales, Scotland and Ireland are available to Familyrelatives subscribers at <www.familyrelatives.co.uk> (see Figure 8-2). The Irish return, dated 1876, is also available to Ancestry UK subscribers – see <www.ancestry.co.uk/search/db.aspx?dbid=48475>. The return for Wales can be seen free on the

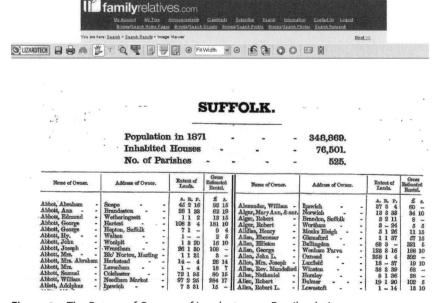

Figure 8-2 The Return of Owners of Land, 1873, on Familyrelatives

Welsh site the Ogre at <www.cefnpennar.com/1873index.htm>, which has those for Scotland and Ireland available via paid download.

There are also several online transcriptions for individual counties. The most extensive of these is available in the UK Genealogy archives at <uk-genealogy.org.uk/datafiles/landtaxsearch.html>, which has over 30,000 records for the counties of Anglesey, Brecknock, Cardigan, Leicester, Worcester, Oxford, Stafford, Middlesex, Rutland and Hertford. The 'Explanatory Statement' from the original publication, which explains a great deal about the survey, is included at <uk-genealogy.org.uk/OwnersofLand.html>. Further county extracts include:

- Oxfordshire <www.genoot.com/eng/oxf/landowners/>
- Norfolk <www.thornburypump.myby.co.uk/1873/>
- Cheshire <www.geocities.com/mar1elene/1873returns.html>
- County Carlow <www.rootsweb.ancestry.com/~irlcar2/Carlow_1871.htm>

The National Farm Surveys of England and Wales, 1940–1943 are described in a National Archives research guide at <www.nationalarchives.gov.uk/catalogue/RdLeaflet.asp?sLeafletID=309>. There is a report on 'Digitising the 1941 National Farm Survey: An Initial Assessment', published in 2006, available at <countryside-quality-counts.org.uk/publications/1941-Farm-Survey.pdf>, thought I am not aware that this has yet led to a digitization project.

The most famous survey of property holdings, though few of us can trace our pedigrees back that far, is the Domesday Book. The National Archives' DocumentsOnline has information about it at <www.nationalarchives.gov.uk/documentsonline/domesday.asp>.

Another medieval source are the Feet of Fines, which are legal records of land purchase going up to the early Tudor period. Chris Phillips' Medieval English Genealogy site has a list of Feet of Fines published (whether in print or online) for each English county at <www.medievalgenealogy.org.uk/fines/counties.shtml>. The site itself has transcriptions and images for some counties, while the Anglo-American Legal Tradition website at <aalt.law.uh.edu> has images of many others. However, the latter provides only images of the original documents written in Latin, and provides no index or transcription.

In fact, Medieval English Genealogy has a great deal of information about similar records at <www.medievalgenealogy.org.uk/sources/public.shtml> with many links to online materials.

Griffith's Valuation

For Ireland, the nineteenth-century property records are all the more important because of the destruction of census records. The sites referred to for Irish census material in Chapter 6 have information on these records, usually under the heading 'Census substitutes'. Among the most important is Griffith's Valuation, also called the Primary Valuation, and there is a range of material from this source online.

The Irish Origins site at <www.irishorigins.com> has an index to Griffith's Valuation and images of the original documents, in a joint venture with the National Library of Ireland and Irish CD-ROM publisher Eneclann.

There are also many local transcriptions, for example:

- The LEITRIM-ROSCOMMON Griffith's database at <www.leitrim-roscommon.com/GRIFFITH/> has a selection of material for parishes in Galway, Leitrim, Limerick, Mayo and Roscommon.
- <freepages.genealogy.rootsweb.ancestry.com/~tyrone/parishes/griffiths/> has some material for Co. Tyrone.
- <www.fermanagh.org.uk/fermanaghpresents/griffiths.htm> has some material for Co. Fermanagh.
- <www.rootsweb.ancestry.com/~irlker/griffith.html> has some material for Co. Kerry.
- From-Ireland has material for Carlow, Laois and Leitrim at <www.from-ireland.net/gene/griffithsval.htm>, which also has links to other sites with Griffith's data.

Links to such material will be found on the Genuki pages for Ireland at <www.genuki.org.uk/big/irl/>, and on the Ireland pages of Census Finder at <www.censusfinder.com/ireland.htm>.

The PRONI has a guide to to Irish valuation records at <www.proni.gov.uk/your_family_tree_series_-_04_-_valuation_records.pdf>.

Insurance records

Useful sources of information on property in London are the surviving fire insurance policies. The Guildhall Library holds records for many insurance companies, and over 50,000 policies from the Sun Fire Office for 1808 to 1839 have been indexed. The index can be found on the Access to Archives website at <www.nationalarchives.gov.uk/a2a>, and detailed instructions on using it are available at <www.history.ac.uk/gh/sun.htm>. The index comprises the name and address of the policyholder, his occupation or status, and the location of property insured. There is general information on the Guildhall Library's fire insurance records at <www.history.ac.uk/gh/fire.htm>.

Crime

The official records of the courts and the prison system contain much information about the individuals who came into contact with the law. The National Archives has a number of research guides devoted to the subject, including:

- Outlawry in Medieval and Early Modern England
- Convicts and Prisoners 1100–1986
- Tracing 19th and 20th Century Criminals
- Criminal Trials, Old Bailey and the Central Criminal Court
- Bankrupts and Insolvent Debtors: 1710–1869
- Bankruptcy Records After 1869
- a number of guides on Assizes

All of these are linked from <**www.nationalarchives.gov.uk/catalogue/ researchguidesindex.asp**> and from the website for this book. The National Archives also has material on 'Ancestors and the Law' in its 'Family History' section at <**www.nationalarchives.gov.uk/familyhistory/guide/ancestors law**>.

Cyndi's List has a page devoted to 'Prisons, Prisoners & Outlaws' at <**www.cyndislist.com/prisons.htm**>, though many of the UK links relate to policing rather than to criminals. Genuki (see p. 18) lists relevant resources under the headings 'Court Proceedings' and 'Correctional Institutions' on national and county pages.

A major online resource is the Proceedings of the Old Bailey site at <**www.oldbaileyonline.org**>, which contains details of almost 200,000 trials from 1674 to 1913, with transcriptions and scanned images from the contemporary printed proceedings free of charge. Sophisticated search facilities allow trials to be selected by keyword, name, place, crime, verdict and punishment, or you can browse the trials by date. The text of trials also contains the names of defendants, victims, jurors and judges, which can be found via the name search, so the site is not only of interest to those with criminal ancestors.

In addition to the records themselves, the site has extensive background material about particular communities, which will be of general interest:

- Black Communities
- Gypsies and Travellers
- Homosexuality
- Irish London
- Jewish Communities

- Huguenot and French London
- Chinese Communities

Additional background includes material on the various types of verdict and punishment. Even if you don't think you have criminal ancestors, this site is worth visiting for the insight it provides into urban life in the period.

The Newgate Calendar was a popular eighteenth-century work with information on notorious criminals, and there are a number of versions online including <**www.exclassics.com/newgate/ngintro.htm**>.

Capital Punishment UK at <**www.capitalpunishmentuk.org**> is a site devoted to all aspects of the subject and has extensive information on those executed in the British Isles.

Records relating to crime and punishment in Scotland are held by the NAS (see p. 199), which has a very comprehensive page on 'Crime and Criminals' at <**www.nas.gov.uk/guides/crime.asp**>.

There are a number of online databases relating to particular courts and gaols:

- For Aylesbury Gaol, Buckinghamshire County Council has an online database of nineteenth-century prisoners at <**apps.buckscc.gov.uk/ eforms/libPrisoners**>.
- Warwickshire County Record Office has a Calendars of Prisoners Database covering the courts at Warwick, Birmingham and Coventry between 1801 and 1900, with details of over 30,000 prisoners. The data-

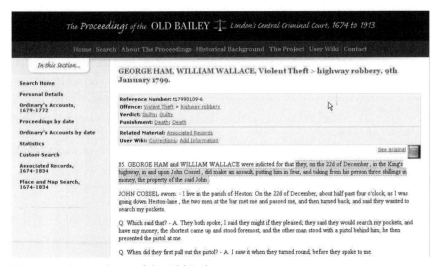

Figure 8-3 Proceedings of the Old Bailey

base can be searched by crime and residence as well as by surname. The URL is a 94-character monster – see the website for this book for a link.

- The National Library of Wales has a Crime and Punishment database at <**www.llgc.org.uk/sesiwn_fawr/index_s.htm**>, with details of crimes and criminals included in the gaol files of the Court of Great Sessions in Wales from 1730 until its abolition in 1830.
- For Dumfries and Galloway there is a database of the Jail Books (1714–1788) and the Bail Bond Registers (1775–1810) at <**www.dgcommunity. net/historicalindexes/jail.aspx**>.

For general information on prisons, the Rossbret Prisons website at <**www. institutions.org.uk/prisons/**> is an essential resource. This has a list of prisons organized by county with historical information and details of the relevant records. There is a PRISONS-UK mailing list, details of which will be found at <**lists.rootsweb.ancestry.com/index/intl/UK/PRISONS-UK. html**>. Historic Herefordshire Online has material on the county's prisons at <**www.smr.herefordshire.gov.uk/post-medieval/prisons/prisons_index. htm**>.

The resources discussed here mostly relate to the modern period. The National Archives has research guides at <**www.nationalarchives.gov.uk/ catalogue/researchguidesindex.asp**> on earlier courts such as the Court of Requests and the Star Chamber. However, you are unlikely to find material relating to individual cases online except where they have been published in print and are available in one of the digital book archives discussed in Chapter 12.

There are many resources online relating to convict transportation to the colonies, and these are discussed in Chapter 11.

Material relating to the legal profession and the police are covered in the following chapter.

9

OCCUPATIONS

Occupational records do not form a coherent category. There are state records only where people were employed by the state itself or where the government sought to regulate qualifications and employment. Otherwise each trade or industry kept its own records. Of course, many of our ancestors, especially those who worked the land, have left no record of their employment at all, other than in the occupation column of a census or a certificate.

Occupational terms

Given that most agricultural and early industrial occupations are now marginal if not actually obsolete, it is not uncommon to encounter unknown terms for occupations in historical records..

The definitive reference work for occupational terminology in any period is the *Oxford English Dictionary* (Figure 9-1). Accessing the online edition at <**www.oed.com**> is described on p. 178.

The most comprehensive listing of occupational terms for the early twentieth century is the Ministry of Labour's 1927 *Dictionary of Occupational*

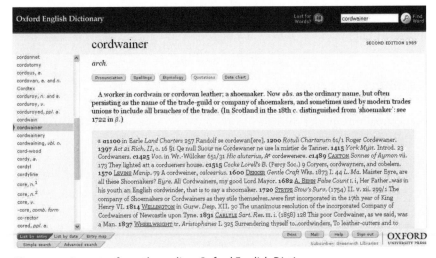

Figure 9-1 An entry from the online *Oxford English Dictionary*

Terms, based on the terms used in the 1921 census, which has something like 30,000 entries and descriptions. It also classifies occupations, so that you can see all the jobs involved in, say, basket-making. Unfortunately, it is a rare publication and is not available online, but it has been published by the Open University on CD-ROM, and this may be available in libraries. You can get an idea of the usefulness of the work from the extract for the pottery industry at <**www.rootsweb.ancestry.com/~engsts/potters1.html**>. A similar US work, The *Dictionary of Occupational Titles*, published by the US Department of Labor in 1971, is available online at <**www.occupational info.org**>, though, of course, you will need to exercise considerable caution if using this to interpret an eighteenth-century British occupation.

The other material available online is, by comparison, very concise. Brief explanations of terms for past occupations are provided in John Hitchcock's 'Ranks, Professions, Occupations and Trades' page at <**homepage.ntlworld. com/hitch/gendocs/trades.html**>, which has around 1,600 occupational terms. The 'Dictionary of Ancient Occupations and Trades, Ranks, Offices, and Titles' at <**freepages.genealogy.rootsweb.ancestry.com/~dav4is/ Sources/Occupations.html**> is a smaller collection of around 750 terms, with the emphasis on the sixteenth and seventeenth centuries. Olive Tree's list of 'Medieval And Obsolete English Trade And Professional Terms' at <**olivetreegenealogy.com/misc/occupations.shtml#med**> may be useful, especially since it includes medieval Latin terms for many occupations, and some older English spellings. Rodney Hall's 'Old Occupation Names' at <**rmhh.co.uk/occup/**> is also useful. For specifically Scottish terminology, look at Scots Family's 'Old Occupations in Scotland' page at <**www.scots family.com/occupations.htm**>.

If you have ancestors in manufacturing or trade, you may also find the Dictionary of Traded Goods and Commodities, 1550–1820 site at <**www. british-history.ac.uk/source.aspx?pubid=739**> useful in identifying precisely what your ancestor made or sold.

General information

The National Archives' Family History Guide (see p. 7) includes material on occupations, under the title 'People at Work' at <**www.nationalarchives. gov.uk/familyhistory/guide/trade/**>, with pages devoted to apprentices, the police, customs and excise officers, coastguards and the legal profession. The National Archives have research guides on the following occupations and professions for which there are state records:

royal warrant holders and household servants	tax and revenue collectors Metropolitan Police
lawyers	Royal Irish Constabulary

teachers	civil servants
nurses	coastguards
railway staff	

There is also a guide on apprentices. All are linked from the research guides home page at <**www.catalogue.nationalarchives.gov.uk/researchguides-index.asp**>.

Genuki has an 'Occupations' page at <**www.genuki.org.uk/big/eng/Occupations.html**>, with a number of links for particular occupations, and links to all the National Archives' research guides mentioned. Cyndi's List has a page of resources relating to occupations at <**www.cyndislist.com/occupatn.htm**> and many other pages which have information on occupations related to particular topics – for example the 'Prisons' page at <**www.cyndislist.com/prisons.htm**> includes links to police history websites.

The Modern Records Centre at the University of Warwick holds records relating to 'labour history, industrial relations and industrial politics'. While it has not put any records online, the main genealogy page at <**www2.warwick.ac.uk/services/library/mrc/subject_guides/family_history/**> has links to genealogical guides for the following occupations:

bookbinders	painters
bricklayers	picture-frame makers
brushmakers	plasterers
bus and cab workers	printing workers
carpenters	quarrymen
carvers	railwaymen
compositors	seamen
gilders	steam engine makers
house decorators	stonemasons
ironfounders	tramway workers
joiners	woodworkers
miners	

There is very little data available on the commercial data services apart from a small amount for the professions (see below). The only significant set of general occupational records online is the apprenticeship material on the British Origins site at <**www.origins.net**>:

- the London City Apprenticeship Abstracts 1442–1850 (100,000 records with 300,000 names of apprentices, their parents, and masters)
- the Apprentices of Great Britain 1710–1774 (350,000 records, about 20 per cent of which relate to Scotland)

The site has additional information about apprenticeship records, and there is a list of City Livery Companies at <**www.britishorigins.com/help/ popup-aboutbo-lonapps2.htm**>. More information about the Livery Companies will be found on the Corporation of London site at <**www. cityoflondon.gov.uk/Corporation/LGNL_Services/Leisure_and_culture/ Local_history_and_heritage/Livery/**>.

In the case of self-employed tradesman or craftsman, it will be worth checking trade directories – see p. 179 – which may well bring the benefit of establishing a workplace address.

Individual occupations

There are many sites devoted to individual occupations, sometimes with just historical information, sometimes with a database of names. Unfortunately, it is not possible here to do more than cite a few examples, but you can find many other links to sites for individual occupations on Cyndi's List and among my own public bookmarks at <**delicious.com/ petex/occupations**>.

Examples of the sites with individual names include:

- the Database of Sugar Bakers and Sugar Refiners at <**www.mawer.clara. net/intro.html**>
- the Biographical Database of British Chemists at <**www5.open. ac.uk/Arts/chemists/**>
- the Coalmining History Resource Centre at <**www.cmhrc.co.uk**>, which has lists of mines at various dates, reports from an 1842 Royal Commission on child labour in the mines, and a database of mining deaths with 90,000 names (Figure 9-2)
- the Institute of Historical Research's lists of Royal Office Holders in Modern Britain at <**www.history.ac.uk/office/**> ('modern' here meaning 'post-medieval')
- Corkcutters in England at <**corkcutter.info**>, with information on the corkcutting industry and a database of corkcutters
- the British Book Trade Index, hosted by the University of Birmingham at <**www.bbti.bham.ac.uk**>, an index of people who worked in the book trade in England and Wales up to 1851. There is a similar project for Scotland run by the National Library of Scotland at <**www.nls.uk/ catalogues/resources/sbti/**>

For many occupations, records are very limited until you get to the twentieth century. The learned professions are a major exception, and these are treated separately below. Likewise any service in the army or navy will have left some, perhaps even many, records for an individual, and these are

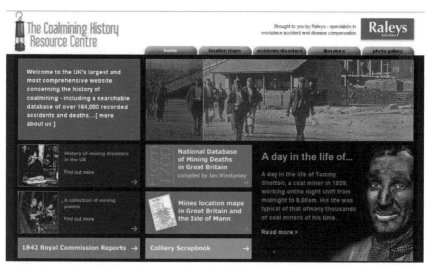

Figure 9-2 The Coalmining History Resource Centre

discussed in Chapter 10. Otherwise, the occupations most likely to have left records are the professions, where formal qualifications and professional bodies are involved. It is always worth checking the website of any relevant professional body, since it may well provide some indication of what records are available and other information on tracing individuals. For example, the Royal College of Nursing has an area of its site at <**www.rcn. org.uk**> devoted to archives, including a factsheet 'Tracing nurses' at <**www.rcn.org.uk/development/library/archives/factsheets/factsheets- tracingnurses**>, and the Royal Institute of Chartered Surveyors has a guide to its Library and a page on family history at <**www.rics.org/Services/ Library/Family+history_c_091006.htm**>.

On the whole, there are few substantial collections of professional records online, but there are two notable datasets available from the Society of Genealogists via commercial data services:

- Teachers' Registrations at Origins , which give details of nearly 100,000 people who taught in England and Wales between 1870 and 1948 – see <**www.originsnetwork.com/help/popup-aboutbo-teachers2.htm**>
- Civil Service Evidence of Age records 1752–1948 at Findmypast – see <**www.findmypast.com/civil-service-evidence-of-age-search-start. action**>

It is also worth checking record office sites for local data collections, such as:

- Lancashire's database of the police officers of the Lancashire County Constabulary, 1840–1925, and some borough police forces at <www.lancashire.gov.uk/education/record_office/records/police.asp>
- Warwickshire's Victuallers Database, which gives details of the county's victuallers in Warwickshire 1801–1828 taken from quarter session records (see Figure 9-3). Unfortunately, this is another instance of a monster nonsense URL – instead start from the council home page at <www.warwickshire.gov.uk> and search for 'victuallers', or follow the link on the website for this book.

There are an increasing number of mailing lists devoted to occupations. They are listed at <www.rootsweb.ancestry.com/~jfuller/gen_mail_occ.html>, and those most relevant to UK family historians are:

BLACKSMITHING	HM-CUSTOMS-WATERGUARD
BRITISH_HATTERS	Itinerantroots
CANAL-PEOPLE	LIGHTHOUSE-KEEPERS
CIRCUS-FOLK	MUSIC-OCCUPATIONS
COALMINERS	ORGAN-BUILDERS
DOCTORS-NURSES-MIDWIVES	PAPER-MILLS-MAKERS
ENG-CANAL-PEOPLE	POLICE-UK
ENG-PUBS-INNS	POSTALWORKERS-UK
ENG-THAMESWATERMEN	RAILWAY-UK
HM-CUSTOMS-EXCISE	SCOTLAND-TINKS-HAWKERS

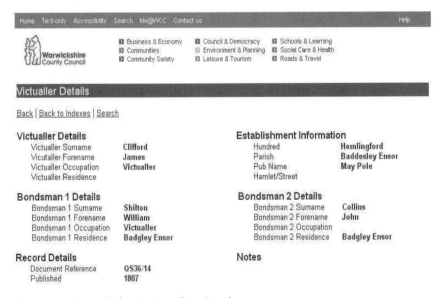

Figure 9-3 Warwickshire's Victuallers Database

SCOTTISH-MINING   UK-PHOTOGRAPHERS
THEATRE-UK   UK-WATCHMAKERS
TOWNCRIERS-UK   VIOLIN-MAKERS
UK-COALMINERS   WOODWORKERS

Many of these are hosted by RootsWeb, where details and archives will be found, linked from <**lists.rootsweb.ancestry.com/index/other/ Occupations/**>. British-Genealogy has a general 'Occupations' discussion forum as well as forums for specific occupations:

Actors & Artistes   Mariners and Ships
Apprentices   Medical Occupations
Canals and Watermen   Miners
Carpenters, Wheelwrights, etc. Occupations – general forum
Clergymen   Photographers and old
Coastguards and Customs Officers   photographs
Cordwainers, Shoemakers,   Policemen
 Saddlers, etc.   Railwaymen
Husbandmen, Yeomen, etc.   Smiths
Labourers   Stone Masons & Builders
Licensed Victuallers, Innkeepers, Tailors and Dressmakers
 etc.   Teachers

All are linked from <**www.british-genealogy.com/forums/forumdisplay. php?f=36**>.

There are even a few societies devoted to the history of trades and occupations. In the case of the railways, for example, there is the Railway Ancestors Family History Society, with a website at <**www.railway ancestors.org.uk**>, while the London & North Western Railway Society has a Staff History Group. Its web pages at <**www.lnwrs.org.uk/SHG/**> offer a family history research guide and a database of staff members (Figure 9-4).

Resources relating to merchant seamen are discussed along with those for the Royal Navy, on p. 144. Photographers are covered on p. 285.

▌ The learned professions

While records for individual trades and occupations are generally sparse and fortuitous, those for the learned professions are much more copious, well organized, and, in many cases, in print.

Most of the relevant material is, of course, specific to a particular profession, but there are a number of general sources to check. Directories, for example, often have lists for individual trades and professions, and you

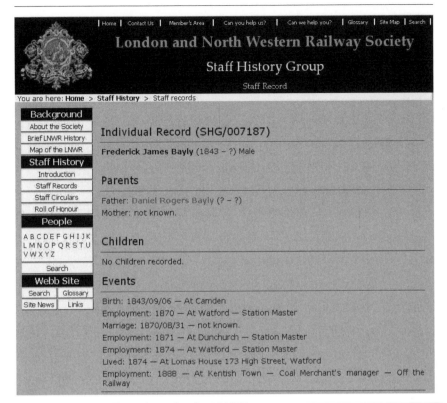

Figure 9-4 The Staff Database for the L&NWR

can expect to find an entry for self-employed professionals in the many directories which are available online. The premier site for directories is the Historical Directories site (see p. 179), and Figure 9-5 shows an example – a list of local dentists from Kelly's 1895 directory for Gloucestershire. All the professional entries here give an address, and many indicate qualifications. In some cases, specific days are listed for surgeries in particular towns.

Some professions have their own directories, such as the clergy's *Crockford's Clerical Directory*. The digital book archives discussed in Chapter 12 may have scans of individual volumes; otherwise a search of the library catalogues mentioned in Chapter 13 will locate a physical copy. The Society of Genealogists, for example, has a considerable collection of such directories, and all are listed in their online catalogue at <**www.sog.org.uk/ sogcat/access/**>. Findmypast (see p. 46) currently has four professional directories available to its subscribers: the 1896 *Clergy List*, the 1925 *Dental Surgeons Directory*, the 1858 *Medical Directory For Ireland*, and the 1913 *Medical Register*.

The learned professions are so called because they require a university degree. This means that the records of the ancient universities can be

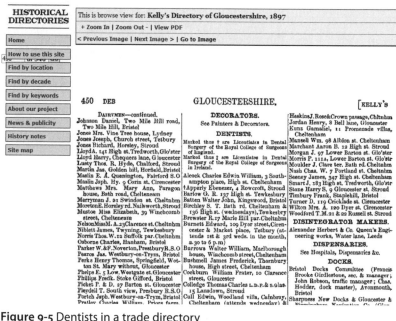

Figure 9-5 Dentists in a trade directory

looked to for information on individual ancestors. For Cambridge, Venn's *Alumni Cantabrigienses*, covering the period 1261–1900, is on the Internet Archive at <www.archive.org/details/texts/>. A search for the title will bring up a list of volumes; alternatively just follow the links from the Wikipedia article at <en.wikipedia.org/wiki/Alumni_Cantabrigienses>. It is also available to Ancestry subscribers at <www.ancestry.com/search/db. aspx?dbid=3997>. A free database is in preparation by John Dawson and an experimental version of this is available at <venn.csi.cam.ac.uk/ ACAD/>.

The equivalent publication for Oxford, Foster's *Alumni Oxonienses*, is also available on the Internet Archive at <www.archive.org/stream/ alumnioxonienseo0fostgoog>. Again, Ancestry has made the material available to subscribers, at <www.ancestry.co.uk/search/DB.aspx?dbid= 8942>. Bob Sanders has a page devoted to 'Oxford University Alumni with Cardiff & Vale Of Glamorgan Connections' at <www.angelfire.com/ga/ BobSanders/ALUMNOX.html>. Familyrelatives at <www.familyrelatives. com> has not only the *Alumni Oxonienses*, but also the *Alumni Dublinense*, which lists staff and students of Trinity College Dublin 1593–1846.

If you know which college an ancestor attended, you may find useful information about the available records by consulting the college website. Balliol College Oxford, for example, has a comprehensive page devoted to tracing past members at <archives.balliol.ox.ac.uk/Past%20members/ trace.asp>.

The legal profession

For the legal profession, a useful place to start is the National Archives' site, which provides a research guide to 'Lawyers: Records of Attorneys and Solicitors' at <www.nationalarchives.gov.uk/catalogue/RdLeaflet. asp?sLeafletID=98>, and pages on the records of attorneys as part of the 'In depth guide to family history' at www.nationalarchives.gov.uk/familyhistory/guide/trade/attorneys.htm.

The Inner Temple is another useful site. It has a list of bibliographical sources for lawyers at <www.innertemple.org.uk/archive/itad/biog_sources.html> and a page devoted to 'The Inns Of Court And Inns Of Chancery And Their Records' at <www.innertemple.org.uk/archive/inns_records.html>, as well as information on 'Legal Education to 1850' at <www.innertemple.org.uk/archive/itad/legal_education.html>. Its Admissions Database at <www.innertemple.org.uk/archive/itad/> has entries covering the period 1547 to 1850. Figure 9-6 shows the entry for John Bishop, with his age, address and date of admission as well as the name and address of his father, and the fact that he is the eldest son.

Medicine

The medical profession has a range of professional bodies to which an ancestor may have belonged, and the websites of these are worth looking at. The Royal College of General Practitioners has a guide to 'Tracing Your Medical Ancestors' at <www.rcgp.org.uk/default.aspx?page=93>. Although it does not itself hold any personal records, the British Medical Association has a page devoted to 'Biographical information: doctors and other professions'

Figure 9-6 A record from the Inner Temple Admissions Database

at <**www.bma.org.uk/ap.nsf/Content/LIBBiographical Information**>. The older establishments all have historical material in their libraries and archives, which may include the publications and perhaps even personal papers of members, so it will be worth consulting any online catalogue.

Alex Glendinning's comprehensive page on 'Was Your Ancestor a Doctor?' at <**user.itl.net/~glen/doctors.html**> includes coverage of overseas sources and medical staff in the armed forces. However, it does not seem to have been checked for some time, and quite a few of the links are broken.

The Guildhall Library has information using its own holdings in 'Sources For Tracing Apothecaries, Surgeons, Physicians And Other Medical Practitioners At Guildhall Library' at <**www.history.ac.uk/gh/apoths. htm**>, but this page will also be of use for doctors outside the capital.

Munk's Roll is a collection of obituaries of members of the Royal College of Physicians, and the College has an online index to it at <**www.rcplondon. ac.uk/heritage/munksroll/**>. Ten volumes have been printed, covering the period from the founding of the College to 1997, and all of these are included in the online index, with detailed biographies for a number of members.

A list of those granted medical licences by the Archbishop of Canterbury is available as a PDF file on the Lambeth Palace Library site, linked from <**www.lambethpalacelibrary.org/content/medicallicences**>. The licences cover the period 1535–1775.

Ancestry has a complete run of the quadrennial UK Medical Registers of the General Medical Council for 1859–1959 at <**www.ancestry.co.uk/search/ DB.aspx?dbid=33538**>, which can be browsed (the entries are in alphabetical order) or searched, though since the index has been created by optical character recognition, it is not entirely reliable. Findmypast's medical registers are mentioned above (p. 46).

DOCTORS-NURSES-MIDWIVES is a mailing list for those with ancestors in the medical profession, details of which will be found at <**lists. rootsweb.ancestry.com/index/other/Occupations/DOCTORS-NURSES-MIDWIVES.html**>.

Further links will be found on the 'Medical & Medicine' page on Cyndi's List at <**www.cyndislist.com/medical.htm**>. The Library of the Wellcome Institute at <**library.wellcome.ac.uk**> has links to more general material on the history of medicine.

The Church

Among the useful guides for anyone starting to investigate clerical ancestry is the Guildhall Library's introduction to 'Sources For Tracing Clergy And Lay Persons' at <**www.history.ac.uk/gh/clergy.htm**>. Although the main focus is London, much of the information is relevant to all ancestors in the

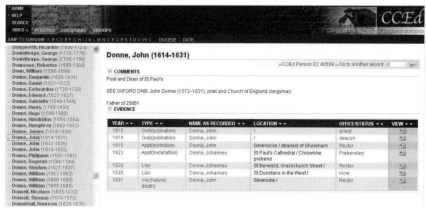

Figure 9-7 Entry for the poet John Donne in CCEd

Established Church. Lambeth Palace Library has a guide to 'Biographical sources for Anglican clergy' at <**www.cofe.anglican.org/about/librarie-sandarchives/anglicanclergysourceguide.pdf**>. The most important online resource is the Clergy of the Church of England Database project (CCEd) at <**www.theclergydatabase.org.uk**>, which aims to document the careers of all Church of England clergymen between 1540 and 1835. The project is still in progress, but it already has details of around 23,000 individuals on the website. Information about the dates and dioceses covered so far will be found at <**www.theclergydatabase.org.uk/upgrade/content.html**>. For each individual the database gives details of his university degree (if known) and a list of appointments, with links to information on sources (Figure 9-7).

London University's Institute for Historical Research has an index to the *Fasti Ecclesiae Anglicanae*, a list of English cathedral clergy up to 1857 at <**www.history.ac.uk/fasti/**>. The first two volumes (of seven) of the equivalent publication for Scotland, the *Fasti Ecclesiae Scoticanae*, are indexed and transcribed at <**www.dwalker.pwp.blueyonder.co.uk/Ministers%20 Index. htm**>. Vol. VII is available (catalogued as Vol. 10) on the Internet Archive at <**www.archive.org/stream/fastiecclesiaescooscot**>, and it will be worth keeping an eye out for other volumes appearing on this site.

CHURCHMEN-UK is a mailing list for those interested in clerical ancestors, and details will be found at <**lists.rootsweb.ancestry.com/index/ other/Occupations/CHURCHMEN-UK.html**>, and British-Genealogy has a 'Clergymen' discussion forum at <**www.british-genealogy.com/ forums/forumdisplay.php?f=39**>.

Mundus at <**www.mundus.ac.uk**> describes itself as a 'gateway to missionary collections in the UK', and will be worth checking if you have missionary ancestors. The site provides information on over 400 collections of overseas missionary materials held in institutions in the

United Kingdom, including collections of personal papers.

For ministers outside the established church, see the links for other denominations in Chapter 7.

Company records

If you think that an ancestor may have worked for, or even owned, a particular company, it will be worth trying to find out whether there are any surviving records. Unless the company is still in existence, and perhaps even then, the records are likely to be in a repository, in which case they should show up in the National Register of Archives at <**www.nationalarchives. gov.uk/nra**> (see p. 195). The NRA's 'Corporate name' search will identify such records, and in many cases link to an A2A record (see p. 193). For example, Figure 9-8 shows the beginning of a substantial page in A2A describing the records of Berger Jenson and Nicholson Limited of Hackney. Lower down the page is a complete history of the company, and a list of the individual documents, which include staff records.

Of course, in the case of a large company, there may well be a website with information about the company's history and staff records. For example, although it is not an official company site, there is 'an electronic history of J.Lyons & Co. and some of its 700 subsidiaries' at <**www.kzwp.com/lyons/**>, which has a 'Pensioners' section including hundreds of death notices,

Figure 9-8 Corporate records in A2A

obituaries of notable senior staff, and lists of the company's war dead.

Trade unions

In the case of nineteenth-century or later workers, there may be information on individual ancestors in the records of the trade unions. Records for the thousands of individual unions which preceded the growth of the large amalgamated unions of the present should be sought in the online catalogues of the local record offices (see Chapter 13). But for general information about trade union records and family history the site to visit is Trade Union Ancestors at <**www.unionancestors.co.uk**>. This not only lists the more than 5,000 unions which have existed over the last 200 years, but provides family trees showing the 'genealogy' of the modern national unions, which may help to identify the likely location of surviving records (Figure 9-9). There are also brief histories of a number of unions, with lists of officers. A partner site, Chartist Ancestors at <**www.chartists.net**>, will be of interest to those with activist ancestors in the 1840s, and contains lists of names from newspapers, court records and petitions.

The Trades Union Congress Library Collections are deposited at the London Metropolitan University, and details will be found on its website at <**www.londonmet.ac.uk/services/sas/library-services/tuc/**>.

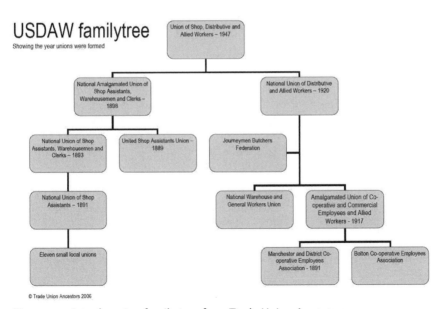

Figure 9-9 A trade union family tree from Trade Union Ancestors

10

THE ARMED FORCES

Even before the mass conscription of the two World Wars, the army and the navy provided an occupation or a career for large numbers of men from all strata of society. There can be few British families without some ancestors who served in the forces.

Because of this, military records have been high on the list for indexing and digitization. The National Archives itself has made them a major focus of its DocumentsOnline service (p. 51), and all the major commercial data services offer a range of military records. There are many sites dedicated to those who have fallen in war, particularly the First World War. Also, the widespread interest in military history means there are a host of well-informed non-commercial sites, which, even if they do not list individual names (and are often not graphically appealing), provide useful historical information.

▍ General information

There are two official sites for information on the armed forces and their records: the National Archives and the Ministry of Defence (MoD). The National Archives provides an extensive series of research guides to help you understand how the historical records are organized and how to locate and understand them. These can be found at <**www.nationalarchives.gov. uk/catalogue/researchguidesindex.asp**>. The 'In depth guide to family history' at <**www.nationalarchives.gov.uk/familyhistory/guide/**> has extensive sections devoted to the Royal Navy, Royal Marines, British Army and Royal Air Force with details of personnel records, operational records, medals and courts martial. The site also has a separate area on military history with a home page at <**www.nationalarchives.gov.uk/militaryhistory/**>, with links to the relevant research guides.

The MoD site at <**www.mod.uk**>, while mainly devoted to the present-day forces, has detailed pages on the location of recent service records, and provides many contact addresses. Each branch of the services has its own website within the MoD's internet domain: <**www.royal-navy.mod.uk**>, <**www.army.mod.uk**> and <**www.raf.mod.uk**>. Beyond these central bodies, there are the individual regiments, ships, squadrons and other units, many of which have their own web pages with historical information. The easiest way to find these is from the official site for the relevant arm of the services, which has links to its constituent units. The MoD site does not offer information about individuals.

Genuki has pages devoted to Military Records at <www.genuki.org.uk/big/MilitaryRecords.html> and Military History at <www.genuki.org.uk/big/MilitaryHistory.html>. Cyndi's List has a page devoted to UK Military at <www.cyndislist.com/miluk.htm>, which covers all branches of the services, while her 'Military Resources Worldwide' page at <www.cyndislist.com/milres.htm> has more general material.

The *London Gazette* (see p. 188) contains details of appointments (of officers) in the armed forces, and the text search facility on the site at <www.gazettes-online.co.uk> can be used to do a name search.

The Scots at War site at <www.scotsatwar.org.uk> concentrates mainly on the twentieth century. It has a Commemorative Roll of Honour with service and biographical information on Scottish servicemen, and detailed genealogical help pages, which will be of interest to anyone with Commonwealth military ancestors.

Britains [*sic*] Small Wars at <www.britains-smallwars.com> covers the period from 1945 up to the present and has extensive information about each war, including in many cases lists of casualties. British Armed Forces and National Service 1947–1963 at <www.britisharmedforces.org> is a site with historical information about the period of national service, the various units active in the period, and 'Servicemen's Tales' from both national service conscripts and regular servicemen.

The Imperial War Museum at <www.iwm.org.uk> has a family history section at <www.iwm.org.uk/server.php?show=nav.00100a>, with several guides to tracing service personnel:

- Tracing Merchant Navy Ancestry
- Tracing Royal Navy Ancestry
- Tracing POWs
- Tracing Army Ancestry
- Tracing Royal Flying Corps and Royal Air Force Ancestry
- Tracing West Indian Service Personnel

The IWM also has an online database with parts of its collections catalogued at <www.iwmcollections.org.uk>. Digitized extracts from some of the materials are available on the site.

There are quite a few sites devoted to particular wars or battles, such as the pages on the Battle of Culloden <www.electricscotland.com/history/

culloden/>. Some are devoted to a war as a whole, such as the Trenches on the Web site at <**www.worldwar1.com**>,which is subtitled 'An Internet History of The Great War'. While you can locate such sites by using a search engine (see Chapter 19), it will often be less time-consuming to start by looking for an article on the engagement on Wikipedia, which will have links to recommended sites and sources.

RootsWeb has a number of mailing lists devoted to particular wars, including:

- NAPOLEONIC
- CRIMEAN-WAR
- BOER-WAR
- WORLDWAR2
- GREATWAR
- WW1-UK
- KOREAN-WAR

WW20-ROOTS-L is devoted to 'genealogy in all twentieth century wars'. Details for all these lists can be found by using the 'Find a mailing list' search at <**lists.rootsweb.ancestry.com**>.

British-Genealogy has discussion forums devoted to the following conflicts:

- English Civil War
- Napoleonic Wars
- American War of Independence
- Crimean War
- Boer War
- World War 1
- World War 2

Links to these will be found at <**www.british-genealogy.com/forums/**>.

▍The Royal Navy and merchant navy

Although the merchant navy is not an arm of the state, it has long been subject to government regulation. There has always been movement between the Royal Navy and the merchant fleet, and many ancestors will have served in both. For those reasons, they are treated here together.

The official Royal Navy site at <**www.royal-navy.mod.uk**> has separate sections for ships, the Fleet Air Arm, submarines, the Royal Marines and naval establishments. The site has an extensive 'History' section at <**www.royal-navy.mod.uk/server/show/nav.3839**>, but there is no material specifically on family history.

The most important gateway to British maritime resources on the web was the National Maritime Museum's Port gateway. Although Port itself is no more, all its material has been incorporated in the Intute gateway at <www.intute.ac.uk> (see p. 260), which has a very extensive section devoted to maritime and naval history. You can go there direct using <www.intute.ac.uk/artsandhumanities/cgi-bin/browse.pl?id=200383>, or select 'History' and then 'Maritime/Naval History' from the home page. The section lists over 800 websites and gives quite detailed descriptions, so you should be able to tell which ones will be of use to you. A search on 'genealogy' within this section bring up 55 resources. As noted on p. 260, Intute has a high quality threshold so any site it includes will be worthwhile. The NMM itself has over 70 research guides devoted to maritime history available on its own site at <www.nmm.ac.uk>. Two of these are devoted specifically to tracing ancestors in the Royal Navy and merchant navy, but others that will be of interest are the guides to passenger lists, shipping companies, *Lloyd's List*, press-gangs, uniforms and medals.

Genuki has a page of merchant marine links at <**www.genuki.org.uk/big/MerchantMarine.html**>, while the Royal Navy is included in its Military Records and Military History pages mentioned above.

A site with a substantial collection of naval resources is Paul Benyon's 'Late 18th, 19th and early 20th Century Naval and Naval Social History' at <**www.pbenyon.plus.com/Naval.html**>. It includes extracts from many different types of sources, from Navy regulation to newspaper extracts, and many include names of individual seamen.

The MARINERS mailing list is for all those whose ancestors pursued maritime occupations, worldwide. The list has its own website at <**www.mariners-l.co.uk**> with sections devoted to individual countries, as well as more general topics such as wars at sea, and shipping companies. The site also has a guide to ranks in both the Royal and merchant navy at <**www.mariners-l.co.uk/GenBosun'sLocker.html**>. The MERCHANT-MARINE mailing list covers Merchant Marines of all countries involved in the Second World War, and details will be found at <**lists.rootsweb.ancestry.com/index/other/Military:_Naval/MERCHANT-MARINE.html**>. There is also a BRITISH-MARINERS list – details at <**lists.rootsweb.ancestry.com/index/other/Occupations/BRITISH-MARINERS.html**>.

In addition to the NMM's site at <**www.nmm.ac.uk**>, almost 300 maritime museums are listed at <**www.cus.cam.ac.uk/~mhe1000/marmus.htm**>.

Records

Since the majority of naval records are held by the National Archives, one of the best places to find out about them is the collection of online research guides at <www.nationalarchives.gov.uk/catalogue/researchguidesindex. asp>, where the relevant materials are grouped under Royal Navy and Merchant Navy. An introduction to the records of merchant seamen will be found at <www.nationalarchives.gov.uk/familyhistory/guide/trade/ merchantnavy.htm>.

The Royal Navy site has details on obtaining service records for those who joined the Navy from 1924 onwards at <www.royal-navy.mod.uk/ server/show/conWebDoc.108/changeNav/3533> (earlier records are at the National Archives).

For a more discursive guide to naval records, Fawne Stratford-Devai's articles on the Global Gazette site are recommended, 'British Military Records Part 2: THE ROYAL NAVY' at <globalgenealogy.com/ globalgazette/gazfd/gazfd48.htm> and 'Maritime Records & Resources' in two parts, at <globalgenealogy.com/globalgazette/gazfd/gazfd50.htm> and <globalgenealogy.com/globalgazette/gazfd/gazfd52.htm>. Among other things, these articles have very useful lists of some of the main groups of records (mainly from the National Archives) which have been micro-filmed by the LDS Church and can therefore be consulted at Family History Centers.

Other guides to tracing seafaring ancestors include Bob Sanders' site at <www.angelfire.com/de/BobSanders/>, which has an extensive collection of material on 'Tracing British Seamen & their ships', including not only naval occupations but also Fishermen, Customs & Excise Officers and Coastguards (be warned, though, that the background colours make some pages hard to read). Len Barnett has what he calls 'a realistic guide to what is available to those looking into merchant mariners' careers' at <www. barnettmaritime.co.uk>.

DocumentsOnline (p. 51) has the following naval records available:

- Registers of Seamen's Services (ADM 139, ADM 188)
- Royal Naval Division service records (ADM 339)
- Royal Naval Officers' Service Records (ADM 196)
- RNVR service records from WW1 (ADM 337)
- WRNS: Women's Royal Naval Service (ADM 318, ADM 336)
- Wills of Royal Naval Seamen (ADM 48)
- French Muster Rolls from the Battle of Trafalgar (HCA 32)
- Medals issued to Merchant Seamen, WW2 (BT 395)

Naval records available on other commercial sites include:

- Findmypast: Royal Naval Division 1914–1919
- Origins: Trinity House Calendars 1787–1854

- Ancestry: British Naval Biographical Dictionary, 1849, and Royal Naval Division Casualties of The Great War, 1914–1924
- The Genealogist: a dozen Navy Lists drawn from the period 1806–1938.
- FamilyRelatives: World War I and II Royal Navy Deaths (1913–21 and 1935–50).

There are many data transcriptions relating to seamen to be found on websites run by individuals. For example, Bob Sanders has an index to O'Byrne's *Royal Navy Biography* of 1849 with details of Royal Navy officers on six separate pages, linked from <**www.angelfire.com/de/BobSanders/ Site.html**>, as well as many other small data collections. The Naval Biographical Database is an ambitious project at <**www.navylist.org**> to 'establish accurate biographical information on those individuals who have served, or supported the Royal Navy since 1660'. So far the site has details of around 15,000 people and 5,000 ships. The site is basically free, though there is a charge for more detailed information

The National Archives has a Trafalgar Ancestors database, launched on the 200th anniversary of the battle, at <**www.nationalarchives.gov.uk/ trafalgarancestors/**>, with over 18,000 names drawn from a wide range of sources (Figure 10-1). There is much further information about the battle and about Nelson. The Age of Nelson at <**www.ageofnelson.org**> has a complete Navy List for the period of the Napoleonic Wars. It also has a project to trace the descendants of those who fought at Trafalgar, as well as its own Trafalgar Roll.

Among the sites devoted to merchant seamen is Irish Mariners at <**www. irishmariners.ie**>, which contains an index of around 23,000 Irish-born

Figure 10-1 Trafalgar Ancestors

merchant seamen extracted from records in the Southampton Civic Archives for the period from late 1918 to the end of 1921. A particular interest of these records is that they include photographs. Welsh Mariners at <www.welshmariners.org.uk> has a database of 22,000 Welsh merchant seamen, 1800–1945, and over 3,000 men active in the Royal Navy 1795–1815, which therefore includes Welshmen at Trafalgar.

A major undertaking is the Crew List Index Project (CLIP) at <www.crewlist.org.uk>. The site does not list names of individuals, but it has a wealth of information about crew lists, and how to locate them, including indexes of the lists held at the National Archives and in local record offices.

Ships

There are a number of sites relating to the ships rather than the seamen who served on them, and these can be useful for background. For example, Gilbert Provost has transcribed details of vessels from the Lloyd's Register of British and Foreign Shipping from 1764 up to 2003 at <www.reach.net/~sc001198/Lloyds.htm>. Michael P. Palmer maintains the Palmer List of Merchant Vessels at <www.geocities.com/mppraetorius/>, which has descriptions of hundreds of merchant vessels, compiled from a variety of sources. Both sites provide names of masters and owners as well as information on the ships themselves. Steve Johnson provides a 'photographic A to Z of British Naval warships, submarines, and auxiliaries from 1880 to 1950s' at <freepages.misc.rootsweb.ancestry.com/~cyberheritage/>. Through Mighty Seas at <www.mightyseas.co.uk> is devoted to the merchant sailing ships of the North West and the Isle of Man and has histories of over 950 vessels.

If you suspect that an ancestor was on a naval vessel, either in port or at sea, on census night in 1901, you should find Jeffery Knaggs' index to the location of Royal Navy ships at <homepage.ntlworld.com/jeffery.knaggs/RNShips.html> of interest. Bob Sanders has a similar list of Ships in UK Ports for the 1881 census at <www.angelfire.com/de/BobSanders/81Intro.html>.

The Army

The National Archives research guides mentioned above are good starting points for tracing army ancestry and there is more stuctured guidance at <www.nationalarchives.gov.uk/familyhistory/military/army/>. Genuki has a page devoted to British Military History at <www.genuki.org.uk/big/MilitaryHistory.html>, and an article by Jay Hall on 'British Military Records for the 18th and 19th Centuries' at <www.genuki.org.uk/big/MilitaryRecords.html>. There is a useful article by Fawne Stratford-Devai devoted to 'British Military Records Part 1: The Army' in *The Global Gazette* at <globalgenealogy.com/globalgazette/gazfd/gazfd44.htm>.

Records

The National Archives catalogue is the main source of information for all service records for individual soldiers. In some cases, the online catalogue includes the names of individual soldiers from documents in WO 97, which comprises discharge papers for the period 1760–1854 (see p. 198). DocumentsOnline includes a range of army records:

- Campaign Medal Index Cards, WW1 (WO 372)
- Selected WW1 and Army of Occupation War Diaries (WO 95)
- Women's (later Queen Mary's) Army Auxiliary Corps service records (WO 398)
- Royal Marines Service Records (ADM 159)
- Prisoner of War interviews and reports, WW1 (WO 161)

Among the records available on the commercial data services are:

- Findmypast: De Ruvigny's Roll 1914–1918, Waterloo medal roll 1815, and other army lists 1656–1888
- The Genealogist: various Army Lists 1806–1938
- Ancestry: WWI Medal Rolls Index Cards, Pension Records and Service Records, 1914–1920; Scottish Soldiers in Colonial America
- Familyrelatives: World War I and II Army Deaths (1913–21 and 1935–50)

The National Roll of the Great War is available at both Findmypast and Ancestry

Regiments

The crucial piece of information about any ancestor in the army is the regiment or unit he served in. A useful area of the army site at the MoD is that devoted to the organizational structure of the army at <**www.army.mod. uk/structure/structure.aspx/**>, which has links to the web pages for the individual regiments, as well as to the special units and the Territorial Army. The pages for each regiment include historical information.

However, over the centuries, regiments have not been very stable in either composition or naming and you are likely to need historical information about the particular period when an ancestor was in uniform. Apart from the official material on the MoD site, the essential resource for regimental history is T. F. Mills' Land Forces of Britain, the Empire and Commonwealth site at <**www.regiments.org**>. Unfortunately, at the time of writing, the home page says simply, 'Sorry, this site is temporarily unavailable'. This is very unfortunate because the site not only provides detailed background information on the regimental system at <**regiments. org/milhist/uk/forces/bargts.htm**>, but also lists the regiments in the army in particular years since the eighteenth century. However, a copy of the site as it was in January 2008 is available on the Waybackmachine at <**www. archive.org**>.

An alternative comprehensive source of information on regiments is Wikipedia. The 'List of British Army regiments' at <**en.wikipedia.org/wiki/ List_of_British_Army_regiments**> gives the present-day regiments and has links to equivalent lists for a number of earlier dates, as well as a useful list of regimental nicknames. There are, as you would expect, quite extensive articles on the individual regiments.

The regimental pages on the Scots at War site at <**www.scotsatwar.org. uk/regpages.htm**> have lists of Scottish regiments with pages devoted to each one. Particularly useful are the regimental 'family trees' showing the origins of the present-day regiments in earlier units (Figure 10-2).

For details of the regiments active in the Indian subcontinent, the Families In British India Society Wiki (see p. 170) is a good source. The entry point for all articles on military subjects is at <**wiki.fibis.org/index. php?title=Category:Military**>. As you would expect, the site also has details of the East India Company's military presence in India.

Many individuals have put up pages on particular regiments, sometimes in relation to a specific war or engagement. There is no single comprehensive

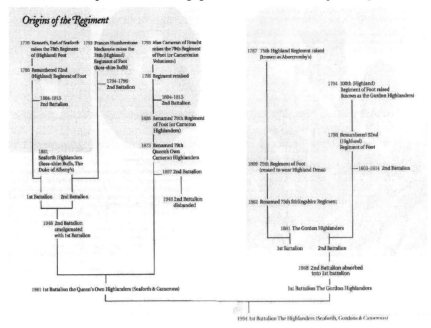

Figure 10-2 Scotsatwar: the origins of the 1st Battalion the Highlanders

listing of these, but you should be able to find them by entering the name of the regiment in a search engine.

There is a very active britregiments mailing list, details of which will be found at <**groups.yahoo.com/group/britregiments/**>. Note that this is a military rather than genealogical discussion forum.

If you need to identify a regimental cap badge, you could have a look at <**www.egframes.net**>. This is a commercial site offering badges for sale, but it has photographs of current badges and a searchable database of regiments. If you want to know what uniform an ancestor wore, or are trying to identify a photograph, the illustrations from two booklets by Arthur H. Bowling on the uniforms of British Infantry Regiments 1660–1914 and Scottish Regiments 1660–1914 are online at <**geocities.com/Pentagon/ Barracks/3050/buframe.html**>.

Otherwise, you will need to browse through some of the online photographic collections, such as Photographs of Soldiers of the British Army 1840 to 1920 at <**www.members.dca.net/fbl/**>.

The Army Museums Ogilby Trust's site at <**www.armymuseums.org.uk**> has details of 136 museums, which can be located by name or by geographical area. For each museum, there is a link to its website if there is one. The National Army Museum in Chelsea has a website at <**www.national-army-museum.ac.uk**>. A list of Scottish military museums is provided on the Scottish Military Historical Society's website at <**www.scottishmilitary research.org.uk/page6.htm**>. Regimental museums can also be found via the regiment's page on the Army website.

▌ The Royal Air Force

The official RAF site is at <**www.raf.mod.uk**>, with a list of squadrons and stations linked from the 'Organisation' page at <**www.raf.mod.uk/ organisation/**>. The History section at <**www.raf.mod.uk/history/**> offers historical material on individual squadrons and stations, with images of squadron badges, and details of battle honours and aircraft. If you have an ancestor who took part in the Battle of Britain, you will want to look at the operational diaries at <**www.raf.mod.uk/bob1940/bobhome.html**>. The home page of the Air Historical Branch at <**www.raf.mod.uk/ahb/**> has links to the websites of individual squadrons and stations. Contact details (non-electronic) for RAF Personnel records are given at <**www.raf.mod. uk/contactus/**>.

So far, Familyrelatives at <**www.familyrelatives.com**> seems to be the only commercial data service with RAF-specific collections, offering WWII RAF Deaths, and RAF lists for 1920, 1922 and1929. DocumentsOnline has the WRAF service records for the First World War (AIR 80) with details of around 30,000 individuals – details at <**www.nationalarchives.gov.uk/**

documentsonline/ww1airwomen.asp>. The RAF site, incidentally, has a section of its site devoted to 'Women in Aviation' at <www.raf.mod.uk/history_old/wia.html>.

Although not strictly RAF records, Ancestry's collection of Royal Aero Club Aviators' Certificates, 1910–1950 at <www.ancestry.co.uk> will include details of many who had been or were to be RAF pilots in the two World Wars. This collection includes around 28,000 index cards and 34 photograph albums.

The RAF Museum has a website at <www.rafmuseum.org.uk>, and the pages for the museum's Department of Research & Information Services at Hendon has information on archive and library material at <www. raf museum.org.uk/research/>.

There do not seem to be any genealogical mailing lists specifically for the RAF, though the general lists for twentieth-century wars mentioned on p. 144 above will cover RAF interests.

▌Medals

The National Archives has two main research guides on military medals and their records:

- Campaign Medals, and other Service Medals at <www.nationalarchives. gov.uk/catalogue/RdLeaflet.asp?sLeafletID=37>
- Gallantry Medals <www.nationalarchives.gov.uk/catalogue/RdLeaflet. asp?sLeafletID=35>

The 'In-depth guide to family history' includes a page on medals in the section for each arm of the services, indicating the records to refer to. There is also a guide to 'Merchant Seamen: Medals and Honours' at <www.national archives.gov.uk/catalogue/RdLeaflet.asp?sLeafletID=133>.

An increasing number of the records relating to medals will be found in DocumentsOnline (p. 51) at <www.nationalarchives.gov.uk/documents online>, which currently includes:

- WW1 Campaign Medal Index Cards (WO 372)
- Recommendations for Honours and Awards (WO 373)
- World War Two Medals issued to Merchant Seamen (BT 395)
- The Victoria Cross Registers (WO 98)

The first of these is particularly important since it includes almost all who served overseas, inlcuding many whose service records do not survive.

Details of gallantry awards were posted in the *London Gazette*, which can be searched at the Gazettes Online website, described in more detail on

United Kingdom: Korea War Medal

| Ribbon: Yellow with 2 light blue stripes. Instituted: 1951. Awarded: For one day's service in Korea, or 28 days at sea in the region, between 2 July 1950 and 10 June 1953. All recipients also received the UN Korea Medal | | |

| World Medals Index | Text List | Ribbon Chart | References |

Figure 10-3 Medals of the World

p. 188. Unfortunately, the dedicated honours and awards search that the site previously offered is no longer available.

There are many other sites devoted to medals. In particular, Wikipedia has an extensive set of pages devoted to British military medals and awards. The most general starting page is <**en.wikipedia.org/wiki/Category: Military_awards_and_decorations_of_the_United_Kingdom**>, but for a specific medal, just type the name of the medal into the search box on the home page at <**en.wikipedia.org**>. For the Victoria Cross, George Cross, George Medal and Military Medal, there are pages listing the recipients and linking to biographies with details of the action for which the award was made. Stephen Stratford has information on gallantry medals, with photographs, at <**www.stephen-stratford.co.uk/gallantry.htm**>.

If you need to identify medals, a good starting point is MedalNet at <**www.medal.net**>, which is devoted to Commonwealth medals. Google's image search at <**images.google.com**> (see p. 321) will quickly find images of a particular medal. McCollum's Militarium has an online 'Medal Identification Tool' at <**ww.military-medal.co.uk/medal-identifier-4. html**>, though it is still a work in progress and not yet complete. Medals of the World has an extensive collection of images of medals and ribbons for many countries at <**www.medals.org.uk**> (Figure 10-3).

▌ Commemoration

There are many online resources which commemorate those who served in the armed forces and particularly those who fell in action.

Debt of Honour Register

The most important collection of online data relating to twentieth-century service personnel who gave their lives is the Debt of Honour Register at <**www.cwgc.org**>. This is on the website of the Commonwealth War Graves

Commission, and was one of the first major databases of genealogical significance to go online when it was launched in 1998. The database contains the names of 1.7 million members of the Commonwealth forces who died in the First and Second World Wars

For all those listed there is name, rank, regiment and date of death, with details either of place of burial or, for those with no known grave, of commemoration. The burial information gives not only the name of the cemetery but also the grave reference and instructions on how to get to the cemetery. Some records have additional personal information, usually including the names of parents and the home address. With many cemeteries holding the dead from particular battles and campaigns, there is often historical information which puts the death in its military context. The database also includes information on 60,000 civilian casualties of the Second World War, though without details of burial location.

The initial search form allows you to specify surname, initials, war or year of death, force (i.e. army, navy, etc.) and nationality. Unless you are looking for an unusual name, it is best to enter as much detail as possible. Figure 10-4 shows a search for the record of the poet Edward Thomas.

From the details given, the database reports that there are 16 records (Figure 10-5). Knowing that Edward Thomas was an officer and died in France, it is straightforward to identify him as the second lieutenant in the Royal Garrison Artillery who died on 9th April 1917.

The list of search results links to a page giving the details for each soldier listed. In the case of Thomas (see Figure 10-6), in addition to the basic details of rank, regiment and date of death, the record shows the names of his parents. The bottom part of the screen gives details of the cemetery and grave. The name of the cemetery links to a page about the cemetery, with further links to plans and photographs.

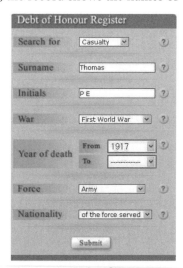

Because the search results sometimes give only the initials of the individuals, it can be quite time-consuming to search for someone whose regiment is unknown, though in some cases an age is given. Unfortunately, next of kin is not always named, so for common names you may need ultimately to look at service records to confirm the identity of a particular entry.

You can also search for individual cemeteries and access a list of graves.

Figure 10-4 Debt of Honour Register search form

A separate project, but one being carried out in association with the CWGC, is the War Graves Photographic Project <**www.twgpp.org**> which aims to 'photograph every war grave, individual memorial, MoD grave, and family memorial of serving military personnel from WWI to the present day'. In January 2009, the site had around one million names in its database, over half of the one-and-three-quarter million names records by the CWGC. Photos of the headstones can be ordered.

In addition to the data in the Debt of Honour Register (see p. 153), the Officers Died site at <**www.redcoat.info/memindex3.htm**> lists officers killed in a whole range of wars from the North American Wars of the eighteenth century to Afghanistan and Iraq in 2004, compiled from various

CWGC
Commonwealth War Graves Commission

Here are the results of your enquiry. There are **9** records which match your search criteria.

Select a name to see more details

No	Surname	Rank	Service Number	Date Of Death	Age	Regiment/Service	Nationality	Grave/Memorial Ref.	Cemetery/Memorial Name
1	THOMAS	Private	4428	18/05/1917	Unknown	South African Native Labour Corps	South African	I. B. 1.	ARQUES-LA-BATAILLE BRITISH CEMETERY
2	THOMAS, PHILIP EDWARD	Second Lieutenant		09/04/1917	39	Royal Garrison Artillery	United Kingdom	C. 43.	AGNY MILITARY CEMETERY
3	THOMAS FORCADOS	Private	7279	15/10/1917	Unknown	Nigeria Regiment, W.A.F.F.	United Kingdom		CALABAR MEMORIAL
4	THOMAS LIMBA	Private	933	22/12/1917	Unknown	Inland Water Transport, Royal Engineers	Indian		FREETOWN MEMORIAL
5	THOMAS MOWUMI	Private	7056	18/04/1917	Unknown	Nigeria Regiment, W.A.F.F.	United Kingdom		IBADAN MEMORIAL
6	THOMAS NJANA	Corporal	8584	21/09/1917	Unknown	Gold Coast Regiment, W.A.F.F.	United Kingdom		KUMASI MEMORIAL
7	THOMAS OBI	Carrier	3791	05/12/1917	Unknown	Nigeria Carrier Corps	United Kingdom		LAGOS MEMORIAL
8	THOMAS OWERRI	Private	97	28/07/1917	Unknown	Inland Water Transport, Royal Engineers	Indian		LAGOS MEMORIAL
9	THOMAS SOREN	Labourer	1853	25/10/1917	Unknown	Indian Labour Corps	Indian	I. H. 4.	LA CHAPELETTE BRITISH AND INDIAN CEMETERY, PERONNE

Figure 10-5 Debt of Honour Register search results

Casualty Details	
Name:	THOMAS, PHILIP EDWARD
Initials:	P E
Nationality:	United Kingdom
Rank:	Second Lieutenant
Regiment/Service:	Royal Garrison Artillery
Unit Text:	244th Siege Bty.
Age:	39
Date of Death:	09/04/1917
Additional information:	Son of Philip Henry Thomas; husband of Helen Thomas. One of the War Poets.
Casualty Type:	Commonwealth War Dead
Grave/Memorial Reference:	C. 43.
Cemetery:	AGNY MILITARY CEMETERY

Figure 10-6 Debt of Honour Register individual record

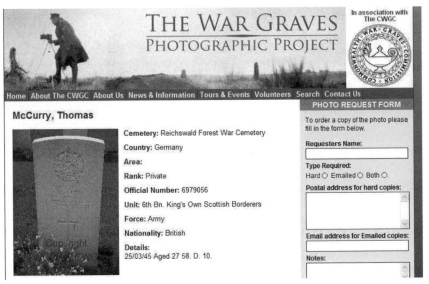

Figure 10-7 The War Grave Photographic Project

books, casualty lists, medal rolls, newspapers, and memorials. The same site has pages devoted to Soldiers [*sic*]Memorials at <**www.angelfire.com/ mp/memorials/memindz1.htm**>.

War memorials

Perhaps as a result of the 90th anniversary of the Armistice, a significant development in the last few years has been the number of sites devoted to domestic war memorials.

The main national project is the Imperial War Museum's UK National Inventory of War Memorials at <**www.ukniwm.org.uk**>. The main database lists around 56,000 war memorials with details of appearance, location and the number of names recorded. This does not include the individual names, but Channel 4's Lost generation website at <**www.channel4.com/ history/microsites/L/lostgeneration/**> has been set up to provide these. Unfortunately neither the memorial search nor the person search were working properly on the occasions I tried the site, though the records themselves are clearly present.

The equivalent project for Ireland, the Irish War Memorials Project, has a site at <**www.irishwarmemorials.ie**>. The site includes many photographs of memorials and often the names of those commemorated and any other text. In addition to a list of memorials, which can be sorted geographically, there is a list of names and regiments.

World War One Cemeteries at <**www.ww1cemeteries.com**> is designed as a guide to the cemeteries of the two World Wars. For each cemetery, it generally has a description and photograph; for some there are lists of names, while for others there is just a list of the regiments represented.

Roll of Honour at <www.roll-of-honour.com> is a site dedicated to listing those commemorated on war memorials. Currently the site has details of over 600 memorials in around half the counties of England. For each memorial the site gives not only the names of the individuals but also, where available, personal details drawn from the Debt of Honour Register (p. 153) or other publications. There are photographs for many of the memorials. The site does not confine itself to those who died, nor to the World Wars, but includes the Boer war and more recent conflicts such as the Falklands.

Alongside these national projects, there are countless local sites, such as:

- Newport's War Dead <www.newportsdead.bravehost.com>
- Dover War Memorial Project <www.doverwarmemorialproject.org.uk>

Not only towns and cities, but individual institutions may have details of their war dead on the web. For example:

- The Bata company's Reminiscence and Resource Centre has details of its fallen employees at <www.batamemories.org.uk/main/eng/00-en-pages/07-Worldwar.html>.
- The Department for Business, Enterprise & Regulatory Reform (the DTI, as was) has a section of its website at <www.berr.gov.uk/aboutus/corporate/history/warmemorial/> devoted to the 300 staff from the department's wartime predecessors who died in the wars. It includes basic biographical details for each individual, including, in some cases, the enumeration of the family in the 1901 census.
- The University of Glasgow's Roll of Honour at <www.archives.gla.ac.uk/honour/> has a database of 4,500 staff and students who served in the First World War (not just those killed). For over 200 of them, there are biographies drawn from the University's records.

11

MIGRATION AND COLONIES

Former British colonies are genealogically important for British and Irish family history for three reasons: they have been the destination of emigrants from the British Isles (both voluntary and otherwise), the source of much immigration, and a place of residence and work for many British soldiers, merchants and others.

There is not space here to deal with internet resources relating to the individual countries, or to overseas records unrelated to immigration or emigration, but good places to start are Cyndi's List at <**www.cyndislist. com**>, which has individual pages for all the countries or regions, and the GenWeb site for the country at <**worldgenweb.org**> (see p. 24). Genuki has links relating to both emigration and immigration at <**www.genuki.org. uk/big/Emigration.html**>. Resources relating to child migration are covered in 'Adoption and child migration' on p. 234.

For the official British records of emigration, the National Archives' 'Emigrants' research guide is the definitive online guide to official records, linked from <**www.nationalarchives.gov.uk/catalogue/researchguides index.asp**>. The National Library of Scotland has details of records of emigration from Scotland in its Scots Abroad databases at <**www.nls. uk/catalogues/online/scotsabroad/**>.

Probably more helpful for the beginner, though, is the National Archives' 'In-depth learning guide' to family history (see p. 7). The section devoted to migrant ancestors at <**www.nationalarchives.gov.uk/familyhistory/ guide/migrantancestors/**> has material on all aspects of migration, with pages devoted to the main destinations, passports, refuges and internees. It does not have coverage of individual immigrant groups. This approach is covered by the Moving Here site at <**www.movinghere.org.uk**>. The most important site for information on immigration to the British Isles, this has sections devoted to Caribbean, Irish, South Asian, and Jewish immigration to England over the past two centuries as well as the subsequent history of the immigrant communities. The site has a catalogue of resources as well as general historical material and individual historical testimony. There is specifically genealogical information for each of these immigrant groups in the 'Tracing Your Roots gallery' at <**www.movinghere.org.uk/galleries/roots/**>.

A useful general starting point for all ethnic groups is The Open Directory (see p. 27) at <**www.dmoz.org**>, which has pages for many groups, linked from <**dmoz.org/Society/Ethnicity/**>. The links collected here are primarily to historical and cultural material, however, and you should not expect to find any genealogical resources beyond what is already on Cyndi's List. For more specifically British resources, it is worth going to <**dmoz.org/Regional/Europe/United_Kingdom/Society_and_Culture/Ethnicity/**>, which links to pages for 14 immigrant communities.

The National Archives has an introduction to naturalization records for family historians at <**www.nationalarchives.gov.uk/familyhistory/naturalisation/**>, and there are research guides for 'Immigrants' and 'Naturalisation and Citizenship' linked from <**www.nationalarchives.gov.uk/catalogue/researchguidesindex.asp**>.

There is a Museum of Immigration at Spitalfields in London which has a website at <**www.19princeletstreet.org.uk**>. The British Empire & Commonwealth Museum in Bristol has a website at <**www.empire museum.co.uk**> with information on the museum and its collections. The Migrations Museum Network at <**www.migrationmuseums.org**> has

Figure 11-1 Material on South Asian migration from MovingHere

details of over two dozen migration museums around the world.

UntoldLondon at <**www.untoldlondon.org.uk**> 'tells you where to look for the history of all of London's races and faiths', with details of and links to relevant material in archives and museums. The 'Cultural Group Histories' page at <**www.untoldlondon.org.uk/archives/TRA37269.html**> is probably the best place to start for information on a particular immigrant group. In addition to immigrants from former colonies, there is also information on groups from a wide range of other countries.

There are a number of general mailing lists relating to migration from and within the British Isles, including:

- ENGLISH-EMIGRANTS <**lists.rootsweb.ancestry.com/index/other/Ethnic-English/ENGLISH-EMIGRANTS.html**>
- WELSH-EMIGRANTS <**lists.rootsweb.ancestry.com/index/other/Ethnic-Welsh/WELSH-EMIGRANTS.html**>
- IRISH-IN-UK <**lists.rootsweb.ancestry.com/index/other/Ethnic-Irish/IRISH-IN-UK.html**>, with a website at <**www.connorsgenealogy.com/IrishUK/**>
- IRISH-SCOTS <**lists.rootsweb.ancestry.com/index/other/Ethnic-Irish/IRISH-SCOTS.html**>

There are also local resources relating to immigrant groups, and these are often part of a local history site, particularly in the case of major cities. For example, the PortCities sites at <**www.portcities.org.uk**> have material on the slave trade for Bristol and Liverpool, while for London there are individual sections devoted to the roles of Chinese, Scandinavian, Jewish, Bengali, Goan, Swahili, Somali and Portuguese communities in the life of the port. For Bristol, there is a comprehensive site devoted to the city's ethnic groups, Identity and the City: a History of Ethnic Minorities in Bristol 1000–2001 at <**www.englandspastforeveryone.org.uk/Counties/Bristol/Projects/EthnicMinorities**> (Figure 11-2). Of course, these sites rarely have specifically genealogical information. For London, the Old Bailey proceedings site has some very substantial articles about individual immigrant communities at <**www.oldbaileyonline.org/static/Communities.jsp**>.

One problem in finding online resources relating to immigration is that search engines (see Chapter 19) will find predominantly materials relating to current immigration practices and issues, and it is much more difficult to identify historical materials by this method. For that reason, it is generally more productive to follow the links from the specialist genealogical and historical sites mentioned in this chapter.

Figure 11-2 Explore Bristol's Past

Passenger lists

Key general records for emigration from the British Isles are passenger lists, and there are a number of sites with information about surviving passenger lists, or with data transcribed from them. Cyndi's List has a 'Ships and Passenger Lists' page at <www.cyndislist.com/ships.htm>. Among other information, this has links to many passenger lists and lists of ship arrivals. Passenger lists specifically for immigration to North America and Australia are covered in the following sections.

Ancestorsonboard at <www.ancestorsonboard.com> is Findmypast's passenger list site, with 24 million records derived from the National Archives' Outward Bound Passenger Lists. These records are also accessible from the main site at <www.findmypast.com>. Subscriptions are described in Table 4-1a.

The Immigrant Ships Transcribers Guild at <www.immigrantships.net> has transcribed over 6,500 passenger lists and is adding more all the time. These can be searched by date, by port of departure, port of arrival, passenger name or captain's name. In addition to its own material, the 'Compass' area of the site at <immigrantships.net/newcompass/pcindex. html> has an enormous collection of links to other passenger list sites.

The Scottish Emigration Database at <www.abdn.ac.uk/emigration>

contains the records of over 21,000 passengers who embarked at Glasgow and Greenock for non-European ports between 1 January and 30 April 1923, and at other Scottish ports between 1890 and 1960.

Ancestry UK has a large number of databases relating to migration, many drawn from published works on English, Scots and Irish migration to North America. While most of the material discussed here concerns those leaving the British Isles, Ancestry has a database of UK Incoming Passenger Lists, 1878–1960, is drawn from the National Archives' BT26 series. There is a name search, and you can also browse the records by port, year and ship. This material is not just a source for immigrants – it also captures those returning from working abroad.

There are a number of mailing lists for immigrant ships, but the most general is TheShipsList, which has its own website at <**www.theshipslist. com**>. SHIPS_FROM_ENGLAND has similar coverage, though with an emphasis on the British Colonies of North America – details are at <**lists. rootsweb.ancestry.com/index/other/Immigration/SHIPS_FROM_ ENGLAND.html**>. Other lists relating to emigration and immigration will be found at <**www.rootsweb.ancestry.com/~jfuller/gen_mail_emi.html**>.

▌ The Americas

The earliest British migrants to North America were either voluntary settlers or transported convicts, though American independence eventually put a stop to the latter. Of course, independence did not put a stop to immigration from Britain and particularly Ireland.

The National Archives has a number of research guides on the British official records relating to British North America and the United States, all linked from <**www.nationalarchives.gov.uk/catalogue/researchguides index.asp**>:

- 'America and the West Indies, Transportation to, 1615–1776'
- 'America and West Indies: Colonies before 1782'
- 'American Revolution'
- 'Emigrants to North America after 1776'

The US National Archives and Records Administration (NARA) has comprehensive information on US immigration records at <**www.archives. gov/genealogy/immigration/**> and naturalization records at <**www. archives.gov/ genealogy/naturalization**>.

For other links relating to emigration to North America, the best starting point is the 'Immigration and Naturalization' page on Cyndi's List at <**www. cyndislist.com/immigrat.htm**>.

US sites of course have a wealth of data relating to immigrants.

For the early period of settlement, Ancestry at <**www.ancestry.com**> has several databases in addition to the passenger lists mentioned above:

- Immigrants to New England 1620–33
- Irish Quaker Immigration into Pennsylvania
- New England Founders
- New England Immigrants, 1700–75
- New England Irish Pioneers
- Scots-Irish in Virginia

A number of immigration datasets are included in a subscription to Ancestry's UK record collection, but for most a subscription to the US Immigration Collection or the Worldwide Membership is required (see p. 44).

Pilgrim Ship Lists Early 1600's at <**www.packrat-pro.com/ships/shiplist. htm**> has details of over 7,100 families and 250 ships from this period.

There are also sites devoted to particular groups of settlers, such as the *Mayflower* Passenger List at <**members.aol.com/calebj/passenger.html**>. The 'Immigration' page on Cyndi's List is the easiest way to find such sites.

In addition to the general passenger list sites mentioned above, there are a number of major databases for ships carrying immigrants to the USA. NARA has a page devoted to Ship Passenger Arrival Records and Land Border Entries (not all of which, of course, constitute immigration) covering the various types of record. The 'Immigration And Ships Passenger Lists Research Guide' at <**home.att.net/~arnielang/shipgide.html**> offers help and guidance on researching ancestors who emigrated to the USA. The most significant databases are:

- Castle Garden at <**www.castlegarden.org/**>, has an online searchable database of 10 million immigrants from 1830 to 1892.
- The Ellis Island Passenger Arrivals (the American Family Immigration History Center) at <**www.ellisislandrecords.org**> has a searchable database of passengers who entered America through Ellis Island between 1892 and 1924.
- Irish Famine Passenger Records in NARA's Access to Archives Databases (AAD) at <**aad.archives.gov/aad/series-list.jsp?cat=GP44**> lists 604,596 persons who arrived in the Port of New York, from 1846-1851.

A smaller index, The Immigrant Servants Database at <**www.immigrant servants.com**> includes details of over 18,000 immigrants identifiable from published records as indentured servants up to 1820.

Harvard has more general historical materials relating to post-independence immigration (i.e. not records of named individuals) at <**ocp.hul.**

harvard.edu/immigration/> on its 'Immigration to the United States, 1789-1930' site.

There is less material online for Canada. Marjorie Kohli's Immigrants to Canada site at <**www.ist.uwaterloo.ca/~marj/genealogy/thevoyage.html**> has an extensive collection of material, and links to many related resources. The National Archives of Canada has information on immigration and citizenship at <**www.collectionscanada.gc.ca/genealogy/022-908-e.html**>, covering both border entry and passenger lists. There is a pilot online database for the passenger list records for the years 1925–35 at <**www.collections canada.gc.ca/databases/immigration-1925/index-e.html**>. The inGeneas site at <**www.inGeneas.com**> also has a database of passenger lists and immigration records: the National Archives of Canada Miscellaneous Immigration Index is free; the index to other material can be searched free, but there is a charge for record transcriptions. Resources relating to the British Home Children settled in Canada will be found on p. 236.

South America has been a much less significant destination for British settlers, but the Glaniad site at <**www.glaniad.com**> provides information on the Welsh in Patagonia.

Australasia

After the United States gained their independence from Britain in 1776, a new destination was required for the undesirables sentenced by the courts to transportation.

There are extensive materials online relating both to convict transportation to Australia, and to later free emigration to Australia and New Zealand. Good starting points are the Australia and New Zealand pages on Cyndi's List at <**www.cyndislist.com/austnz.htm**> and <**www.cyndislist.com/newzealand.htm**> respectively. Another worthwhile site is the Australian Family History Compendium, which has a list of online sources at <**www.cohsoft.com.au/afhc/**>. For information on the official records held by the British state, see the National Archives' Research Guides.

The University of Wollongong has a database of the First Fleet convicts <**firstfleet.uow.edu.au**>, with details of crime and conviction, and much supporting material about the fleet. The First Fleet 1788 site at <**www.jag10.freeserve.co.uk/1788.htm**> includes officials and marines as well as convicts, and also lists the provisions carried on the supply ships. Convicts to Australia at <**convictcentral.com**> has extensive material on the transported convicts, including the names of all those on the first, second, and third fleets, and details of all convict ships to the various states. The National Archives of Ireland has a database of Transportation Records 1788–1868 at <**www.nationalarchives.ie/topics/transportation/search01.html**> (see Figure 11-3).

Figure 11-3 An entry from the National Archives of Ireland's Transportation Records

In addition to the passenger list sites mentioned above, links to passenger lists for Australasia will be found at <**www.nationalarchives.ie/genealogy/transportation.html**>.

Australian government agencies have much information relating to convicts and free settlers online. The National Archives of Australia website at <**www.naa.gov.au**> has a section devoted to 'Migration, citizenship and travel' at <**www.naa.gov.au/collection/explore/migration/**>, which includes information on the relevant records and their locations.

Making Australia Home at <**www.naa.gov.au/whats-on/records-releases/making-australia-home.aspx**> is a National Archives project that aims to provide 'migrants and their families with better access to records that document their arrival and settlement in 20th-century Australia'. The NAA name search linked from this page can be used to search immigration and naturalization records by selecting this option from the 'Category of records' field.

Ancestry Australia at <**www.ancestry.com.au**> has a substantial collection of databases relating to convicts and free settlers, including:

- NSW Free Settlers, 1826–1922, with almost nine million names
- The List of Convicts with Particulars, 1788–1842, with physical descriptions of around 23,000 convicts
- Convict Savings Bank Books, 1824–1886

There are also relevant materials on the websites of the individual states. For example, the Victoria Public Record Office has an online database of Immigration to Victoria 1852–1889 at <**proarchives.imagineering.com.au**>. The Archives Office of Tasmania has a number of name indexes at <**www. archives.tas.gov.au/nameindexes**> which include convicts, arrivals, and naturalizations. There is also a Colonial Tasmanian Family Link Database with about 500,000 entries about Tasmanian families. New South Wales has all nineteenth-century civil registration indexes online at <**www.bdm. nsw.gov.au/familyHistory/searchHistoricalRecords.htm**> and Indexes to Assisted Immigrants at <**www.records.nsw.gov.au/archives/indexes_to_ assisted_immigrants_366.asp**>. Comprehensive links to Australian archives are on the Archives of Australia site at <**www.archivenet.gov.au**>.

Archives New Zealand has a website at <**www.archives.govt.nz**> with a 'Migration Reference Guide' at <**www.archives.govt.nz/docs/pdfs/Ref_ Guide_Migration.pdf**>. The Registrar General's site at <**www.bdm.govt. nz**> has information on births, deaths and marriages but no online data.

The online Encyclopedia of New Zealand at <**www.teara.govt.nz**> has considerable material relating to settlement, with sections devoted to particular communities. There is extensive coverage of English, Scots, Welsh and Irish settlement.

There are dozens of mailing lists for Australian and New Zealand genealogy, all listed at <**www.rootsweb.ancestry.com/~jfuller/gen_mail _country -aus.html**> and <**www.rootsweb.ancestry.com/~jfuller/gen_mail_country- nez.html**>. The main general lists are AUSTRALIA, NEW-ZEALAND, and GENANZ, while the remainder are devoted to specific topics: AUS- CONVICTS, AUS-IMMIGRATION-SHIPS, AUS-IRISH, AUS-MILITARY, AUS-NSW-COLONIAL-HISTORY, convicts-australia, TRANSCRIPTIONS- AUS and TRANSCRIPTIONS-NZ. There are also lists for individual states, regions, and even towns.

▌ Africa and the Caribbean

A good starting point for researching Black British ancestry is the BBC's family history site, which offers an introduction to Caribbean family history by Kathy Chater at <**www.bbc.co.uk/history/familyhistory/get_started/ caribbean_01.shtml**>. This provides some historical background and discusses the relevant records. The National Archives has pages devoted to 'Caribbean Histories Revealed' at <**www.nationalarchives.gov.uk/caribbean history/**>, which provides information about the region and the migrations to and from it, with an extensive collection of links and a very substantial bibliography. 'Black Presence. Asian and Black History in Britain 1500– 1850' is another National Archives site at <**www.nationalarchives.gov.uk/ pathways/blackhistory/**> which provides a concise introduction to the historical background of migration from the Caribbean and the Indian subcontinent.

CaribbeanGenWeb at <www.rootsweb.ancestry.com/~caribgw/> has areas devoted to all the islands of the Caribbean. Though there are considerable differences in scope, as each island site has its own maintainer, all have message boards to make contact with other researchers, and many have substantial collections of links. You should also find information on civil registration, parish registers and other records. Another useful collection of genealogy links for the Caribbean will be found on the Candoo site at <www.candoo.com/genresources/>, including lists of relevant microfilms in the LDS Church's Family History Centers.

The Caribbean Surnames Index (CARSURDEX) at <www.candoo.com/surnames/> offers a discussion forum which can be used to post details of the families being researched. The postings can be read by anyone but registration (free) is required to respond or post a message yourself.

The main mailing list for West Indian ancestry is CARIBBEAN – see <lists.rootsweb.ancestry.com/index/other/Newsgroup_Gateways/CARIBBEAN.html>. Details of other West Indies mailing lists will be found at <www.rootsweb.ancestry.com/~jfuller/gen_mail_country-wes.html>. The GEN-AFRICAN list (see <lists.rootsweb.ancestry.com/index/other/Newsgroup_Gateways/GEN-AFRICAN.html>) covers the genealogy of Africa and the African diaspora. There are also genealogical mailing lists for individual African countries – see <www.rootsweb.ancestry.com/~jfuller/gen_mail_african.html>. The CARIBBEAN-FREEDMEN and ENGLAND-FREEDMEN mailing lists may be of interest to descendants of freed slaves. Details of both are linked from <lists.rootsweb.ancestry.com/index/other/Ethnic-African/>.

While there is still relatively little specifically genealogical material online for those with Black British ancestry, the web offers an increasing amount of general historical information relating to black immigration and the history of black communities in Britain.

Resources relating to the BBC's *Windrush* season, broadcast in 1998, at <www.bbc.co.uk/history/british/modern/windrush_01.shtml> include a factfile and oral testimony from those who came to Britain on the *Windrush*. This is part of the 'Multiculture' area of the BBC's site which has a range of material relating to Black History and the British Empire. The Black Presence in Britain at <www.blackpresence.co.uk> is a blog devoted to black British history and has articles on a number of aspects, including parish and military records.

As mentioned above, the PortCities sites for Bristol and Liverpool, linked from <www.portcities.org.uk>, have material on the slave trade centred on these ports, while the London site has pages devoted to the capital's Somali and Swahili-speaking communities.

The Parliament website has extensive historical material on 'Parliament and the British Slave Trade 1600–1807' at <**slavetrade.parliament.uk/slavetrade/**>, while the National Archives has materials on slavery and its abolition at <**www.nationalarchives.gov.uk/slavery/**>.

It's worth using a search engine searching for the phrase 'black history' with the name of a town. This will turn up sites such as Birmingham Black History at <**www.birminghamblackhistory.com**>, or Brighton and Hove Black History at <**www.black-history.org.uk**>.

One of the most significant local projects is the Black and Asian Londoners Project (BAL), run by the London Metropolitan Archives (LMA). It aims to create an online database of Black and Asian Londoners between 1536 and 1840, with names and area of residence based on information from church registers, family papers in the LMA and material from the British Library and the India Office. The home page is at <**www.corpoflondon. gov.uk/Corporation/lma_learning/dataonline/lz_baproject.asp**> and the database can be searched on name, street, borough, place of origin, or

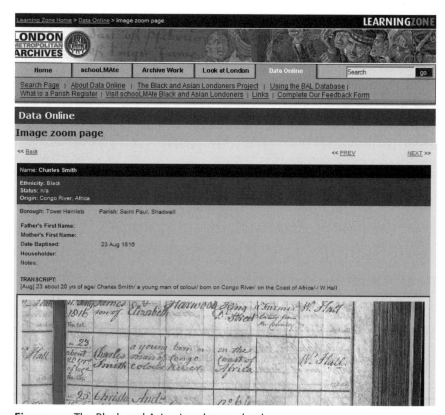

Figure 11-4 The Black and Asian Londoners database

occupation. The results of a search are images of the original records – Figure 11-4 shows the baptism of Chas. Henry Smith, 'a young man of colour', at St Paul, Shadwell.

CASBAH is a project which aims to identify and map national research resources relevant to Caribbean studies and the history of Black and Asian peoples in Britain. The CASBAH website at <www.casbah.ac.uk>, while aimed primarily at academic researchers, is useful to anyone researching Black History in Britain because it provides links to around 120 other relevant websites, particularly libraries with relevant collections. A number of relevant organizations have useful websites, for example the Archives & Museum of Black Heritage at <www.aambh.org.uk> (this requires Macromedia Flash, and does not seem to work with Firefox) and the Black and Asian Studies Association <www.blackandasianstudies.org.uk>.

The Open Directory's African-British page at <dmoz.org/Society/ Ethnicity/African/African-British/> is a good starting point for web resources relating to African and Afro-Caribbean immigration into Britain, though the listing does not specialize in genealogical sources.

Black Search at <www.black-search.co.uk> is a UK-based web directory of Black websites from around the world. It has a genealogy page, which can be found by following the 'History and Culture' link from the home page.

For convict transportation to the West Indies, see the National Archives' Research Guides mentioned under 'The Americas', above.

India

While some countries above were net recipients of migrants from the British Isles, the history of migration between Britain and the Indian subcontinent is more complex. Initially India was the temporary home of many young men in the army, trade or colonial administration. Those who chose to remain gave rise to an Anglo-Indian population. After independence, the flow was reversed, with many migrants from India, Pakistan and, later, Bangladesh settling in Britain.

A number of the resources mentioned in the previous section cover Asian immigration to Britain as well as Black immigration.

The British Library has a whole set of pages devoted to 'Asians in Britain' at <www.bl.uk/reshelp/findhelpsubject/history/history/asiansinbritain/ asiansinbritain.html>, including an outline of Asian immigration and contemporary material from various walks of life. The National Archives' materials relating to Black and Asian Britons have been mentioned above, and there is also a research guide to 'Family History Sources for Indian Indentured Labour' at <www.nationalarchives.gov.uk/catalogue/RdLeaflet. asp?sLeaflet ID=400>.

Local history sites for the major cities are always worth checking. For example, the Liverpool Museums sites host material on 'The Indian Presence in Liverpool' at <**www.liverpoolmuseums.org.uk/hamlyn/ip/**> with photos, biographies, and recordings of the immigrant families who came to the city in the twentieth century.

The British Library site is also useful for ancestors from the British Isles who lived or worked in India, as it includes the India Office website. This has pages for family historians at <**www.bl.uk/reshelp/findhelpsubject/ history/genealogy/indiaofficerecordsfamilyhistory/familyresearch.html**>, with information on the various types of genealogical source. The India Office Family History Search at <**indiafamily.bl.uk**> has a database of 300,000 births, baptisms, marriages, deaths and burials in the India Office Records, mainly for Europeans, for the period 1600–1949. Following the links to Sources leads to a list of the original document extracted.

Apart from the British Library, the most important site for the British in India is that of the Families in British India Society at <**www.fibis.org**> with a free online database of selected records of the India Office and East India Company held by the British Library and elsewhere. The records include transcriptions of civil, ecclesiastical, maritime and military records covering the period from 1737 to 1947. Amongst almost 200,000 records are details of ships sailing to India, and their occupants, plus births, marriages and deaths of persons in British-administered territories in India. Many records are of soldiers of the Indian Army and of the British Army regiments which served in India. The database can be searched from <**search. fibis.org**>. The FIBIWiki at <**wiki.fibis.org**> contains research guides, lists sources, and provides general background information about the culture, society and history of India during the period of British rule.

Findmypast at <**www.findmypast.com**> (see p. 46) has a number of datasets relating to British India, including:

- Bengal Civil Service Gradation List 1869
- India Office List 1933
- East India Register & Army List 1855
- Indian Army & Civil Service List 1873
- East India Company's Commercial Marine Service Pensions List 1793-1833

The Honorable East India Co site at <**www.honeastindiaco.com**> has birth, marriage and death notices of people who worked for or were associated with the Company, collected from various newspapers and publications.

Military sites mentioned in Chapter 10 may have information about the British Army in India.

There are two genealogical mailing lists relevant to the Indian subcontinent, BANGLADESH and INDIA. Details will be found at <lists.rootsweb. ancestry.com/index/intl/BGD/BANGLADESH.html> and <lists.rootsweb. ancestry.com/index/intl/IND/INDIA.html> respectively. RootsWeb hosts genealogical mailing lists for a number of other Asian countries, listed at <lists.rootsweb.ancestry.com/index/>. There is also an INDIA-BRITISH-RAJ list, though this is devoted to general historical and cultural topics rather than to genealogical issues as such. Subscription details and a link to the archive of messages will be found at <lists.rootsweb.ancestry.com/index/intl/IND/INDIA-BRITISH-RAJ.html>.

European immigration

For guidance about immigrants to Britain from continental Europe, the best starting points are the pages for the relevant country at Cyndi's List (p. 21) and WorldGenweb (p. 24) and the general immigration sites given at the start of this chapter. However, three particularly significant groups are covered here in more detail.

Jews

There are many sites devoted to Jewish genealogy, though not many are specifically concerned with British Jewry. A general history of Jews in Britain is provided in Shira Schoenberg's Virtual Jewish History Tour, which has a page devoted to England at <www.jewishvirtuallibrary.org/jsource/vjw/England.html>. JewishGen at <www.jewishgen.org> is a very comprehensive site with a number of resources relevant to Jewish ancestry in the British Isles. These include an old but still useful article on researching Jewish ancestry at <www.jewishgen.org/infofiles/ukgen.txt>, and the London Jews Database <www.jewishgen.org/databases/londweb.htm>, which has over 9,000 names, taken principally from London trade directories. (Jeffrey Maynard, who compiled this database, has a number of other small datasets on his Anglo-Jewish Miscellanies site at <www.jeffreymaynard.com>.)

The Jewish genealogical magazine *Avotaynu* has a 'Five-minute Guide to Jewish Genealogical Research' at <www.avotaynu.com/jewish_genealogy. htm>. The National Archives has a research guide 'Anglo-Jewish History, 18th–20th Centuries: Sources in The National Archives' online at <www. catalogue.nationalarchives.gov.uk/Leaflets/ri2183.htm>. The Jewish Historical Society of England at <www.jhse.org> has a few general articles and a useful 'Chronology of the Jews in Britain'. The site's bibliographies and links will direct you to further sources of information. As usual, Cyndi's List has a good collection of links at <www.cyndislist.com/jewish.htm>.

The Jewish Genealogical Society of Great Britain's website at <www. jgsgb.org.uk>, has a substantial collection of links to Jewish material in

Britain and worldwide. It also has a number of data files available for down-loading at <www.jgsgb.org.uk/downl2.shtml>. *Avotaynu* has a Consolidated Jewish Surname Index at <www.avotaynu.com/csi/csi-home.html> with over half a million names. There is a varied collection of material relating to London Jews on Jeffrey Maynard's site at <www.jeffreymaynard.com>. The Channel 4 Guide to Genealogy has material on tracing Jewish ancestry at <www.channel4.com/history/microsites/U/untold/resources/geno/geno3a.html>.

The regional Jewish newspaper *The Jewish Telegraph* has a 'Roots Directory' at <jewishtelegraph.com/roots.html> where people can post contact messages.

The JewishGen Family Finder (JGFF) at <www.jewishgen.org/jgff/> is a 'database of ancestral towns and surnames currently being researched by Jewish genealogists worldwide', with around 80,000 surnames submitted by 60,000 Jewish genealogists.

The Holocaust Martyrs' and Heroes' Remembrance Authority has made its central database of Shoah Victims' Names available online at <www.yadvashem.org>. The database contains some three million names of Holocaust victims. Basic searches can be made on surname, forename and locality, while the advanced search facilities offer more precise matching possibilities using year of birth and death, as well as permitting up to four locations to be specified.

For details of Jewish archives in the UK, consult the University of Southampton's 'Survey of Jewish archives in the UK and Ireland' at <www.archives.soton.ac.uk/jewish/> which gives details and locations. There are two sites devoted to particular archives:

- The Susser Archive, relating to Jews in South West England, at <www.thorngent.eclipse.co.uk/susser/>
- The Rothschild Archive at <www.rothschildarchive.org>

There are two general Jewish mailing lists: the JEWISHGEN list, hosted by JewishGen at <www.jewishgen.org/JewishGen/DiscussionGroup.htm> and RootsWeb's JEWISH-ROOTS list at <lists.rootsweb.ancestry.com/index/other/Religion/JEWISH-ROOTS.html>. John Fuller lists another three dozen mailing lists for Jewish genealogy at <www.rootsweb.ancestry.com/~jfuller/gen_mail_jewish.html>, but these are all specific to particular geographical areas, whether as sources of emigration, or as destinations of migrants. A similar list is at Cyndi's List, <www.cyndislist.com/jewish.htm#Mailing>. Only one list is specifically relevant to Jewish communities in the British Isles, the BRITISH-JEWRY mailing list, details of which are at at <lists.rootsweb.ancestry.com/index/other/Ethnic-Jewish/BRITISH-

JEWRY.html>. There is also a Jewish Roots forum on British-Genealogy at <www.british-genealogy.com/forums/forumdisplay.php?f=187>.

Huguenots

Cyndi's List has links to Huguenot resources at <www.cyndislist.com/ huguenot.htm>, while basic information on the Huguenots will be found on Olive Tree Genealogy at <olivetreegenealogy.com/hug/overview.shtml>.

There are two main mailing lists: HUGUENOTS-WALLOONS-EUROPE and a general Huguenot mailing list, both hosted at RootsWeb (subscription details at <lists.rootsweb.ancestry.com/index/other/Religion/>). The former has its own website at <www.island.net/~andreav/> with a good collection of links and its own surnames list.

The Huguenot Surnames Index at <www.aftc.com.au/Huguenot/Hug. html> will enable you to make contact with others researching particular Huguenot families.

The Huguenot Society of Great Britain & Ireland has a website at <www. huguenotsociety.org.uk>. Information about the Huguenot Library, housed at University College London, will be found at <www.ucl.ac.uk/ Library/huguenot.shtml>.

There are also sites with local information: the Institute of Historical Research site has pages on the French Protestant Church of London at <ihr. sas.ac.uk/ihr/associnstits/huguenots.mnu.html>, while the England GenWeb Project has material on Cambridgeshire Huguenots at <www. rootsweb.ancestry.com/~engcam/HuguenotsandWalloons.htm>.

Gypsies

There are two starting points on the web for British gypsy ancestry. The Romany & Traveller Family History Society site at <www.rtfhs.org.uk>, apart from society information (including a list of contents for recent issues of its magazine), has a page on 'Was Your Ancestor a Gypsy?'. This lists typical gypsy surnames, forenames and occupations. The site also has a good collection of links to other gypsy material on the web. The Gypsy Lore Society Collections at the University of Liverpool site at <sca.lib.liv. ac.uk/collections/colldescs/gypsy/index.htm> has information about, and photographs of, British gypsy families, as well as a collection of links to other gypsy sites.

Directories of gypsy material can be found in the Open Directory at <dmoz.org/Society/Ethnicity/Romani/> and there is more specifically genealogical material on Cyndi's List at <www.cyndislist.com/peoples. htm#Gypsies> on a page entitled 'Unique Peoples & Cultures'.

Romani.org at <www.romani.org> is a general site devoted to the Romani people, and there is an online publication for Romani culture and

Figure 11-5 BBC Kent's Romany Roots site

history, The Patrin Web Journal, at <**www.geocities.com/~patrin/**>. BBC Kent has a Romany Roots site at <**www.bbc.co.uk/kent/romany_roots/**>. Although it has no specifically genealogical material, there are many articles on Romany history and culture, and the message board is used for genealogical queries (Figure 11-5). The Romany Wales project at <**www. valleystream.co.uk/romhome.htm**> has information on the Romany people in Wales, with histories of a number of individual families.

Wikipedia has a wide range of articles on Romany history and culture. The best starting point is the 'Romnichal' article at <**en.wikipedia.org/ wiki/Romnichal**>.

There is a UK-ROMANI mailing list for British gypsy family history, details of which will be found at <**lists.rootsweb.ancestry.com/index/ other/Ethnic-Romani/UK-ROMANI.html**>. Ancestry's Gypsy message board will be found at <**boards.ancestry.co.uk/topics.ethnic.gypsy/ mb.ashx**>. British-Genealogy has a Romanies forum at <**www.british-genealogy.com/forums/forumdisplay.php?f=424**>.

12

PRINT SOURCES

While the most important records for family historians are the usually handwritten public records, there are important sources of information in print, and not just where manuscript records have been transcribed.

Books

Digital archives

A significant development in the last couple of years has been the start of major projects to put digitized books online. These have received some bad publicity because many books still in copyright have been digitized without the permission of the copyright owners, and major academic and public libraries have been criticized for deals with commercial organizations. But the effect for genealogists has been very beneficial in that large numbers of eighteenth- and nineteenth-century books, many of them far from easy to find, have become available online via book digitization projects. Those of most interest to family historians fall into two groups. First, there are many topographical works devoted to describing various parts of the country – for any town or county you should be able to find a guidebook from the early twentieth century or earlier. Second, there seem to be quite a few books from historical publishing societies, some of which include transcriptions of historical records, so there is plenty of chance of finding transcribed parish registers, poll books and the like on these sites.

Google is the major commercial company involved in book digitization, after Microsoft abandoned its Live Search Books programme in May 2008. Google Books at <**books.google.com**> has books both from publishers and from university libraries. Where a book comes from a publisher, you will find either that only the publication details are available with no access to the content, or that there is a 'limited preview', with perhaps 10 per cent of the pages viewable online. Even if you only get the publication details, these will help you find a second-hand copy or search the library catalogues mentioned in Chapter 13. In the case of out-of-copyright books, you should be able to download the entire book as a PDF file. The libraries who are

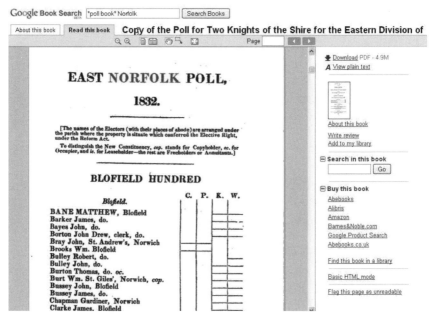

Figure 12-1 A Norfolk Poll Book in Google Books

working with Google are listed at <**books.google.com/googlebooks/partners. html**>. They include the Bodleian Library in Oxford, a dozen of the most important US university libraries, as well as a number of European libraries. All books have been fully indexed and are visible to Google's main search engine (though not to any other search engine), so you can search for individual names. Figure 12-1 shows an 1832 poll book for East Norfolk on Google Books, scanned from a copy in the Stanford University Library.

The Open Content Alliance is a non-profit group set up to create a free digital archive. Its textual material is available from the Text Archive area of the Internet Archive at <**www.archive.org/details/texts/**>. It also draws considerably on the collections of American libraries, including some of the major public libraries, though it seems to have less historical UK material than Google Books. Notably, it includes a large amount of material from Microsoft's Live Search Books. Unlike Google Books, however, this project has no agreements with publishers and therefore does not include material that is still in copyright.

A related but distinct project, run by the Internet Archive, is the Open Library at <**www.openlibrary.org**>, which has the primary aim of providing a web page for every book ever published. Alongside records for some 30 million books, it has scanned copies of around one million of these. The search facility on the home page allows you to restrict your search to the scanned volumes.

One of the sites included in Open Content Alliance is the much older Project Gutenberg, which has its own site at <**www.gutenberg.org**>. This is a long-standing project to digitize out-of-print books, which now hosts over 25,000 texts. The text were created by retyping them, not by scanning. Although the main focus of the project has been literary texts (including translations), there seem to be quite a few Victorian works of topography and social history. For example, there is Edwin Waugh's *Home-Life of the Lancashire Factory Folk during the Cotton Famine* and E. V. Lucas' *Highways & Byways in Sussex*. It is well worth using the 'Full Text' field on the advanced search page to see if there is any text with material on places your ancestors came from. The texts are all provided in plain text form or formatted for the web. If you are using a dialup connection, it is useful that Project Gutenberg also makes its texts available as compressed ZIP files for faster downloading.

One thing to note is that since all these sites are US-based, it is the copyright status in the United States which is relevant. This means that any book published before 1923 is regarded as out of copyright, even though such a work would, if the author died after 1938, still be in copyright in the UK in 2009.

In addition to these general book archives, there are several sites which concentrate on genealogy books. The most significant is the Family History Archives site at FamilySearch, which has a collection of over 25,000 digitized books from the Family History Library (see p. 206) and a number of

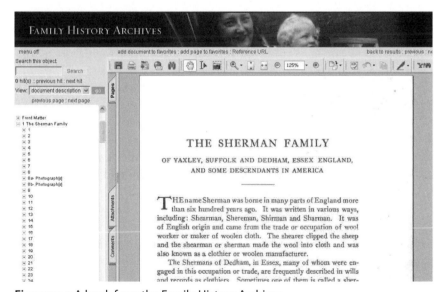

Figure 12-2 A book from the Family History Archives

other US genealogical libraries. They include many hard-to-find printed family histories, and some are even scanned typescripts. The basic search includes author, title and surname, but there is an additional option to include a full text search (though this will be rather slow and may well give you too many results to be useful). Helpfully, the initial list of matching books includes a description and the main surnames covered. The books are presented in PDF format, but cannot be downloaded as a whole – each page is a separate PDF file (Figure 12-2). If you are already on the FamilySearch site, select Historical Books from the Search Records menu; otherwise, go to <**www.lib.byu.edu/fhc**>.

Library Ireland has around 70 out-of-copyright books and countless articles on Irish history and genealogy at <**www.libraryireland.com**>. These include a number of works on Irish names and a growing collection of directories (see below).

The commercial data services (see Chapter 4) also tend to offer digitized reference books, though these are only accessible with a subscription to the sites. For example, Ancestry has a 'Dictionaries, Encyclopedias and Reference' collection, with around 60 books relating to the UK. These can be searched without a subscription from <**search.ancestry.co.uk/search/ CardCatalog.aspx?cat=41**>. You can use the filter option in the right-hand column of this page to narrow the list down to books which include material for a particular county.

Current reference works

It is important not to overlook general reference books, not perhaps for information on individual ancestors (unless they were specially notable), but for authoritative historical and geographical information about the British Isles. While many older editions are available in digitized versions in the book archives discussed above, in many cases current editions are also available online. An important set of reference works is those published by Oxford University Press, particularly:

- the *Oxford English Dictionary* <**dictionary.oed.com**> (see Figure 9-1)
- the *Oxford Dictionary of National Biography* <**www.oxforddnb.com**>
- the *Oxford Reference Collection* <**www.oxfordreference.com**>

These are available only to subscribers, and the individual subscriptions are quite hefty. However, thanks to a national agreement with the Museums, Libraries and Archives Council, most public libraries in the UK have subscriptions, and if you are a member of your local library this will almost certainly extend to allowing you access from your own computer at home. You will need a library card, as the login requires a library card number from a participating library instead of a username and password. Details should be given on the library area of your local authority website, which will probably also have links to the correct login pages. There is information about this scheme at <www.oup.com/online/library> and a list of libraries at <www.oup.com/oxforddnb/info/freeodnb/libraries/>. The scheme also extends to the Republic of Ireland.

The *Encyclopedia Britannica* <www.britannica.com> is widely available on the same basis. Some earlier editions are now in the public domain, in the USA at least, and available free online. The 1911 edition is at <www.1911encyclopedia.org> as well as a number of other sites – see Wikipedia's article on this edition at <en.wikipedia.org/wiki/Encyclop% C3%A6dia_Britannica_Eleventh_Edition> (which also draws attention to some of the most notable problems of relying on this edition).

Directories

For the family historian, the most important class of printed books are the nineteenth-century trade and post office directories. These provide descriptions of individual towns and villages, along with the names of some or all tradespeople and householders. A large number of these have been digitized and published on CD-ROM, but an increasing number are available either complete or in part on the web. There are also directories relating to the military and the professions, but these are discussed with other occupational records in Chapters 9 and 10.

Rod Neep's British-Genealogy site has some general information about trade directories and how they can help with your research at <www. british-genealogy.com/resources/books/directories/>. There are individual pages listing the published directories for the following counties: Bedfordshire, Berkshire, Buckinghamshire, Cornwall, Cumberland, Derbyshire, Gloucestershire, Nottinghamshire, Oxfordshire, and Staffordshire. An article by David Tippey, 'Using Trade Directories in your Research', is available at <www.genealogyreviews.co.uk/tippey_ directories.htm>.

The major site for directories is the Digital Library of Historical Directories site at <www.historicaldirectories.org>. This is the fruit of a lottery-funded project based at the University of Leicester. The aim of the project is to place online digitized trade directories from England and Wales from 1750 to 1919. It is intended to be representative rather than comprehensive, with one directory for each county and each major town for the 1850s, 1890s and 1910s, with additional decades to follow. The project is now complete and offers a total of 675 directories.

You can browse by county or decade, or you can select the keyword option to do a more advanced search. This allows you to specify, if you

Figure 12-3 Digital Library of Historical Directories: a page from White's 1855 *History, Gazetteer & Directory of Suffolk*

wish, a county, a decade, a publisher, and any names or other terms (a particular occupation, perhaps). The search results list all matching directories, but does not list the pages with individual hits – you need to select the directory you want to examine. This will bring up the title page of the directory and tell you how many occurrences of your keywords there are. To examine the relevant pages, you need to click on the 'Next hit' button. You can also simply browse the directory, page by page. The display shows a page at a time, and pages can be printed or saved (see Figure 12-3).

Although this is by far the largest collection of directories, there are many other sites which have material from directories. In some cases, there is simply a name index to the printed volume, such as that for Pigot's *Commercial Directory for Surrey* (1839), which is on the Genuki Surrey site at <**homepages.gold.ac.uk/genuki/SRY/**>. This provides text files with page references for names and places. While not a substitute for online versions of the directories, these listings at least indicate whether it is worth locating a copy of the directory in question. Another approach is to place scanned images on the web, along with a name index, as on Nicholas Adams' site, which provides Pigot's 1830 and 1840 directories for Herefordshire at <**freepages.genealogy.rootsweb.ancestry.com/~nmfa/ genealogy.html**>. Finally, some sites offer a full transcription, with or without a name index. For Derbyshire, for example, there are Rosemary

Lockie's pages devoted to the 1835 Pigot's *Commercial Directory for Derbyshire* at <**www.genuki.org.uk/big/eng/DBY/Pigot1835/about.html**> and Ann Andrews' transcription of all the Derbyshire entries from Kelly's *Directory of the Counties of Derby, Notts, Leicester and Rutland*, 1891, at <**www.andrewspages.dial.pipex.com/dby/kelly/**> (Figure 12-4).

There are also some partial transcriptions, usually for individual towns or cities, such as Brian Randell's material for Exeter at <**genuki.cs.ncl. ac.uk/DEV/Exeter/White1850.html**> taken from White's *Devonshire* directory of 1850. Rob Marriott and Davina Bradley's site devoted to Ashover in Derbyshire has entries for the town from six different directories at **www. ashover.org/drct.htm**>.

Since directories were compiled on a county basis, the easiest way to find them online is to look at the relevant county page on Genuki. Alternatively, you could use a search engine to search for, say, [Directory AND Kelly AND Norfolk] or [Directory AND Pigot AND Lancashire] to locate the publications of the two main nineteenth-century directory publishers. (See Chapter 19 for information on search engines and formulating searches.) County record offices have good collections of local directories, so it will be

---

The Andrews Pages |Genealogy and Local History| Derbyshire> Kelly's Directory, 1891> This page

Calow, Derbyshire

Kelly's Directory, 1891

Derbyshire transcripts of Kelly's Directory from:
Kelly's Directory of the Counties of Derby, Notts, Leicester and Rutland
pub. London (May, 1891) - p.73

CALOW is a small village and township, in the Chesterfield division of the county, parish, union, petty sessional division and county court district of Chesterfield, 2 miles east from Chesterfield, on the Bolsover road. The chapel of St. Peter, erected in 1869, is a building of stone in the Early Gothic style, consisting of an apsidal chancel, nave and a tower on the south-west with spire erected in 1887 by Mrs. Walker and containing 3 bells, the lower stage of the tower forms a porch : there are 200 sittings. The Rev. Hezekiah Astley Kemp Hawkins has been curate in charge since 1888 and resides at Devonshire Street, Chesterfield. There are Congregational and Primitive Methodist chapels. The charities are £2 11s. yearly. Coals and ironstone are found here. Earl Manvers is lord of the manor and principal landowner. The soil is strong clay ; subsoil, clay. Two-thirds of the land is pasture ; wheat and oats are grown here. The area is 1,339 acres ; rateable value, £2,281 ; the polulation in 1881 was 563.

WALL LETTER BOX cleared at 6.20 p.m. Letters through Chesterfield, the nearest money order & telegaph offfice, arrive at 7.30 a.m.

National School (mixed and infants ; average attendance, 77 children & 35 infants ; Miss Elizabeth Mercer ; mistress ; Miss Mary A Surguy & Miss Maria England, assistant mistresses

Clark Alison
Coulston John, Spring house
Oliver John, The Lawn
Ward John, Rose cottage

COMMERCIAL

Adlington Elizabeth (Mrs.), farmer
Arnold John, shopkeeper
Ball Manton, farmer
Beresford Mary (Mrs.), shopkeeper

◄ Previous Page

Next Page ►

▼ Village Links

Figure 12-4 The entry for Calow, Derbyshire, from an 1891 Kelly's directory

worth looking at the online catalogues. Familia at <**www.familia.org.uk**> lists the directory holdings for many public libraries. With few exceptions the directories available online date from before the First World War, so for more recent directories you will almost certainly need to visit the relevant CROs or local libraries.

The British Library, of course, has many trade and post office directories, which can be located by searching the online catalogue at <**catalogue.bl. uk**> – see p. 202. Since directory titles are very varied, the best way to search is to enter the town/county and the word 'directory' in the 'Type word or phrase' field and select 'Word from title' in the 'Search by' field. You can then sort the results by year.

As mentioned above (p. 178), Library Ireland has a number of transcribed directories.

Three of the commercial data services described in Chapter 4 have significant directory holdings. TheGenealogist at <**www.thegenealogist. co.uk**> (see p. 47) has around 80 trade and post office directories, the latest

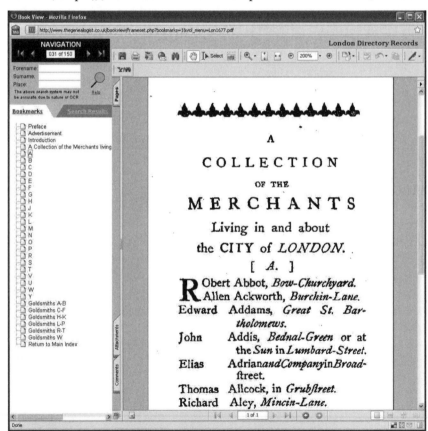

Figure 12-5 The 1677 *Little London Directory* at TheGenealogist

of which is for 1956. Around half of them are for London and include the 1677 *Little London Directory*, which seems to be the earliest directory available online (Figure 12-5). Each directory is displayed as a single PDF file.

Familyrelatives at <**www.familyrelatives.com**> (see p. 49) has around 30 Pigot's directories for individual English counties for the period 1828–40, and half a dozen twentieth-century directories for Irish counties. There is a free search which, for the English directories, just tells you the number of hits. For the Irish directories, the results show two lines of text from a matching entry. In each case, to view the original page image you need to be a subscriber. The images are not available to pay-per-view customers.

Ancestry has a collection of 1,780 UK telephone books from the BT Archives, providing 'near full county coverage for England as well as containing substantial records for Scotland, Ireland, and Wales'. They cover the period from the very first phone books in 1880 up to the privatization of British Telecom in 1984. Obviously the information is quite limited, but the ability to find an address in years other than those for which you have certificates or census records is very useful. There is no name search. Digitized images of the original pages are organized by period, place and year; then you have to locate the right page within the volume by narrowing down the correct page number. So finding an individual entry for larger towns in the later years can be quite time-consuming. With a common surname, there may be a problem in identifying the correct individual,

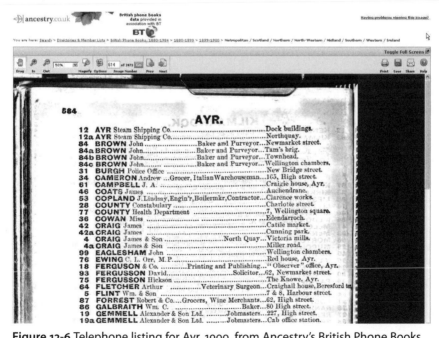

Figure 12-6 Telephone listing for Ayr, 1900, from Ancestry's British Phone Books

since usually only initials are given rather than a forename. The early books have relatively few individuals but have many business addresses, so can be used in the same way as trade directories.

More recently, Ancestry has added a collection of 'City and County Directories 1600s–1900s', information on which is given at <**www.ancestry. co.uk/search/db.aspx?dbid=1547**>. In the initial release (January 2009), there seem to be between one and a dozen directories per English county, with a few for Scotland and Wales, and one for the Isle of Man. Each directory page displays as a separate image in Ancestry's image viewer. You can browse through any directory, but there is also a name search.

Newspapers

Until quite recently, the only way to read historical newspapers, particularly for local titles, was to go to the British Library Newspaper Library or the reference library in the locality. However, there are now several major and many minor newspaper digitization and indexing projects which are making newspapers easier to consult.

The Genuki county pages are a good way of finding links to local newspapers on the web, and Cyndi's List has a 'Newspapers' page at <**www. cyndislist.com/newspapr.htm**>. There are, of course, many sites relating to present-day newspapers including Kidon Media-link, which has links to the websites of UK newspapers at <**www.kidon.com/media-link/uk.php**>.

British Library

The most important site for British newspapers is that of the British Library (BL). This has a general page for newspapers and comics at <**www.bl.uk/ reshelp/findhelprestype/news/**>, which is a gateway to an extensive set of pages with links to newspapers sites on the web, including London National Newspapers, Scottish Newspapers, Irish Newspapers, English and Welsh Newspapers, Channel Islands and Isle of Man Newspapers, Newspapers Around the World, and Other Newspaper Libraries and Collections. Details of the BL's own resources are on the British Library Newspaper Collections page at <**www.bl.uk/reshelp/findhelprestype/news/blnewscoll/**>, and these comprise over 52,000 newspaper and periodical titles from all over the world, dating from the seventeenth to the twenty-first century.

The BL used to have a separate Newspapers Catalogue but this has now been incorporated into the Integrated Catalogue at <**catalogue.bl.uk**>. However, you can still search the newspapers separately, though the URL is a 125-character monster consisting of apparently random letters and numbers, so to get to it you need to select 'Search the Integrated Catalogue' from the catalogue home page, then 'Catalogue subset search', then 'Newspapers'. To find the newspapers for a particular town or city, you need

INTEGRATED
CATALOGUE
Catalogue: Newspapers

| Home | About | Search | Results | Previous searches | My folder | Blank order form |

| Selected records: | View selected | Email/print/save | Create subset | Add to My folder |

| Whole set: | Select all | Deselect | Rank | Refine | Filter |

You searched for (W-newspaper heading= liverpool) in Newspapers. Sorted by: Date Range, then Title

Records 1 – 10 of 417

Quick tips – for this page

Seeing strange characters in some of the records?   Last Browse

| Go to record | | Jump to text | ← Previous page | Next page → |

#	Title	Edition	Place	Date Range
1	☐ Williamson's Liverpool Advertiser and Mercantile Register.		England Merseyside Liverpool.	1756 to 1759
2	☐ Williamson's Liverpool Advertiser and Mercantile Chronicle.		England Merseyside Liverpool.	1759 to 1793
3	☐ The Liverpool Chronicle.		England Merseyside Liverpool.	1767 to 1768
4	☐ Liverpool Phoenix or, Ferguson's Weekly Gazette.		England Merseyside Liverpool.	1794 to 1795
5	☐ Billinge's Liverpool Advertiser and Marine Intelligencer.		England Merseyside Liverpool.	1794 to 1828
6	☐ Gore's Liverpool General Advertiser.		England Merseyside Liverpool.	1795 to 1795
7	☐ Liverpool Trade List.		England Merseyside Liverpool.	1798 to 1800
8	☐ Liverpool Phoenix, and Saturday's Advertiser.		England Merseyside Liverpool.	1800 to 1800
9	☐ Gore's General Advertiser		England Merseyside	1800 to 1876

Figure 12-7 Search results for 'Liverpool' in the Newspaper Library catalogue, sorted by date

to select 'Newspaper place heading' in the 'Search by' field and then enter the name of the place in the field to the right.

Each entry in the web catalogue contains full details of the title (including any title changes), the place of publication (the town or city and the country) and the dates which are held. The results can be sorted by any of these fields, which means you can get a historical list of newspapers for a particular town (see Figure 12-7).

The BL has made a small selection of newspapers available online in the Olive ActivePaper Archive at <**www.uk.olivesoftware.com**>, which has digitized copies of a number of editions of:

Figure 12-8 The *Daily News* in the ActivePaper Archive

- *Daily News*
- *News of the World*
- *Penny Illustrated*
- *Manchester Guardian*
- *Weekly Despatch*

There are a number of short runs of each paper for individual years. Each newspaper page comes up as a separate image in the browser window. In this view only the headlines are easily legible, but clicking on an article brings up an enlarged version so you can read the body text. There is a also a text search facility, which brings up only the individual articles. You can also download a complete edition in PDF format. Figure 12-8 shows the front page of the *Daily News* for 10th November 1918.

In October 2007, the BL released the fruits of a major digitization project for nineteenth-century British newspapers. The aim of the Newspapers Digitisation Project is to make available resources for the study of the nineteenth century as seen through the pages of 'London national newspapers, English regional newspapers, home country newspapers from Scotland, Wales and Northern Ireland, and titles in specialist areas such as Victorian radicalism and Chartism'. The project, which covers the whole of the period 1800–1900, is described at <**www.bl.uk/reshelp/findhelprestype/news/ newspdigproj/ndproject/**>, with a link to the list of the papers included.

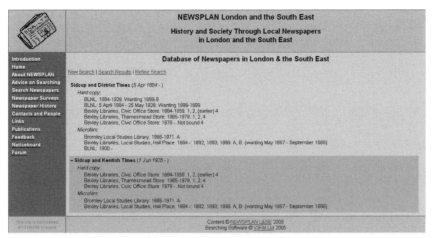

Figure 12-9 Details of the *Sidcup and District Times* in Newsplan

However, access to the site is limited: it is accessible from computers within a British library building, in Further and Higher Education institutions in the UK, and libraries which have taken out a subscription with the project's commercial partner, Gale. (Gale, in fact, make a wide range of digitized publications available to UK libraries – see the list at <**www.gale. cengage.co.uk/products/**>.)

Public libraries

The websites for other major libraries and archives discussed in Chapter 13 will have sections on their newspaper holdings. Unfortunately Familia (see p. 204) does not include newspaper holdings for public libraries.

A particularly useful programme is Newsplan, which gives details of newspapers and information on libraries and record offices where they can be consulted. Newsplan comprises a number of independent regional sites. The main Newsplan website has details for two regions:

- London and the South East at <**www.newsplan.co.uk/laser_newsplan/**> – 2,500 titles
- West Midlands at <**www.newsplan.co.uk/wm_newsplan/**> – 1,100 titles

Other regions have their own websites, and the list of regions is given on the BL's Newsplan page at <**www.bl.uk/reshelp/bldept/news/newsplan/ newsplan.html**>. However, at the time of writing, the links for the Northern and North Western Regions were dead.

Figure 12-9 shows a sample record in Newsplan.

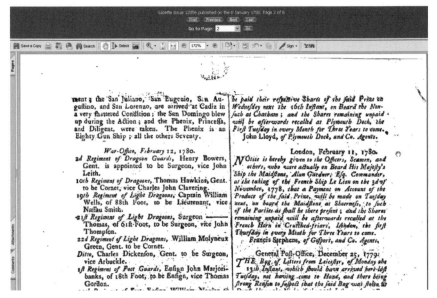

Figure 12-10 The *London Gazette*, 8th January 1780

Individual newspapers

Many of the larger newspapers have their own digital archives covering, in most cases, the entire run of the paper from its first to its most recent edition. These tend to be subscription services, though the option often includes a very inexpensive 24-hour subscription. Initial searches are usually free. You may well find that your local public library has access to some of these, particularly in the case of the national dailies. Users in Further and Higher Education are likely to have access via an institutional subscription. Digital archives for national dailies include:

- *The Times* <archive.timesonline.co.uk>
- the *Guardian/Observer* <archive.guardian.co.uk>
- the *Scotsman* <archive.scotsman.com>
- the *Irish Times* <www.irishtimes.com/search/archive.html>

The *Jewish Chronicle* at <www.thejc.com> has an archive of issues from 1841 onwards. There is a free trial search, but full access to the archive is only for those who subscribe to the newspaper itself.

Another important site for historical newspapers is Gazettes Online at <www.gazettes-online.co.uk>. This a major project to make the entire archive of the London, Edinburgh and Belfast Gazettes available on the web. These are the UK's official newspapers of record, stretching back to 1665 and containing official announcements of many types, including the award of medals, official appointments (including promotions of officers in the armed forces) and insolvency notices. Although there is a browse option, this covers only the most recent issues; for historical material, you need to select the advance search, in which you specify a date range and the words or phrases to look for.

The pages are black and white scans (*not* greyscale) and are displayed in PDF format, one file to a page (see Figure 12-10).

One thing to note about the text search is that the index it uses has been created by optical character recognition and therefore contains many errors. Unlike the census, where you can try and imagine what a letter might have looked like to a transcriber, it is very difficult to predict OCR errors, since typically these are caused by unevennesses in the printing and random marks on the paper (especially print-through from the other side of the sheet, as you can see in Figure 12-10). This is particularly the case with older issues.

Historical collections

In addition to the digital archives created by individual newspapers, there are a number of broader-based historical collections as well as non-commercial projects for individual local newspapers.

The Internet Library of Early Journals at <**www.bodley.ox.ac.uk/ilej/**> is a joint project by the universities of Birmingham, Leeds, Manchester and Oxford to place online digitized copies of eighteenth- and nineteenth-century journals, in runs of at least 20 years. The project comprises:

* *Gentleman's Magazine*
* *The Annual Register*
* *Philosophical Transactions of the Royal Society*
* *Notes and Queries*
* *The Builder*
* *Blackwood's Edinburgh Magazine*

The Nineteenth-Century Serials Edition is a free, online edition of six nineteenth-century periodicals and newspapers at <**www.ncse.ac.uk**>:

* *Monthly Repository* (1806–37) and *Unitarian Chronicle* (1832–33)
* *Northern Star* (1838–52)
* *Leader* (1850–60)
* *English Woman's Journal* (1858–64)
* *Tomahawk* (1867–70)
* *Publishers' Circular* (1880–890)

The NewspaperArchive at <**newspaperarchive.com**> is a subscription site with around a dozen English, Scottish and Irish papers for shorter or longer runs. You can see what is available by selecting the 'Browse Available Papers' option. There is a very large collection of US papers, as well as titles from Canada, Denmark, Jamaica and South Africa.

Ancestry has a Historical Newspaper Collection with significant runs of three UK newspapers:

- *The Times*
- *Edinburgh Advertiser*
- *Staffordshire Sentinel*

There are also other short runs, from a single month to several years, of a dozen other newspapers. All are listed at <**search.ancestry.co.uk/search/ CardCatalog.aspx?cat=38**>. As with the reference works on Ancestry (see p. 44), you can filter this list for particular localities.

Indexes

There are also a number of online indexes to individual editions of newspapers, particularly local papers. These are generally non-commercial and therefore inevitably limited in scope, without digital images, though some include transcriptions.

- The *Belfast Newsletter* is served by an index for the period 1737–1800 at <**www.ucs.louisiana.edu/bnl/**> and a number of digitized copies for 1796–1803 on the Act of Union site at <**www.actofunion.ac.uk/news. php**>.
- There is a surname index for the *Surrey Advertiser* for 1864 –67 at <**www. newspaperdetectives.co.uk**>.
- The Georgian Newspaper Project at <**www.bathnes.gov.uk/BathNES/ leisureandculture/recordsarchives/Georgian/default.htm**> aims to abstract and index the *Bath Chronicle* for the years 1770-1800. So far the database covers 17 completed years up to 1799.
- The *Cambrian* was the first newspaper to be published in Wales, and Swansea's Cambrian Index Online at <**www.swansea.gov.uk/index. cfm?articleid=5673**> covers the newspaper in the period 1804–1930.
- North Lincolnshire has a surname index to the Star series of newspapers started on 26 October 1889 as the *North Lindsey Star*. The Star Surnames Index, covering births, marriages and deaths 1891–1959, is at <**www. northlincsgov.uk/NorthLincs/Leisure/libraries/familyhistory/Surnames/**>.
- Richard Heaton has a collection of nearly 850 Extracts and full Transcripts of mainly English and Irish, Georgian and early Victorian

Regional Newspapers <freepages.genealogy.rootsweb.ancestry. com/~dutillieul/ZOtherPapers/Index.html>.

The National Library of Scotland (see p. 202) has a 'Guide to Scottish Newspaper Indexes', which provides details of Scottish newspaper titles that have an index (not necessarily online, or even digital), along with the dates covered and the libraries that have a copy. So far it includes 183 titles and can be found at <www.nls.uk/collections/newspapers/indexes/>.

Obituaries

There are a number of sites with information about newspaper obituary notices. Cyndi's List has a page devoted to obituaries at <www.cyndislist. com/obits.htm>, though almost all the sites listed relate only to the USA.

Free Obituaries On-Line at <www3.sympatico.ca/bkinnon/obit_links6. htm> has links to sites providing obituaries – many are newspaper sites – for Australia, Canada, England, Ireland, Jamaica, New Zealand, Scotland and the USA.

The Obituary Daily Times is a daily index of published obituaries at <www.rootsweb.ancestry.com/~obituary/>, which has over ten million entries, mainly from US newspapers. The site is an index only – you need to refer to the original newspaper to see the text.

Ancestry subscribers can search a substantial obituaries database. The search page for the UK and Ireland material is <www.ancestry.com/search/ obit/?uk&dbid=8960>. There is no indication of which sources are included.

Obituary Lookup Volunteers at <freepages.genealogy.rootsweb. ancestry.com/~obitl/> holds lists of those prepared to look up obituaries in particular newspapers or libraries. There are separate pages listing volunteers for England, Wales, Scotland and Ireland, as well as a number of other countries. However, the coverage of the British Isles is extremely limited.

RootsWeb has around 40 mailing list for obituaries, including ENGLAND-OBITS, ENGLISH-OBITS, IRELAND-OBITS and SCOTLAND-OBITS, as well as a number for former British colonies. All are listed at <lists. rootsweb.ancestry.com/index/other/Obituaries/>.

All national newspapers and many local papers have a website, and these will generally carry the obituaries from recent editions.

13

ARCHIVES AND LIBRARIES

Archives and libraries are often seen as the antithesis of the internet, but this is largely illusory, certainly from the genealogical point of view. With only a limited range of British genealogical resources reproduced as images on the web, you will often need to go to the relevant record office or a suitable library to check the information you have found online against original documents (or microfilms of them). It will be years before all the core sources are completely available online. Technologically, it is in fact a trivial matter to take records which have already been microfilmed and put images of them online. But to be usable, such online images need to be supported by indexes, and the preparation of these requires substantial labour and investment. As mentioned in Chapter 4, delivering images via the web has implications for running costs, even where production costs are minimal.

If you are going to look at paper records, then catalogues and other finding aids are essential. Traditionally, these have been available only in the reading rooms of record offices themselves, so a significant part of any visit has to be spent checking the catalogues and finding aids for whatever you have come in search of. But the web has allowed repositories to make it much easier to access information about their collections and facilities. At the very least, the website for a record office will give a current phone number and opening times. Larger sites will provide descriptions of the holdings, often with advice on how to make the most of them. Increasingly, you can expect to find catalogues online and, in some cases, even place orders for documents so that they are ready for you when you visit the repository.

All this means you can get more out of a visit to a record office, because you're able to go better prepared. You can spend more time looking at documents and less trying to locate them. And if you can't get to a record office, you will be able to give much more precise information than previously to someone visiting it on your behalf.

This chapter looks at what the major national repositories and the various local institutions provide in the way of online information.

Gateways to archives

There are a number of sources of information about repositories and the archival collections they hold.

The ARCHON Directory at <www.nationalarchives.gov.uk/archon/> acts as a gateway for all British archives. The site is hosted by the National Archives (see p. 196) and its intention is to provide 'information on all repositories in the United Kingdom and all those repositories throughout the world which have collections of manuscripts which are noted in the indexes to the UK National Register of Archives'. There is a page devoted to each archival repository in the British Isles, including the Republic of Ireland. In addition to basic details such as contact information, opening times and a link to any website, it also provides links to catalogue entries in the National Register of Archives (see below).

There are also search facilities which make it possible to search across the directory, so, for example, you could search for all archives in a given town or county. Although it is probably easier to use the Genuki county pages to find county record offices (see p. 203), the ARCHON Directory is better for locating other repositories and archives with relevant material.

Access to Archives (A2A) is a national project, funded by government and the Heritage Lottery Fund, to 'create a virtual national archives catalogue, bringing together a critical mass of information about the rich national archival heritage and making that information available globally from one source via the World Wide Web'. The website at <www.

Figure 13-1 The ARCHON Directory's list of repositories in the South West

nationalarchives.gov.uk/a2a/> offers search facilities across 400 catalogues with seven-and-a-half million items. This includes material from many county record offices. The search allows you to look for a word or phrase (which includes names) in a specific repository, over a whole region, or indeed over all regions'. You can also restrict the search to material you have not previously seen by searching only for items added since a particular date.

North of the border, the Scottish Archive Network (SCAN) at <**www. scan.org.uk**> has a similar remit – among its aims are 'the linking of archives large and small, public and private, throughout Scotland, and the creation of a unique knowledge base on Scottish history and culture'. It has a directory with contact details for all Scottish repositories at <**www.scan. org.uk/Directory/**>. There is an online catalogue at <**www.scan.org.uk/ catalogue**> which provides consolidated access to the catalogues of over 50 repositories in Scotland, with over 20,000 archives. The Research Tools pages at <**www.scan.org.uk/researchrtools/**> (note the 'r' before 'tools') include examples of documents, a glossary of Scottish terms, and material on handwriting. There is also a Knowledge Base with answers to questions frequently asked in Scottish archives. Oddly, this does not have its own page but is available as a pop-up link from other pages, such as the Research Tools page.

SCAN hosts or runs a number of other related websites, notably Scottish Handwriting, which is discussed on p. 271.

Archives Network Wales at <**www.archivesnetworkwales.info**> is a similar site for Wales, with descriptions of archival collections in 20 Welsh record offices, universities, and other bodies.

There are two more general gateways. Michael (Multicultural Inventory of Cultural Heritage in Europe) is an international programme covering 'digital collections from museums, archives, libraries and other cultural institutions from across Europe'. The main page is at <**www.michael-culture.org**> and Michael-UK is at <**www.michael-culture.org.uk/mpf/ pub-uk**>. The easiest way to find family history material is to click on the 'Subject/theme' link on the home page and then select 'Genealogy' from the drop-down list labelled 'Subject'. At the beginning of 2009, this brought up a list of 116 digital resources from records offices and museums.

Cornucopia at <**www.cornucopia.org.uk**> is 'an online database of information about more than 6,000 collections in the UK's museums, galleries, archives and libraries'. Unlike Michael-UK it does not offer genealogy as a subject heading, but a search for 'genealogy' brings up over 200 records, mostly for record offices and local studies centres.

The National Register of Archives

The National Register of Archives 'contains information on the nature and location of manuscripts and historical records that relate to British history' and has an online index at <**www.nationalarchives.gov.uk/nra/**>. This contains reference details for around 150,000 people, families and corporate bodies relating to British history, with a further 100,000 related records. The materials themselves are held in record offices, university libraries and specialist repositories. The search engine allows you to search by:

- Corporate Name – combined search of the Business Index and the Organizations Index
- Personal Name – combined search of the Personal Index and the Diaries and Papers Index
- Family Name
- Place Name – lists businesses, organizations and other corporate bodies by place

Figure 13-2 shows the results of a place name search in the NRA, while Figure 13-3 shows the full details for one of the search results. This gives not only the repository but also the reference number used by the record office in question. An obvious use of the NRA is to locate the parish registers for a particular place.

It is important to note that unlike A2A, the NRA catalogue cannot be used to search for the contents of archives, only the description and location, so a search on family name will only find archives deposited by or

Figure 13-2 Place name search for 'Burslem' in the National Register of Archives

Figure 13-3 Full entry for a record in the NRA

relating to the family, not individual documents which mention someone with that surname.

National archives

The National Archives

The National Archives is the main national repository for the UK, and its website at <**www.nationalarchives.gov.uk**> has a number of sections relevant to genealogists, with a main 'Family History' page at <**www. nationalarchives.gov.uk/familyhistory/**>. For detailed information on the National Archives' records for individual areas of interest, there are over 300 research guides, all linked from an alphabetical index at <**www. nationalarchives.gov.uk/catalogue/researchguidesindex.asp**>. For a more informal introduction to family history research at the National Archives, see the 'Family History' pages at <**www.nationalarchives.gov.uk/ familyhistory/**>, under 'Learning guides'. The 'Visit Us' menu links to pages with all you need to know when visiting the National Archives, including details of opening hours. Probably the most important page if you have never previously visited the Archives is the advice on planning your visit at <**www.nationalarchives.gov.uk/visit/plan.htm**>.

There is an enormous amount of material on the site that is relevant to genealogists and these resources are not described here but in the relevant chapters. There are links to the online data collections (the 1901 census and DocumentsOnline) from the 'Search the archives' menu and the 'Family History' page.

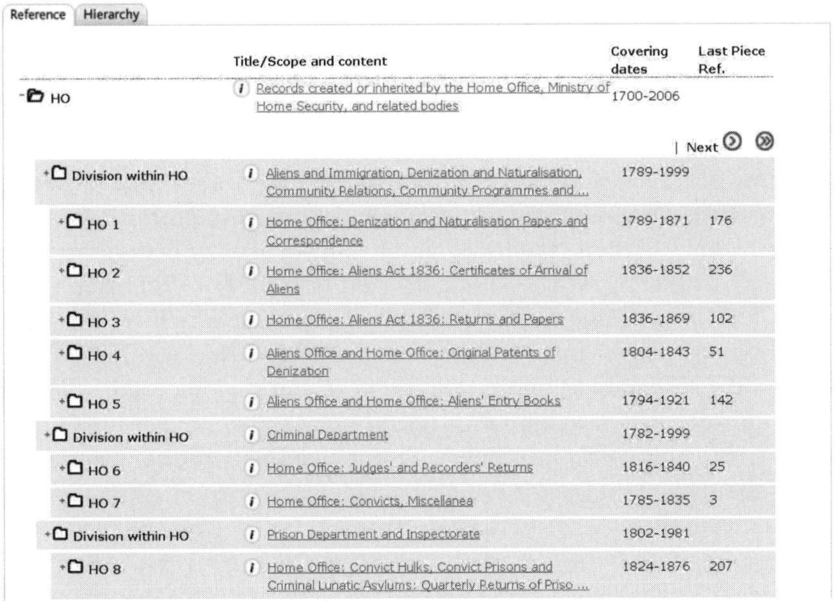

Reference | Hierarchy

	Title/Scope and content	Covering dates	Last Piece Ref.
- HO	Records created or inherited by the Home Office, Ministry of Home Security, and related bodies	1700-2006	

| Next

	Title/Scope and content	Covering dates	Last Piece Ref.
+ Division within HO	Aliens and Immigration, Denization and Naturalisation, Community Relations, Community Programmes and ...	1789-1999	
+ HO 1	Home Office: Denization and Naturalisation Papers and Correspondence	1789-1871	176
+ HO 2	Home Office: Aliens Act 1836: Certificates of Arrival of Aliens	1836-1852	236
+ HO 3	Home Office: Aliens Act 1836: Returns and Papers	1836-1869	102
+ HO 4	Aliens Office and Home Office: Original Patents of Denization	1804-1843	51
+ HO 5	Aliens Office and Home Office: Aliens' Entry Books	1794-1921	142
+ Division within HO	Criminal Department	1782-1999	
+ HO 6	Home Office: Judges' and Recorders' Returns	1816-1840	25
+ HO 7	Home Office: Convicts, Miscellanea	1785-1835	3
+ Division within HO	Prison Department and Inspectorate	1802-1981	
+ HO 8	Home Office: Convict Hulks, Convict Prisons and Criminal Lunatic Asylums: Quarterly Returns of Priso ...	1824-1876	207

Figure 13-4 Series list for Home Office records (HO)

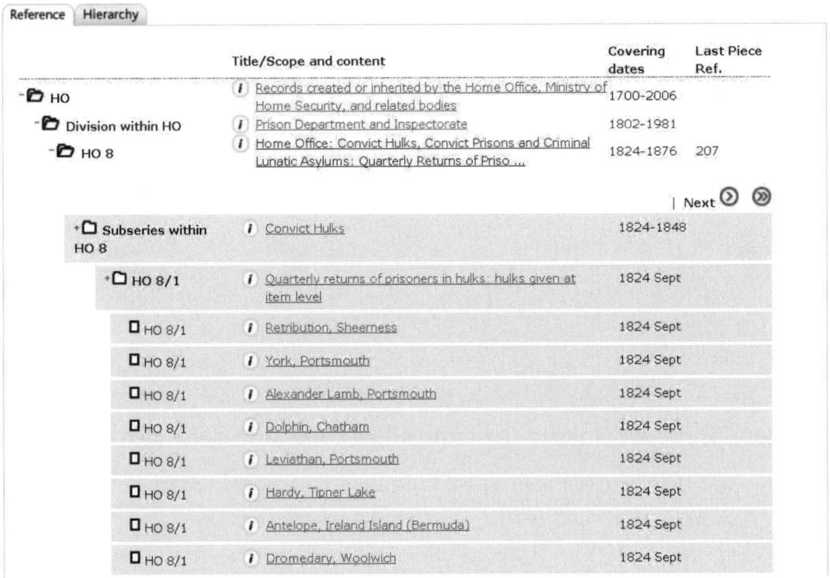

Reference | Hierarchy

	Title/Scope and content	Covering dates	Last Piece Ref.
- HO	Records created or inherited by the Home Office, Ministry of Home Security, and related bodies	1700-2006	
- Division within HO	Prison Department and Inspectorate	1802-1981	
- HO 8	Home Office: Convict Hulks, Convict Prisons and Criminal Lunatic Asylums: Quarterly Returns of Priso ...	1824-1876	207

| Next

	Title/Scope and content	Covering dates	Last Piece Ref.
+ Subseries within HO 8	Convict Hulks	1824-1848	
+ HO 8/1	Quarterly returns of prisoners in hulks: hulks given at item level	1824 Sept	
HO 8/1	Retribution, Sheerness	1824 Sept	
HO 8/1	York, Portsmouth	1824 Sept	
HO 8/1	Alexander Lamb, Portsmouth	1824 Sept	
HO 8/1	Dolphin, Chatham	1824 Sept	
HO 8/1	Leviathan, Portsmouth	1824 Sept	
HO 8/1	Hardy, Tipner Lake	1824 Sept	
HO 8/1	Antelope, Ireland Island (Bermuda)	1824 Sept	
HO 8/1	Dromedary, Woolwich	1824 Sept	

Figure 13-5 List of piece numbers for the class HO 8

The Catalogue

One of the most important facilities on the National Archives' website is the online catalogue at <**www.nationalarchives.gov.uk/catalogue/**>, with around 10 million entries. There are two ways to use the catalogue: you can browse or you can search.

In browsing, you start from the list of all the department codes denoting the various government departments which created the records in question, and you will then get a list of all the individual document series from that department. Figure 13-4 shows the start of the list of all the document series for Home Office Records (department HO), which would be of interest if you had an ancestor who was a criminal or was naturalized. The titles of the series are sometimes rather terse, but clicking on the tile will bring up a detailed description. Clicking on the series number itself opens up a menu listing of all the individual pieces within that series. Figure 13-5 shows the start of the list for HO 8, records for the prison hulks.

Of course, this is all very well if you are familiar with the records in question, or are working with a reference book. If not, it is probably easier to enter the catalogue via the Search option. You can search on up to three keywords, and the results will list every relevant document together with its full catalogue reference for all the series whose titles or descriptions contain the relevant words. If there are a lot of matches in different series, the results page will list the departments and the number of results in each; clicking on that number will bring up a list of the individual documents.

Figure 13-6 Search results in class WO 97 (Royal Hospital Chelsea: Soldiers Service Documents)

You can also specify a series to narrow down the search. Where a document relates to a specific individual, it is indexed under that person's name, so you can, rather surprisingly, search the catalogue for an individual ancestor. Figure 13-6 shows an entry for my great-great-great-grandfather Christopher Christian in class WO 97 (Royal Hospital Chelsea: Soldiers Service Documents). Note that to search on two keywords, you need to link them with AND; if you just type in two words, they are treated as a phrase.

In itself, the online catalogue is very straightforward to use, but it cannot simplify the organization of the actual records, which have been created independently by individual government departments over the past 900 or so years. In order to make the most of the catalogue, you will need to be familiar with the way in which the records you are looking for are organized. The research guides, linked from <**www.catalogue.nationalarchives. gov.uk/researchguidesindex.asp**>, cover all the major series of records of interest to genealogists. *Tracing Your Ancestors in the National Archives* and specialist books on individual record series (for example, *A Guide to Naval Records in the National Archives of the UK*) are recommended reading. A useful feature of the online catalogue search is that the search results pages start with a drop-down list of relevant research guides.

Other catalogues
In addition to the main catalogue, there are a number of specialist catalogues on the site. Those of most interest to genealogists are:

- the E179 database of tax records, discussed on p. 120
- the Equity Pleadings database, which currently contains details of around 30,000 Chancery Pleadings
- the Hospital Database, which includes the location and covering dates of administrative and clinical records
- the Manorial Documents Register (MDR), which shows the whereabouts of manorial documents in England and Wales, with county sections for: Berkshire, Buckinghamshire, Cumberland, Hampshire, Isle of Wight, Lancashire North of the Sands, Middlesex, Norfolk, Surrey, Westmorland, the three Ridings of Yorkshire, and all of Wales

All are linked from the 'Search the archives' page at <**www.national archives.gov.uk/searchthearchives/**> (select 'More…' from the 'Search the archives' menu on the home page).

National Archives of Scotland
The National Archives of Scotland has a website at <**www.nas.gov.uk**>, with a Family History section at <**www.nas.gov.uk/familyhistory/**>. The

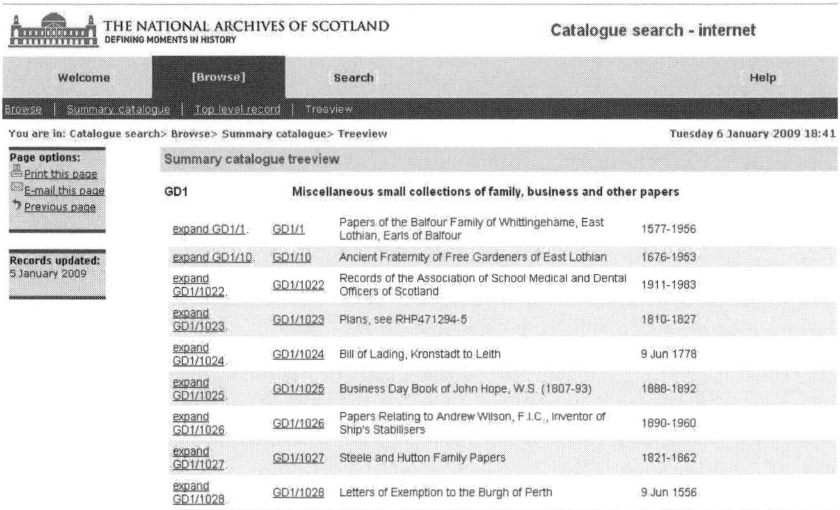

Figure 13-7 The NAS catalogue

material in the NAS is indexed in the SCAN online catalogue (see p. 194).

The site offers a comprehensive collection of guides, covering a wide range of subjects, including: adoption, chancery records, crafts and trades, crime and criminals, customs and excise, deeds, divorce, education, emigration, estate records, inheriting lands and buildings, lighthouses, military records, the poor, sasines, taxation records, valuation rolls, and wills and testaments.

The NAS has a number of catalogues and indexes. These are all listed at <**www.nas.gov.uk/catalogues/**> (click on the 'Doing research' menu on the home page). The main NAS catalogue is at <**www.nas.gov.uk/online Catalogue/**>. It works in much the the same way as the National Archive's catalogue (see Figure 13-7).

The Public Record Office of Northern Ireland

The Public Record Office of Northern Ireland (PRONI) has a website at <**www.proni.gov.uk**>. The site offers extensive information for genealogists, including descriptions of the major categories of record and about two dozen leaflets on various aspects of Irish genealogical research. Links to all these aids are provided on the 'Records Held' page at <**www.proni. gov.uk/index/research_and_records_held.htm**>. There is also a FAQ page at <**www.proni.gov.uk/index/about_proni/frequently_asked_questions.htm**>.

PRONI has an online catalogue, eCATNI, launched in January 2009 and there is a prominent link on the home page. For a number of types of record, the catalogue entries include individual names, for example, private papers, criminal records, wills, land records, and many other types of legal

Search Results

PRONI Reference	Date(s)	Title/Description	Item	
BELF/1/1/2/128/35	1942	Edward Blackburn - bigamy. Bill No. 64	Y	View
BELF/1/2/2/18/19	1 January 1908	Robert Moorhead, Joseph Blackburn and Robert	Y	View
D562/70	21 May 1753	Geo. Blackburn the Elder, Great Footstown	Y	View
D562/727	c.1730	Geo. Blackburn, Kintrim (?) v. Corker. Case	Y	View
D562/977	27 November 1746	Edward Blackburn to Randall Moore Account	Y	View
D562/1157	26 December 1740	Bond for £100. Nathaniel Blackburn, Seddan	Y	View
D562/14346	26 May 1824-1825	A letter from A. Blackburn at Parsonstown	Y	View
D848/32A	No Date	Petition for admission of John Blackburn	Y	View
D848/32B	1 August 1802	Indenture of apprenticeship from John Blackburn	Y	View
D1075/37	4 July 1892	Letters of administration from Mary Blackburn	Y	View
D1928/L/117	1701-1843	Blackburn's tenement, Lurgan, Co. Armagh	N	View
D2121/4/307	28 July 1885	Proposal for dwelling house. Henry Blackburn	Y	View
D2777/9/9	17 November 1876	Draft letter from O'Hagan to Colin Blackburn	Y	View
D3000/77	c.1650-c.1800	Typescript genealogical notes relating to the Blackburn family, Loughgall, Co. Armagh	N	View
DIO/2/9/783	14 August 1911	Nomination of the Rev. T. Havelock Blackburn	Y	View

Figure 13-8 eCATNI: results of a seach for 'Blackburn'

record. It is therefore worth searching the catalogue for any family name you are researching. Figure 13-8 shows the results of a search for 'Blackburn'.

In addition to the catalogue, the site has several indexes of use to genealogists, including:

- the Geographical Index (for locating any administrative geographical name, with Ordnance Survey Map reference number)
- the Prominent Person Index
- the Presbyterian Church Index
- the Church of Ireland Index

The last two cover only those records which have been microfilmed by PRONI. There are plans to add other church records, and school records. All are linked from the 'Online guides and indexes' page. Unfortunately this has a 125-character URL, so either follow the link from the website for this book, or, from the PRONI home page, click on 'Search the Archives', then 'Online guides and indexes'.

PRONI has three important online databases of primary records, all linked from the home page:

- a database of half a million men and women who signed the Ulster Covenant and Declaration in 1912, with scanned images of the signatures
- Freeholders' Records, an index of pre-1840 voter registration records
- Will Calendars (see p. 119)

National Archives of Ireland

The National Archives of Ireland has a website at <**www.nationalarchives. ie**>. Among other things, this has help for beginners, information on the main types of Irish genealogical record, and a good list of links to websites for Irish genealogy. The NAI has no online catalogue, but there are two online databases of interest to genealogists:

- Ordnance Survey Parishes Index
- Ireland-Australia Transportation

These can be accessed from the 'Searchable finding aids' page at <**www. nationalarchives.ie/search/databases.html**>. There is information on various aspects of Irish genealogy at <**www.nationalarchives.ie/ genealogy/**>, including guides to the various types of relevant record.

The national libraries

The British Library has a number of collections of interest to genealogists. The home page of the BL is at <**www.bl.uk**>, while the Integrated Catalogue is at <**catalogue.bl.uk**>. The catalogue is also included in COPAC, discussed on p. 205.

The India Office records held by the British Library do not have their own online catalogue, but a comprehensive guide to them will be found at <**www.bl.uk/reshelp/findhelpregion/asia/india/indiaofficerecords/ indiaofficehub.html**>. Some of the material can be found on Access to Archives <**www.nationalarchives.gov.uk/a2a/**> – on the A2A search page select 'British Library, Asia, Pacific and Africa Collections' from the 'Location of Archives' field. The NRA at <**www.nationalarchives.gov.uk/ nra/**> also contains entries for material in the India Office records.

The British Library's newspaper collection is discussed in detail on p. 184.

The National Library of Scotland has a website at <**www.nls.uk**>. Its main catalogue is at <**main-cat.nls.uk**> and various other catalogues are linked from <**www.nls.uk/catalogues/online/**>. Among these, Scots Abroad at <**www.nls.uk/catalogues/online/scotsabroad/**> will be of interest to those descended from Scottish emigrants. The site also has an introduction to Scottish family history at <**www.nls.uk/family-history/**>.

The National Library of Wales website at <**www.llgc.org.uk**> provides links to a number of online catalogues from <**www.llgc.org.uk/index. php?id=catalogues**>. The most useful of these for genealogists are:

- the main catalogue
- Crime and Punishment (see p. 125)
- Marriage Bonds

The Digital Mirror area of the site includes 'Welsh Biography Online', which has information on the lives of eminent Welsh people, and links to online collections of maps and photographs.

The NLW also maintains another useful though not genealogical database, Wales on the Web. This is a gateway of web resources relating to all aspects of Wales and has its own website at <**www.walesontheweb.org**>.

The National Library of Ireland has a website at <**www.nli.ie**>, with a family history section at <**www.nli.ie/en/family-history-introduction. aspx**>. This covers all the main sources in the library which are of use to family historians, and has lists of parish registers. There are several online catalogues, searchable separately or combined, all linked from <**hip.nli.ie**>. There is also a newspaper catalogue at <**www.nli.ie/newsplan/**>. There are catalogues of the photographic collections, linked from the family history page. The site also hosts the web pages of the Office of the Chief Herald at <**www.nli.ie/en/heraldry-introduction.aspx**>.

For access to online catalogues of the UK national libraries, see the information on COPAC, p. 205, below.

County record offices

There are several ways to locate a county record office (CRO) website. Each Genuki county page provides a link to relevant CROs, and may itself give contact details and opening times. The ARCHON Directory (see p. 193) allows you to locate a record office by county or region. Finally, CROs can be found via the website of the relevant county council (you may even be able to make a guess at its URL, as it will often be something like <**www.essexcc.gov. uk**>) or via the UK government portal at <**www.direct.gov.uk**> (see p. 17), which links to the websites of all arms of national and local government.

There is a wide variation in what CROs provide on their websites. At the very least, though, you can expect to find details of location, contacts, and opening times, along with some basic help on using their material. However, most offer substantial background material on the area and specific collections, and even online catalogues. Even better, a number of CROs are engaged on major digitization projects, some of which are mentioned elsewhere in this book. Much of the manuscript material held by CROs is catalogued on ARCHON (see p. 193).

Public libraries

Public libraries, although they have little in the way of manuscript collections, have considerable holdings in the basic sources for genealogical research. For example, many central libraries have microfiche of the GRO indexes and microfilm of local census returns, as well as local printed material.

The UK Public Libraries page at <**dspace.dial.pipex.com/town/square/ ac940/ukpublib.html**> is a general site devoted to Public Libraries. It provides links to library websites, and to their OPACs (Online Public Access Catalogues) where these are available over the internet.

For public libraries in the Irish Republic, the country's public library portal Library.ie has links to the websites and online catalogues at <**www. library.ie/weblog/public-libraries/**>.

For genealogists, a more useful starting point is the Familia website at <**www.familia.org.uk**>. This is designed to be a comprehensive guide to genealogical holdings in public libraries, with a page for every local authority in the UK and the Republic of Ireland, listing the principal public libraries within the authority which have family history resources, along with contact details, opening times, etc. It then outlines the genealogical holdings under the following main headings:

- Births, deaths and marriages
- Census records
- Directories
- Electoral registers
- Poll books
- International Genealogical Index
- Unpublished indexes
- Parish registers
- Periodicals
- Published transcripts
- Other materials

Unfortunately, however, the project's host organization lost its funding some years ago and it seems that the site is now moribund – the pages for individual libraries seem not have been updated since May 2006 and many of the links to library websites are no longer working. Of course, it's unlikely that the materials listed will have ceased to be available, but it would be unwise to rely on the contact details or any information about the location of resources.

A useful resource for locating individual books in public libraries is Worldcat at <**www.worldcat.org**>, a global library catalogue. If you enter a book title, it will bring up a record for the book. If you then enter your postcode, it will list the closest libraries which hold copies of the book.

University libraries

While university libraries are not of major importance for genealogical research, all have special collections which may include personal papers of notable individuals. There are some significant university collections relating to occupational, religious and ethnic groups, some of which are mentioned in the relevant chapters of this book. They are also likely to have collections of local material which, while probably not of use in constructing a pedigree, may be of interest to the family historian looking for local topographical and historical information.

There is no single central index to university library holdings but COPAC is a major consortium of 60 research libraries, including three of the four copyright libraries (Cambridge University Library, the Bodleian in Oxford, and Trinity College, Dublin), as well as the British Library, and the National Libraries of Scotland and Wales (see p. 202). The COPAC website at <**www.copac.ac.uk**> provides access to a consolidated catalogue for all member institutions.

All university libraries are included on the ARCHON site at <**www.nationalarchives.gov.uk/archon/**>, which provides contact details and has catalogue entries for archival material (i.e. not books or periodicals) relating to individuals, families and organizations. The Archives Hub at <**www.archiveshub.ac.uk**> is a site which offers descriptions of archival collections in over 170 academic libraries.

University library sites do not generally cater for family historians, but the University of London's Helpers site at <**www.helpers.shl.lon.ac.uk**> is an exception in that it is specifically designed to assist with research about individuals – the name stands for 'Higher Education Libraries in your PERsonal history research'. It includes a database which lists and describes the holdings in the University's colleges and institutions that may be useful in genealogical research, and has guides to using Higher Education libraries.

Bear in mind that university libraries are not open to the general public and that you will normally need to make a written application in advance in order to have access, particularly in the case of manuscript material.

Family History Centers

The LDS Church's Family History Centers (FHCs) are valuable not just because they hold copies of the IGI on CD-ROM, microfiche copies of the GRO indexes, and other materials, but because any UK genealogical material which has been microfilmed by the Church can be ordered for viewing in an FHC, and this includes many parish registers. Also, their computer suites provide free access to some commercial genealogical data.

Contact details for FHCs are given on the FamilySearch site at <**www.familysearch.org**> – clicking on the 'Library' tab (at the top of most main screens) and then selecting 'Family History Centers' will lead to a search page. Genuki provides a quick way to get listings from this search facility:

the page at <**www.genuki.org.uk/big/LDS/**> has links which will search automatically for all FHCs in England, Scotland, Ireland and Wales on the FamilySearch site. The site of the LDS Church in the UK at <**www.lds.org. uk**> has a database of FHCs, reached by following the 'Find a Family History Library' link at <**www.lds.org.uk/family_history.php**>, which will give the FHCs in a particular city or region, or search for those nearest to a particular postcode.

The key to exploiting this immense wealth of material is the Family History Library (FHL) catalogue, which can be consulted online at the FamilySearch site. The search page at <**www.familysearch.org/Eng/ Library/FHLC/frameset_fhlc.asp**> offers searches by place, surname, or, for published works, author. If you search by place, you will get a list of the various types of records available for it. Figure 13-9 shows the initial results of a place search for Lenham in Kent, while Figure 13-10 shows the expanded entry for 'Church records', with descriptions of the various items available.

Place Details	FAMILY HISTORY LIBRARY CATALOG	THE CHURCH OF JESUS CHRIST OF LATTER-DAY SAINTS
		View Related Places

Place:	England, Kent, Lenham
Topics:	England, Kent, Lenham - Census England, Kent, Lenham - Church records England, Kent, Lenham - Church records - Indexes England, Kent, Lenham - Land and property England, Kent, Lenham - Manors England, Kent, Lenham - Manors - Court records England, Kent, Lenham - Occupations England, Kent, Lenham - Poorhouses, poor law, etc. England, Kent, Lenham - Taxation

Figure 13-9 Search results for Lenham, Kent, in the FHL catalogue

Topic Details	FAMILY HISTORY LIBRARY CATALOG	THE CHURCH OF JESUS CHRIST OF LATTER-DAY SAINTS

Topic:	England, Kent, Lenham - Church records
Titles:	Archdeacon's transcripts, 1564-1813; Bishop's transcripts, 1611-1905 Church of England. Parish Church of Lenham (Kent) Births and baptisms, 1779-1837 Independent Church (Lenham) Bishop's transcripts, 1874-1908 Church of England. Chapelry of Charing Heath (Kent) Churchwarden accounts and vestry minutes, 1681-1918 Church of England. Parish Church of Lenham (Kent) Parish register extracts, 1559-1905 Church of England. Parish Church of Lenham (Kent) Record of members, 1849-1860 Church of Jesus Christ of Latter-day Saints. Lenham Hill Branch (Kent) Record of members, ca. 1795-1877 Church of Jesus Christ of Latter-day Saints. Bromley Branch (Kent)

Figure 13-10 Search results for Lenham, Kent, in the FHL catalogue – Church records

Title Details	FAMILY HISTORY LIBRARY CATALOG	THE CHURCH OF JESUS CHRIST OF LATTER-DAY SAINTS

View Film Notes

Title:	Archdeacon's transcripts, 1564-1813; Bishop's transcripts, 1611-1905
Authors:	Church of England. Parish Church of Lenham (Kent) (Main Author)

Notes:	Microreproduction of original records housed at the Canterbury Cathedral Archives, Canterbury, Kent.
	Some early pages damaged.
	The church was named for St. Mary.
	Canterbury Cathedral Archives no.: DCa/BT/112; DCb/BT1/141; DCb/BT2/174

Subjects:	England, Kent, Lenham - Church records

Format:	Manuscript (On Film)
Language:	English
Publication:	Salt Lake City : Filmed by the Genealogical Society of Utah, 1991-1992
Physical:	on 4 microfilm reels ; 35 mm.

Figure 13-11 FHL catalogue search Title Details

Film Notes	FAMILY HISTORY LIBRARY CATALOG	THE CHURCH OF JESUS CHRIST OF LATTER-DAY SAINTS

View Title Details

Title:	Archdeacon's transcripts, 1564-1813; Bishop's transcripts, 1611-1905
Authors:	Church of England. Parish Church of Lenham (Kent) (Main Author)

Note	Location Film
Archdeacon's transcripts: Baptisms, marriages and burials 1564-1813 (missing: 1565/6, 1570/1, 1573/4, 1578/9, 1594/5, 1629/30, 1633/4, 1640/1-1660/1, 1664/5, 1665/6, 1670/1, 1774/5, 1775/6)	FHL BRITISH Film 1751918 Item 3
Bishop's transcripts: Baptisms, marriages and burials 1611-1813 (missing: 1613/4, 1621/2, 1627/8, 1631/2, 1640/1, 1642/3-1662/3, 1716/7, 1795/6)	FHL BRITISH Film 1736839 Item 3
Bishop's transcripts contd.: Baptisms,marriages and burials 1813-1824	FHL BRITISH Film 1786623 Item 6
Bishop's transcripts contd.: Baptisms and burials 1824-1873, 1876-1882, 1897-1898, 1904-1905 Marriages 1824-1837	FHL BRITISH Film 1786624 Item 1

Numbers 1-4 of 4 film notes

Figure 13-12 FHL catalogue – Film Notes

In order to find the microfilm reference for one of the entries, you need to click on it to bring up the 'Title Details' screen (Figure 13-11). This tells you the repository where the material is held (or was at the time of filming), together with the repository's reference for the material. This means you could even use the FHL catalogue as a partial catalogue to county record offices.

Finally, clicking on the 'View Film Notes' button at the top left brings up detailed information on the microfilms relating to this item (Figure 13-12) with an exact description of what is on each film, together with the film reference which you can now use to order the film at an FHC.

The Society of Genealogists

The Society of Genealogists is home to the premier genealogical library in the country and its website is at <**www.sog.org.uk**>. General information about the library is at <**www.sog.org.uk/library/intro.shtml**> and the library catalogue is available online at <**www.sog.org.uk/sogcat/sogcat. shtml**>. There are two types of search: the default browse search takes you to the first item in the catalogue which matches your search criteria, or the 'Power Search' allows you to select items based on up to three fields.

In order to use the library, you need to be a member of the Society or pay a search fee (see <**www.sog.org.uk/visit.html**>). But even if you are not in a position to use the library itself, the comprehensive nature of the Society's collections makes the catalogue a valuable guide to which parish registers, for example, have been transcribed, or what has been published on a particular surname. If you are not already familiar with the Library and its catalogue, it will be worth looking at the tutorial, particularly if you want to search for place names or surnames.

The Society also runs free 'open access sessions' where non-members can use the Society's computer facilities to access a number of commercial data services. Details are at <**www.sog.org.uk/library/openaccess.pdf**>.

Beyond the British Isles

If you need to consult archives outside the UK and Ireland the best general starting points will be the pages for individual countries on Cyndi's List – each of these has a section headed 'Libraries, Archives & Museums'. This will have links to not only the national archives, but also major provincial archives. Of course, if the country is not English-speaking you may not be able to make full use of the site, but you will often find at least some basic information in English and an email address for enquiries.

The UNESCO Archives Portal at <**www.unesco-ci.org/cgi-bin/portals/ archives/page.cgi?d=1**> provides links to national and other archives around the world.

The Family History Centers have microfilmed records from many countries, and searching on a country in the Family History Library Catalog will list the various types of record and what has been filmed (see p. 206).

14

SURNAMES, PEDIGREES AND FAMILIES

The resources discussed in Chapters 4 to 11 contain direct transcriptions of, or indexes to, primary genealogical sources. But alongside these are 'compiled' sources, the material put together by individual genealogists. Many people are now putting their pedigrees on the internet on a personal website – Chapter 20 explains how to do this yourself, and Chapter 19 looks at how to locate such material. But there are a number of public sites to which people can submit details of the surnames they are interested in, or even entire pedigrees, so that others can contact them. This chapter also looks at sites devoted to the genealogies of royal and noble families, as well as the pedigrees of well-known people. Sites devoted to surname origins and distribution are discussed in Chapter 16.

█ Surname interests

One of the best ways to make progress with your family tree is to get in touch with others who are interested in the same surnames. In some cases you will end up encountering cousins who may have considerable material relating to a branch of your family, but at the very least it is useful to discover what resources others have looked at. If you find someone who is doing a one-name study, they may even have extracts from primary sources they are prepared to share with you.

Before the advent of the internet, making such contacts was quite difficult. It involved checking a range of published and unpublished sources, looking through the surname interests in family history magazines, and consulting all the volumes of directories such as the annual *Genealogical Research Directory*, which was issued in print or on CD up until 2007 (see <members.ozemail.com.au/~grdxxx/>). You will still need to do all this, of course, not least because quite a few genealogists are still not online and this is the only way to find out about *their* researches. The SoG's leaflet 'Has it been done before?' at <**www.sog.org.uk/leaflets/done.pdf**> provides a comprehensive overview of the various offline resources to check. But the internet now offers a much easier way both of locating and of inviting such contacts.

County surname lists

If you have already made some progress with your family history and have got back far enough to know where your ancestors were living 100 or so years before your birth, then you should check the relevant county surname list – a directory of genealogical research interests for a particular county.

Surname lists do not provide genealogical information as such: they are just registers of interests, like a printed research directory, and for each surname they give the email address of the researcher who submitted it, and usually a date range for the period of interest (see Figure 14-1). Some lists also have links to the websites of submitters.

There is at least one surname list for almost every county in the UK and Ireland, and Genuki keeps a central list of these at <**www.genuki.org.uk/ indexes/SurnamesLists.html**>. Many counties are included in Graham Jaunay's national Online Names Directories for England, Wales, Ireland and Scotland at <**www.list.jaunay.com**>, which are run in connection with Genuki. These cover around 70 per cent of the British Isles – all Welsh counties, most Scottish and Irish counties, and half the English counties. Within each national directory, you can search on an individual county or do a general search. Figure 14-1 shows the results of a search for any name in Northumberland in the Online English Names Directory. Clicking on the name in the 'Subscriber' column links will bring up a mail window in your browser with the email address of the person to contact, or you can read the email address from the status bar at the bottom of the browser when you move your mouse over the link. Surname lists for Australia,

Online English Names Directory

Search in the County of 'NBL' for the keyword ''.

Names 1–88 of 88

County	Family name	Place	Date range	Subscriber	Submitted
NBL	ADDISON	Berwick On Tweed; Tweedmouth	1775-1875	Jenny	14 Jul 2007
NBL	ALNWICK	All County	all dates-onwards	James N. Alnwick	23 Feb 2008
NBL	ANDERSON	Alwinton; Cheviot Hills Areas	all dates-	Heather	23 Feb 2008
NBL	ANDERSON	All County	1600-1975	Terri	2 Aug 2008
NBL	ARCHER	Location: ?	1750-1875	Teresa Colbeck	18 Aug 2007
NBL	ATKINSON	Warkworth; Branton; Alnwick	1800-onwards	Aillin O'brien	11 Aug 2007
NBL	AUSTIN	Walbottle; Newburn	before-1850	Bill	8 Mar 2008
NBL	BLAIR	Blyth; Cowpen; Whalton; Ponteland	-	Sue Horsman	15 Nov 2008
NBL	BOLAM	Gosforth; Earsdon	1750-1850	Helen K	26 Jan 2008
NBL	BOWES	Morpeth	1875-1925	Eric Codling	2 Jun 2007
NBL	BREWIS	Location: ?	1825-1850	Bev Price	29 Sep 2007
NBL	BROWELL	All County	1900-1950	Christine Smith-Stephens	1 Mar 2008

Figure 14-1 Northumberland entries from the Online English Names Directory

Canada, New Zealand and the USA are also available on this site.

Alongside Graham Jaunay's lists, there are around 40 other county-based surname lists, with a few for smaller areas. Although these lists are not formally connected with Genuki, many of them have a long-standing relationship with the relevant Genuki county page. Links to any lists relevant to a county will be found on the Genuki county page as well as on the central surname list page.

For other countries, look at the section headed 'Queries, Message Boards & Surname Lists' on the page for the country on Cyndi's List at <**www.cyndislist.com**>, but do not expect to find the same level of coverage as there is for the British Isles.

In addition to the county surname lists, there are a number of surname lists relevant to UK emigration and immigration. These are discussed in Chapter 11 (see p. 158 ff).

Obviously, you should also consider submitting your surname interests to the relevant national or county lists so that other people can contact you. The exact method of doing this varies from list to list: on some there is a web page with a submission form; on others you will need to email the list-maintainer. Be sure to follow the instructions, as many list-maintainers expect you to submit your interests in a particular format (to make processing of submissions easier to automate) and may ignore something sent in the wrong format.

One problem with surname lists is that someone who has made a submission may forget to update their entries if they subsequently change their email address, so you will occasionally find contact details that are no longer valid. Unfortunately there is nothing you can do about this – it is a fact of life on the internet – and there is no point in asking the surname list manager where a particular submitter can be contacted if their stated email address is no longer valid. Obviously if you change your own email address, you'll need to contact the owner of any surname list you have submitted to. For Graham Jaunay's lists, there are online forms for changing an email address, and you will need to 'refresh' your entries annually to keep them listed.

Guild of One-Name Studies

The Guild of One-Name Studies at <**www.one-name.org**> is an organization for those who are researching all people with a particular surname, rather than just their own personal pedigree. It has a searchable Register of One-Name Studies online at <**www.one-name.org/register.shtml**>, which gives a contact address (not necessarily electronic) for each of the 7,500 or so surnames registered with the Guild.

Unlike the county lists, the surname interests registered with the Guild cover the whole world – this is, in fact, a requirement for membership. So, even though the person who has registered a particular one-name interest may not have ancestors in common with you, there is still a good chance that they have collected material of interest relating to your surname. In particular, a Guild member is likely to have a good overview of the variants of their registered surname. This makes the Guild's list of surnames worth checking even, or especially, if you are only just starting your researches. In contrast, the county surname lists are probably not very useful until you have got back at least three generations.

Society of Genealogists
The SoG has three indexes for surnames and pedigrees:

- Surname Document Collection – a variety of documents and transcripts, including original certificates and wills, for around 10,000 surnames
- Pedigrees Collection – 3,000 surnames
- Members' birth briefs – 28,000 surnames from four-generation pedigrees submitted by SoG members

All are linked from the 'Searching for surnames and families' page at <**www. sog.org.uk/library/surnames_and_families.shtml**>. For each of these, the site lists only the surname, with no indication of dates or location, and you will need to consult the original document. In some cases you can order copies by post – the Search & Copy Service is described at <**www.sog.org. uk/library/searches.shtml**> – but otherwise you will need to visit the Society's library.

RootsWeb
One of the most useful sites for surname interests is RootsWeb at <**www. rootsweb.ancestry.com**>, which has a wide range of surname-related resources, all linked from <**resources.rootsweb.ancestry.com/~clusters/ surnames/**>. There is a separate page for each listed surname (see Figure 14-2) with:

- links to personal websites at RootsWeb which include the name
- search forms for a number of databases hosted by RootsWeb
- links to any mailing lists for the surname (see below)

The most general surname resource at RootsWeb is the Roots Surname List (RSL) at <**rsl.rootsweb.ancestry.com**>. This is a surname list attached to the ROOTS-L mailing list, the oldest genealogy mailing list on the internet, and contains well over a million entries submitted by around

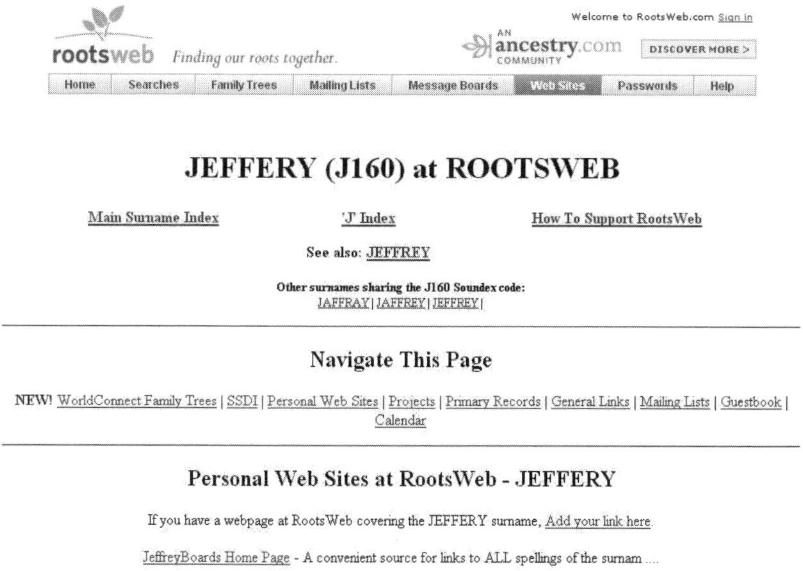

Figure 14-2 A RootsWeb surname page

200,000 individual genealogists. You can enter a geographical location to narrow your search, using Chapman county codes (see p. 244) and/or three-letter country codes – there is a list of standard codes at <**helpdesk. rootsweb.ancestry.com/codes/**>. However, you may need to do a couple of searches to make sure you find all relevant entries as some people spell out English counties in full or use the two-letter country code UK instead of ENG. If you check the list regularly, a useful feature is that you can restrict your results to those added or updated recently. Submitter details are not given on the search results page, but there is a link to them from the user ID of the submitter.

Discussion forums

Mailing lists, newsgroups and other types of discussion forum are described in detail in Chapter 18, but it is worth noting here that there are many groups devoted to individual surnames. Even if you do not participate in any of them, it will still be worth your while to look through the archives of past messages to see if anyone else is working on the same family or on the same geographical area.

John Fuller's list of mailing lists has information on those dedicated to individual surnames at <**www.rootsweb.ancestry.com/~jfuller/gen_mail. html#SURNAMES**>. Many of these surname lists are hosted by RootsWeb and can also be found from the general list of mailing lists at <**lists. rootsweb.ancestry.com**> or via the individual surname pages at <**resources.**

Surnames matching Jeffery

New entries are marked by a +, modified entries by a *, and expiring entries by an x. Clicking on the highlighted code words ·
the name and address of the researcher who submitted the surname. (If no names are listed below this line, then none were for

Alternate Surnames (Click for a detailed list of alternates)

See the Jeffery resource page for more searches

You might have to scroll left or right to view all of the information

Surname	From	To	Migration	Submitter	Comment
JEFFERY	-----	1860	MELBOURNE AUSTRALIA	gildtime	
Jeffery	1500	1999	worldwide	Ktimbrel	Adoptee of Samuel 1902?
Jeffery	1600	1986	Illogan,CON,ENGl>Ballarat,VIC,AUS>Dunedin, NZL	bevjef	
Jeffery	1600	now	Hartland>Northam>DEV,ENG	ldeleuw	
jeffery	1600	1900	cornwall to yorks	annipeel	mary daughter of william
Jeffery	1600	1650	Southease,SSX,ENG	hstvns	
Jeffery	1624	now	SCT>NS>ON,CAN	davidbel	
Jeffery	1650	1860	"Medstead,HAM,ENG"	Mswitzer	
Jeffery	1650	1750	Frant,SSX>Goudhurst,KEN,ENG	bjashton	Robert 1664-1715
Jeffery	1650	now	Richmond Co VA	lfarbry	
Jeffery	1670	now	Cornwall, England>USA	greg08	St Levan, Penberth, Newlyn (West)
Jeffery	1680	1796	CAM,ENG	ruddles1	

Figure 14-3 Search results in the Roots Surname List

rootsweb.ancestry.com/~clusters/surnames/>.

Alongside the surname mailing lists, there are web-based message boards or discussion forums for individual surnames. One of the largest sites hosting such discussion lists is GenForum at <**genforum.genealogy.com**>, which must have message boards for at least 10,000 surnames. Ancestry. com has a large set of surname message boards at <**boards.ancestry.com**> – follow the link to 'United Kingdom and Ireland', and then the link to the relevant part of the UK. You do not need to be an Ancestry subscriber to use these.

In many cases, these boards relate to a surname mailing list hosted by RootsWeb. This means that you can contribute your own query via the web without having to subscribe to a mailing list. A particularly useful feature is that the individual boards can be searched, which makes it possible to find messages relating to particular places, something which is essential for common and widespread surnames.

Family history societies

Every family history society has a register of members' interests, and it will be worthwhile checking the societies which cover the areas where your ancestors lived. If you're lucky, the list will be available online. For example, the Shropshire FHS offers a database of 20,000 members' interests at <www.sfhs.org.uk/memberinterests.asp>, which can be browsed, or searched for a specific surname. The Sussex Family History Group at <www.sfhg.org.uk> has both a public members' interests area and a more extensive one for members only. Bear in mind that not all these members will be contactable by email and societies generally do not publish members' postal addresses online, so you may need to consult the society's journal for contact details. For a list of FHS websites consult the 'Family History and Genealogy Societies' page on Genuki at <www.genuki.org.uk/Societies/>.

Personal websites

Many genealogists have a personal website (see Chapter 20), and locating such sites can be a useful step in making contact with someone who shares your genealogical interests or even some of your ancestors. Cyndi's List has a 'Personal Home Pages Index' at <www.cyndislist.com/personal.htm> with sub-pages for each letter of the alphabet. Of course, this includes only a fraction of the personal genealogical websites, and really you need to use a search engine to get more inclusive coverage. Unfortunately just typing a surname in a search engine will not be very helpful. You need to search for a surname and the word 'genealogy' and/or the phrase 'surname list' (see Chapter 19).

Pedigree databases

The surname interest resources do not provide genealogical information, they simply offer contact details for other genealogists who may share your interests. But there are several sites which allow genealogists to make their pedigrees available on the web. You can, of course, do this by creating your own website, as discussed in Chapter 20, particularly if you want to publish more comprehensive information. But if you just want to make your pedigree available online, these sites provide an easy way to do it. Even if you do not make your own pedigree available, many others have, and it is worth checking these sites for overlap with your own family tree.

There are two ways of getting your own pedigree into one of these databases. Some of them have facilities for you to create your pedigree entirely online, while the commoner method is to upload a GEDCOM file containing your pedigree. Information about GEDCOM files and how to create them will be found on p. 335, Chapter 20.

There is not space here to give more than a brief account of some of the most important sites, but for a comprehensive list of pedigree databases consult the 'Databases – Lineage-Linked' page on Cyndi's List at <www.cyndislist.com/lin-linked.htm>.

Free databases

FamilySearch at <www.familysearch.org> has been discussed as a source of record transcriptions in Chapter 7 (p. 101), but the site also includes two data collections with user-submitted information. Ancestral File goes back to 1978, starting life as a CD-ROM collection, initially as a way for members of the LDS Church to deposit the fruits of their researches but in fact open to submission from anyone with genealogical information. The Pedigree Resource File is a more recent database compiled from submissions to the FamilySearch website and also published on CD-ROM.

In Ancestral File a successful search on an individual name brings up an individual record with links, on the left, to a full pedigree, a family group record and submitter details (see Figure 14-4). Unfortunately, there is only a postal address for the submitter, no email address, and it may well be out of date, considering the age of some of the data.

In the Pedigree Resource File a search produces a similar individual record with details of the submitter, but no link to a pedigree. A useful feature is that it gives you the submission number – clicking on this will do a search for all individuals in the same submission. The submitter details will include a postal address, and may also have a link to the submitter's website. As discussed in Chapter 7, you can search all four FamilySearch databases at once by selecting 'All Resources' from any of the search pages (see Figure 7-2), and the results are then listed separately for each database.

Probably the largest collection of pedigrees is on RootsWeb, whose WorldConnect data has a home page at <**worldconnect.genealogy.**

Figure 14-4 An individual record in Ancestral File

rootsweb.ancestry.com>. It currently contains over 550 million entries for around five million surnames, submitted by about a quarter of a million users. Ancestry's World Tree provides access to the same database at <**www.ancestry.myfamily.com/trees/awt/**> (this is freely accessible and does not require a subscription to Ancestry).

The initial search page form provided on RootsWeb allows you to search on surname and given name, and the search results pages then list each matching entry with further details and offer a link to the home page for the database in which the entry is found or to the specific person. If you get too many results to cope with, a more detailed search form provides options to narrow down your search with dates, places, names of parents, etc.

Figure 14-5 shows the results of an advanced search on WorldConnect for the surname Collyer, with birth or christening in Surrey. Clicking on the name of the individual takes you to their data, while the link on the right takes you to details of the submitted database in which this individual is found, including the email address of the submitter. On the Ancestry site you need to register with your name and email address, free of charge, before you can search. However, the initial search form is more comprehensive. Data from World Tree are also included in general searches carried out on the Ancestry site at <**www.ancestry.myfamily.com/search/**>.

GenCircles at <**www.gencircles.com**>, started by Cliff Shaw in 2001, is a free service that currently has over 90 million individuals (see Figure 14-6). You need to register before using, but there's no subscription. GenCircles offers a facility called SmartMatching, which compares the individuals in

RootsWeb's WorldConnect Project
Global Search

Names: 554,461,147 Surnames: 4,951,296 Databases: 418,657

Results 1-20 of 244

Name	Birth/Christening		Death/Burial		Database	Order record?	Other Matches
	Date	Place	Date	Place			
Collyer,	1631	Godalming Parish, Surrey Co, England	25 Feb 1631	Godalming Parish, Surrey Co, England	rjpowder		Census Newspapers Histories
🔍📷	Father: Edward Collyer Mother: Joan Harward						
Collyer, Abraham	1835	Surrey			steveferring		Census Newspapers Histories
🔍📷	Father: Francis Collyer Mother: Living						
Collyer, Abraham	1835	Surrey			steve_biggs		Census Newspapers Histories
🔍📷	Father: Francis Collyer Mother: Unknown						
Collyer, Ada	1867	Lambeth, Surrey			haydencowan		Census Newspapers Histories
🔍📷📖	Father: Joseph Collyer Mother: Clara Henrietta Owen						
COLLYER, Ada	ABT 1850	Lambeth, Surrey, England			chari81		Census Newspapers Histories
🔍📷📖	Father: Henry COLLYER Mother: Elizabeth LEE						
Collyer, Agnes	26 APR 1876	Horsell, Surrey, England	16 JUN 1961		3306507		Census Newspapers Histories
🔍📷	Father: Richard Collyer Mother: Ellen Mundy Spouse: Lancelot Kirkland						

Figure 14-5 Search results on WorldConnect

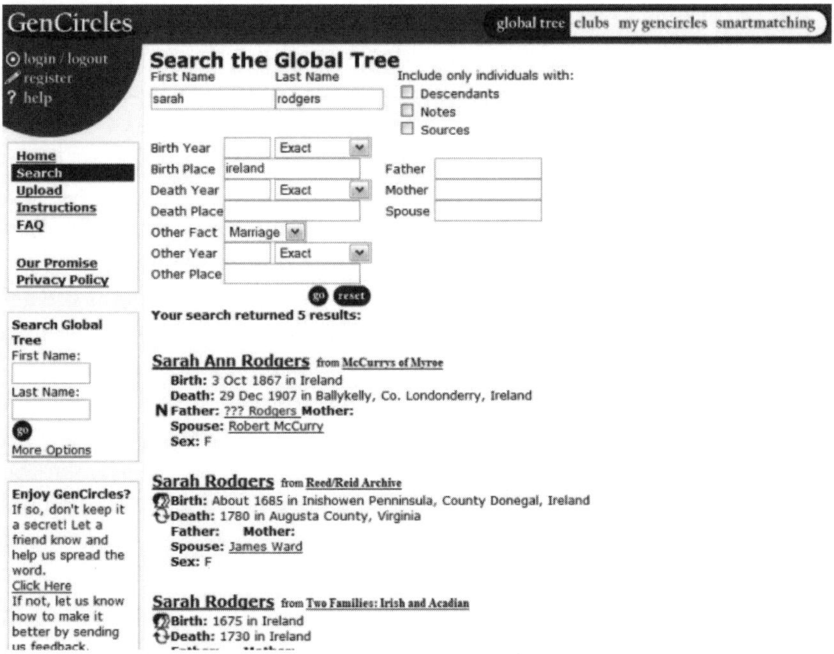

Figure 14-6 Search results in GenCircles

your file against all other individuals submitted to detect any matches.

MyHeritage <**www.myheritage.com**> is a relatively new service, but already has almost 300 million individuals in over six million family trees. The site provides a free downloadable program Family Tree Builder. At the end of 2007 MyHeritage took over GenCircles and therefore includes all that site's records in its database.

Another free service is GeneaNet, a French-run site at <**www.geneanet. org**> which started in 1996. This allows you to upload a GEDCOM file, but it also has its own free software GeneWeb, which you can either use on the site or download. It has entries for more than 240 million individuals. Additional facilities are available as part of 'privileged membership' for €40 per year. For some entries you can only see the contact details, for others a pedigree is available.

GEDCOM Index at <**gedcomindex.com**> does not itself host any pedigrees, but indexes thousands of GEDCOM files found elsewhere on the web – there are over 450,000 individuals for the UK. Links to the files are organized by country, then county, then surname.

A interesting experiment is WikiTree at <**wikitree.org**>, a collaborative project launched in April 2005 to develop an online pedigree database with a wiki page for each individual. However, it has a relatively small number of users and very few of the pages offer much detail about individuals.

Subscription databases

Alongside the free pedigree databases, there are a number of commercial services, all of which require a subscription. I should perhaps point out that I have not subscribed to any of these services and the material in this section is based on the publicly available information the sites provide.

GenServ at <**www.genserv.com**>, started by Cliff Manis in 1991 as an email only service – this was before the invention of the web – is among the oldest pedigree databases on the internet, with over 23 million individuals in over 16,000 GEDCOM files. It is a slightly unusual service in that you *must* submit some of your own material in order to subscribe. Once you have done this you can have a free 60-day trial subscription, while a regular subscription is $12/£8 per year, which allows you to do unlimited searches (though only so many per day). Details of how to subscribe are given at <**www.genserv.com/gs/gsh2sub.htm**>. A more limited trial (one surname search for any one email address) is available under the 'Sample Search' option at <**www.genserv.com/gs3/samplesearch.html**>.

OneGreatFamily at <**www.onegreatfamily.com**> was launched in the summer of 2000 and now holds details of over 190 million ancestors. It represents a more sophisticated approach to online pedigrees. Rather than just seeing itself as a repository for a copy of your data, it acts as a substitute for a traditional genealogy program. Like GenCircles, it has facilities for matching your own data with other trees on the site. Subscriptions are $14.95, $29.95 and $74.95 for one, three and twelve months respectively. There is also a seven-day free trial, though you have to give credit card information in order to sign up for this, and it automatically turns into a subscription if you do not cancel. To view pedigrees on the site you need to download the Genealogy Browser, which is a plug-in for your web browser. To find out more, it is worth reading Dick Eastman's very positive account of using the site at <**www.onegreatfamily.com/static-tpls/pr-eastman 06-21-00.htm**>.

Genes Reunited

Halfway between the free and the subscription services is Genes Reunited at <**www.genesreunited.co.uk**>. The site, launched in November 2002, is an offshoot from the very successful Friends Reunited, and is one of the most popular UK genealogy sites. (In fact it was launched as Genes Connected but the name was changed in 2004 to make the link more obvious.) I have termed it 'semi-free' because it is a mix of a free and a subscription service. You do not have to subscribe in order to enter or upload your pedigree, nor to carry out searches on the database. But you need to be a subscriber in order to make contact with the person who submitted an individual you find a possible match with. Genes Reunited does not give you the email address

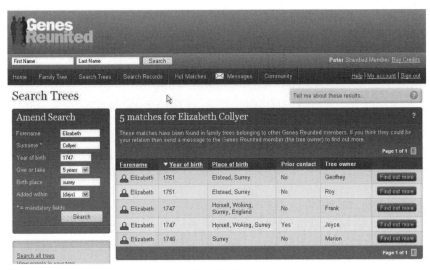

Figure 14-7 Search results in Genes Reunited

of a submitter; instead you type in a message on the site and Genes Reunited actually sends it. This offers some measure of privacy protection, since subscriber email addresses are not visible on the site and are never given out. The subscription is £9.95 per year. There is also a 'Gold Membership' which includes unlimited access to the site's data collections described in Chapters 4 and 5. The site provides several message boards and there are brief articles for the novice genealogist.

One irritating problem is that individuals are listed only with a birth year. Christening dates are not used, even in the absence of a birth date, so there will be no date given for that individual if there is only a christening date in the GEDCOM file.[7]

To help you find matches in the trees of others, the site has a 'Hot Matches' feature, which automatically compares people in your pedigree with all the others on the site. Some of its matching is very loose – you can find someone born in Cornwall matched with someone of the same name from Aberdeen – but it also shows you how many matches there are in another tree. Anything over 20 matches is likely to mean an overlap with your own tree. In any case, you can contact the submitter to compare notes.

Currently Genes Reunited claims to have over 181 million names in its

---

7   A fudge to get round this, more or less, is to do a search and replace in your GEDCOM file before uploading it, substituting 1 BIRT for every occurrence of 1 CHR. This is preferable to entering a guessed-at birth year for everyone in your database, which is both bad practice *and* hard work.

family trees. Although this is fewer than some of the sites mentioned above, the site's UK focus means that it must have the largest number of British and Irish ancestors of any pedigree database. Another consideration is the connection with Friends Reunited (with around 11 million registrations). This suggests Genes Reunited probably contains many submissions from people who do not regard themselves as serious family historians and who are unlikely to use any of the other resources discussed in this chapter. It may, therefore, be particularly good for contacting reasonably close cousins, particularly if there are recent branches of your family you have lost touch with. On the other hand, there may also be entries from people who will not bother to respond to a contact. If my own experience is anything to go by, this is one of the most useful contact sites – I have had dozens of useful contacts over a period of four years.

Record-based matching

Another approach to matching individuals is taken by LostCousins at <www.lostcousins.com> launched in September 2004. In this service, you don't submit general details of ancestors for matching, but the full reference to the record of an ancestor in census indexes. This approach means that matching will be very accurate and unambiguous, and unlike other types of pedigree database, you won't find vague or incomplete entries.

The site started off with just the 1881 census index (see p. 81), but now includes the 1841 census, as well the 1880 US census and 1881 Canadian census.

Unfortunately, the site gives no indication of how many individuals have been submitted, so it's not possible to assess the likelihood of a match. Since matches can only be made on ancestors alive in 1841, you will not get any contacts with anyone more remotely related to you than about fifth cousins.

To use the site requires registration and login. Once you have entered details of an ancestor you will automatically receive an email when a match is found. Registration is free.

Limitations

One point to bear in mind is that, with the exception of Genes Reunited and LostCousins, the majority of the individuals in these databases were born in the US, so in spite of the number of entries you should not be surprised if you do not find matches for your UK ancestors in them. However, as many American pedigrees have some roots in the British Isles, it is still well worth checking them. Also, as more British genealogists submit their family trees to such sites, they become more useful for British genealogy.

The material on these sites consists entirely of submissions from individual genealogists. The completeness and accuracy of information is therefore highly variable, though some sites do basic checks in order to detect obvious errors, such as a death date earlier than a birth date. It is therefore best to regard these databases as a way of contacting people with similar interests, rather than as direct resources of data. It would be very unwise to incorporate such material directly into your own genealogy database without thorough checking. The obvious exception here is LostCousins, where matching is tied to a specific census record, and you don't have access to a pedigree as such.

In some cases checking will be simple – the example in Figure 14-4 gives a christening date and parish, which should be easy to check; in others the information may be of little value, perhaps just a year and a country. There is no way to tell for certain in any of these databases what sources submitters have drawn their information from. But that does not lessen the advantage of these databases over the surname resources discussed earlier in this chapter, namely that they provide information about individuals and families, not just about surnames. This should make it fairly easy to establish whether the submitter is interested in the same family as you, something that may be particularly important for a common surname.

The problem with all compiled sources is that there is no guarantee of reliability, and indications of the original source for an event may be missing or simply wrong. The errors in indexes to primary sources will normally be restricted to misreadings of original documents or mistyping of the entries, but in the individual submissions, information is often fragmentary – years rather than full dates, for example – and errors can be more serious. Some of the submissions are obviously nothing more than guesswork.

To get an idea of how badly wrong some of the information is, it is instructive to look for someone whose details are well known. Charles Darwin was born near Shrewsbury on 12 February 1809 and baptized at St Chad's, Shrewsbury. He married Emma Wedgwood on 29 January 1839, and died at Downe, Kent, on 16 April 1882. A search for Charles Darwin in the IGI produces a whole host of results. Among them is the baptism entry from the registers of St Chad's, but the remainder are all from individual submissions, and some are bizarre indeed. One is for a 'Carlos Roberto Darwin', with the correct birth and death years, but the place given simply as England; another has him born in 'Shrewsbury, Northampton, England'; and one has Charles Darwin, born 1809, Downe, Kent, died 16 April 1682, and married to Julia Wedgwood.

Within limits, even inaccurate data can be useful if it's backed up by an accurate source citation – at least you get a pointer to a document that might be worth consulting. But in most cases the only source information in these collections are the contact details submitter. If you're lucky, you may also get link to a personal genealogy website. But in the IGI, for example, the contact details are merely postal addresses which could be as much as 25 years old. If you're very unlucky, you may even find *no* useful submitter details: some IGI entries simply say something completely unhelpful like, 'Record submitted after 1991 by a member of the LDS Church. No additional information is available. Ancestral File may list the same family and the submitter. No source information is available.'

Rights

If you are intending to submit your own pedigree to one of these databases, there is one important issue you need to be aware of. On some sites, when you upload material to a database you grant the site ownership of your pedigree or unlimited rights to use the material as they see fit. This is not necessarily as unreasonable as it might sound. With FamilySearch your data file will be permanently archived in the LDS Church's Granite Mountain Records Vault, ensuring preservation, and it is unrealistic to expect an archive to keep track of the legal ownership of thousands if not millions of files over many decades. Also, FamilySearch makes the data freely accessible online and its CD-ROMs are sold more or less at cost. On the other hand, it is perhaps understandable that some people baulk at allowing the fully commercial exploitation of their data without royalty by some sites, when they are already paying a subscription.

It is therefore important to check the terms and conditions of any pedigree database before you submit your own material. Of the sites mentioned here, RootsWeb, GenCircles, Genes Reunited, and GenServ make no claim on material submitted, and you retain complete rights over your GEDCOM, including editorial control.

Privacy

Another issue in placing your pedigree online is the privacy of living individuals. This is nothing to do with data protection, as is often thought – much of your information comes from public sources and there can be no legal bar in the UK to publishing it online, or indeed in any other medium, as long as it is accurate. The real issue is that people can be distressed, understandably, if they find their personal details published online by someone else. Because of this all the online pedigree databases have a policy on publishing information about living individuals. Here are some typical policies:

- RootsWeb has facilities which make it possible for you to remove living people entirely, or clean their entries of specific pieces of information,

but it does not check your efforts.
- GenesReunited has a condition that you do not include living individuals without their permission, but they do not check or modify the submitted data.
- GenCircles uses a number of techniques for identifying individuals and then ensures that they are not displayed, though the submitter can still see the information.

If you're going to submit to a site that doesn't have its own privacy protection mechanism, you will need to remove living individuals or least their details. Most genealogy software programs have facilities for doing this: it may be an explicit option in the Export to GEDCOM process, or you may have to select those people who are to be included. If in doubt, excluding everyone born less than 100 years ago is a sensible policy. Ideally, exclude those born than less than 100 years ago only if they have no death or burial date. Figure 14-8 shows how this is done in Personal Ancestral File, using the Advanced Focus/Filter option on the Search menu.

There are a number of stand-alone tools for purging GEDCOM files of sensitive information – see the 'Software & Computers' page on Cyndi's List at <**www.cyndislist.com/software.htm#Privacy**>. Note that this is something that will also be necessary if you put a pedigree on a personal website (see Chapter 20). The issue of online privacy is discussed further on p. 383.

Genetics and DNA testing

With the advent of consumer genetic testing, there is now a scientific method of establishing kinship to add to the traditional historical methods. The ease and affordability of DNA testing has improved rapidly in recent years, giving rise to all sorts of expectations about what this can do for the genealogist. This is not the place to debate the merits and limitations of DNA testing in validating pedigrees, never mind the technicalities, but it clearly provides a method of confirming or establishing links between individuals.

The use of DNA testing in genealogy is not directly an internet development, but the web provides the mechanism by which the results of individual tests can be matched, and DNA projects for specific surnames rely on the internet for collaboration.

There is plenty of online information about DNA testing aimed at a genealogical audience. For example:

- Genuki has a concise page on 'DNA testing for Genealogy' at <**www.genuki.org.uk/big/bigmisc/DNA.html**>.

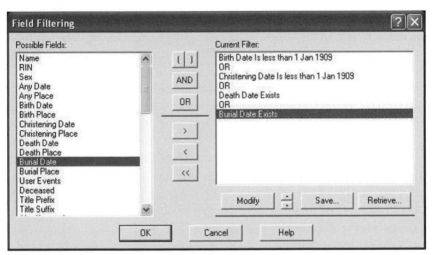

Figure 14-8 Filtering out living persons in Personal Ancestral File

- The World Families Network has useful FAQ at <**www.worldfamilies. net/faq**>. Though mainly about the site's own facilities, much of the information, especially the 'Understanding Genetic Genealogy FAQ' is of general relevance.
- The International Society of Genetic Genealogy (ISoGG) at <**www.isogg. org**> is a non-commercial organization whose mission is 'to advocate for and educate about the use of genetics as a tool for genealogical research, and promote a supportive network for genetic genealogists'. There is a section of the site for 'DNA-Newbies', which explains basic concepts and provides a useful glossary.
- Ancestry.com's DNA site has a comprehensive FAQ at <**dna.ancestry. com/faq.aspx**>.
- Roots Television (see p. 370) has videos on DNA in genealogy at <**www. rootstelevision.com/players/player_dna.php**>, including a number of lectures.
- Probably the most comprehensive set of links, including over a dozen testing companies, is Kerchner's DNA Testing & Genetic Genealogy Info and Resources Page at <**www.kerchner.com/dna-info.htm**>. The site also has a substantial glossary of DNA testing terminology at <**www. kerchner.com/anonftp/pub/glossary.pdf**>.

There are hundreds of DNA testing projects based on individuals with a shared surname, and many have a website and/or mailing list, which should give you the possibility of discussing whether there might be a connection, even if you're not involved in the project. The majority of these projects concentrate on Y-DNA, so are only relevant to the paternal line and only to male descendants. This does mean, however, that it is closely related to surname inheritance. MtDNA testing, which relates to the maternal line and is applicable to descendants of both sexes, is also available, though of course it cannot relate to a particular surname.

In a search engine, entering the phrase 'surname DNA project' along with the surname of interest should be adequate to locate most of these. If you get no initial results, repeat the search but without the quote marks. There is a substantial list of projects at <**www.worldfamilies.net/ surnames/**>. This site also provides free web pages for DNA projects.

If you have had a DNA test carried out, there are also sites where you can post the details of your own genetic markers in the hope of a match, or search for matches from the existing submissions, for example:

- Ybase at <**ybase.org**>
- Mitosearch at <**www.mitosearch.org**>

This means that you do not need to be part of a surname project in order to make use of DNA testing.

Ancestry.com's DNA site <**dna.ancestry.com**>, mentioned above, offers its own test kits and lets you upload test results from other services to try and find matches.

There is a general mailing list devoted to this topic, GENEALOGY-DNA, details of which will be found at <**lists.rootsweb.ancestry.com/index/ other/DNA/GENEALOGY-DNA.html**>. RootsWeb also hosts mailing lists for a number of individual DNA projects, listed at <**lists.rootsweb.ancestry. com/index/other/DNA/**>, including ISoGG's DNA-NEWBIE list.

Cyndi's List has a general page devoted to the subject under the heading 'Genetics, DNA & Family Health' at <**www.cyndislist.com/dna.htm**> and there are links to individual surname projects on the 'Surname DNA Studies and Projects' at <**www.cyndislist.com/surn-dna.htm**>.

Royal and notable families

The web has a wide range of resources relating to the genealogy of royal houses and the nobility, as well as to famous people and families. For initial orientation, Genuki's page on 'Kings and Queens of England and Scotland (and some of the people around them)' at <**www.genuki.org.uk/big/ royalty/**> provides a list of Monarchs since the Conquest, Kings of England, Kings of Scotland, Queens and a selection of the most notable Queens, Kings, Archbishops, Bishops, Dukes, Earls, Knights, Lords, Eminent Men, Popes and Princes. There is also a detailed table of the Archbishops of Canterbury and York, and the Bishops of London, Durham, St David's and Armagh, from AD 200 to the present day at <**www.genuki.org.uk/big/eng/**

History/Archbishops.html>.

Cyndi's List has a page with over 200 links relating to Royalty and Nobility at <**www.cyndislist.com/royalty.htm**>.

The best place for genealogical information on English royalty is Brian Tompsett's Directory of Royal Genealogical Data at <**www3.dcs.hull.ac.uk/ public/genealogy/royal/catalog.html**>, which contains 'the genealogy of the British Royal family and those linked to it via blood or marriage relationships.' The site provides much information on other royal families, and includes details of all English peerages at <**www3.dcs.hull.ac.uk/ genealogy/royal/peerage.html**>. It can be searched by name, by date, or by title. A nineteenth-century descent of Queen Victoria from Adam will be found on Library Ireland at <**www.libraryireland.com/Pedigrees1/ RoyalFamilyEngland.php**>. Another massive database devoted to European nobility will be found on the WW-Person site at <**www8. informatik.uni-erlangen.de/html/ww-person.html**>. Family History UK has a family tree of the royal families of Europe at <**www.tree.family history.uk.com/fproyal.php**>. Unlike most other examples, this data is stored in a database which can provide ancestor and descendant trees (in fact it uses the TNG software, mentioned on p. 351).

The official website of the royal family is at <**www.royal.gov.uk**> which, among other things, offers family trees of the royal houses from the ninth-century kingdom of Wessex to the present day in PDF format linked from <**www.royal.gov.uk/output/Page10.asp**>.

Burke's Peerage & Gentry at <**www.burkes-peerage.net**> has a series of indented lineages of the rulers of England, Scotland and subsequently Great Britain among the free resources on its website at <**www.burkes-peerage.net/articles/roindex.aspx**> – see Figure 14-9. The main resources on the site are available via its subscription service, and comprise data from the published books, including:

- *Burke's Peerage & Baronetage*, 107th edition, including Knights, Scottish Chiefs and Scottish Feudal Barons
- *Burke's Landed Gentry*, 19th edition, The Kingdom in Scotland
- *Burke's Landed Gentry*, 19th edition, The Ridings of York
- *Burke's Landed Gentry*, 19th edition, The Principality of Wales
- *Burke's Landed Gentry*, 19th edition, The North West
- *Burke's Landed Gentry*, 18th edition
- *Burke's Landed Gentry*, Irish Families (Irish supplement to the 15th edition of *Burke's Landed Gentry*)

You can browse an index of *Burke's Peerage and Gentry* free of charge. This has links to brief entries for individuals and families, with full entries available only to subscribers. Subscriptions are £7.95 for 72 hours or £64.95 for a year, and you may find that your library has a subscription.

Genuki has part of *The English Peerage* (1790) online at <**www.genuki. org.uk/big/eng/History/Barons/**>, with information on a number of barons and viscounts of the period. Leigh Rayment's Peerage Page at <**www. leighrayment.com**> has comprehensive information on the peerages, baronetage, House of Commons, the orders of chivalry and the privy council.

For Wales, a major project is underway at Aberystwyth University to digitize the Welsh Genealogies compiled by the late Dr Peter Bartrum, covering the period 300–1500, some of which have been published in 26 volumes. This will include all known genealogical information about Welsh historical figures of the period, including royalty and nobility. Details of the project can be found at <**www.aber.ac.uk/aberonline/en/archive/2006/11/ uwa11506/**>, and the home page of the university's Department of Welsh at <**www.aber.ac.uk/cymraeg-welsh/**> will have a link to the site when it goes live in summer 2009.

Wikipedia has extensive coverage of royal and noble lineages of many countries. The easiest place to start from is the category page for family trees at <**en.wikipedia.org/wiki/Category:Family_trees**>.

Royal and noble titles for many languages and countries are explained in the 'Glossary of European Noble, Princely, Royal, and Imperial Titles' at <**www.heraldica.org/topics/odegard/titlefaq.htm**>.

Figure 14-9 Burke's Peerage and Gentry: Lineage of James VI & I

Alongside royalty and nobility, you can almost certainly find information on the web on any other genealogically notable group of people. Thus there are sites devoted to everyone from the *Mayflower* pilgrims at <www. mayflowerhistory.com/Passengers/passengers.php> (and many other sites) to the *Bounty* mutineers on Paul Lareau's Pitcairn And Norfolk Islands Genealogy site at (<www.lareau.org/bounty.html>). The ancestry of the US presidents will be found on a number of sites, and <www3.dcs. hull.ac.uk/genealogy/presidents/presidents.html> provides a tree for each of them. The ancestry of Tim Berners-Lee, inventor of the World Wide Web, can be found at <www.wargs.com/other/bernerslee.html>. The Famous Family Trees Blog has links to many pedigrees of royalty and the famous at <famousfamilytrees.blogspot.com>. Mark Humphrys has a site devoted to the Royal Descents of Famous People at <humphrysfamilytree. com/famous.descents.html>. There are, of course, countless sites devoted to biblical genealogies.

There are also plenty of pedigrees for other fictional families online. For example, the BBC has family trees for the characters in *Eastenders* at <www. bbc.co.uk/eastenders/characters_cast/>, while Wikipedia has family trees for the Simpsons, Harry Potter, the Sopranos and others, all linked from <en.wikipedia.org/wiki/Category:Fictional_family_trees>.

There are a number of relevant mailing lists including:

- GEN-ROYAL <lists.rootsweb.ancestry.com/index/other/Royalty_and_ Nobility/GEN-ROYAL.html>
- BRITISH-NOBILITY <lists.rootsweb.ancestry.com/index/intl/UK/ BRITISH-NOBILITY.html>
- PLANTAGENET <lists.rootsweb.ancestry.com/index/intl/UK/ PLANTAGENET.html>
- SCT-ROYAL <lists.rootsweb.ancestry.com/index/intl/SCT/SCT- ROYAL.html>
- GEN-ANCIENT <lists.rootsweb.ancestry.com/index/other/ Miscellaneous/GEN-ANCIENT.html>

Lists for further countries will be found at <www.rootsweb.ancestry. com/~jfuller/gen_mail_nobility.html>. Yahoo has over 200 discussion groups for royal and noble genealogy, listed at <dir.groups.yahoo.com/dir/ Family___Home/Genealogy/Royal_Genealogies> (note the three underscores in the address).

Clans

Some information on Scottish clans will be found among the surname resources discussed earlier in this chapter, but there is also more specific material online. The most comprehensive coverage of clans is provided by Wikipedia. It has a substantial 'Scottish clan' article at <**en.wikipedia.org/ wiki/Scottish_clan**>, which includes a listing of all clans recognized by the Lord Lyon Court (see below). For each name, there is a link to an article on the individual clan. Many of these articles are quite substantial.

Another site with good coverage is Electric Scotland, which has a list of 'Official Scottish Clans and Families' at <**www.electricscotland.com/ webclans/clanmenu.htm**> with links to information, albeit less copious than Wikipedia's, on the individual clans.

Both of these sites have clan maps, and there is a further map on the Scots Family site at <**www.scotsfamily.com/clan-map.htm**>. Of special interest because of its early date is interest is Lizars' 1822 'Map of the Highlands of Scotland denoting the districts or counties inhabited by the Highland Clans' which is available on the National Library of Scotland site at <**www.nls.uk/maps/scotland/thematic.html**>.

A general mailing list is CLANS, details of which can be found at <**lists. rootsweb.ancestry.com/index/intl/SCT/CLANS.html**>, and RootsWeb has almost 200 mailing lists for individual clans, listed at <**lists.rootsweb. ancestry.com/index/intl/SCT/**>. However, even those for large and well-known clans seem to have few messages, so they are probably of less use than the lists devoted to the surnames.

You can expect to find copies of older books on the clans in the digital book archives discussed in Chapter 12. For example, *The Scottish Clans and their Tartans*, published by W. & A. K. Johnston around 1900, is available at the Internet Archive and has colour plates of the tartans.

Heraldry

Heraldry is intimately connected with royal and noble families, and there is quite a lot of material relating to it on the web. The authoritative source of information about heraldry in England and Wales is the website of the College of Arms at <**www.college-of-arms.gov.uk**>. Its FAQ page deals with frequently asked questions about coats of arms. The SoG has a leaflet on 'The Right to Arms' at <**www.sog.org.uk/leaflets/arms.pdf**>.

For Scotland, the Lord Lyon King of Arms is the chief herald, with a website at <**www.lyon-court.com**>. The Public Register of All Arms and Bearings in Scotland has been digitized and is available on ScotlandsPeople (see Chapter 4), which gives information on these records at <**www. scotlandspeople.gov.uk/content/help/index.aspx?r=554&1283**>. Information on heraldry in Ireland will be found on the web pages for the Office of the Chief Herald on the National Library of Ireland's website at <**www. nli.ie/en/heraldry-introduction.aspx**>. There has been considerable uncertainty about the legal status of Irish arms granted after independence from

Britain, and the issues are discussed in some detail in Sean J. Murphy's article 'An Irish Arms Crisis' at <**homepage.eircom.net/~seanjmurphy/ chiefs/armscrisis.htm**>.

Burke's Peerage and Gentry has its International Register of Arms online at <**www.armorial-register.com**>. This is not an official register and is not in any sense comprehensive – it contains only the arms of those who have paid to register them in the index. The site has a substantial list of heraldry societies.

The Heraldry on the Internet site at <**www.digiserve.com/heraldry/**> is a specialist site with a substantial collection of links to other online heraldry resources, and Cyndi's List has a page of heraldry links at <**www.cyndislist. com/heraldry.htm**>. The British Heraldry site at <**www.heraldica.org/ topics/britain/**> has a number of articles on heraldry. The Heraldry Society will be found at <**www.theheraldrysociety.com**>, while the Heraldry Society of Scotland has a site at <**www.heraldry-scotland.co.uk**>.

For the meaning of terms used in heraldry, an online version of Pimbley's 1905 *Dictionary of Heraldry* is at <**www.digiserve.com/heraldry/pimbley. htm**>, while there is an online version of James Parker's *A Glossary of Terms used in Heraldry* (1894) at <**www.heraldsnet.org/saitou/parker/**>. Burke's Peerage has a 'Guide to Heraldic Terms' taken from the 106th edition of *Burkes's Peerage & Baronetage* at <**www.burkes-peerage.net/articles/ heindex.aspx**>. Heraldic terms will also be found in the 'Knighthood, Chivalry & Tournament Glossary of Terms' at <**www.chronique.com/ Library/Glossaries/glossary-KCT/glssindx.htm**>. Google Books at <**books.google.com**> (see p. 175) has the full text of a number of older works on heraldry, including William Berry's 1810 *An Introduction to Heraldry* and Hugh Clark's 1775 *A Short Introduction to Heraldry*.

Biography

The *Oxford Dictionary of National Biography* is the definitive national reference work for the lives of notable people, and information on access to the online edition is given on p. 178. Its website at <**www.oup.com/oxforddnb/ info**> has some freely accessible material, including biographies for notable brewery founders and shopkeepers. There is a free index which provides the name and dates of all those in the dictionary. There are also some quite substantial articles on groups of people who played an important role in British history, such as the Women's Social and Political Union, the Chartists, and the Pilgrim Fathers, though these do not generally provide any genealogical information.

The Bolles Collection has the index and epitome (i.e. a synopsis of each entry) for the 1903 edition of the *Dictionary of National Biography* online, containing brief biographies of over 30,000 notable individuals – follow the link to the DNB from <**www.perseus.tufts.edu/cache/perscoll_Bolles. html**>. The easiest way to locate a particular individual is to use the search facility on this main page.

The *Dictionary of Ulster Biography* was published in 1993 and all articles are available online at <**www.ulsterbiography.co.uk**>.

Locating living people

The surname lists and databases already discussed will put you in touch with other genealogists who have made their researches – or at least their research interests – public, but you can also use the internet to locate long-lost relatives or their descendants, or simply people with a particular surname.

Phone numbers

BT provides an online directory enquiry service at <**www.thephonebook. bt.com**> and this will give you an address, postcode and phone number. You need to give a location – either a town or the first part of a postcode – so you cannot do a national search. Also, your search will fail if it gives too many results, so a search on surname only may not work if it is a common one and/or the location is too broad, e.g. a large town.

The internet is particularly useful for foreign phone numbers, since only a small number of major reference libraries in the UK have a full set of international directories. Infospace has worldwide telephone listings available from <**www.infospace.com/home/white-pages/world**>. Infobel's 'Telephone Directories' pages at <**www.infobel.com/teldir/**> has links to Yellow Pages, White Pages, Business Directories, Email Addresses and Fax Listings from 184 countries. International dialling codes are at <**kropla. com/dialcode.htm**>.

Historical telephone directories for the UK are available at Ancestry and are described on p. 183.

Electoral registers

The electoral registers are a traditional resource for establishing who lives at which address, and therefore for tracing living people. The problem with the printed registers is, of course, that they are not indexed, so unless you have an approximate idea where someone lives, they are actually of little use in tracing living people, unless you have a great deal of time to spare. However, the modern electronic register does not have this drawback. The registers are held by local authorities and can be inspected at various locations in the area, but are not made available online. However, an edited version can be searched online on a number of commercial websites, including:

- 192.com at <www.192.com> (100 credits valid for six months for £41.07)
- TraceSmart at <www.tracesmart.co.uk> (5 credits valid for one month £3.49)
- The UK Electoral Roll at <www.theukelectoralroll.co.uk> (unlimited searches, monthly subscription for £6.25)
- Ukroll.com at <www.ukroll.com> (unlimited searches for 30 days for £8.47)

The prices given here are those for the cheapest packages, but there are other schemes available for those with a need for heavier use. You can find other similar services by conducting a search on 'UK electoral register' on any search engine.

Findmypast (see Chapter 4) has a 'Living Relatives' section. The Electoral Roll search costs 10 units (<70p) and gives full details of all matching individuals. The advanced search includes an option to specify other people living in the same household. If you already have pay-per-view credits with Findmypast, you can use these for searches in Living Relatives. However, Living Relatives is not included in subscription packages. The data is taken from the latest electoral roll.

Apart from the cost, the other limitation with these services is that individuals can request that their details are excluded from the commercial available data and obviously will not be findable by this method.

While the electoral rolls give more details than the phone book in that the full name is included, this will not necessarily be sufficient to identify a specific individual unless he or she has an uncommon name or you know the names of other family members who are likely to be living at the same address,

192.com gives you the initial search free but you need to pay to see the full details. However, the initial results list all the people living in a particular household, which will often help you identify the individual you want.

Most of these sites also include civil registration searches, though since this data is freely available elsewhere (see Chapter 5) it is not worth subscribing just for this.

Email addresses

Finding email addresses is not straightforward. For a start, there are no directories of email addresses which are authoritative in the way that phone books are for phone numbers. There are simply too many email addresses and they are changing all the time. Also, there is no single place to register them. However, there are a number of directories of email addresses on the web.

The Yahoo directory has links to many sites providing general or specific email address searches at <**uk.dir.yahoo.com/Reference/Phone_Numbers_ and_ Addresses/Email_Addresses/**>.

One point to bear in mind is that it is easy for these databases to add an email address by extracting it from a message sent to a mailing list, or if it is provided on a web page. However, it is quite impossible for a database to know when the address ceases to be valid (perhaps because the person concerned has changed their internet provider), so the databases are full of old, no longer valid email addresses as well as current ones. Except for fairly unusual names, you will find multiple entries, and since email addresses often give no clue to the geographical location of the person it may be hard to identify the one you are looking for. Also, people posting messages to mailing lists often use pseudonyms.

Another way to find an email address is simply to use a standard search engine to look for the relevant name, but success will depend on the person concerned having a web page or having sent messages to a publicly archived mailing list or newsgroup, or contact details on someone else's website, and the search could be time-consuming.

All in all, looking for an email address is likely to be a time-consuming and problematic task.

Social networking

Social networking sites such as FaceBook at <**www.facebook.com**> can, in principle, be used for locating people, though you will generally need to be a member yourself in order to identify and contact people. But these suffer the same problem as email address searches: with just a name to go on, there's little chance of being sure you have the right person, though if you're lucky, there may be a photograph, which may help.

Probably the most useful site for the UK is Friends Reunited at <**www. friendsreunited.com**>, which is designed to put people in touch with former schoolmates or work colleagues. If you know where someone went to school or where they used to work, the problem of identifying the right person is greatly reduced.

Adoption and child migration

While the resources discussed so far can be useful for tracing people when you know their names they may be of little use in the case of adoption or child migration, and you will need to go to sites specifically devoted to these issues.

The FamilyRecords portal has brief information on UK adoption records at <**www.familyrecords.gov.uk/topics/adoption.htm**> and more informa-tion, including details of the Adoption Contact Register, is available on the GRO site at <**www.gro.gov.uk/gro/content/adoptions/**>. GROS has a page on 'Adoption in Scotland' at <**www.gro-scotland.gov.uk/regscot/adoption. html**>. For Ireland, a National Adoption Contact Preference Register was launched early in 2005 – details at <**www.adoptionboard.ie/ preferenceRegister/index.php**>. Searching in Ireland has a page for Irish-born adoptees at <**www.netreach.net/~steed/search.html**>.

Adoption Search Reunion is a site run by the British Association for Adoption and Fostering at <**www.adoptionsearchreunion.org.uk**>, with a range of useful resources. Probably the most important is the Location Adoption Records database, which helps identity places where you may find relevant records. You can search by the name or location of a maternity or other home, by the organization or local authority which arranged the adoption, and even by the name of a staff member. The site also offers advice about making contact and links to other useful websites.

The Salvation Army offers a Family Tracing Service and their website has a section devoted to family tracing, with a home page at <**www1.salvation army.org.uk/familytracing**>.

The UK Birth Adoption Register at <**www.ukbirth-adoptionregister.com**> is a site for adoptees and birth parents to register their interest in making contact. A one-off registration fee of £10 is required to place your details in the database. The UK Adoption Tracing Service has an Adoption Contact

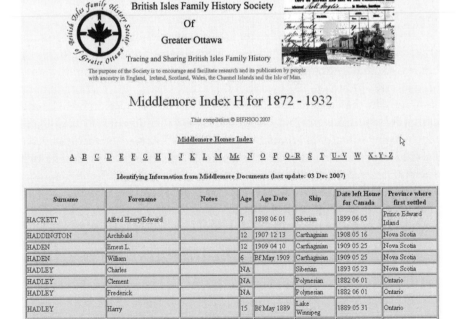

Figure 14-10 BIFHSGO index of Home Children

Register at <www.adoptiontrace.co.uk> with a £3 registration fee.

Cyndi's List has a page devoted to Adoption resources worldwide at <www.cyndislist.com/adoption.htm>, and John Fuller has an extensive list of mailing lists relating to adoption at <www.rootsweb.ancestry.com/~jfuller/gen_mail_adoption.html>, though many of these are for specific localities.

For child migration, the Department of Health has a very comprehensive leaflet 'Information for former British child migrants'. This provides information on the various agencies involved in child migration from the UK (and the relevant dates), with contact details and links to websites. Unfortunately it has a 106-character URL, so start from the DoH Publications page at <www.dh.gov.uk/en/Publicationsandstatistics/Publications> and make use of the Publications and letters library search. Alternatively follow the direct link from the website for this book. A Select Committee report from 1998 on 'The Welfare of Former British Child Migrants' at <www.parliament.the-stationery-office.co.uk/pa/cm199798/cmselect/cmhealth/755/75504.htm> provides a historical perspective.

Government sites in the receiving countries are also likely to have information relating to local records. For example, the National Archives of Australia has a factsheet on 'Child migration to Australia' at <www.naa.gov.au/about-us/publications/fact-sheets/fs124.aspx>. Library and Archives Canada has an online database of Home Children (1869-1930) at <www.collectionscanada.gc.ca/databases/home-children/>.

Child Migrants Trust is a charity which helps reunite families of former child migrants. Its website at <www.childmigrantstrust.com> provides a history of child migration and links to websites of many organizations for former child migrants. BRITISHHOMECHILDREN is a mailing list for 'anyone who has a genealogical interest in the 100,000 British Home Children who were emigrated to Canada by 50 child care organizations 1870-1948' – details at <lists.rootsweb.ancestry.com/index/intl/CAN/BRITISHHOMECHILDREN.html>. The British Isles Family History Society of Greater Ottawa has general information about Home Children and a database of child migrants 1872–1932 (see Figure 14-10).

A more general resource which may be of use is Look4them at <www.look4them.org.uk>, an umbrella site run by nine organizations involved with tracing missing people. LookUpUK at <www.lookupuk.com> is a site for tracing both missing persons and those separated by adoption, with a number of message boards and other resources.

15

GEOGRAPHY

Maps and gazetteers are essential reference tools for family historians, and while the internet cannot offer the wealth of material available in reference libraries and record offices, let alone the British Library Map Library (see p. 258), there are nonetheless many useful resources online. Historical maps are quite rare, and the web has proved an ideal medium for making them much more readily accessible, with the result that family historians are now able to make more use of them.

Good starting points for online maps and gazetteers are the 'Maps, Gazetteers & Geographical Information' page on Cyndi's List <www.cyndislist.com/maps.htm> and the Genuki county pages.

Gazetteers

While your more recent ancestors perhaps all came from places you are familiar with, the more lines you follow the more likely you are to come across somewhere you've never heard of or don't know the location of. Although your local library will have some suitable gazetteers to help you locate them, you will almost certainly find that online sources offer a much wider range of information and are, of course, much more readily to hand.

Modern

As you'd expect, one site that provides a gazetteer is the Ordnance Survey, which has a link to its place name gazetteer from the home page at <www.ordnancesurvey.co.uk>, or you can go direct to <www.ordnancesurvey.co.uk/oswebsite/freefun/didyouknow/>. This claims to have 250,000 place names. The search results will give you the county or unitary authority in which the place is located, a grid reference, latitude and longitude, with a link to the OS Get-a-map facility (see p. 245). Although the search does not allow wildcards, you can give part of the name – as little as two letters – if you're not sure of the spelling, or suspect you've got an old spelling. Obviously, the fewer letters you enter, the longer the search will take and the more results you'll need to examine. 'Place' is a very broad concept in this gazetteer – it covers not only towns and villages, but even many individual farms and named geographical features.

Given the comprehensive nature of the OS gazetteer, it might seem there would be little scope for competition. But the Gazetteer of British Place Names at <**www.gazetteer.co.uk**>, although it includes a mere 50,000 names, provides details about the present-day administrative divisions a place belongs in. It also includes 'commonly accepted spelling variations of place names including an exhaustive coverage of Welsh and Gaelic spellings'. The National Gazetteer of Wales at <**homepage.ntlworld.com/ geogdata/ngw/**> is a similar site, covering around 6,000 Welsh places, with Welsh and English names.

Although created for a very different purpose, Archaeology UK's UK Placename Finder at <**www.digital-documents.co.uk/archi/placename. htm**> may be useful. It includes around 160,000 places and provides a sophisticated search facility. Search results show counties and grid references with a link to two general mapping sites discussed below, Multimap and StreetMap.

Historical

Of course, a significant problem in using present-day gazetteers for the family historian is that the information they give may not be appropriate for earlier historical periods. In particular, the county name given for a place will be its modern administrative county, and for places now in a unitary authority or a post-1974 county a modern gazetteer will not even indicate which county a place used to be in. For this reason historical gazetteers are an essential online resource.

The most important historical gazetteer for the UK is A Vision of Britain through Time at <**www.visionofbritain.org.uk**>, which describes itself as 'A vision of Britain between 1801 and 2001. Including maps, statistical trends and historical descriptions'. The site provides many different types of material – descriptive, statistical, graphical – and will take some time to explore, but the starting point is the main page for any place. This gives a descriptive nineteenth-century gazetteer entry, and links to a collection of 'Travellers' Tales' and historical information under the title 'A vision of . . .'. The latter provides the most detailed information about the place, with sub-pages containing statistical information under headings such as population, industry, life and death, and social structure (see Figure 15-1). In many cases, there is a map showing the boundaries of the place in question.

The site has three descriptive gazetteers:

- John Marius Wilson's *Imperial Gazetteer of England & Wales* (1872)
- Frances Groome's *The Ordnance Gazetteer of Scotland* (1885)
- John Bartholomew's *Gazetteer of the British Isles* (1887)

The Bartholomew descriptions are fairly concise (particularly for smaller places), while Wilson's are more extensive. Note that the Bartholomew gazetteer includes the present-day Republic of Ireland. To access the entries from these, you need to go to the Descriptive gazetteer search at <**www. visionofbritain.org.uk/descriptions/**>.

The 'Travellers' Tales' comprise the complete texts of a dozen important works of travel literature, mainly from the nineteenth century, but including some earlier works.

The site has a useful facility to help with places: the Administrative Unit Search, which provides information on historical units of administration. For an individual village, for example, it will tell you not only which county it is (or rather was) in, but the Poor Law or Registration District, any ancient hundred it was part of, and the like. While none of this will help you locate a place on the map, it will indicate which records may have information on a place.

Genuki has a number of historical gazetteers which are likely to be useful for family history. The main Genuki Gazetteer at <**www.genuki.org.uk/big/ Gazetteer/**> is intended in the first instance to make it easier to locate the

Figure 15-1 A Vision of Britain

GENUKI
Contents

GENUKI Gazetteer

	Place name	County	Search type	
	moreton	- Any -	Complete word	New Search

County	OS Grid Ref or Lat/Lng	Gazetteer Place entry	Genuki Parish or Township
Buckinghamshire	SP706352	Maids Moreton	Maids Moreton
Berkshire	SU560904	North Moreton	North Moreton
"	SU561885	South Moreton	South Moreton
Cheshire	SJ260900	Moreton	n/k
Cornwall	SS270070	Little Moreton	Launcells
"	SS270070	Moreton	"
"	SS280080	Moreton Mill	"
"	SS270080	Moreton Pound	"
Devon	SS435263	Moreton	Bideford
Dorset	SY800890	Moreton	Moreton
Essex	TL530070	Moreton	n/k
Gloucestershire	SP200320	Moreton in Marsh	Moreton in Marsh
"	SO784094	Moreton Valence	Moreton Valence

Figure 15-2 The Genuki Gazetteer: results for 'Moreton'

appropriate page on Genuki for information about a particular place. It includes the locations of nearly all the civil parishes at the time of the start of civil registration in 1837 (which form the basis of Genuki's town and parish pages), but smaller places are gradually being added and for some counties coverage is *very* comprehensive, e.g. Cornwall with over 13,000 places. You can either view the locations of matching places on a Google map or as a list (see Figure 15-2). From the latter, you can go to a fuller gazetteer entry or the relevant Genuki parish or township page.

The Genuki Church Database at <**www.genuki.org.uk/big/churchdb/ search.html**> (see Figure 15-3) provides the locations of all churches within a given distance of a particular place (the default is three miles). Results link to the Genuki parish page, if there is one.

Genuki also has a searchable database of places in the 1891 census at <**www.genuki.org.uk/big/census_place.html**> (covering England, Wales and the Isle of Man only). The results give the county, district and sub-district, as well as the piece number and the LDS microfilm number. There is a limited wildcard facility, in that you can truncate a name to as little as the first four letters. If you type in the name of a district or sub-district, you get a list of all the places it comprises, with their piece numbers.

Another useful tool is Darren Wheatley's Parish Finder at <**www. parishfinder.co.uk**>. This allows you not only to search for the county and grid reference for any parish, but you can also search for neighbouring parishes and discover the distances between parishes.

Scotland

While Scotland is included in many of the gazetteers already mentioned, there is also a major project for a specifically Scottish gazetteer based at the University of Edinburgh and accessible at <**www.geo.ed.ac.uk/scotgaz/**>, the Gazetteer for Scotland, which is described as 'a vast database of information on places, people and families in Scotland'. Although there is a 'place search', this cannot actually be used to find towns and villages. Instead you need to use the 'any words' search at <**www.geo.ed.ac.uk/scotgaz/Anyword.html**>, and select parishes and settlements – or you could even try Attractions, Council Areas, Families, Famous People, Geographical Features or Historical Counties. This takes you to a descriptive entry for the place with details of location, and a link to a very schematic county map, though no grid reference is given. The site includes many entries from Groome's *Ordnance Gazetteer for Scotland* (1882–85) – a 'quill and parchment' icon on a place entry indicates a link to an extract from Groome.

Ireland

For Ireland, there are a number of online sources to help you locate historical places. The National Archives of Ireland has an OS Parish List Index at <**www.nationalarchives.ie/search/index.php?category=17&subcategory=145**> (or go to the Finding Aids page at <**www.nationalarchives.ie/search/databases.html**> and follow the Ordnance Survey link). The Irish Times' Irish

Figure 15-3 The Genuki Church Database: Moreton, Cheshire

Ancestors site has a place name search at <**scripts.ireland.com/ancestor/ placenames/**>. The IreAtlas at <**www.seanruad.com**> is a database of all Irish townlands, with details of the county and civil parish. It does not give map references. Irish Ancestries has an Irish Placename Finder at <**www. irishancestries.com/databases/irish-townlands.php**>.

The Public Record Office of Northern Ireland has a 'Geographical Index of Northern Ireland' at <**www.proni.gov.uk/index/local_history/ geographical_index.htm**>, which lists counties, baronies, Poor Law Unions, dioceses, parishes and townlands in the six counties. The index is only browsable, not searchable, but there are several different routes through the material to help you find a specific place. However, I couldn't find any way of getting a single listing of all the places with a particular name.

The Placenames Database of Ireland <**www.logainm.ie**> gives both the Irish and English names of a place, along with the coordinates and the administrative units into which a place falls. For larger places, street names are included, and the database also covers topographical features such as islands and valleys. Coordinates use the the Irish National Grid, which is explained briefly on Wikipedia at <**en.wikipedia.org/wiki/Irish_national_ grid_reference_system**>, and this page has links to more detailed information.

Library Ireland has a transcription of Samuel Lewis's 1837 *Topographical Dictionary of Ireland* at <**www.libraryireland.com/topog/**>.

With the exception of the 'Geographical Index of Northern Ireland', all these resources cover the whole island of Ireland.

Counties and towns

As well as these national gazetteers, there are many resources for counties and larger towns. It is not possible here to give a comprehensive listing – the easiest way to find them is to go to the Genuki page for the relevant county at <**www.genuki.org.uk/big/**>. A number of local government sites provide gazetteers of their area, for example:

- Gazetteer of Greater Manchester Placenames at <**www.manchester2002-uk.com/towns/gazetteer1.html**>
- Devon Library Services' Historic Devon Gazetteer at <**www.devon.gov. uk/localstudies/100169/1.html**>
- The North West Kent Family History Society's West Kent Parish Gazetteer at <**www.nwkfhs.org.uk/parindex.htm**>
- Clare County Library's transcription of the entries for Clare places in the *Parliamentary Gazetteer of Ireland, 1845* at <**www.clarelibrary.ie/eolas/ coclare/history/parliamentary_gazeteer_1845.htm**>

There are also many small-scale scans and transcriptions for individual places of material from historical gazetteers. If there is a Genuki page for a particular town or village, it will normally start with a brief description taken from a nineteenth-century source. Trade directories, discussed on p. 179, will also give the location of a place and other information.

For London, see p. 253.

Administrative geography

All towns and villages in the British Isles have a place in the administrative geography of the constituent counties, and this has not necessarily remained constant over the last few hundred years. A number of the gazetteers already mentioned include information on the administrative units to which towns and villages belong, most notably A Vision of Britain (p. 238). But there are also some resources specifically devoted to this issue, which is important because it has a bearing on where records are likely to be found.

Genuki provides a general overview of Administrative Regions and, as well as pages for the individual counties, has material on 'Local Government Changes in the United Kingdom' at <**www.genuki.org.uk/big/Regions/ UKchanges.html**> with detailed tables for England, Wales, Scotland and Northern Ireland. The situation in the Republic of Ireland is more straightforward as the pre-independence counties remain. The Gazetteer of British Place Names, mentioned above, has maps of the old counties as well as the new counties and unitary authorities at <**www.gazetteer.co.uk**>. It is also well worth looking at their 'Additional notes for historians and genealogists' at <**www.gazetteer.co.uk/section4.htm**>, which explains the difference between the historic counties, the 'registration counties' used by the GRO, and the nineteenth- and twentieth-century administrative counties and county boroughs.

Genuki has maps of the counties of England, Wales and Scotland at <**www.genuki.org.uk/big/Britain.html**> and of Ireland at <**www.genuki. org.uk/big/Ireland.html**>. Each Genuki county page also has a description of the county, usually drawn from a nineteenth-century directory.

If you are from outside the UK and are not familiar with the counties and other administrative divisions you will find Jim Fisher's page 'British Counties, Parishes, etc. for Genealogists' at <**homepages.nildram.co. uk/~jimella/counties.htm**> useful.

Where counties have changed their boundaries over the years, the individual Genuki county pages will provide relevant details. The complex set of changes which, in less than a hundred years, saw parts of the home counties, and indeed the whole of Middlesex, incorporated into the capital are dealt with on the Genuki London site at <**homepages.gold.ac.uk/genuki/ LND/parishes.html**>.

Genealogists almost always refer to pre-1974 counties and any genealogical material on the internet is likely to reflect that. This is why there are no pages on Genuki for Tyne and Wear or the present-day divisions of Wales. But non-genealogical sites will tend to locate places in their current counties, even if the material is from the nineteenth century – a number of the sites with photographs discussed in Chapter 17 do this, for example.

Counties are often referred to by three-letter abbreviations, the Chapman County Codes, e.g. SFK for Suffolk. A list of these can be found on Genuki at <**www.genuki.org.uk/big/Regions/Codes.html**>. There is a brief account by Colin Chapman of the origin of the codes at <**www.lochinpublishing. org.uk/chapman_cc.htm**>.

Overseas

Gazetteers may be even more important if you have ancestors who migrated. It is not possible here to cover individual countries outside the British Isles, but there are a number of places to look. As you would expect, Cyndi's List has links to many online gazetteers. They are included in the 'Maps, Gazetteers & Geographical Information' page at <**www.cyndislist. com/maps.htm**> under two distinct headings: 'Historical Maps, Atlases & Gazetteers' and 'National Gazetteers & Geographic Information', of which the latter has the most useful entries.

The National Library of Australia has a useful page devoted to 'Gazetteers of the World and Beyond' at <**www.nla.gov.au/map/worldgazetteers.html**> (the 'Beyond' indicates the inclusion of a planetary gazetteer). This page has not only links to online sources, but details of a number of gazetteers available in print and on CD-ROM.

The most comprehensive world gazetteer is the Getty Thesaurus of Geographic Names Online at <**www.getty.edu/research/conducting_ research/vocabularies/tgn/**>. Even for the UK this is useful, since it includes geographical, and some historical, information. However, it is not intended to be comprehensive, and concentrates on larger places. For example, it gives only one place in Ireland called Inch, while the Irish Ancestors site (see p. 241) lists a dozen.

If these resources fail to find your place, it is worth checking Wikipedia at <**en.wikipedia.org**>, which has many articles on individual places all over the world, and not just the major towns and cities. Otherwise, see whether there is a mailing list devoted to the country you are interested in – listed by John Fuller at <**www.rootsweb.ancestry.com/~jfuller/gen_mail. html**> – and post a query. There will almost certainly be people on the list with suitable reference works to hand or even local knowledge.

Modern maps

As with gazetteers, the OS website at <**www.ordnancesurvey.co.uk**> is the obvious starting point for any information about present-day mapping of the British Isles. This provides a facility called Get-a-map at <**www. getamap.co.uk**>, which allows you to call up a map centred on a particular place. You can search by place name, postcode, or OS grid reference. Alternatively, you can just click on the map of the UK and gradually zoom in to your chosen area. The maps are free for personal use (including limited use on personal websites). There is also an option to go to the nineteenth-century OS maps discussed in 'Historical maps', below.

A relatively unknown source of OS maps for England is the MAGIC (Multi-Agency Geographic Information for the Countryside) site at <**www. magic.gov.uk**>, shown in Figure 15-5. The site is designed to provide information for countryside management, shown in a number of layers, over a base map, which is a monochrome modern OS map. MAGIC has a number of advantages over the Get-a-map service. The first is that you can get a much higher level of detail – the Get-a-map site has a maximum scale of 1:25,000, while MAGIC allows you to go up to 1:101.[8] Also, it shows a much larger area: a rectangle 6x4km, compared with a 2km square in Get-a-map. The only disadvantage of the site is that the maps can be quite slow to load.

Another useful feature of MAGIC is that it shows modern civil parish boundaries. While it is true that in urban areas these won't match historical ecclesiastical boundaries, for rural areas the site provides the closest thing we have to an online parish map. Because this site is designed for specialist use, it is more complex to use than those designed for the general public. To access the maps, from the home page you need to choose Interactive Map, then choose Administrative Areas from the top field, and enter a place, postcode or grid reference in the lower. There are many options once you are viewing a map. A Map Tools tab gives access to a range of tools, including the ability to identify an area, and to save a map as a GIF file. You can also bookmark the current view.

There are five main sites that provide free UK street maps. Streetmap at <**www.streetmap.co.uk**> allows searches by street, postcode, place name, OS grid, Landranger grid, latitude/longitude or telephone code. Multimap at <**www.multimap.com**> offers similar facilities: the initial search option offers place or postcode, while the advanced search includes building and street. Google Maps launched a UK map site in spring 2005 at <**maps. google.co.uk**>, though this shows only streets, and doesn't indicate even

---

8   The British Library has a useful page showing different map scales at <**www.bl.uk/ reshelp/findhelprestype/maps/mapscales/mapscales.html**>.

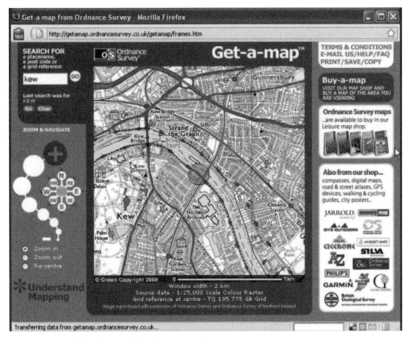

Figure 15-4 The National Archives in Get-a-map

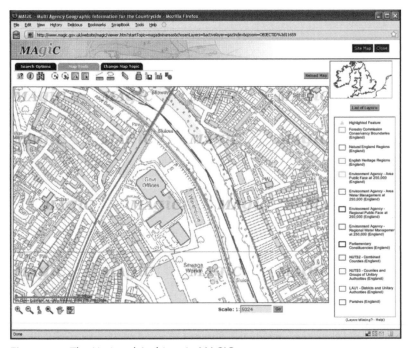

Figure 15-5 The National Archives in MAGIC

quite major landmarks (e.g. Canterbury Cathedral, Stonehenge). It is less well known that 192.com provides also street maps in addition to its directory service at <**www.192.com/maps**>. OpenStreetMap at <**www.openstreet map.org**> is a non-commercial collaborative street mapping site, which includes not only street names, but also the names and locations of buildings like churches and pubs.

Genuki has instructions on 'How to find a present day house, street or place in the U.K. (or to find only the Post Code)' by using the Royal Mail site or the Multimap site at <**www.genuki.org.uk/big/ModernLocations.html**>.

For aerial photographs, there are two main options. Multimap provides photographs which, for the most populous parts of the country, are at a high level of detail. There is also an option for a 'Bird's Eye' view (see Figure 15-6), which allows you to see the facades of individual buildings.

Google Maps has a satellite mapping option covering the whole country (and indeed the whole world), though resolution varies from area to area. There are various levels of zoom, options to rotate and tilt the images, and very quick panning. The same images can be viewed in Google Earth, a free downloadable viewer for satellite maps at <**earth.google.com**>. This has the advantage of an overlay showing roads and street names. It also offers a 'placemark' facility so that you can keep a permanent marker for places you want to view again. Because of the amount of data transferred, Google Earth requires a broadband connection and a fairly recent Windows PC. With an older machine you will need to check whether your graphics card is supported before downloading.

At the start of 2008, 192.com added aerial photographs for London to its mapping facility at <**www.192.com/maps/**>. To access them, you need to zoom in so that the scale at the bottom of the image indicates not more than 100 metres and then click on the 'Super Zoom' button on the left-hand edge of the image.

Historical Aerial Photography at <**www.oldaerialphotos.com**> is a commercial site offering aerial photographs for sale. Unfortunately, the site does not offer any preview – you have to select the location you want using a Multimap street map and order on that basis, though there are samples to let you judge scale and resolution. Photographs are supplied either as prints or as digital images on CD in TIFF format. The site also includes a note, 'We also have photography from the 1940s and other decades for this area that are not yet available to search online'.

A similar service is offered by UK Aerial Photos at <**www.ukaerial photos.com**>, which includes aerial photos from the 1940s as well as from recent years. The photographs are JPEG images, which are sent by email. This site does offer a preview of the photo.

Figure 15-6 Multimap: Bird's Eye view of Cambridge Market

Historical maps

The best-known site for historical maps is Old-maps at <**www.old-maps. co.uk**>. This is a free site, run by a commercial mapping company, which has scans of the First Series of 6-inch Ordnance Survey maps of England, Wales and Scotland. These maps date from the latter half of the nineteenth century.

You can either do a place name search to locate the map for the area you are interested in, or use the county gazetteer to select from a list. The initial map image that comes up when you select a place is too small for you to see any but the most obvious geographical detail, but once you zoom in, the resolution is generally sufficient to read small text. In all but the most heavily built up areas, individual buildings and plots of land can be made out clearly. However, while the resolution is good, the scans are black and white rather than greyscale, which tends to give poor results where the original has shading or where text is overlaid on map detail ('old-maps' is overprinted in blue on all the maps).

Apart from the main map from the First Series, there are also later OS maps going up to the 1930s, which will allow you to look for later features and trace the development of a locality. You cannot download any of the maps, though of course you can take a screenshot, and the maps are available for purchase.

Another site with nineteenth-century Ordnance Survey maps is the London Ancestor's collection of maps from the report of the 1885 Boundary Commission, which includes Ireland (Old-maps does not). All are linked from the home page at <**www.londonancestor.com**>. For Wales and Scotland, only a selection of counties and towns is included. Because these maps have been scanned as greyscale images, they are generally preferable to the scans on Old-maps when looking at urban areas. However, since the aim of these maps was to show the names and boundaries of electoral divisions, detail is sometimes obscured by overwritten text or hand-drawn lines. Figure 15-7 offers a comparison using the area around Trafalgar Square: on the left is the black and white scan at Old-maps, while on the right is the same area in greyscale on the London Ancestors' site.

The Boundary Commission county maps are at a smaller scale and therefore less detailed than the 6-inch maps on Old-maps, which means they are less good for rural areas, though they do have the advantage of showing parish boundaries very clearly.

Another source for OS maps is British History Online (see p. 261), which has 1-inch maps for the whole of Great Britain and 6-inch maps for around 20 major cities at <**www.british-history.ac.uk/map.aspx**>. You can search by place name or postcode, though the latter option didn't seem to be working when I tried it.

Many individuals have scanned classic historical maps and map editions. The most extensive volunteer-run site is Genmaps at <**freepages.genealogy. rootsweb.ancestry.com/~genmaps/**>, which covers England, Wales and Scotland, with an enormous collection of maps for the counties, as well as many for individual towns and cities. The site doesn't give a figure for the total number of maps available, but it must be a couple of thousand – there are 350 just for Yorkshire, and even Rutland is represented by 40 maps. Genmaps also has an extensive collection of links to other historical map

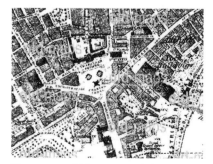

Figure 15-7 Old-maps and the Boundary Commission maps compared

sites, including those of several dozen commercial map dealers, many of whom have low-resolution scans on their sites. However, it looks like these links have not been checked for some time, as quite a few of them are dead.

Other personal projects include Tom Arnold's scans of Samuel Lewis' county maps of Wales and Ireland dating from around 1840. These are linked from <**homepage.ntlworld.com/tomals/index2.htm**>. John Speed's early seventeenth-century maps of around 30 English towns and cities (plus Edinburgh) have been digitized by Professor Maryanne Horowitz of Occidental College, Los Angeles ,and are available at <**faculty.oxy.edu/ horowitz/home/johnspeed/**>. Maproom.org has maps from Cary's *Traveller's Companion* of 1790, showing main roads and distances, at very high resolution at <**www.maproom.org/00/07/**>.

There are also maps from some more modern printed works which are likely to be of interest. For example, Alan Gresley has scanned the town plans from the 1910 edition of Baedeker's *Great Britain Handbook for Travelers* at <**contueor.com/baedeker/great_britain/**>.

Your Maps Online at <**www.yourbooksonline.co.uk**> used to be a free site, but now requires a £12.99 annual subscription, though there is also a £3.99 'low resolution tariff'. The site currently boasts over 500 maps. Many of these have been scanned at very high resolution, and are therefore excellent quality, though you need to be prepared for some long downloads if you have a dialup connection. You can get an overview of what's available by following the 'Take the Tour' link on the home page.

Mapseeker is a commercial site with a collection of historical maps under the heading 'Genealogy Map Resources' at <**www.mapseeker.co.uk/ genealogy/**>. Particularly useful are the city maps for Birmingham, Edinburgh, Liverpool and Manchester. There are good-quality scans of a section of maps viewable free of charge, and many more are available for purchase.

There is no online map collection from the British Library, though the BL's Images Online website at <**www.imagesonline.bl.uk**> includes some digitized maps. These can be found by selecting the 'Maps and Lanscapes' link from the Subject Index.

The National Library of Wales' 'Digital Mirror' has maps from Thomas Taylor's 1718 work *The Principality of Wales exactly described*, the first atlas of Wales, at <**www.llgc.org.uk/index.php?id=132**>.

Another source for historical maps online may be the sites of commercial map-dealers, many of whose websites have scans of the maps they have for sale. For example, Heritage Publishing at <**www.heritagepublishing. com**> has scans of some of John Speed's 1610 maps of the British counties. It is well worth using a search engine to locate sites which have the phrase 'antique maps' and the town or county of your choice.

Local projects

In addition to the sections for individual counties on Genmaps and Your Maps Online, there are many sites with map collections for individual counties and towns.

The University of Portsmouth's Geography department hosts two county collections, each with a very comprehensive range of historical county maps going back to the sixteenth century:

- Old Hampshire Mapped at <www.geog.port.ac.uk/webmap/hantsmap/hantsmap/hantsmap.htm>
- Old Sussex Mapped at <www.envf.port.ac.uk/geo/research/historical/webmap/sussexmap/sussex.html>

For County Durham, Pictures in Print at <www.dur.ac.uk/picturesinprint/> is a collaborative project between the British Library and the various holders of map archives in Durham to produce an online catalogue for the maps of the county along with digital images (see Figure 15-8). To view the images, you will need to download a plug-in.[9] There are several different search categories, of which the place search is likely to be the most useful. The subject search is also useful, though it is better to select from the list of subject index terms rather than try to guess the subject headings.

Tomorrow's History at <www.tomorrows-history.com> is a local history site for the North East of England, with a map viewing system which allows you to compare maps from any two periods since the mid-nineteenth century.

Here's History Kent at <www.hereshistorykent.org.uk> has maps of historic towns with historical areas and buildings marked on an overlay over the OS map or an aerial view – search for a town then select 'GIS Mapping' from the sidebar.

Lancashire has a wide selection of OS maps for the county at a variety of scales at <www.lancashire.gov.uk/environment/oldmap/>, covering the period from the First Series up to the 1950s, along with some older county maps.

For Cornwall, A Cornish Sourcebook has around 30 maps of the county dating from 1654 at <cornovia.org.uk/maps/>.

A particularly good site is Cheshire's E-mapping Victorian Cheshire at <maps.cheshire.gov.uk/tithemaps/TwinMaps.aspx>, which allows you to compare a nineteenth-century map of an area (including the 1840s tithe

---

9   The plug-in downloads automatically for Internet Explorer, but may need to be manually installed for other browsers.

Title:	Plan & section of the Clarence rail way from the River Tees near Haverton Hill in the parish of Billingham to Simpasture farm in the parish of Heighington as set out to be made under an act of Parliament of the 9th of Geo. IVth. Together with the proposed alterations amendments and extensions also the additional branches therein & therefrom all in the county of Durham
Creator:	Ducote, A.
Date:	[1829?]
Contents description: includes sections of the line and branches	
Retrieve full record	

Title:	Durham
Creator:	Rowe, Robert, 1775-1843
Date:	[1830]
Contents description: map of Durham county. County boundary, wards, seats of the nobility and gentry, and mail coach roads coloured. Shows railways. Indicates the distance from London to principal towns, and the distances between market towns within the county. Text on map: 'some detached parts of the county of Durham are situate in Northumberland, too far north to be inserted in this map. -See the map of Northumberland'. From Teesdale's New British atlas... revised and corrected... (London, 1830) Revised ed. of Rowe's 1813 map but with all reference to Rowe erased, additional roads, railways, and asterisks denoting parliamentary representation added, and other changes. Watermark is 1830.	
Retrieve full record	

Title:	Durham
Creator:	*Creator not certain*
Date:	[183?]
Contents description: map of Durham county with the county boundary and mail roads coloured. Also shows lead mines in Weardale and coal pits near Gateshead and Whickham. Indicates Darlington-Stockton railway, and the Breckon Hill to Billingham line. Possible variant and updated version of the original map published in J. Pigot and Co.'s British Atlas (London, Manchester, 1831). Evidence from the indications of railway development shown on this map dates it to the latter part of 1838 (see record no. 532).	

Figure 15-8 Catalogue entries for railway maps from Pictures in Print

maps) with a modern map. Figure 15-9 shows the village of Newton, now part of Chester, in the tithe and modern maps. (Since tithe maps are primary sources for genealogists they are discussed in more detail in Chapter 8 on p. 121)

Parish maps

Maps of the ancient ecclesiastical parishes are among the most useful for the family historian. Of the national collections, the London Ancestor's Boundary Commission maps and MAGIC show more recent parish boundaries, but there is no guarantee that these match the older boundaries.

The definitive parish maps for an older period are those published in *Historic Parishes of England & Wales*, details of which are given on the University of Exeter site at <**sogaer.exeter.ac.uk/geography/research/ historical/historic_parishes.shtml**>. These maps used to be available on CD, though this service has been discontinued. However, Higher and Further Education users can download copies of the maps from the AHDS History site at <**ahds.ac.uk/history/collections/hpew.htm**>. The reason for mentioning them here is that the authors, Roger Kain and Richard Oliver, allow the maps to be published online, and you will find a number of them

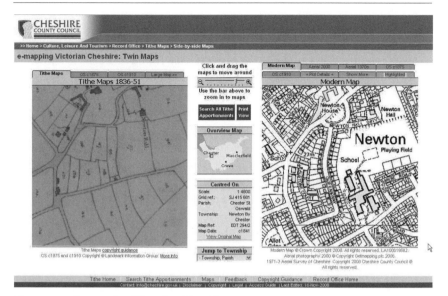

Figure 15-9 E-mapping Victorian Cheshire

available on Genuki parish pages, such as Brian Randell's pages for Devon parishes at <**www.cs.ncl.ac.uk/genuki/DEV/indexpars.html**> and my own for Sussex at <**homepages.gold.ac.uk/genuki/SSX/parishes.html**>.

For many parishes, you will find a map of the historical boundaries on A Vision of Britain (p. 238).

If you just need to see the location of a parish relative to the surrounding area, many Genuki county pages have a map showing the parishes within the county. Also, most family history societies have a map on their website showing the location of the parishes for their area. Look at Genuki's list of FHSs at <**www.genuki.org.uk/Societies/**>.

London

There is an enormous wealth of online maps for London, many of which show individual streets. Genmaps has scans of over 170 historical maps, plans and panoramas of London at <**freepages.genealogy.rootsweb. ancestry.com/~genmaps/genfiles/COU_Pages/ENG_pages/lon.htm**> from the 1560s to 1920, including John Roque's detailed 24-sheet map of 1746 and many plans of City wards. The site also has many county maps for Middlesex, though these are mostly not at the same level of detail.

The Collage server at <**collage.cityoflondon.gov.uk**> includes many maps and plans among its 20,000 or so images, mainly drawn from the Guildhall Library's Print Room. Particularly useful is the place search, which links to plans of individual City wards and parishes. There are also many views of individual streets, as well as insurance plans showing the locations of individual buildings. High resolution digital files of the images can be purchased online.

If you are trying to find a London street mentioned in a census which no longer appears on the A–Z, the Lost London Streets site will be worth looking at. This gives an A–Z reference with details of what happened to the street. It covers over 3,500 streets that have undergone a name change or have disappeared altogether over the last 200 years. Unfortunately the original site was closed down a few years ago, but a copy of all the pages as of August 2005 is available at the Internet Archive: go to <**www.archive. org**> and enter the URL **members.aol.com/WHall95037/london.html**. Alternatively, use the direct link from the website for this book.

GenDocs' Victorian London Street index will be found at <**homepage. ntlworld.com/hitch/gendocs/lon-str.html**>. For over 61,000 streets this gives a postal district or locality and metropolitan borough, but no more precise location. For an earlier period, The London Ancestor has a street index to W. Stow's 1722 *Remarks on London: Being an Exact Survey of the Cities of London and Westminster…* at <**www.londonancestor.com/stow/ stow-strx-all.htm**>.

UCLA's Department of Epidemiology has an area of its website at <**www. ph.ucla.edu/epi/snow.html**> devoted to John Snow, one of the founders of the subject, and this includes a number of London maps from the mid-nineteenth century. These have been scanned at very high resolution and are of exceptional quality, as you can see from Figure 15-10, which shows Charing Cross in 1818, before the development of Trafalgar Square.

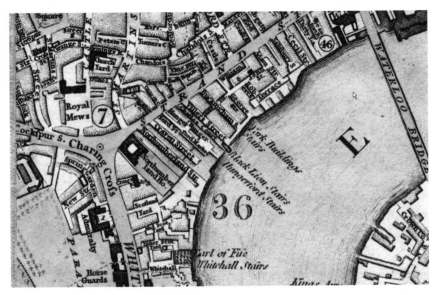

Figure 15-10 Map of London in 1818 from the UCLA Department of Epidemiology

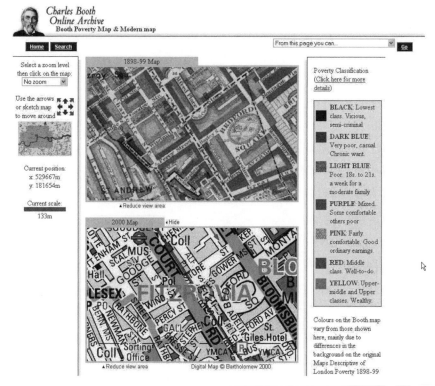

Figure 15-11 Charles Booth Online Archive, Booth Map & Modern Map

MOTCO has historical maps and panoramas of London from 1705 onwards at <www.motco.com/map/>. Some maps have place indexes – for example Stanford's 1862 Library Map of London and its Suburbs has an index to around 5,000 streets, with a link to the relevant portion of the map.

One of the most famous London maps, Charles Booth's 1889 Map of London Poverty, is available on the LSE's Charles Booth site at <**booth.lse. ac.uk**>, which shows Booth's original map against a modern one (Figure 15-11).

Other sites with London maps include:

- Old London Maps at <**www.oldlondonmaps.com**>
- Maps of London at <**www.maps-of-london.com**>
- MAPCO (Map and Plan Collection Online) at <**archivemaps.com/ mapco/london.htm**>

Scotland

Scotland is particularly well served by historical map digitization projects, and there are two outstanding sites for maps of the country.

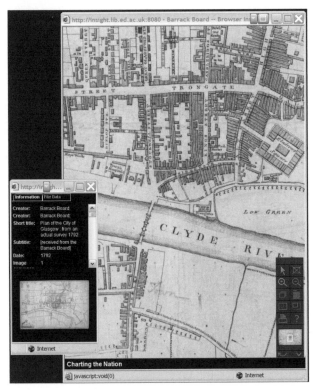

Figure 15-12 A 1792 plan of Glasgow from Charting the Nation

Charting the Nation at <**www.chartingthenation.lib.ed.ac.uk**> is run by the University of Edinburgh Library and has maps for the period 1550–1740. (In fact, there are some later maps, as the site includes The Board of Ordnance collection of military maps and architectural plans dating from around 1690 to about 1820.) While some of the maps are at too large a scale to be of any genealogical utility, there are others, such as the 1792 map of Glasgow (Figure 15-12), which are detailed enough to show individual streets and buildings. Unlike most map sites, rather than selecting a map and then having to load a map viewer, here you start the map viewer first and then select which map you want to look at. There are two different viewers, the second and more sophisticated of which requires the download and installation of a plug-in. The basic viewer can be slightly confusing at first, as it uses several different windows. It also requires your browser to have any pop-up blocker disabled – consult your browser's online help to find out how to do this.

The other major site for Scottish maps is that of the National Library of Scotland, which has over 6,000 maps in its Digital Library at <**www.nls. uk/maps/**>, including:

- Maps of the whole of Scotland 1560–1928 (around 1,300 maps)
- County maps of Scotland, 1580–1928
- Military Maps of Scotland, eighteenth century
- Ordnance Survey maps, 1847–1930
- Ordnance Survey town plans, 1847–1895

To view many of the maps requires a plug-in (called ExpressView), which you will need to download.

The OS town plans are probably the most useful to the family historians, covering 62 towns in over 1,900 sheets at an extraordinary level of detail. The quality of the scans is excellent. Other notable items include Bartholomew's 1912 *Survey Atlas of Scotland*.

Maps of the Scottish clans are discussed on p. 230.

Ireland

Probably the most useful set of maps of Ireland for the genealogist are the Boundary Commission county maps on the London Ancestor site at <**www. londonancestor.com/maps/maps-ireland.htm**>. For Counties Roscommon and Leitrim, there is a very comprehensive set of maps showing Roman Catholic and civil parishes, as well as Poor Law Unions, at <**www.leitrim-roscommon.com/LR_maps.html**>.

The University of Wisconsin-Madison has some maps of Ireland, including a Poor Law map, at <**history.wisc.edu/archdeacon/famine/map. html**>. The Perry-Castañeda Library has a 1610 town plan of Dublin at <**www.lib.utexas.edu/maps/historical/dublin_1610_1896.jpg**>.

University College Cork has a collection of Irish county maps at <**www. ucc.ie/celt/mapsireland.html**>, taken from an 1881 atlas.

Irish Townland Maps at <**www.pasthomes.com**> is a commercial site offering maps of Irish townlands from the 1830s. An annual subscription costs $25, which allows you to browse the site, and you can then purchase maps at two different resolutions. Maps are provided in PDF format, and two sample maps show the size and resolution available.

Map collections

For guides to archival map collections, the British Cartographic Society's 'A Directory of UK Map Collections' at <**www.cartography.org.uk/default. asp?contentID=705**> is a very comprehensive starting point. This is part of the site's 'Map Curators Toolbox' [*sic*], which contains much useful information about maps and mapping. The Toolbox home page is <**www. cartography.org.uk/default.asp?contentID=64**> (there seems to be no link to this from the BCS home page).

The catalogues of the archives and libraries mentioned in Chapter 13 include map holdings. The National Archives has a research guide 'Maps in the Public Record Office', linked from <**www.nationalarchives.gov.uk/ catalogue/researchguidesindex.asp**>.

The national libraries all have significant map collections which are described on their websites:

- British Library <**www.bl.uk/reshelp/bldept/maps/maplibover/ mapliboverview.html**>
- National Library of Scotland <**www.nls.uk/collections/maps/**>
- National Library of Wales <**www.llgc.org.uk/index.php?id=collections02**>.
- National Library of Ireland <**www.nli.ie/en/printed-maps-introduction. aspx**>

Finding maps

Of course, there are many more maps online than it has been possible to mention here, particularly for local areas. Some of the larger sites mentioned have good collections of links, but there are two other obvious places to look for links to other online maps. First, the Genuki page for a county or parish (start from <**www.genuki.org.uk/big/**>) should have a range of links to relevant maps, and some of the parish pages have a map of the parish.

For older maps on a worldwide basis, probably the best starting point is the Map History gateway at <**www.maphistory.info/webimages.html**>, maintained by Tony Campbell, former Map Librarian of the British Library. The Europe page at <**www.maphistory.info/imagebi.html**> has links to over 60 sites with individual maps or map collections for the British Isles.

ABCgenealogy has a number of links to a number of maps and map collections for the UK and Ireland at <**www.abcgenealogy.com/Maps/ Europe/**>.

For map collections of local coverage it will always be worth checking the websites of the relevant record offices, whose online catalogues are also good places to start looking for details of the maps which aren't online.

Interactive mapping

One upshot of the increasing range of interactive facilities online is that it is now possible to have customized maps identifying places relevant to your family tree. Google, in particular, allows web designers to take a map from Google Maps and plot particular locations on it from a data source. You can see some of the possibilities from the Genuki gazetteer (p. 239), with its 'plot places on a map option' and from Nations' Memorybank (Figure 17-10), which uses this feature to indicate the location of a photograph.

Obviously setting this up on a website of your own requires considerable technical knowledge, but MapYourAncestors at <**www.mapyourancestors.**

com> is a free service which enables you to plot the locations of your ancestors' dwellings or events in their lives on a Google map. Putting these locations in a sequence makes it possible to follow the travels or migrations revealed by records. The site is rather short on documentation, but there is an article about it by Dick Eastman at <**blog.eogn.com/eastmans_online_genealogy/2007/07/map-your-ancest.html**>.

The similarly named Map My Ancestors is a piece of software designed to provide a similar function for anyone using Google Earth (see p. 247). The program costs £10 to download from <**www.familytreeassistant.com**>, but there is also a free trial version, and there are examples on the site of what the program does.

16

HISTORY

While family history is concerned mainly with individual ancestors, their lives and the documents that record them cannot be understood without a broader historical appreciation of the times in which they lived. The aim of this chapter is to look at some of the general historical material on the internet that is likely to be of use to family historians.

General resources

There are, of course, many resources online relating to particular aspects of British and Irish history, but it is mainly those covering local and social history which are most likely to be of use to the family historian. Even so, the material online is as nothing to the immense body of print publications on the subject. A good guide to this material is the Royal Historical Society Bibliography at <**www.rhs.ac.uk/bibl/bibwel.asp**>. Designed as an 'authoritative guide to what has been written about British and Irish history from the Roman period to the present day', it has over 450,000 entries. Particularly useful for family historians are the county listings for all parts of the British Isles.

Intute (see p. 26) is probably the best general gateway to historical resources online. Its 'History' page at <**www.intute.ac.uk/artsandhumanities/history/**> has a wide range of subheadings, many of which are not relevant to genealogical interests, but the following sections are likely to include interesting resources:

- Agricultural/Rural History
- Archives
- Ecclesiastical/Church History
- Family History
- Historical Geography
- Imperial and Colonial History
- Local/Regional History
- Maritime/Naval History
- Military History/Wars and Conflicts

- Oral History
- Palaeography
- Population/Environment History
- Social History

▌ Local history

For introductory material on local history the Local History page on the BBC History site at <www.bbc.co.uk/history/trail/local_history/> is a good starting point. As well as describing what is involved in local history, it looks at how to approach the history of a factory, a landscape and a village, by way of example. The National Archives' site has a local history section at <www.nationalarchives.gov.uk/localhistory/> with introductory material and an in-depth guide to the relevant national records.

If you want guidance on where to find information and sources, then the 'Getting Started' page on the *Local History Magazine* website at <www.local-history.co.uk/gettingstarted.html> will prove useful. Sites with information on repositories which hold sources for local history are covered in Chapter 13.

It would be unrealistic to expect much of the printed material on local history to be available online, but the *Victoria County History* (VCH) at <www.victoriacountyhistory.ac.uk> has a lottery-funded project to create an online edition. This project is still in the early stages – there are 16 county websites with varying amounts of material, all linked from the map on the home page. Where material is online it is in fact hosted by British History Online at <www.british-history.ac.uk>, the site run by the University of London's Institute of Historical Research, As well as the VCH, this has an increasing number of other local history sources. Many of the older volumes of the VCH are available in the Internet Archive at <www.archive.org/details/texts/>.

Chris Phillips, who runs the very useful Medieval English Genealogy site at <www.medievalgenealogy.org.uk>, has compiled an index to place names mentioned in the titles of topographical articles in the published volumes of the VCH. This can be found at <www.medievalgenealogy.org.uk/vch/>. His page for the individual VCH counties link to online editions if available.

For Scotland, the *Statistical Accounts of Scotland* at <edina.ac.uk/statacc/> are a major source. These accounts are descriptive rather than financial and were published in two sets of volumes, one dating from the 1790s and the other from the 1830. There is a chapter devoted to every parish, each compiled by the local minister, and they offer 'a rich record of a wide variety of topics: wealth, class and poverty; climate, agriculture, fishing and wildlife; population, schools, and the moral health of the people'.

There is an increasing amount of material online for individual cities, towns and villages. County record offices are among those exploiting the web to publish online resources for local history, and there are a number of lottery-funded projects to put local history material online. Most larger cities have substantial historical material on their websites. Some of the more notable sites are:

- PortCities <www.portcities.org.uk> (ports of Bristol, Hartlepool, Liverpool, London, Southampton)
- Tomorrow's History <www.tomorrows-history.com> (North East of England)
- Knowsley (Lancs) Local History <history.knowsley.gov.uk>
- Digital Handsworth <www.digitalhandsworth.org.uk>
- Wiltshire Community History <www.wiltshire.gov.uk/community/>
- The Kingston Local History project at <fass.kingston.ac.uk/research/local-history/projects/klhp/> (Kingston-on-Thames)
- Recording Uttlesford History <www.recordinguttlesfordhistory.org.uk>
- The Gaelic Village <www.ambaile.org.uk/en/> (Scottish Highlands and Islands)
- TheGlasgowStory <www.theglasgowstory.com>
- Gathering the Jewels <www.gtj.org.uk> (Wales)
- Powys Heritage Online <history.powys.org.uk>

Some of these have online data as well as general historical material. The photographic collections mentioned on p. 281 are also useful for local history.

It is also well worth checking the website of the Local Heritage Initiative at <www.lhi.org.uk>. This programme was launched in 2000 to 'help communities bring their local heritage to life', and the clickable map on the home page leads to a list of projects for the selected region.

There are many sites with small data extracts for local areas, often a single parish, examples of which will be found in Chapter 8. But a more comprehensive approach is represented by the Online Parish Clerk (OPC) schemes. Each county scheme has volunteers transcribing historical records for individual parishes. So far, there are schemes for Cornwall, Cumberland & Westmorland, Devon, Dorset, Hampshire, Kent, Lancashire, Somerset, Sussex and Wiltshire. Links to the websites of these projects, which will link in turn to the pages for individual parishes, will be found on Genuki's OPC page at <www.genuki.org.uk/indexes/OPC.html>. Many Genuki county and parish pages themselves include descriptive extracts from historical directories and have links to other local transcriptions.

One often overlooked aspect of history which influenced our ancestors' lives is the climate. Climate History in the British Isles at <**www.booty.org. uk/booty.weather/climate/histclimat.htm**> allows you to see whether a particular year was affected by any severe meteorological events, national or local.

Societies

There are at least as many groups devoted to local history as there are family history societies, though of course not all of them have websites. A comprehensive listing for all parts of the UK and Ireland is provided by *Local History* magazine in the Local History Directory at <**www.local-history. co.uk/Groups/**>. This gives contact details including email addresses and websites where available. It also includes the many county-based record societies, whose print publications are such an important source for family historians. The British Association for Local History has select list of links to local history society websites at <**www.balh.co.uk/directory.php**>.

Mailing lists

LOCAL-HISTORY is a general mailing list for the British Isles, which is hosted by JISCmail, the national academic mailing list service. You can see the archive of past messages for the list at <**www.jiscmail.ac.uk/cgi-bin/ webadmin?A0=local-history**>, and there are also instructions on how to subscribe.

There are two other places to look for genealogical discussion forums relating to local history. ONE-PLACE-STUDY is a mailing list for those involved in studying a single parish or group of parishes, details of which can be found at <**lists.rootsweb.ancestry.com/index/other/Miscellaneous/ ONE-PLACE-STUDY.html**>. British-Genealogy also hosts a discussion forum for one-place studies at <**www.british-genealogy.com/forums/ forumdisplay.php?f=177**.

Curious Fox at <**www.curiousfox.com**> is a site which provides message boards for local history and genealogy. While most discussion forums are county based, this is different in that it is based on a gazetteer of over 50,000 town and villages in the British Isles (including 3,000 in Ireland), each with its own page. You can search for the settlement name, generate lists of nearby villages and hamlets, and get links to the exact location on Multimap and Old-maps. You can also search by family name. The site calls itself 'semi commercial': you can join and use the site free of charge, but a subscription of £5 provides additional facilities, including an automatic email when someone adds a message relating to a town or village you have stored as a place of interest. Without a subscription you can only contact subscribers.

Most of the genealogical mailing lists for counties, areas, and individual places are useful for local history queries, and there are some lists which specifically include local history in their remit. For example, the sussexpast group on Yahoo Groups at <**groups.yahoo.com/group/sussexpast/**> describes its interests as 'Discussions and questions/answers on archaeology, local history, museums and architecture in Sussex'. Lists which are more explicitly focused on the history of individual localities include:

- LANARK-HISTORY
- LONDON-LIFE
- WALES-LOCAL-HISTORY

Details of all three will be found in RootsWeb listings for Scotland, England and Wales, respectively, at <**lists.rootsweb.ancestry.com/index/**>.

Social history

Although the web provides material on any aspect of social history you care to name, from slavery to education, it is difficult to know what you can expect to find on a given topic in terms of quality and coverage. In view of the large number of possible subjects which come under 'social history', and the very general application of these headings (education, poverty, etc.), using a search engine to locate them can be quite time-consuming. Also, of course, searching on these terms will bring up many sites that have nothing to do with the history of the UK. However, if you know any terms that refer only to British and Irish historical material ('1840 Education Act', 'Poor Law', etc.) this will make searching easier. Local history sites such as those discussed above are likely to include some material on social history and local museums, and may provide useful links to non-local material.

For more recent local and social history, local newspapers are an important source, and these are discussed on p. 184.

Where aspects of social history are bound up with the state, you can expect to find some guidance on official sites. The National Archives, for example, has research guides on Education, Enclosures, Lunacy and Lunatic Asylums, Outlawry, and the Poor Law, among other subjects – see <**www.nationalarchives.gov.uk/catalogue/researchguidesindex.asp**>. Records relating to crime and punishment are discussed on p. 125ff.

A comprehensive guide to social history sites is beyond the scope of this book, but the following examples may give a taste of some of the resources on the internet.

Professor George P. Landow's Victorian Web includes an overview of Victorian Social History at <**www.victorianweb.org/history/sochistov. html**> with a considerable amount of contemporary documentation. This site, incidentally, was one of the first to use the web to make linked historical materials available.

The Workhouses site at <**www.workhouses.org.uk**> provides a comprehensive introduction to the workhouse and the laws relating to it, along with lists of workhouses in England, Wales and Scotland and a guide to workhouse records. The Rossbret Institutions site at <**www.institutions. org.uk**> has information not only on workhouses but on a wide range of institutions, including Asylums, Almshouses, Prisons, Dispensaries, Hospitals, Reformatories, and Orphanages. The County Asylums site at <**www.countyasylums.com**>, though mainly about the buildings themselves, will also be of interest.

GenDocs has a list of 'Workhouses, Hospitals, Lunatic Asylums, Prisons, Barracks, Orphan Asylums, Convents, and other Principal Charitable Institutions' in London in 1861 at <**homepage.ntlworld.com/hitch/gendocs/ institute.html**>.

Hidden Lives at <**www.hiddenlives.org.uk**> is a site devoted to children in care between 1881 and 1918. It has details of around 170 care homes (Figure 16-2) and many histories of individual children (not named). There are useful links to other online sources relating to children and poverty. Another site devoted to children is Small and Special at <**www.smalland special.org**>, a collection of resources relating to the early years of The Hospital for Sick Children at Great Ormond Street. The site includes a database of patient admission records 1852–1914, articles on the early history of the Hospital and a gallery of images. Access to detailed case notes on individuals requires (free) registration.

The Powys Heritage Online project mentioned above has sections devoted to crime and punishment, education and schools, religion in Wales, and care of the poor, at <**history.powys.org.uk/history/intro/ themes.html**>, which make use of original documents and photographs.

Scots Origins has a number of articles on aspects of Scottish social history at <**www.scotsorigins.com/help/popup-resarticles-so.htm**>, including the fishing and weaving industries, the Poor Law, and religion.

Electric Scotland has a substantial account of the 'Social History of the Highlands' at <**www.electricscotland.com/history/social/**>, taken from a nineteenth-century work. The site has much other material on Scottish history.

Finally, the Spartacus Educational site at <**www.spartacus.schoolnet. co.uk**> is a model of what can be done with historical material on the web. It has information on many topics in social history since the mid-eighteenth century, such as child labour, the railways, the textile industry and female emancipation. The site contains both general information and historical documents. The pages devoted to the textile industry, for example,

Figure 16-2 Hidden Lives

at <**www.spartacus.schoolnet.co.uk/Textiles.htm**>, contain general information on the machinery, the various occupations within the industry and
the nature of daily life in the textile factory, but also include biographical
material on individual inventors, entrepreneurs and factory workers, the
latter taken from interviews before a House of Commons Committee in 1832.

Names

Origins

A regular topic in discussion forums is the origin of surnames. When
talking about surnames, though, the term 'origin' has two distinct meanings: how the name came about linguistically (its etymology); and where it
originated geographically (its home). Unfortunately there is little reliable
information on the web relating to the first of these. The authoritative
sources for British surname etymologies are the modern printed surname
dictionaries, which are not available online. If you are lucky you may find a
surname site that quotes and gives references for the relevant dictionary
entries for your particular surname, but in the absence of source references
you should treat etymological information given on genealogy websites as
unreliable. Even where sources are given, you should be cautious – some of
the older surname dictionaries cited are the work of amateurs rather than
scholars. Indeed, even the works of the latter may have been invalidated
by subsequent research, particularly because we now have much more
extensive information on surname distribution and variant forms than
was available even 20 years ago.

Cyndi's List has a page devoted to surnames in general at <**www. cyndislist.com/surn-gen.htm**>, though many of the links are for surname *interests* (covered in Chapter 14) rather than surname origins.

Wikipedia has a number of articles on surnames, which seem to be quite sound. The most general one is at <**en.wikipedia.org/wiki/Family_name**>, and this has links to related articles. However, the Wikipedia pages for individual surname etymologies, which are generally unsourced and frequently unsound, are of little value.

In fact, there seems to be no very satisfactory site for surname etymologies. Nonetheless, you can find brief etymologies for the commoner surnames at Behind the Name's page on 'English Names' at <**surnames. behindthename.com**> and on About.com's 'Glossary of Last Name Meanings and Origins' page at <**genealogy.about.com/library/surnames/ bl_meaning.htm**>.

However, many older printed works on British surnames are available online, usually at the digital book archives discussed on p. 175. For example, the following can all be found at Google Books and the Internet Archive:

- William Arthur, *An Etymological Dictionary of Family and Christian Names With an Essay on their Derivation and Import* (1857)
- Charles Bardsley, *Dictionary of English and Welsh Surnames* (1901)
- Mark Lower, *English Surnames. An Essay on Family Nomenclature, Historical, Etymological,and Humorous* (1849)
- Mark Lower, *Patronymica Britannica. A Dictionary of the Family Names of the United Kingdom* (1860)

None of these is a substitute for a modern surname dictionary, though William Arthur's 'Essay On The Origin And Import Of Family Names' at <**www.searchforancestors.com/surnames/origin/essay.html**> is still a useful brief introduction to the general sources of surnames. However, these older works may include sources for older usages of a name, which can be helpful.

SURNAME-ORIGINS-L is a US-based mailing list devoted to the etymology and distribution of surnames, and details can be found at <**members.tripod.com/~Genealogy_Infocenter/surname-origins.html**>.

Variants

There is no definitive online source to help you to decide whether surname X is in fact a variant of surname Y, or what variant spellings you can expect for a surname. However, if a name has been registered with the Guild of One-Name Studies, the Guild's online register at <**www.one-name.org/ register.shtml**> may give some indication of major variants, and it will be worth contacting the person who has registered it. Posting a query about variants on one of the many surname mailing lists and query boards (see Chapter 18) would also be a sensible step.

The Thesaurus of British Surnames is a project to develop an online thesaurus of British surname variants. The ToBS website at <**www.tobs.org. uk**> does not have details of individual variants but has a number of resources relating to the issues of surname matching, including papers on the problems of identifying surname variants, and a comprehensive bibliography on the subject.

There are a number of computerized surname-matching schemes. The most widely used, though it has severe shortcomings, is Soundex, which is described at <**www.archives.gov/research_room/genealogy/census/ soundex.html**>. A more recent development is the proprietary NameX, which is used by Origins and Findmypast, and is briefly described at <**www. namethesaurus.com/Thesaurus/FAQ.htm**>. The ToBS website has links to online versions of some of these at <**www.tobs.org.uk/links/online.html**>.

Distribution

Looking at the geographical distribution of a surname in a major database such as FamilySearch at <**www.familysearch.org**> can sometimes be helpful. However, you should be cautious about drawing etymological inferences from distributional information in this sort of database, because not all parts of the country are equally well represented.

The most important site for surname distribution is National Trust Names at <**www.nationaltrustnames.org.uk**>, which draws on a project based at University College London. You can get distribution maps for the 1881 census or the 1998 electoral register, and the maps, even those for 1881, show the relative frequency for each postcode area, effectively the catchment area of each post town (Figure 16-3). From the initial distribution map, you can get statistical information about frequency, though it does not give a breakdown for each area. The data covers England, Wales and Scotland.

Harry Wykes has a site devoted to Surname Distribution Analysis at <**www.wykes.org/dist/**>, which produces distribution maps for individual surnames. To use the site, you need to have the 1881 census on CD-ROM, and you can then extract and upload the data for a surname, from which the site will create a distribution map, which you can then download.

GROS has an Occasional Paper on 'Surnames in Scotland over the last 140 years' linked from <**www.gro-scotland.gov.uk/statistics/publications- and-data/occpapers/surnames-in-scotland-over-the-last-140-years.html**>. Two linked PDF documents show the most common surnames in the Scottish counties in 1901 and 2001.

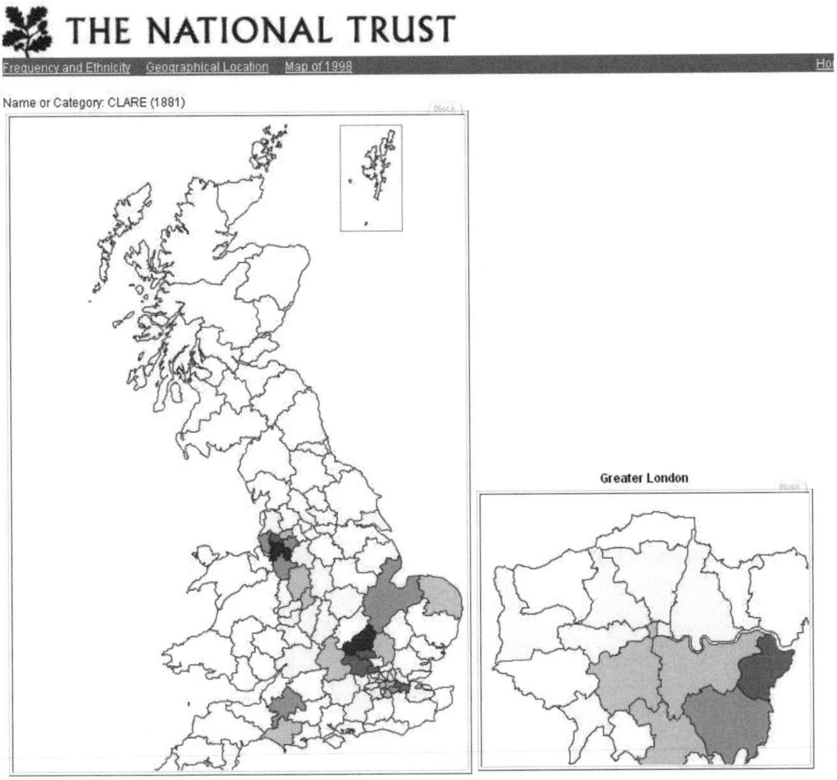

🍃 THE NATIONAL TRUST

Name or Category: CLARE (1881)

Figure 16-3 1881 distribution of the surname Clare at National Trust Names

The classic Victorian work on the subject is Henry Guppy's 1890 work *Homes of Family Names of Great Britain*, which is available at the Internet Archive (see p. 176).

For a list of the commonest surnames in various parts of the world, see Wikipedia's article at <**en.wikipedia.org/wiki/List_of_most_common_ surnames**>.

Philip Dance's Modern British Surnames site at <**www.modbritnames. co.uk**> is designed as a guide to the resources for the study of surname frequency and distribution.[10] The site includes discussion of the various approaches to surname origins, and has interesting statistical material. A site covering local names is Graham Thomas' Gloucestershire Names and their Occurrence at <**www.grahamthomas.com/glocnames.html**>.

---

10   Sadly, Philip died in October 2008. If the site cannot be maintained at its current location, it seems likely that the content will be given a permanent home elsewhere.

Forenames

Oxford University Press's *Concise Dictionary of First Names* has a free searchable database of British forenames at <www.askoxford.com/dictionaries/name_dict/>, and this is the best place to start for the origins of any forename. Behind the Name at <www.behindthename.com> is a very comprehensive site devoted to the etymology and history of first names. In addition to English and Irish names it has details for a number of other countries and regions, as well as a listing of Biblical names. What's In a Name at <www.whatsinaname.net> has well-sourced information about forenames and forename variants.

About.com has a page of links for 'Naming Patterns for Countries & Cultures' at <genealogy.about.com/od/naming_patterns/Naming_Practices_Patterns_for_Countries_Cultures.htm>, which includes links for British and Irish names, as well as many others. A search for ["naming patterns"] in a search engine will reveal many other sites devoted to this topic. Anne Johnston has a useful list of diminutives for common Christian names at <www.nireland.com/anne.johnston/Diminutives.htm>. The website for the OLD-ENGLISH mailing list (see p. 271) has a listing of Latin equivalents of common forenames at <homepages.rootsweb.ancestry.com/~oel/latingivennames.html>.

For present-day forename frequencies, the authoritative sources are government sites. The National Statistics site at <www.statistics.gov.uk> has a number of reports on the current and historical frequency of first names. There are details of links to various pages relating to forename frequency at <www.statistics.gov.uk/cci/nscl.asp?id=7557>. GROS has a paper on 'Popular Forenames in Scotland, 1900–2000' at <www.gro-scotland.gov.uk/statistics/publications-and-data/occpapers/popular-forenames-in-scotland-1900-2000.html>.

Image Partners has a forename thesaurus which attempts to match variant forename spellings at <www.imagepartners.co.uk/Thesaurus/Forenames.aspx>, and Edgar's Name Page has 'A Brief Discussion of Nicknames and Diminutives' at <www.geocities.com/edgarbook/names/other/nicknames.html>.

Understanding old documents

One of the main things genealogists need help with is making sense of old documents, whether it is a census entry or a sixteenth-century will. In some cases it's just a matter of deciphering the handwriting, in others it is understanding the meaning of obsolete words, and in older documents the two problems often occur together. While the internet hardly provides a substitute for the specialist books on these subjects, there are quite a few resources online to help with these problems.

Handwriting

As the mistakes in census transcriptions show, even fairly modern handwriting can often be problematic to read, and once you get back beyond the nineteenth century the difficulties become ever greater. Few genealogists bother to go on palaeography courses, but there are some outstanding online resources to help you.

The English Faculty at Cambridge University provides an online course on English Handwriting 1500–1700 at <**www.english.cam.ac.uk/ceres/ ehoc/**> with high-quality scans of original documents (Figure 16-4). There are extensive examples of every individual letter in a variety of hands, as well as examples of the many abbreviations found in documents of this period. A series of graded exercises gives you an opportunity to try your own skills at transcribing original manuscripts.

The National Archives also has an online palaeography tutorial at <**www. nationalarchives.gov.uk/palaeography/**>. The interactive part of the site offers 10 graded documents to try your hand at transcribing, with a pop-up alphabet for the hand, and there are another 30 example documents on the site. The 'Where to start' page offers tips for transcribing and covers some common abbreviations.

The Scottish Archive Network's dedicated palaeography website Scottish Handwriting at <**www.scottishhandwriting.com**> concentrates on the period 1500–1750 . It includes a '1 Hour Basic Tutorial' and has detailed pages devoted to the forms of some of the more challenging individual letters. A problem solver suggests techniques for making sense of problem words and letters.

Dave Postles of the University of Leicester has materials relating to an MA in Palaeography online at <**paleo.anglo-norman.org**>. The site has two areas, one devoted to medieval and the other to early modern palaeography.

Dianne Tillotson has a site devoted to all aspects of Medieval Writing at <**medievalwriting.50megs.com/writing.htm**> and there is useful material on abbreviations at <**medievalwriting.50megs.com/scripts/abbreviation/ abbreviation1.htm**>.

The website for the OLD-ENGLISH mailing list at <**homepages. rootsweb.ancestry.com/~oel/**> includes pages on Old Law Hands and Court Hand with scans of plates from Andrew Wright's 1776 *Court Hand Restored* showing examples of all the common letter shapes of the period. Both are linked from <**homepages.rootsweb.ancestry.com/~oel/contents. html**>.

While most palaeography sites deal with the early modern and medieval periods, there is also help for those struggling with Victorian hands. For example, the FreeBMD page on 'Reading the Writing' at <**www.freebmd.**

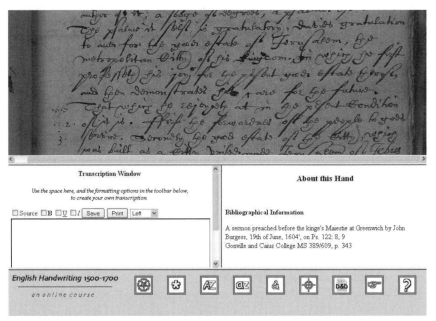

Figure 16-4 English Handwriting 1500–1700

org.uk/handwriting.html> shows how the shape of nineteenth-century pen nibs affects the thickness of the stroke, and also looks at how to deal with difficult scans.

If you have to deal with languages other than English, 'How do I read an old document?' at <**script.byu.edu**> may be worth consulting, as it offers help with both manuscript and printed documents in English, German, Dutch, Italian, French, Spanish, and Portuguese. It does not have additional original documents, but points to those on some of the other sites mentioned above.

Dates and calendars

There are a number of useful resources on the web to help you make sense of the dates and calendars used in older genealogical sources.

There are two particular types of dating which are generally unfamiliar to modern readers. The first is the dating of documents, particularly legal ones, by regnal years, i.e. the number of years since the accession of the reigning monarch (so *1 January 2009* is *1 January 56 Eliz. II*). The Regnal Year Calculator at <**www.albion.edu/english/calendar/Regnal_Years.html**> will convert regnal years for the period from the Norman Conquest to George I. There is a useful table of regnal years up to Queen Victoria at <**www.amostcuriousmurder.com/kingdateFS.htm**>.

Second, particularly in early documents, Saints' days are a common method of identifying a date. The On-line Calendar of Saints' Days at <medievalist.net/calendar/home.htm> should enable you to decode these, and the Catholic Encyclopedia's 'Dates And Dating' page at <www.newadvent.org/cathen/04636c.htm> is also useful.

In September 1752 Britain switched from the old Julian calendar to the Gregorian. For information on this change see Mike Spathaky's article 'Old Style And New Style Dates And The Change To The Gregorian Calendar' at <www.cree.ie/genuki/dates.htm>. Calendars through the Ages has the text of the Calendar Act of 1751, which instituted this change, at <webexhibits.org/calendars/year-text-British.html>, with a calendar for 1752 showing the missing days. Steven Gibbs has a conversion routine for the Julian and Gregorian calendars at <www.guernsey.net/~sgibbs/roman.html>, which may be useful if you are consulting records from countries which switched either earlier (most of Europe) or later (Russia) than the UK. Calendopaedia, the Encyclopaedia of Calendars, at <calendopedia.com> has extensive information on calendars including information on the dates lost in the switch from the Julian to the Gregorian calendar for all the individual countries in Europe at <calendopedia.com/gregory.htm>.

To find out what day a particular date fell on, consult Genuki's Perpetual Calendar at <www.genuki.org.uk/big/easter/>, which also gives the dates of Easter. The years 1550 to 2049 are covered.

Chris Phillips provides a comprehensive guide to chronology and dating at <www.medievalgenealogy.org.uk/guide/chron.shtml>, as part of a site devoted to medieval genealogy, while the Ultimate Calendar Webpage at <www.ecben.net/calendar.shtml> has over 250 links to online resources for all contemporary and historical calendars.

Translation

Latin

For medieval genealogy and for legal records up to the 1730s, you will often encounter texts written in Latin. Even in English texts, Latin phrases, or, worse, abbreviations for them, are not uncommon. Latin has also, of course, been much used for inscriptions.

General help in reading Latin documents will be found at <italiangenealogy.tardio.com/index.php?name=News&file=article&sid=24>. The Latin Dictionary and Grammar Aid at <archives.nd.edu/latgramm.htm> provides a grammar and links to other useful resources. Be warned, however, that these cover classical Latin and not the Latin of medieval and early modern Britain. Lynn H. Nelson's 'Latin Word List' at <www.the-orb.net/latwords.html> seems to be based on the Vulgate and will therefore be of use for Christian Latin terms. There is Java applet based on the above dictionary at <www.sunsite.ubc.ca/LatinDictionary/> which gives Latin to

English and English to Latin translations for a word entered. The digital books archives discussed in Chapter 12 have scans of older Latin dictionaries, which will be perfectly adequate for genealogical purposes.

There is a list of 'Hard Little Words: Prepositions, Adverbs, Conjunctions (With Some Definitions of Medieval Usage)' at <**home.c2i.net/kwhitefoot/ HardLittleWords.html**>. The Latin Primer at <**www.xmission. com/~nelsonb/latin.htm**> has a concise list of essential vocabulary for genealogists. Ancestry solutions has a list of 'Latin terms found in genealogical and historical records' at <**www.ancestrysolutions.com/Defslatin. html**>, with a link to a brief guide to reading Latin. Eva Holmes has three articles on translating Latin linked from <**www.suite101.com/articles. cfm/italian_genealogy**>.

These sites do not include feudal land-tenure terms, and will not be sufficient to enable you to translate a medieval charter, but they can certainly help with Latin words and phrases embedded in English prose.

Latin abbreviations are often used, particularly in set phrases, and the FAQ for the soc.genealogy.medieval newsgroup has a list of some of those commonly found in genealogical documents at <**users.erols.com/wrei/ faqs/medieval.html#GN13**>.

There is a LATIN-WORDS mailing list which is for 'anyone with a genealogical or historical interest in deciphering and interpreting written documents in Latin from earliest to most recent twentieth century times, and discussing old Latin words, phrases, names, abbreviations and antique jargon'. Subscription details will be found at <**www.rootsweb.ancestry. com/~jfuller/gen_mail_trans.html**> and the list archive is at <**archiver. rootsweb.ancestry.com/th/index/LATIN-WORDS**>.

Other languages

The Dictionary of the Scots Language site at <**www.dsl.ac.uk/dsl/**> provides electronic editions of two key works of Scottish lexicography, the *Dictionary of the Older Scottish Tongue* (DOST) and the *Scottish National Dictionary* (SND). Between them, these two dictionaries cover the use of Scots words from the twelfth century to the present day. A search can be conducted in either or both works. Quite apart from their general interest, an obvious use for genealogists is to help with understanding Scottish wills and other legal documents. A wide-ranging glossary of Scottish terms will be found on The Wedderburn Pages at <**pagespro-orange.fr/euroleader/ wedderburn/glossary.htm**>, including both archaic and modern terms.

With the release of the 1911 census, which allowed non-Anglophone families to record their household using Welsh or Irish, you may need recourse to a dictionary to translate the family relationships and the occupations. For Welsh, consult the Welsh–English / English–Welsh On-line

Dictionary provided by the Department of Welsh, Lampeter at <**www. geiriadur.net**>. There is an online Irish dictionary with basic vocabulary at <**www.irishdictionary.org**>, and a list of the Irish words for family relationships at <**www.irishgaelictranslator.com/articles/?p=30**>. Detailed help in dealing with the Irish language entries in the 1911 census is given in Chapter 15 of *Census: The Expert Guide*.

Technical terms

Genealogists encounter technical terms from many specialist areas, and have the additional difficulty that it may not be apparent whether a term is just specialized or in fact obsolete. The definitive resource for such questions remains the *Oxford English Dictionary* – see p. 178 for details of online access, and Figure 9-1 for a sample entry. Some terms may be important enough to deserve their own entry in an encyclopedia, in which case consult Wikipedia at <**en.wikipedia.org**> or, if you have access, the online edition of *Encyclopædia Britannica* (again, see p. 178).

Other places to turn when you encounter this sort of problem include the rather inappropriately named OLD-ENGLISH mailing list, which is for 'anyone who is deciphering old English documents to discuss interpretations of handwriting and word meanings', or the OLD-WORDS mailing list 'for the discussion of old words, phrases, names, abbreviations, and antique jargon useful to genealogy'. Details of how to subscribe to these lists are at <**www.rootsweb.ancestry.com/~jfuller/gen_mail_trans.html**>. You can also browse or search the archives for them at <**archiver.rootsweb.ancestry. com/th/index/OLD-ENGLISH**> and <**archiver.rootsweb.ancestry.com/th/ index/OLD-WORDS**> respectively. Bear in mind that the contributors to the lists have widely varying expertise, and you will need to evaluate carefully any advice you receive. However, the companion website for the OLD-ENGLISH list at <**homepages.rootsweb.ancestry.com/~oel/**> has an excellent collection of material, as well as some useful links at <**homepages. rootsweb.ancestry.com/~oel/links.html**>.

Guy Etchells has a list of 'Leicestershire Agricultural Terms' taken from a work of 1809 at <**freepages.genealogy.rootsweb.ancestry.com/~ framland/framland/agterm.htm**>. Old terms for occupations are discussed on p. 128.

Legal

Even where they are not written in Latin many early modern texts, particularly those relating to property, contain technical legal terms that are likely to mean little to the non-specialist, but which may be crucial to the understanding of an ancestor's property holdings or transactions. A useful list of 'Legal Terms in Land Records' will be found at <**users.rcn.com/deeds/**

legal.htm>, while the equivalent but distinct terminology for Scotland is explained in the Customs & Excise notice 'Scottish Land Law Terms' (the URL is the 187-character address given on p. xii, so instead follow the link from the website for this book). These are both guides to present-day usage, but in view of the archaic nature of landholding records this should not be a hindrance. A more specifically historical glossary is provided on the Scottish Archive Network site at <www.scan.org.uk/researchrtools/glossary.htm>, and legal terms are included in The Wedderburn Pages mentioned above. The Manorial Society of Great Britain has a glossary of manorial terms at <www.msgb.co.uk/glossary.html>.

Medical

Death certificates of the last century, and earlier references to cause of death, often include terms that are unfamiliar. Some can be found in one of the online dictionaries of contemporary medicine, such as MedTerms at <www.medterms.com> or the University of Newcastle's On-line Medical Dictionary at <cancerweb.ncl.ac.uk/omd/>. But for comprehensive coverage of archaic medical terms, refer to Antiquus Morbus at <www.antiquusmorbus.com>, which has old medical terms in English, Latin, German, French, and many other European languages. Each entry comes with a bibliographical reference, and there are links to around 20 further online sources for the medical terms. Within the English section, there are individual lists for occupational diseases, poisons, and alcoholism; there is also a separate list of Scots terms. Cyndi's List has a 'Medical & Medicine' page at <www.cyndislist.com/medical.htm>.

Measurements

Leicester University's palaeography course materials, mentioned on p. 271, include a number of useful lists covering terms likely to be found in old legal documents: land measurement terms, the Latin equivalents of English coinage, and Roman numerals. See the Medieval palaeography pages at <paleo.anglo-norman.org/medfram.html>.

Steven Gibbs's site, mentioned on p. 273, has facilities for converting to and from Roman numerals at <www.guernsey.net/~sgibbs/roman.html>.

Details of old units of measurement (though not areal measurements) can be found at <www.fergusoncreations.co.uk/home/shaun/metrology/english.html>, while both linear and areal measures are covered by <www.johnowensmith.co.uk/histdate/measures.htm>. There is a comprehensive Dictionary of Measures at <www.unc.edu/~rowlett/units/> which includes a useful article on 'English Customary Measures' at <www.unc.edu/~rowlett/units/custom.html>. Cyndi's List has a page devoted to 'Weights and Measures' at <www.cyndislist.com/weights.htm>.

Medieval

There are a number of general guides to medieval terms, including NetSERF's Hypertext Medieval Glossary at <**netserf.cua.edu/glossary/ home.htm**>. The useful Glossary Of Medieval Terms is now only available in the Wayback Machine: go to <**www.archive.org**> and enter the URL **cal. bemidji.msus.edu/History/mcmanus/ma_gloss.html**. Resources for the terminology of heraldry are discussed on p. 230.

Value of money

An obvious question when reading wills, tax records and the like is the present-day equivalent of the sums of money quoted. While there can be no definitive answer – goods are now cheaper than ever, while labour is much more expensive – there is plenty of material online to give you an idea of what things were worth.

There is a very detailed analysis of the historical value of sterling in a House of Commons Research Paper 'Inflation: the Value of the Pound 1750–1998', which is available online in PDF format at <**www.parliament. uk/commons/lib/research/rp99/rp99-020.pdf**>. For a longer time span, there are two tables covering the period from the thirteenth century to the present day at <**www.johnowensmith.co.uk/histdate/moneyval.htm**>.

Measuring Worth is a site with a great deal of information on this topic. Its page on the 'Purchasing Power of British Pounds from 1264 to 2007' at <**www.measuringworth.com/calculators/ppoweruk/**> enables you to find the modern equivalent of an amount in pounds, shillings and pence in a particular year. There is also a useful page on 'Five Ways to Compute the Relative Value of a UK Pound Amount, 1830 to Present' at <**www.measuring worth.com/ukcompare/**> (Figure 16-5). This page clearly makes the point that there is no simple way to equate historical sums of money with a

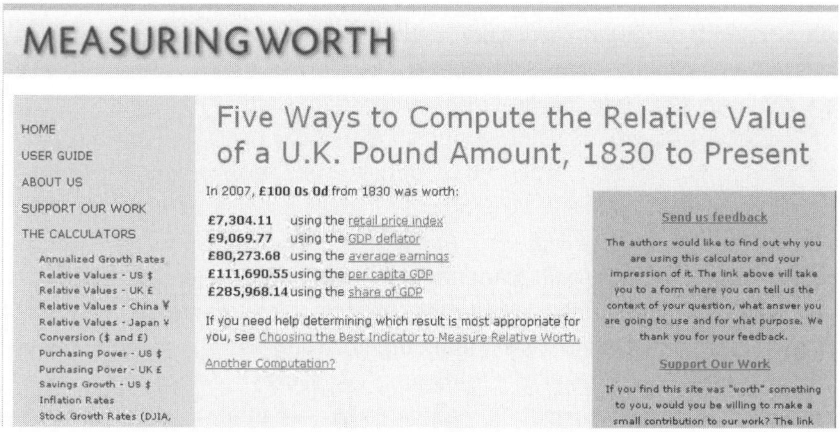

Figure 16-5 Measuring Worth

modern equivalent. Other pages on this site, all linked from the left-hand navigation bar, have information on things like the UK and US inflation rates since the 1660s and the pound–dollar conversion rate for the last 200 years.

Alan Stanier's 'Relative Value of Sums of Money' page at <**privatewww. essex.ac.uk/~alan/family/N-Money.html**> has statistics for the wages of various types of worker, mainly craftsmen and labourers, but also domestic servants and professionals.

The National Archives' website offers a 'Currency converter' at <**www. nationalarchives.gov.uk/currency/**> with information both on relative value and on buying power. Scottish Archive Network (see p. 194) provides a Scots Currency Converter at <**www.scan.org.uk/researchrtools/scots_ currency.htm**>, though unfortunately this requires Internet Explorer and Microsoft Office Web Components to work.

For the most recent period, the Retail Price Index is the official source, and its home is the Office for National Statistics, which has a home page for the RPI at <**www.statistics.gov.uk/cci/nugget.asp?id=21**> and an Adobe Acrobat file with data going back to the birth of the RPI in June 1947 at <**www.statistics.gov.uk/downloads/theme_economy/Rp02.pdf**>.

An excellent collection of links to sites with information on the historical value of the pound and other currencies is Roy Davies's 'Current value of Old Money' page at <**projects.exeter.ac.uk/RDavies/arian/current/ howmuch.html**>, which includes an extensive list of printed sources.

There is an Excel spreadsheet with data on the 'Wages and the cost of living in Southern England 1450–1700' linked from <**www.iisg.nl/hpw/ dover.php**>, with individual figures for Oxford, Cambridge, Dover, Canterbury and London.

Finally, if you are too young to remember the pre-decimal system of pounds, shillings and pence, then 'What's A Guinea?' at <**www.wilkiecollins. demon.co.uk/coinage/coins.htm**> will enlighten you.

17

PHOTOGRAPHS

Among the many reasons for the success of the web is the ease with which it can be used to make images available to a wide audience. The questions of cost and commercial viability that face the printed photograph do not really apply on the web – apart from the labour involved, it costs effectively nothing to publish a photograph online. The widespread availability of inexpensive scanners and the popularity of the digital camera mean that more and more people have the equipment to create digital images. While few archives are in a position to publish a significant fraction of their photographic holdings in print, online image archives are mushrooming, and some offer very substantial collections.

Photographs are, of course, primary historical sources. But you are not particularly likely to come across a picture of your great-great-grandmother on the web (unless she was, say, Queen Victoria), so for the genealogist online photographs mainly provide historical and geographical background to a family history, rather than primary source material.

The web is also a good source of information for understanding and managing your own family photographs, and there are sites devoted to dating, preservation, restoration, and scanning.

Cyndi's List has a page with links for 'Photographs and Memories' at <**www.cyndislist.com/photos.htm**>, covering all aspects of photography and family history. Information on using search engines to locate images online is covered in Chapter 19 on p. 321. Present-day aerial photographs tend to be provided by mapping sites and are covered in Chapter 15, p. 247.

▌National collections

For photographs of historic buildings, there are two national sites for England. The National Monuments Record's (NMR) Images of England site at <**www.imagesofengland.org.uk**> is intended to be 'an internet home for England's listed buildings' with good-quality photographs and descriptions of every listed building in the country. There are over 300,000 listed properties included on the site. You can do a quick search without further ado, while the free registration gives you access to more sophisticated standard and advanced searches. Search facilities include search by county or town, building type, period, or person (an architect or other individual associated with a building). Thumbnail images link to full size images with a description.

ViewFinder is run by English Heritage at <**viewfinder.english-heritage. org.uk**>. This aims to make part of the NMR's image archive available online. Whereas Images of England contains contemporary photographs, the ViewFinder images are older. The site has around 25,000 images in a number of collections drawn from individual photographers. The largest collection, with over 13,000 photographs, represents the work of Henry W. Taunt, an important Oxford photographer of the late nineteenth and early twentieth century. London is well served by these collections, with many street views and material relating to the Port of London. There is also a project relating to 'England at Work', with 5,000 images illustrating England's industrial heritage (click on 'Photo Essays' on the home page, and then select 'England at Work' from the subject drop-down list). The photographs come in three sizes: a small thumbnail, a basic view of about 450x300 pixels, which you can save, and an enlarged view of around 700x480 pixels which your browser won't let you save. Even though the

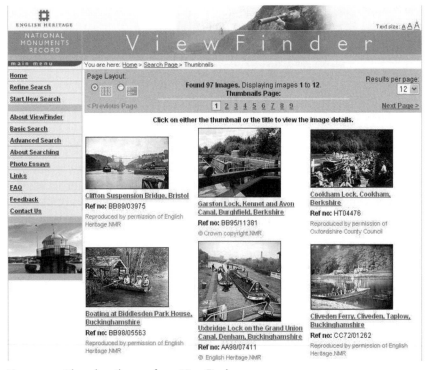

Figure 17-1 Thumbnail page from ViewFinder

images are historical, the search is based on present-day counties, not the pre-1974 counties. Another English Heritage image collection, though more of interest to historians and archaeologists, is PastScape at <**pastscape. english-heritage.org.uk**>.

A similar collection for Scotland is Historic Scotland Images at <**www. historicscotlandimages.gov.uk**>, which, like ViewFinder, has contemporary photographs. These are displayed both as thumbnails and very high-quality images, though unfortunately the thumbnails do not identify the location. There is a keyword search, or you can browse by category.

The National Library of Wales' Digital Mirror offers six online collections relating to Wales and Welsh photography at <**www.llgc.org.uk/index. php?id=133**> and has information about the National Collection of Welsh Photographs at <**www.llgc.org.uk/index.php?id=introduction2**>.

If you have ancestors who came from or worked in one of the British colonies, it will be worth looking at Images of Empire at <**www.images ofempire.com**>, which is 'the largest dedicated online resource of still and moving images on the British colonial period'. It is run by the British Empire and Commonwealth Museum and includes material from nearly 150 photographic collections, which can be viewed either by searching or by browsing the collections individually. A selection of material can be viewed under ten thematic headings (e.g. domestic life, transport).

Local collections

Record offices and libraries have substantial collections of photographic material, and this is increasingly being made available online, in many cases with lottery funding. Some of these collections are purely photographic, while others include scanned prints, drawings and even paintings. The following will give you some idea of the sort of material available.

For London, PhotoLondon at <**www.photolondon.org.uk**> is designed as a gateway to historic photographs in the capital's libraries, museums and archives. When initially launched, it included material from the collections of the Guildhall Library, the London Metropolitan Archives, Westminster City Archives, the Museum of London and the National Monuments Record, and selections from individual boroughs, with descriptions. However, at the time of writing, the site is closed for redevelopment, and the only material available is the *Database of 19th Century Photographers and Allied Trades in London: 1841-1901*. There is no indication as to the future scope of the site.

Collage (see Figure 17-2) is the Guildhall Library's contribution to PhotoLondon at <**collage.cityoflondon.gov.uk**>, and has around 20,000 images of the capital. As well as maps, plans, engravings and photographs

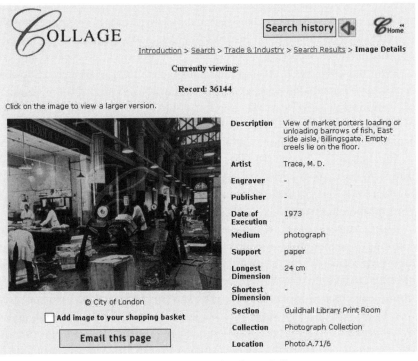

Figure 17-2 Photograph of Billingsgate Market from Collage

of places, there is a large collection relating to trades and industries, including the City livery companies.

For suburban London, the Ideal Homes site at <**www.ideal-homes.org. uk**> includes historical photographs for the six South-East London Boroughs. The images are not accessible from the home page, but from the home page for each borough there are links from the right-hand navigation bar. Thumbnails link, in turn, to larger images with a description.

Glasgow's Mitchell Library, which houses the City Archives, offers the 'Virtual Mitchell Collection' at <**www.mitchelllibrary.org/virtualmitchell/**> – note the three l's in the URL – which is a selection from the images in the collection covering 'street scenes and buildings, but also scenes of past working lives and of social life in the city.' Searches can be made by street name or subject.

West Sussex Record Office has an online database, West Sussex Past Pictures, at <**www.westsussexpast.org.uk/pictures/**>, with details of 31,000 photographs held in the record office, of which around 8,000 are available online. The online database provides record office references so that scans of photographs can be requested if the image is not already online.

Picturesheffield.com at <**www.picturesheffield.com**> is an online version of Sheffield Local Studies Library's computerized image system. Funded from the Heritage Lottery Fund, the site contains around 11,000 photographs, about a third of the Library's collection. Low resolution images (typically around 350x200 pixels at 72 dots per inch) can be downloaded from the site free of charge, and high-resolution photographic prints can be purchased.

Picture The Past at <**www.picturethepast.org.uk**> is the website for the North East Midland Photographic Record, a project run by the local authorities of Derby, Derbyshire, Nottingham, and Nottinghamshire, and intended to 'conserve and make publicly accessible the photographic heritage of the North East Midlands'. The site currently holds around over 70,000 images, including many of individual streets and houses. There is a comprehensive search facility – you can specify a county or a place, and enter individual keywords (though the site does not indicate what keywords are used in the database). Individual images are presented on-screen at around 250x190 pixels, and you can order high-quality prints online. A useful feature of the database is that each image has a link to a present-day map showing the approximate location. Many pictures are accompanied by quite detailed historical notes (see Figure 17-3). There is also a facility for those with local historical knowledge to contribute additional information.

It is always worth checking a relevant record office website for photographic collections. Even if there is little or no material on the web, you can expect to find information about their holdings. For example, Greater Manchester CRO has details of its Documentary Photography Archive at <**www.gmcro.co.uk/Photography/DPA/dpa.htm**>, which is an important collection for family historians because it includes many family photographs up to the 1950s. Photographs are usually an important part of official local history sites for specific places (see p. 261).

Figure 17-3 A Derby street scene from Picture the Past

Personal sites

Alongside these efforts by public bodies, there are many images published on the web by individuals. For example, Old UK Photos at <**www.old ukphotos.com**> has a growing collection of old photos of places, mainly taken from old postcards.

In particular, there are many present-day photographs of parish churches, such as:

- Richard's Church Albums at <**freepages.genealogy.rootsweb.ancestry. com/~temples/**> has photographs of over 2,000 churches in all parts of England.
- The Old Scottish Borders Photo Archive at <**www.ettrickgraphics.com/ bordersindex.htm**> has views of border towns.
- Kevin Quick has photographs of Bedfordshire and Buckinghamshire churches, as well as general views of Bucks towns and villages at <**www. countyviews.com**>.
- Churches of the World is a fairly new site at <**www.photosofchurches. com**>, which has started with photos of Anglesey churches.
- Essex Churches at <**www.essexchurches.info**> has photos of 380 of Essex's churches to date.

Commercial photographs

The commercial picture libraries have not been slow to exploit the web as a means of providing a catalogue for prospective purchasers of their material or services. The reason that these resources are useful to non-professional users is that access to the online catalogues and databases is usually free, though the image size and quality is likely to be reduced, and the scans may have some overprinting to prevent them being used commercially.

For example, PastPix <**www.pastpix.com**> is a subscription service with over 20,000 historical photographs, mainly from the UK, but the collection can be searched free of charge. There is a whole range of photographs of places and occupations, though the picture size for casual visitors is quite small (registered users have access to larger images). One irritation with this site is that it seems to require Internet Explorer and is completely unusable with either Firefox or Opera.

Perhaps the most important commercial site with old photographs for the UK is the Francis Frith Collection at <**www.francisfrith.com**>. Frith was a Victorian photographer whose company photographed over 7,000 towns and villages in all parts of the British Isles, from 1860 until the company closed in 1969. The entire stock was bought by a new company, which now sells prints. While the aim of the website is to act as a sales medium, it has reasonable size thumbnails (under 400x274 pixels) of all 120,000-odd pictures in the collection, which can be located by search or via a listing for each (present-day) county without the need to make a purchase. There are also some historic aerial photographs. The site allows you set up an 'album' to store the pictures you want to view again.

Frith's photographs and many other commercial photographs of towns and villages were issued as postcards, which means that postcard sites may have material of interest. For example, there is a collection of Isle of Wight postcards at <**members.lycos.co.uk/bartie**>; Eddie Prowse has an online collection of postcards of Weymouth and Portland at <**www.eprowse.fsnet. co.uk**>; Photo-Ark at <**www.photo-ark.co.uk**> has postcards (as well as other photographs) for Derbyshire, Lancashire, Lincolnshire, Nottinghamshire, and Yorkshire. Postcardworld at <**www.postcardworld. co.uk**> is a commercial site with postcards of all parts of the UK, with good-quality scans on the site.

Professional photographers

In one sense, professional photographers are just another occupational group (see Chapter 9). But their role in creating a unique part of the recent historical record makes them of interest not just to their descendants. Information about their working lives can be important in dating and locating family photographs.

A useful site for information on UK photographers is the New Index of Victorian, Edwardian & Early 20th Century UK Photographers at <**www. thornburypump.myby.co.uk/PI/**>. This has a database of photographers (which, however, can only be searched by county) and links to many other sites. Roger Vaughan has a list of several hundred Victorian photographers at <**freepages.family.rootsweb.ancestry.com/~victorianphotographs/pixs/ carte.htm**>, while PhotoLondon (see p. 281) has a Directory of London Photographers 1841–1908 at <**www.photolondon.org.uk/directory.htm**>. Another useful site is Christine Hibbert's Victorian Photographers of Britain 1855–1901, which lists photographers, with towns and dates. Unfortunately, the site itself closed down at the beginning of 2008, but the content is still available at the Internet Archive – go to <**www.archive.org**> and enter **mywebpage.netscape.com/hibchris/instant/aboutme.html** in the 'Waybackmachine' field. Details of almost 150 'Jersey Photographers and Studios' will be found on the Jerseyfamilyhistory site at <**jerseyfamily history.co.uk/?page_id=11**>.

The 'Photographs and Memories' page on Cyndi's List at <**www.cyndis list.com/photos.htm**> lists a number of other sites with dates and places for British professional photographers, including some for specific towns or counties (including Ayrshire, Liverpool and Sussex).

UK-PHOTOGRAPHERS is a mailing list for the discussion and sharing of information regarding the dating of photographs produced by professional photographers in England and Wales between 1850 and 1950. Information on subscribing will be found at <**lists.rootsweb.ancestry.com/ index/other/Occupations/UK-PHOTOGRAPHERS.html**>, which has a link to the archive of past messages.

Portraits

While most of the online historic photographs are of places, there are some photographs of individuals. The military is particularly well represented. For example, Fred Larimore's site devoted to Nineteenth Century British And Indian Armies And Their Soldiers at <**www.members.dca.net/fbl/**> has a collection of photographs for the period 1840 to 1920, in some cases with information about the individual shown and commentary on uniform details. Other sites with military photographs are mentioned on p. 148.

The website of the Roger Vaughan Picture Library at <**www.rogerco. freeserve.co.uk**> has around 3,000 Victorian and Edwardian studio photographs, with links to other sites with many more. Most of the subjects aren't named, so this is more useful for help with dating and information on professional photographers.

Buckinghamshire has a online database of Victorian prisoners in Aylesbury Gaol at <**apps.buckscc.gov.uk/eforms/libPrisoners/**>, around a quarter of which have photographs (Figure 17-4).

Many school photographs will be found online. For a simple example,

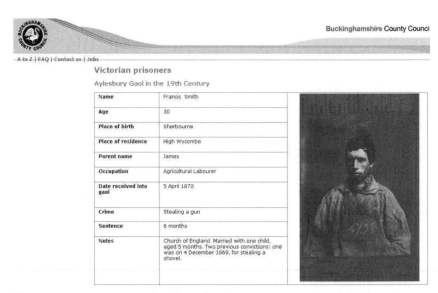

Figure 17-4 An entry in Buckinghamshire's Victorian Prisoners database

see Kennethmont School's page at <**www.kinnethmont.co.uk/k-school. htm**>, which offers a selection of group photos from 1912 onwards with many pupils and teachers identified by name (yes, the site and the school differ in spelling!). Jeff Maynard has a more extensive collection for Harrow County School with form and sports team photos going back to the 1920s at <**www.jeffreymaynard.com/Harrow_County/photographs.htm**>, with something for almost every year.

A good way to find photographs for particular schools is to check the website of the school itself, if it still exists. Most official school sites have the format <**www.*name-of-school.name-of-localauthority*.sch.uk**> though some have their own independent domain – a general search on the school name in a search engine will quickly find the site. A local history site may include school photographs, too. (Incidentally, if you come across a site called World School Photographs, ignore it – it seems to be solely designed to collect personal information, and has *no* school photographs.)

As well as these individual efforts, there are online photo archives to which you can contribute scans of your own material. Perhaps the best known is the 'genealogy photo archive' DeadFred at <**www.deadfred.com**>, which has almost 50,000 records for around 12,000 surnames, but the 'Photographs and Memories' page on Cyndi's List at <**www.cyndislist.com/ photos.htm**> has many more, under the heading 'Lost & Found'.

▌Dating, preservation, restoration

The web can be useful in connection with your own photographs, if you need to date them or if you need advice on preservation or restoration.

Kennethmont School 1937

Mr Fowlie, Headmaster, Andy Munro, Billy McDonald, Jas Greig, Jim Andrew, Sandy Andrew, Bill Pirie, Jim Dey, Gordon Watt

Margt Stewart, Winifred Beattie, Mary Cruickshank, Daisy Morgan, Harriet Simpson, Jean Lawson, Annie Fraser, Helen Borthwick, Isobel Dey

Margt Innes, Twin Rennie, Clare McRobbie, Annie Souter, Annabella Mackie, Janet Mackie, Helen Skinner, Twin Rennie, Williamina McDonald

Alexander Simpson

Figure 17-5 Kennethmont School photograph from 1937

For help with the dating of old photographs, Andrew J. Morris' site 19th Century Photography at <**ajmorris.com/roots/photo/**> provides a detailed account of the various types of photographic process and technique. The Roger Vaughan Picture Library has a section devoted to dating portraits at <**www.cartes.freeuk.com/time/date.htm**> with examples of (approximately) dated photographs for years between 1860 and 1952. *Your Family Tree* magazine has a useful article from its March 2006 edition 'Clues from your old photos' at <**www.yourfamilytreemag.co.uk/resources/yft/beginoldphotos.pdf**>

The Open University has a unit 'Picturing the family' at <**openlearn.open.ac.uk/course/view.php?id=2688**>, an online tutorial (designed to take 12 hours) which 'looks at some of the ways photographs can reveal, and sometimes conceal, important information about the past', with around a hundred photographs for analysis and interpretation.

If you are interested in preserving and restoring old photographs, Colin Robinson has information about their care and conservation at <**www.colinrobinson.com/care.html**>, while David L. Mishkin's article on 'Restoring Damaged Photographs' at <**www.genealogy.com/10_restr.html**> covers the various approaches to restoration. (If you access this site via a UK ISP, you will get an irritating page which asks if you want to go to the UK Ancestry site – you need to click on the 'Remain on Genealogy.com' link.)

If you want to scan photographs and restore them digitally, it is worth looking at Scantips <**www.scantips.com**>, which not only has extensive advice about scanning in general but also includes a page on 'Restoration of genealogical photos' at <**www.scantips.com/restore.html**>. About.com has a series of articles by Kimberley Powell on 'creating and editing digital photos' at <**genealogy.about.com/cs/digitalphoto/a/digital_photos.htm**>.

These sites offer advice not just on the obvious topic of repairing the signs of physical damage but also on correcting tonal problems with faded originals. Sites devoted to digital restoration generally assume you are using Adobe Photoshop, but the principles transfer to other graphics editing packages, though there may be some differences in terminology.

A general source of help with old photographs is the RootsWeb mailing list VINTAGE-PHOTOS, which is devoted to 'the discussion and sharing of information regarding vintage photos including, but not restricted to, proper storage, preservation, restoration, ageing and dating, restoration software, photo types and materials used, restoration assistance, and scanning options'. Information on how to join the list will be found at <**lists.rootsweb.ancestry.com/index/other/Miscellaneous/VINTAGE-PHOTOS.html**>, which also provides links to the list's archives. The GenPhoto list at Yahoo Groups is a mailing list about photography specifically for family historians. Its coverage includes identifying old photographs, and using digital photography and scanning to share and preserve family photos. You can read archived messages and join the group at <**groups.yahoo.com/ group/genphoto/**>. The Photo Identification Discussion Group is also on Yahoo Groups, at <**groups.yahoo.com/group/photoid**>, and is devoted to 'techniques for identifying the date and subjects of old photographs.' Archived messages can be read only once you have joined the group.

Digital preservation

While modern digital photographs don't need 'preservation' as such, appropriate archiving is essential if future generations are to see them. Digital photographs may not get torn or faded, but image files can easily become corrupted or destroyed, as can the physical media on which they are stored. Also, it's a lot easier to write a name and a date on the back of a print than to attach the same information securely to a file. Good starting points for this issue are the articles 'Archiving & Preserving Digital Photography' by Christopher Auman at <**blogcritics.org/archives/2005/02/04/092057. php**>, and 'Digital Life Preservers; How To Organize, Archive, And Protect Your Valuable Photos' by Howard Miller at <**shutterbug.com/techniques/ digital_darkroom/0905digitallife/**>.

If you're serious about digital preservation, then an important consideration is the long-term stability of the storage media. Authoritative guidance is available in a report from the US National Institute of Standards and Technology at <**www.creativetechs.com/tips/SVC-backup/StabilityStudy. pdf**>. The body of the article is very technical, but the conclusions are probably all you need.

Photo sharing

In the last few years, we have seen increasing possibilities for collaboration on the web, and an example of this are photo sharing sites, which make it possible for individuals to share their photos online without going to the trouble of setting up a personal website. The best known of these is probably Flickr at <**www.flickr.com**>, which allows users to maintain a collection of online photos free of charge. Photos can either be entirely public or you can restrict access to selected family members and friends, making it an easy way to share new digital photos of family events or scans of historical photos. Where photos are public, they can be located via the search facility, so sites like Flickr can be used as a way of finding contemporary photos of places in addition to the official geographical collections mentioned at the beginning of this chapter. Even the smallest village is likely to be represented by a dozen or more photographs showing the major buildings and the surrounding landscape – see Figure 17-6. (You can, incidentally, see photos of the author in his earliest youth at <**www.flickr.com/photos/**

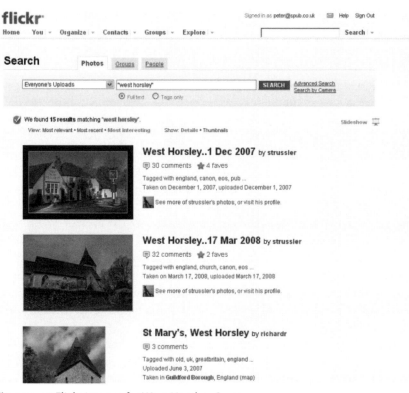

Figure 17-6 Flickr images for West Horsley, Surrey

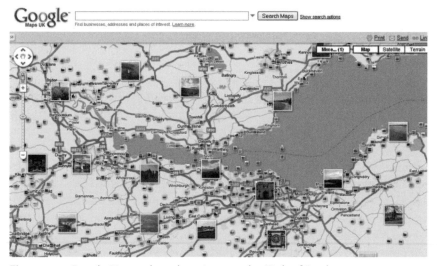

Figure 17-7 Google Maps: photo locations on the Firth of Forth

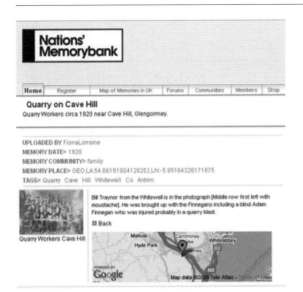

Figure 17-8 Nations' Memorybank: Quarry workers in Co. Antrim, 1920

petex/sets/72157603870404149/>.)

You can get a list of similar sites from the Wikipedia entry on photo sharing at <**en.wikipedia.org/wiki/Photo_sharing**>, which also provides an overview of the various types of photo-sharing site.

Google Maps at <**maps.google.co.uk**> (see p. 245) includes a facility for people to attach a photo to a particular location. To see which locations have photos, you need to click the 'More' button at the top left of the key map and then tick the Photos option (see Figure 17-7).

Wikimedia Commons at <**commons.wikimedia.org**> also has many user-submitted photographs of places – just search on the place name in the search box on the home page.

Geograph at <**www.geograph.org.uk**> takes a similar but more methodical approach: it invites people to submit photographs of the main geographical features for every 1km grid square of the British Isles.

Nations' Memorybank at <**nationsmemorybank.com**> is something more than a photo-sharing site, since it also contains text by the contributors about the places and events. Indeed some of the texts are quite extensive. The example shown in Figure 17-8 shows a group of workers from Glengormy in Co. Antrim. As you can see, the site uses Google Maps (see p. 245) to locate the memory geographically, and you can select a place which has memories attached to it by zooming in on the map of the British Isles on the 'Map of Memories in UK' link on any page. If you register (free of charge), you can upload your own material.

If you can't find a photo of a particular place or building on Flickr or one of the other photo-sharing sites, you could use Genealogy Photos at <**photoexchange.ourgenealogy.co.uk/pe**>. This acts like a lookup exchange (see p. 377) for photographs, aiming to 'help amateur genealogists get in contact with amateur photographers in a certain area who have volunteered to take specific photographs of buildings, landmarks etc.'. You select a country and county and you will get a list of contacts and the areas which they cover. The countries included are Australia, Canada, England, France, New Zealand, Northern Ireland, Scotland, South Africa, Sweden, Switzerland, The Netherlands, USA and Wales.

18

DISCUSSION FORUMS

One of the most useful aspects of the internet for anyone researching their family history is that it is very easy to 'meet' other genealogists online to discuss matters of common interest, to exchange information and to find help and advice. The specific issues of locating other people with interests in the same surnames and families are dealt with in Chapter 14. This chapter looks at the three main types of online discussion forum: mailing lists, newsgroups and web-based forums.

Mailing lists

Electronic mailing lists provide a way for groups of people to conduct online discussions via email. They are simply a logical extension of your electronic address book – instead of each member of a group having to keep track of the email addresses of everyone else, this list of email addresses is managed by a computer called a 'list server'. This arrangement allows people to add themselves to the list, or remove themselves from it, without having to contact all the other members.

You join a list by sending an email message to a list server. Thereafter you receive a copy of every message sent to the list by other list members; likewise, any message you send to the list gets circulated to all the other subscribers.

Finding lists

The first genealogical mailing list, ROOTS-L, goes back to a period long before the internet was available to the general public – its first message was posted in December 1987. There must now be well over 50,000 English-language mailing lists devoted to genealogy.

Every mailing list is hosted on a specific server, which is responsible for dealing with all the messages, and a large proportion of the genealogy lists (over 30,000) are hosted by RootsWeb, whose main mailing lists page will be found at <lists.rootsweb.ancestry.com>. The 'browse mailing lists' link on this page takes you to a list of subject categories, which is useful for finding lists devoted to a particular topic. General, not geographically specific, lists for the UK (which includes those for occupations, for example) are linked from <**lists.rootsweb.ancestry.com/index/intl/UK/**>. Individual pages for England, Ireland, Scotland and Wales have links to lists for local and regional interests. There is no master listing of all RootsWeb lists, so it can be hard to find those which do not fall into obvious categories. The keyword search on the home page will help, though it only searches for the exact words in the names and descriptions of lists, with the result that, for example, searches on 'navy' and 'navies' produce quite different results. However, if you know the name of the list, this limitation is not a problem.

A general mailing list site that hosts around 15,000 genealogy lists is Yahoo Groups at <**groups.yahoo.com**>. Most of the groups hosted here are listed under the **Family & Home | Genealogy** category on the home page, though there are many others for particular countries and areas, which can be found by using the search facility.

In spite of the large number of lists, it is a simple matter to find those which might be of interest to you, as there are two sites which compile this information. The more definitive is John Fuller and Chris Gaunt's Genealogy Resources on the Internet site which has a comprehensive listing of genealogy mailing lists at <**www.rootsweb.ancestry.com/~jfuller/gen_mail. html**>, subdivided into the following categories:

Countries Other Than USA	General Information/Discussion
USA	Jewish
Surnames	LDS
Adoption	Native American
African-Ancestored	Newspapers
Cemeteries/Monuments/Obituaries	Nobility/Heads of State/Heraldry
Computing/Internet Resources	Occupations
DNA Studies/Testing	Religions/Churches
Emigration/Migration Ships and	Societies
Trails	Software
Family History, Folklore, and	Translations and Word Origins
Artifacts	Vital Records (census, BDM)
Freedmen	Wars/Military
Genealogical Material	Uncategorized

The 'uncategorized' lists include a number devoted to topics of general interest, such as the GEN-MEDIEVAL and SHIPWRECK lists.

However, more useful for those with UK interests is Genuki's Mailing Lists page at <**www.genuki.org.uk/indexes/MailingLists.html**>. This has the advantage of listing only those relevant to British and Irish genealogy. It also includes lists which, although of interest to UK genealogists, are not categorized under the UK by John Fuller or RootsWeb, notably war-related lists such as AMERICAN-REVOLUTION, BOER-WAR or WARBRIDES. The organization of the Genuki listing makes it easier to find lists of interest: at the top of the page are those devoted to general topics, but the main body of the page gives all the lists for each county in the British Isles. Another advantage over John Fuller's pages, which give only subscription information, is that the Genuki listing has links to the web page for each list, so you can easily find further information or access the list archives, if they are publicly accessible.

The most generally useful mailing lists are probably those for individual counties. RootsWeb has lists for every county in the British Isles and these are good places to find discussion of or ask questions about the areas where your ancestors lived and about local records.

As well as the lists for each county as a whole, there are many devoted to areas within a county, and to particular towns and villages. Staffordshire, for example, is covered not only by a general list, STAFFORDSHIRE, but also by lists for local areas such as the Black Country and the Potteries, as well as a number of individual towns such as Walsall and Sedgley. Staffordshire interests are also covered by the broader MIDMARCH and SHROPSHIRE-PLUS lists.

Alongside such geographically-based lists, there are general lists covering particular topics in relation either to the entirety of the British Isles, or to some constituent of it. Examples of these are lists like AUS-CONVICTS, BRITREGIMENTS, RAILWAY-UK and UK-1901-CENSUS. Other lists are mentioned in Chapters 8, 9, 10, 14 and 15.

There are also many mailing lists for individual surnames. These are discussed in detail on p. 213.

John Fuller has a regular electronic newsletter called NEW-GENLIST which carries announcements of new lists added to his sites. Subscription details will be found at <**lists.rootsweb.ancestry.com/index/other/Miscellaneous/NEW-GENLIST.html**>, which also has a link to the archive of past announcements.

Of course Genuki and John Fuller only have details of lists relating to genealogy. If you want to find mailing lists on other topics, there is unfortunately no definitive catalogue – in fact such a thing would be impossible to compile and maintain. However, since most mailing lists have either a website of their own or at least a listing somewhere on the web, a search engine can be used to locate them.

List archives

Many genealogy mailing lists, including almost all those hosted by RootsWeb, have an archive of past messages. The RootsWeb list archives can be found at <**archiver.rootsweb.ancestry.com**>. Not all list archives are open to non-members of the relevant list, but where a RootsWeb list has open membership it is not very common to find that the archive is closed. On Yahoo Groups the home page for each list has a link to 'Messages', which contains all past messages in reverse order of date. For many Yahoo groups, however, you have to join the lists to see the messages.

List archives have several uses. First, they allow you to get an idea of the discussion topics that come up on the list and judge whether it would be worth your while joining. Also, an archive will give you some idea of the level of traffic on the list, i.e. how many messages a day are posted. Finally, they provide a basis for searching, whether by the list server's own search facility, or by a general search engine such as those discussed in Chapter 19. This means that you can take advantage of information posted to a mailing list without even joining it, though of course you will need to join to post your own messages.

Joining a list

In order to join a list you need to send an email message to the list server, the computer that manages the list, instructing it to add you to the list of subscribers. The text of the email message must contain nothing but the correct command.

Although the basic principles for joining a list are more or less universal, there are a small number of different list systems and each has its own particular features.

Many lists are run on 'listserv' systems (listserv is the name of the software that manages the lists). To join one of these you need to send a message to listserv@*the-name-of-the-list-server*, and the text of the email message should start with the word **SUB** (short for 'subscribe'), followed by the name of the list and then your first and last names. So to join WW20-ROOTS-L, a list for the discussion of genealogy in all twentieth-century wars, you would send the message shown in Figure 18-1 (supposing your name was John Smith):

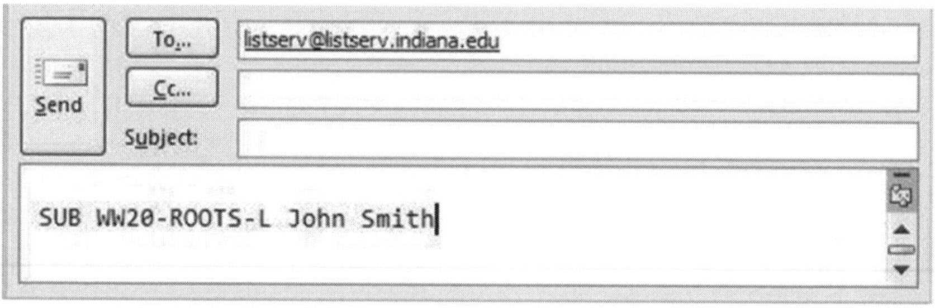

Figure 18-1 Subscribing to a mailing list

You need to specify the list name because this particular list server could be managing many different lists.

On systems such as RootsWeb, however, there is usually a special subscription email address for each list. This is typically formed by adding the word *request* to the list name. So to join the GENBRIT-L list, for example, you send your joining command to GENBRIT-L-request@ rootsweb.com and the text of the message itself only needs to say *subscribe*, as shown in Figure 18-2.

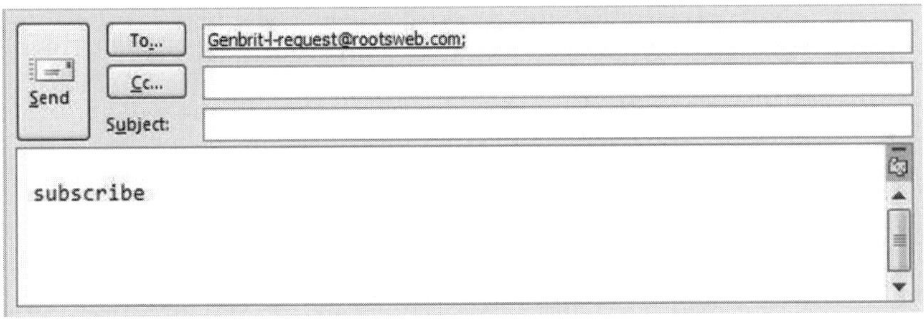

Figure 18-2 Subscribing to a RootsWeb mailing list

Yahoo Groups uses a similar system, but with distinct addresses for subscribing, unsubscribing, contacting the list owner.

You should not need to worry about which subscription format to use: any site with details of mailing lists, such as Genealogy Resources on the Internet, should give explicit instructions on how to join the lists mentioned. On Yahoo Groups the home page for each group gives subscription instructions. RootsWeb does the same.

Because these messages are processed by a computer, you should send *only* the commands – there is no point in sending a message to an automatic system saying, 'Hello, my name is… and I would like to join the list, please.' Also, it is a good idea to remove any signature at the end of your email message, so that the list server does not attempt to treat it as a set of commands.

Incidentally, do not be worried by the word 'subscription'. It does not mean you are committing yourself to paying for anything, it just means that your name is being added to the list of members.

If you have more than one email address you need to make sure that you send your joining message from the one you want messages sent to. Most mailing lists will reject an email message from an address it does not have in its subscriber list. If you want to be able to use more than one email address to post messages to a list, you will need to ask the list administrator to add additional addresses for you.

Some lists have web pages with an online form for joining. In this case

Address	What it's for
The list server	Automatic control of your subscription to the lists. Messages sent to this address are not read by a human, and can only consist of specific commands.
The list itself	This is the address to be used for contributions to the discussion. Anything sent to this address is copied to all the list members. A common beginner's mistake is to send a message meant for the list server to the list address, and hundreds or even thousands of people receive your 'unsubscribe' message.
The list owner/ administrator	This is for contacting the person in charge of the list. For most lists, it should only be needed if there is some problem with the list server (e.g. it won't respond to your messages) or something the automated server can't deal with that requires human intervention (e.g. abusive messages). For closed lists, you will probably need to use this address rather than the list server address in order to subscribe.

Table 18-1 Mailing list addresses

you simply type your email address in the box. There is a similar system for the mailing lists at Yahoo Groups, though here you have to register (free) before you can join any of its lists. Once you have signed in, you can click on the subscribe button for any list and it will bring up a page where you can select your subscription options and join the list.

When you join a list you will normally get a welcome message. You should make sure you keep this, as it will give you important information about the list and the email addresses to use. There are few things more embarrassing online than having to send a message to everyone on a mailing list asking how to unsubscribe because you have lost the welcome message which contains the instructions.

There are some circumstances in which you will not be able to join a list by one of the methods discussed here: some lists are 'closed', i.e. they are not open to all comers. This is typically the case for mailing lists run by societies for their own members. In this case, instead of sending an email to the list server you will probably need to contact the person who manages the list, providing your society membership number, so that he or she can check that you are entitled to join the list and then add you.

Digests

Many mailing lists have two ways in which you can receive messages. The standard way is what is called 'mail mode', where every individual message to the list is forwarded to you as soon as it is received. However, some older email systems were not able to cope with the potentially very large number of incoming messages, so lists also offered a 'digest mode'. In this, a bunch of messages to the list are combined into a single larger message, so reducing the number of messages arriving in the subscriber's mailbox. Even though few of us nowadays are likely to be affected by this sort of technical limitation, some people do not like to receive the dozens of mail messages per day that can come from a busy list, and prefer to receive the messages as a digest.

However, there are also disadvantages to this. For a start, you will need to look through each digest to see the subjects of the messages it contains, whereas individual messages with subject lines of no interest to you can quickly be deleted unread. Also, if you want to reply to a message contained within a digest your email software will automatically include the subject line of the *digest*, not just the subject of the individual message within the digest you are replying to. The result is that other list members will not be able to tell from this subject line which earlier message you are responding to. If your email software automatically quotes the original message in reply, then you will need to delete almost all of the quoted digest if you are not to irritate other list members with an unnecessarily long message, most of which will be irrelevant (see 'Netiquette', p. 306). Unless you have only a slow internet connection and your email software does have offer a filtering facility (see below), there is no good reason to subscribe in digest mode.

There are a number of different ways of arranging to receive a list in digest form. With the lists on RootsWeb there is a different subscription address, containing -D- instead of -L-, so subscription messages for the digest form of the GENBRIT list go to GENBRIT-D-request@rootsweb.com. On listserv systems, once you have joined a list you should send a message with the text set LISTNAME digest to change to digest mode, and set LISTNAME nodigest to switch back to mail mode. On lists with a web subscription form, you may be able to choose between mail and digest on the form.

Text formatting

Email software generally allows you to send messages in a number of different formats, and normally you do not need to worry about exactly how your mail software is formatting them. When you start sending messages to mailing lists, however, you may find that this is an issue you need to consider. The reason for this is that some mailing lists will not accept certain types of formatting, and even if they do, some recipients of your formatted messages may have difficulties.

The standard format for an email message is plain text. This can be handled by any list server and any email software. However, most modern email software will let you send formatted text with particular fonts and font sizes, colour, italics and so on, i.e. something much more like what you produce with your word processor, and some software even uses this as the default. The way it does this is to include an email attachment containing the message in RTF format (created and used by word processors) or HTML format (used for web pages).

You may feel that this is exactly how you want your email messages to look. But if someone is using email software that can't make sense of this format they may have trouble with your message. They may even receive what looks like a blank message with an attachment, and many people are, rightly, wary of opening an attachment which could contain a virus, particularly if it's attached to a suspicious-looking blank message. The only way they will be able to read your message is by saving the attachment as a file and then opening it with the relevant piece of software, and no one will thank you for sending a message requiring all that extra work. Indeed, people using text-based email on some systems, such as UNIX, may not even have access to software for reading such files.

Also, messages with formatting are inevitably larger than plain text messages, so people have to spend more time online to download them, which, while trivial for an individual message, could be significant for someone who is a member of a few busy lists. All things considered, there is really no good reason for using formatted text in mailing-list messages.

Different lists and list systems deal with this problem in a variety of ways. Yahoo Groups allows you to choose whether you receive messages from the list as HMTL or as plain text. RootsWeb does not permit the use of HTML or RTF formatting at all, and will not allow messages with formatted text to get through.

If you need to find out how to turn off the formatting features of your email software, RootsWeb has a useful page on 'Sending Messages in Plain Text' at <**helpdesk.rootsweb.ancestry.com/listadmins/plaintext.html**>. The page shows you how to do this for over 20 of the widely used email packages, but even if it does not include the software or the version you use, it should give you an idea of what to look for in your own email software.

The only formatting feature that can be really useful in an email message is the ability to highlight words to be stressed, and the traditional way of doing this in a plain text message is to put *asterisks* round the relevant word. One thing *not* to do, in genealogy mailing lists anyway, is put words in upper case – this is traditionally reserved for indicating surnames.

Filtering

If you do not want to subscribe to mailing lists in digest mode, you can still avoid cluttering up your inbox with incoming messages from mailing lists. Most email software has a facility for *filtering* messages, i.e. for moving them automatically from your incoming mailbox to another mailbox when it spots certain pieces of text in the header of the message. You will need to consult the online help for your email software in order to see exactly how to do it, but Figure 18-3 shows a 'rule' in Microsoft Outlook which will filter all mail received from the GENBRIT mailing list into a dedicated mailbox called *genbrit*. This does not reduce the number of messages you receive, but it keeps your list mail separate from your personal mail and you can look at it when it suits you. Since GENBRIT can give rise to as many as 100 messages a day, this is the only practicable way to deal with the volume.

If you have registered your own internet domain and use this for your email, you can set up a separate email address which you just use for list mail.

Other uses of mailing lists

Although, in general, mailing lists allow all members to send messages, and messages are forwarded to all members, there are two types of list that work differently.

Some lists are not used for discussion at all, but only for announcements. Typically, this sort of list is used by an organization to publish an email

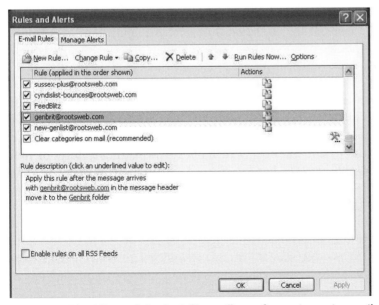

Figure 18-3 This Microsoft Outlook filter will transfer any incoming mail from 'genbrit@rootsweb.com' to a dedicated mail folder

newsletter. It differs from a normal list in that you will not be able to send messages, only receive the announcements. The electronic newsletters mentioned in Chapter 21 (p. 366) are in fact mailing lists of this type.

Normally, mailing lists allow only members of the list to send messages to it, and messages from non-members are rejected. But there are a few lists that accept messages from non-members, for example to allow people to submit information to a project. In a case like this you will not be able to join the list yourself but will be able to send messages to it. Genuki uses a system like this for users to report errors or submit additional information, which is automatically circulated via a mailing list to all Genuki county maintainers. In fact, from the non-members' point of view this is just a special email address, and the fact that it is actually a list is not even apparent.

Newsgroups

Before the internet was dominated by the World Wide Web, the other main type of discussion technology was the newsgroup. Originally access to newsgroups required special software, a 'newsreader', but now most people who access newsgroups use the web-based archive at Google Groups <**groups.google.com**>, which also allows the posting of new messages. This service includes Google's own discussion forums and an archive of newsgroups, which can be browsed from <**groups.google.com/groups/ dir?sel=33554433**>.

Unlike mailing lists and web-based forums, there have never been many newsgroups devoted to genealogy: there are 30 English-language groups and 11 for other European languages. Around half of these are now defunct or moribund; those which remain heavily used are the ones for which RootsWeb provides a 'mailing list gateway', i.e. a linked mailing list, so that you can treat a group just as if it were a mailing list. A full list of these is shown in Table 18-2. The most useful for British and Irish ancestors are GENBRIT, GENIRE, and GENCMP, which covers the use of computers in family history. In addition to the archive at Google Groups, all past messages are archived at <**archiver.rootsweb.ancestry.com**>. The main difference between these and other RootsWeb mailing lists is their very broad subject coverage – there is just a single newsgroup for all UK genealogy, GENBRIT, and none for the individual counties. Also, because some of these have been in existence a very long time (in internet terms, anyway), they hold a very substantial body of genealogical knowledge in their past messages.

Table 18-2 Genealogy newsgroups and their equivalent mailing lists

Newsgroup	Gatewayed mailing list at RootsWeb
alt.genealogy	ALT-GENEALOGY
fr.comp.applications.genealogie (in French)	GEN-FF-LOG
fr.rec.genealogie (in French)	GEN-FF
soc.genealogy.african	GEN-AFRICAN
soc.genealogy.australia+nz	GENANZ
soc.genealogy.benelux	GEN-BENELUX & GENBNL-L
soc.genealogy.britain	GENBRIT
soc.genealogy.computing	GENCMP
soc.genealogy.french	GEN-FR
soc.genealogy.german	GEN-DE
soc.genealogy.hispanic	GEN-HISPANIC
soc.genealogy.ireland	GENIRE
soc.genealogy.italian	GEN-ITALIAN
soc.genealogy.jewish	JEWISHGEN
soc.genealogy.marketplace	GEN-MARKET
soc.genealogy.medieval	GEN-MEDIEVAL
soc.genealogy.methods	GENMTD
soc.genealogy.misc	GENMSC
soc.genealogy.nordic	GEN-NORDIC
soc.genealogy.slavic	GEN-SLAVIC
soc.genealogy.west-indies	CARIBBEAN

Web forums

A third type of discussion group is the web-based forum. There is no single term for these but they are often called 'message boards' or 'bulletin boards'. These work in very much the same way as Google's web-based news service: a website acts as a place where people can post messages for others to read. While using a web-based system is in some ways easier than using mailing lists, these forums have a significant disadvantage: as there is no way to select a whole group of messages for reading, you have to look separately at every single message of interest, each of which is delivered to you as a separate web page. If you want to read every message, this will be *very* tedious.

Unfortunately, there is no comprehensive list of such discussion forums, as a number of ISPs have a system for their subscribers to set up web-based discussion groups, and there are sites like Yahoo Groups (see p. 294) or MSN Groups at <**msnusers.com**>, who provide such facilities for all comers. (In fact the distinction between mailing lists and web-based discussion is not absolutely clear-cut. Yahoo Groups, for example, allows you to read messages on the web rather than receiving them as email.)

The main UK site for genealogy discussion forums is British-Genealogy at <**www.british-genealogy.com/forums**>. This has forums devoted to every county and in some cases, there are forums for individual places within the county. There are also topic-based forums, covering areas such as the census, emigration and a number of occupations, though quite a few of these do not seem to be very active. A convenient overview of all the available forums will be found at <**www.british-genealogy.com/forums/archive/**>.

Another site for UK and Irish interests is RootsChat at <**www.rootschat.com**>. This has discussion forums for all parts of the British Isles, including every individual county (Figure 18-4 shows some of the messages on the Cheshire forum.). Within the counties, there are separate forums for lookup

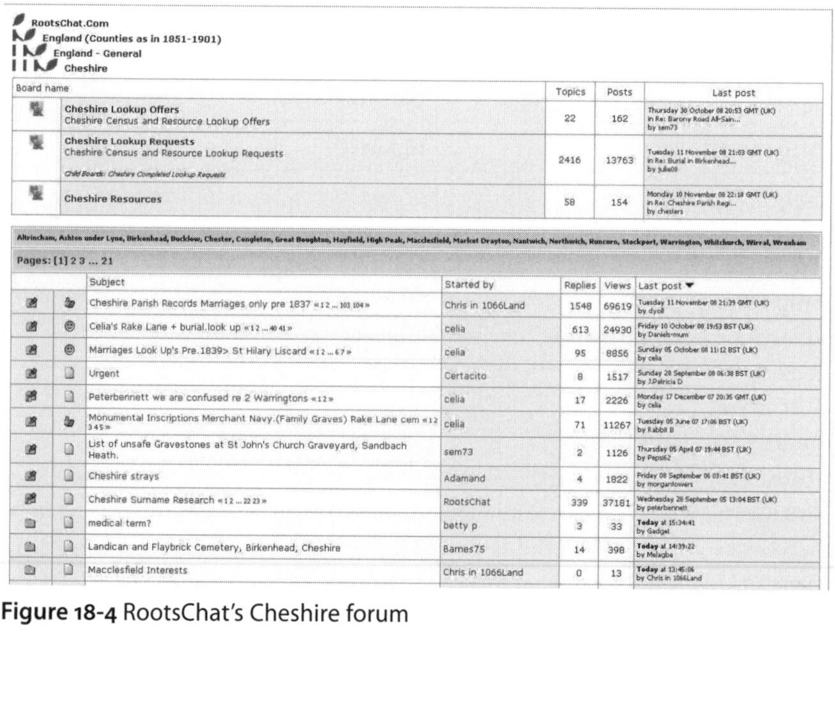

Figure 18-4 RootsChat's Cheshire forum

offers and requests, and details of online resources. There are also forums for the English-speaking former colonies, and a few general topics such as the armed forces and photo restoration.

TalkingScot provides forums for those with Scottish ancestry at <**www. talkingscot.com**>. It has separate discussion groups for the various types of genealogical record as well as individual groups for Scottish emigration to particular countries or regions.

One of the major sites providing discussion forum facilities for genealogy is Genealogy.com's GenForum at <**genforum.genealogy.com**>. There are forums for over 100 countries, including all parts of the British Isles. On the page for each country there is also a link to 'Regions for this Country' which leads to forums for individual counties or major towns, though not every county has its own forum. There is a forum for each US state, and around 80 devoted to general topics (e.g. emigration, Jewish genealogy, marriage records), including 20 or so devoted to computers and genealogy software. There are thousands of forums relating to individual surnames.

Ancestry/RootsWeb also offers message boards at <**boards.ancestry.com**> and <**boards.rootsweb.com**>, covering over 160,000 topics and surnames. There are boards for all parts of the UK and Ireland, with at least one for every pre-1974 county. There are also boards for most other countries and many of the individual counties in each US state. A wide range of general topics have a dedicated message board:

Adoptions	Methods
Ancestry Daily News	Migration
Ancestry.com	Military
Cemeteries & Tombstones	Newspaper Research
Census	Occupations
Crime	Organizations and Societies
Disasters	Orphans and Orphanages
DNA Research	Pioneer Programs
Ethnic / Race	Projects
Folklore, Legends & Family Stories	Religions and Religious
Genealogy Software	Research Groups
Government	Research Resources
Immigration and Emigration	Reunion Announcements
Institutions	RootsWeb
Major Events	Royalty and Nobility
Medical	Volunteer Projects
Medieval History	

You can browse or search the many boards dedicated to individual surnames from the 'Find a Board' option on the main page, and the 'Search the Boards' option at the top of the page will help you find messages on particular topics.

Forums on other providers can be found by using a search engine, and a link to any forum relating specifically to UK genealogy should be found on the relevant county page on Genuki.

Netiquette

Electronic discussion forums are social institutions and, like face-to-face social institutions, they have a set of largely unwritten rules about what counts as acceptable or unacceptable behaviour. While individual groups may spell some of these out in an FAQ or a welcome message, the core rules are common to all online discussion groups and are often referred to collectively as 'netiquette', short for 'internet etiquette'. Many systems make some of these rules explicit conditions for their use, and list/forum owners usually exclude members who persistently ignore them.

The 'official' Netiquette Guidelines are at <**tools.ietf.org/html/rfc1855**> – section 2.1.1 covers email. Virginia Shea's book *Netiquette*, the complete text of which is online at <**www.albion.com/netiquette/book/**>, offers more extensive advice. Malcolm Austen has some brief but useful 'Notes on List Etiquette' at <**mno.org.uk/email-list-etiquette/**>.

Frequently Asked Questions (FAQ)

Once you have been reading a particular discussion forum for some time, you will realize that certain questions come up again and again. Needless to say, regular members of a discussion forum don't relish the thought of repeatedly taking the time to answer these basic questions, so many major mailing lists and forums have what is called an FAQ, a file of 'frequently asked questions'. The FAQ for a mailing list is normally posted to the list periodically, but the actual frequency varies from list to list.

If you are thinking of asking a question on a particular list for the first time, and especially if you are just starting to research your family tree, it's a good idea to consult the FAQ. This will give you a guide as to what are considered appropriate or inappropriate issues to discuss and above all provide answers to some of the most obvious questions asked by beginners.

The easiest way to find the FAQ for a mailing list is to search the list archive. On a web-based system, there may be a link from the home page or a 'sticky' message, which remains permanently at the top of the list of messages.

There is a long-standing FAQ for the soc.genealogy.britain newsgroup and the GENBRIT mailing list at <**www.woodgate.org/FAQs/socgbrit.**

html> and a relatively new replacement for it, still under development, at <**www.genealogy-britain.org.uk**>. Because of their general coverage, these are well worth looking at even if you don't intend to post messages to GENBRIT.

Query etiquette

Here are some of the main dos and don'ts relevant to genealogical forums:

- Make sure that any messages you send are relevant to the forum topic, as:
  - a Welsh genealogy query in a Hampshire forum is a waste of everyone's time;
  - discussion of politics and religion, unless strictly relevant to a genealogical issue, is likely to cause friction.
- Give an explicit subject line so people can see what topic your question relates to – avoid one word subjects, especially if that word is 'help' or 'problem'.
- Read the FAQ if there is one.
- Don't ask factual questions you can easily find the answer to online for yourself.
- Don't post the same query in several different places. If you're not sure which is the right place, ask.
- Always be polite and considerate in responding to others. It's perfectly possible to be critical, should the need arise, without being rude.
- Don't quote the entirety of a previous message in a reply, particularly if your reply comes right at the bottom – just quote the relevant part.[11]
- Don't post a reply to the list or group if your answer is going to be of interest only to the sender of the original message – email that person directly.
- Don't advertise goods or services – there are other places designed for this.
- Don't expect other people to look up records for you unless the forum explicitly permits lookup requests.
- Don't post messages containing other people's data or data from CD-ROMs. This is more than bad manners, it's copyright infringement. (See p. 383ff.)

---

11   One of the great religious schisms on the internet is between the 'top-posters' and the 'bottom-posters', who have different views on where in the message one should add one's own remarks when replying. For discussion of the relative merits of differing posting styles, see the Wikipedia article at <**en.wikipedia.org/wiki/Posting_styles**>.

Starting your own discussion group

There are many websites that allow you to start your own discussion group. As mentioned above, you may find that your own ISP provides facilities to set one up on their website. Alternatively, you could look at using Yahoo Groups at <**groups.yahoo.com**> or MSN Groups at <**msnusers.com**>. The advantage of using well-known services like these is that people will be much more likely to come across your group.

RootsWeb hosts an enormous number of genealogical mailing lists and is a good place to create a new one. Details of how to request a new mailing list will be found at <**resources.rootsweb.ancestry.com/adopt/**>. There is detailed coverage of mailing list administration at <**helpdesk.rootsweb. ancestry.com/listadmins/**>.

Bear in mind that maintaining a mailing list or discussion group could end up requiring a significant amount of your time if it becomes popular. Unless a list is small, it is certainly much better for it to be maintained by more than one person so that responsibilities can be shared. On the other hand, a mailing list for a particular surname is not likely to generate nearly as much mail as one on a general topic. RootsWeb provides detailed information about the responsibilities of list owners on their system at <**helpdesk.rootsweb.ancestry.com/listadmins/duties.html**>, and other sites that provide discussion forums will provide something similar.

Which discussion group?

Which mailing lists or forums you read will, of course, depend on your genealogical interests. The main general group for British genealogy is soc. genealogy.britain and its associated mailing list, GENBRIT. However, if you are not already familiar with mailing lists, you may not want GENBRIT to be the first one you join – you could be a bit overwhelmed with the 50-plus messages per day arriving in your mailbox. Also, it can be a rather boisterous group.

If you know where your ancestors came from, it may be more useful to join the appropriate county mailing lists (see <**www.genuki.org.uk/indexes/ MailingLists.html**>). There are fewer messages, and more of the postings are likely to be relevant. You will certainly have a better chance of encountering people with whom you share surname interests, not to mention common ancestors. Other useful lists are those for special interests, such as coalminers or the Boer War.

You might think that the best thing to do is join the lists for all your surnames of interest, and there are thousands of lists and web-based forums devoted to individual surnames. However, they differ widely in their level of usefulness. Some have very few subscribers and very few messages, while, particularly in the case of reasonably common English surnames, you may well find lists dominated by US subscribers with mainly post-colonial interests. But with a reasonably rare surname in your family tree, particularly if it is also geographically limited, it is very likely that some other subscribers on a surname list will share your interests. Whereas the relevant county mailing list is certain to be useful, with surname lists it's more a matter of luck.

The simplest way to see whether any discussion forum is going to be worth joining is to look at the archives for the list to see the kind of topics that are discussed. This also has the advantage that you can get a rough idea of how many messages a month you would be letting yourself in for. You could also simply join a group and 'lurk', i.e. receive and read the messages without contributing yourself.

19

SEARCH ENGINES

One of the most obvious features of the internet that makes it good for genealogical or indeed any research is that it is very large, and the amount of material available is rapidly increasing. It is impossible to get an accurate idea of the size of the web, but it is reasonable to assume that it is at least 20 billion pages, and that figure does not include any data held in online databases.[12] But the usefulness, or at least accessibility, of this material is mitigated by the difficulty of locating specific pages. Of course, it is not difficult to find the websites of major institutions, but much of the genealogical material on the web is published by individuals or small groups and organizations, which can be much harder to find. Also, since there is no foolproof way to locate material, a failed search does not even tell you that the material is not online.

The standard tool for locating information on the web is a search engine. This is a website that combines an index to the web and a facility to search the index. Although many people do not recognize any difference between directories, gateways and portals on the one hand, and search engines on the other, they are in fact very different beasts (which is why they are treated separately in this book) and have quite different strengths and weaknesses, summarized in Table 19-1.

These differences mean that directories, and particularly gateways and portals, are likely to be good for finding the home pages of organizations and projects, but much less well suited to discovering sub-pages with information on individual topics. Even genealogy directories with substantial links to personal websites and surname resources probably don't include

---

12   Panda's February 2007 article 'The size of the World Wide Web' at <**www.pandia. com/sew/383-web-size.html**>, which gathers together a number of estimates, concludes that 'the number of web pages must be somewhere between 15 and 30 billion – and probably closer to the latter'. In July 2008 Google claimed to have indexed one trillion unique URLs – see <**googleblog.blogspot.com/2008/07/we-knew-web-was-big.html**>. They also claim that 'the number of individual web pages out there is growing by several billion pages per day'. To put this in perspective: the British Library catalogue includes a mere 14 million books, with at best probably five billion pages between them.

Directories, gateways and portals	Search engines
Directories and gateways list websites according to general subject matter.	Search engines list individual web pages according to the words on the page.
Directories are constructed and maintained by intelligent humans. In the case of genealogy gateways you can assume the compilers actually have some expertise in genealogy.	Search engines rely on indexes created automatically by 'robots', software programs which roam the internet looking for new or changed web pages.
Directories and particularly specialist gateways for genealogy categorize genealogy websites intelligently.	While some search engines know about related terms, they work at the level of individual words.
Directories are selective (even a comprehensive gateway like Genuki only links to sites it regards as useful).	Search engines index everything they come across.
Directories, offering a ready-made selection, require no skill on the part of the user.	The number of results returned by a search engine can easily run into six or seven figures, and success is highly dependent on the searcher's ability to formulate the search in appropriate terms.
Gateways often annotate links to give some idea of the scope or importance of a site.	A search engine may be able to rank search results in order of relevance to the search terms, but will generally attach no more importance to the website of an individual genealogist than to that of a major national institution.

Table 19-1 Comparison of directories, etc., with search engines

more than a fraction of those discoverable via a search engine. A directory or gateway might give you a link to the home page of a body like the Society of Genealogists, but only a search engine will take you straight to the page for the opening times. And if you are looking for pages which mention the name of one of your ancestors, there is little point in using a directory or gateway. You have to use a search engine.

There are quite a few different search engines, but the overwhelming majority of searches are carried out using one of the four main search engines:

Google[13]	<www.google.com>
Yahoo Search	<search.yahoo.com>
Windows Live Search	<www.live.com>
Ask	<www.ask.com>

For a comprehensive set of links to search engines, see Yahoo's listing for Search Engines & Directories at <dir.yahoo.com/Computers_and_internet/internet/World_Wide_Web/Searching_the_Web/Search_Engines_and_Directories/>.

Using a search engine

In spite of the more or less subtle differences between them, all search engines work in basically the same way. They offer you a box to type in the 'search terms' or 'keywords' you want to search for, and a button to click on to start the search. The example from Yahoo Search shown in Figure 19-1 is typical. Once you've clicked on the 'Search the Web' button, the search engine will come back with a page containing a list of matching web pages (see Figure 19-2), each with a brief description culled from the page itself, and you can click on any of the items listed to go to the relevant web page. Search engines differ in exactly how they expect you to formulate your search, how they rank the results, how much you can customize display of the results, and so on, but these basics are common to all.

Figure 19-1 The Yahoo Search home page at <search.yahoo.com>

Most search engines will report the total number of matching web pages found, called 'hits', and if there is more than a pageful (typically 10 or 20), it will provide links to subsequent pages of hits. (In Figure 19-2, you can see this information just above the first search result.) Usually the words you have searched on will be highlighted in some way.

On some search engines, such as Ask and Live Search, the first few hits may well be 'sponsored results', i.e. paid entries more or less relevant to your search terms. For any search on the word 'genealogy', these are most

13   If you access Google from a UK ISP, you will be redirected automatically to <www.google.co.uk>.

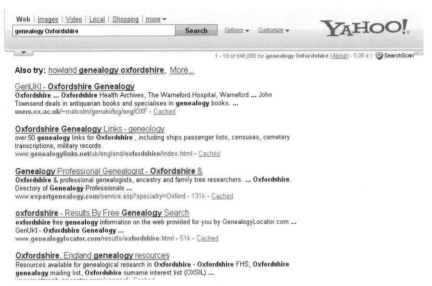

Figure 19-2 Results of a search on Yahoo Search

likely to be for some of the commercial data services that are described in Chapter 4.

▌ Formulating your search

Your success in searching depends in part on your choice of search engine, which is discussed on p. 326, but is also greatly dependent on your skill in choosing appropriate search terms and formulating your search.

In this chapter I have put search terms between square brackets. To run the search in a search engine type in the text between the brackets *exactly*, but don't include the square brackets themselves. Note that the figures given for the number of hits have indicative status only – they were correct when I tried out these searches, but the indexes used by search engines grow daily, so you will not get identical results. Also, there is no way to verify the accuracy of the figures except where they are very low. But the differences between the various *types* of search and formulation should be of the same order.

Basic searching

There are actually several different types of search offered by search engines. In the basic search – the one you get if you don't select any options and just type in words to be searched for – the results will include all web pages found that contain *all* the words you have typed in the search field. This means that the more words you type in, the fewer results you will get. If you type in any surname or place name on its own, unless it's a fairly unusual one, you will get thousands of hits. So it's always better to narrow down your search by entering more words if possible. This type of search is called an AND search.

AND and OR are just the most commonly used parts of a general technique for formulating searches called Boolean logic.[14]

Looking for alternatives

One thing to avoid in a basic search is entering a set of alternatives, because then you will miss some, perhaps many, relevant pages. Supposing you have ancestors who were Grimsby trawlermen, it might seem like a good idea to enter both [trawlerman] and [trawlermen], possibly adding [trawler] for good measure. But each extra word reduces the number of matching pages found. On Google, a search for [Grimsby trawlerman] produces 689 hits, [Grimsby trawlermen] 917 hits, while the combination [Grimsby trawlerman trawlermen] gives only 48. (In fact, for plurals of common words you don't need to do this: Google will automatically include results for [towns] in a search for [town].) The same will happen if you give alternative surname spellings: for example Google gives around 366,000 hits for [Waymark] and 151,000 for [Wymark], but [Waymark Wymark] produces just 36, a tiny number of pages which have both variants.

The AND search is not suitable for looking for alternatives, unless you really do require pages that have both of them. What you need instead is an OR search, which will retrieve all pages containing at least one of the search words.

All the main search engines offer the option of doing an OR search. There are normally two ways to do this. First, all search engines have an Advanced Search page (there will be a link to this located near the search box on the main page, often to the right, as in the Yahoo Search in Figure 19-1). This will offer you a wide variety of things to specify about what you are looking for but near the top should be options to 'look for all of the words' and 'look for any of the words'. The first of these is for words which *must* be included, the latter where any *one* of the alternatives you give will do. Figure 19-3 shows how to find your trawlerman ancestors on Google's Advanced Search page at <**www.google.com/advanced_search**>. You'll find very similar options in other search engines. As you'd expect, this gives you more results than any of the individual AND searches.

Windows Live Search also has an Advanced Search page, which can be accessed from the link on the home page or any page of search results.

---

14 This topic can be handled only briefly here. For more information on using Boolean expressions for searching, look at the help pages of the search engines or the BrightPlanet tutorial at <**www.brightplanet.com/tutorials/67-tutorial-part-4.html**>.

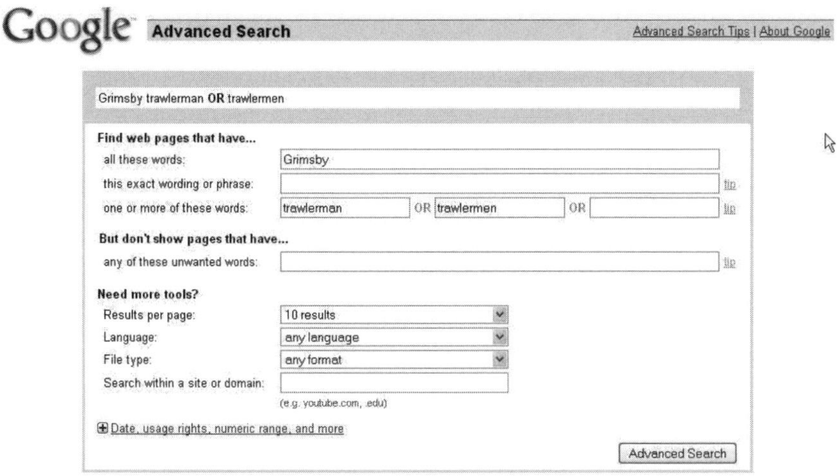

Figure 19-3 An OR search on Google's Advanced Search page

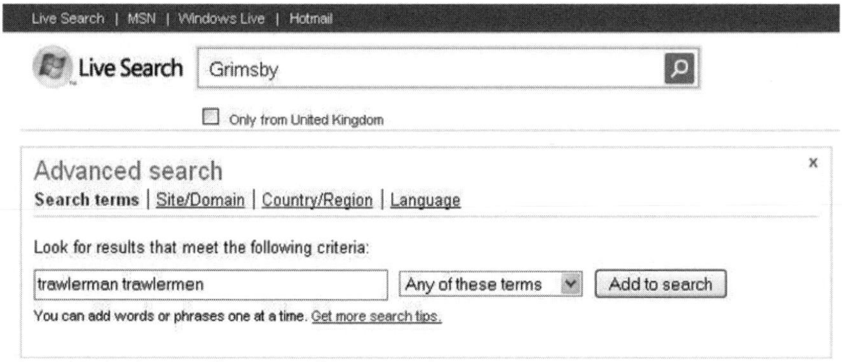

Figure 19-4 Creating an OR search with Windows Live Search

However, Live Search does not use a comprehensive form like Google, which shows all the options at once. Instead, you enter each group of search terms and select whether you want:

- all of these terms
- any of these terms
- this exact phrase
- none of these terms

Figure 19-4 shows how to enter the terms for an OR search. When you click on the 'Add to search' button your search terms are translated into the correct syntax in the search field.

The other way to create an OR search – and one which is much quicker once you know what you're doing – is simply to type in the correct formulation directly in the search field. Strictly, the correct way to do this is shown in the following example:

[Grimsby AND (trawlerman OR trawlermen)]

But given that the default search is an AND search, this is equivalent to

[Grimsby (trawlerman OR trawlermen)]

which is what Windows Live search requires.

However, many search engines are more relaxed. For example, Yahoo and Google only require the OR, not the AND or the parentheses:

[Grimsby trawlerman OR trawlermen]

All of them also seem to accept the strict syntax, so that will be the best approach if you can't find specific information about this topic on the help pages.

You can use the same principles to construct more complex searches:

[Robinson AND (genealogy OR "family history") AND
(Nottingham OR Notts) AND (cobbler OR cordwainer)]

which Google would allow you to enter as

[Robinson genealogy OR "family history" Nottingham OR Notts cobbler
OR cordwainer]

Google provides another way of finding related word forms. If you search Google for [apprentices indenture] you will see that the first few results include pages with the words 'apprentice', 'apprenticeship', and 'indentured'. This technique is called 'stemming' and is an extremely useful tool to reduce the number of alternatives you have to include explicitly in your search terms. It is used by default. If you don't want the variant forms included in search results, prefix your search term with a + sign. None of the other main search engines provides this feature.

Exclusion
Often you will find yourself searching on a word that has several meanings or distinct uses, in which case it can be useful to find a way of excluding some pages. The way to do this is to choose a word which occurs only on

pages you don't want, and mark it for exclusion, which most search engines do by prefixing with a hyphen. For example [Bath Somerset -water] would be a way to ensure that your enquiry about a town in Somerset was not diluted by material on Somerset plumbers.[15]

There is one very common problem when searching for geographical information which this technique can help to alleviate: names of cities and counties are used as names for ships, regiments, families and the like; also, when British emigrants settled in the colonies they frequently reused British place names. This means that many searches which include place names will retrieve a good number of irrelevant pages.

If you do a search on [Gloucester], for example, you will soon discover that there is a Gloucester County in Virginia and in New Brunswick, a town of Gloucester in New South Wales and in Massachusetts (not far from the town of Essex), and you probably do not want all of these included in your results if you are looking for ancestors who lived along the Severn. Then there is HMS Gloucester, the Duke of Gloucester, pubs called the Gloucester Arms and so on. Likewise, if you're searching on [York], you do not really want to retrieve all the pages that mention New York.

Obviously it would be rather tedious to do this for every possibility, but you could easily exclude those which an initial search shows are the most common, e.g. [Gloucester -Virginia] or [York -"New York"]. (Another way to cut down on these irrelevant results would be to search for [Gloucester England], though this will miss many personal genealogy sites, where the country is often taken for granted.)

Another case where this technique would be useful is if you are searching for a surname which also happens to be that of a well-known person: [Gallagher -Oasis] or [Pankhurst -Emmeline -Sylvia -Christabel] will reduce the number of unwanted results you will get if you are searching for the surnames Gallagher or Pankhurst, and do not want to be overwhelmed with hundreds if not thousands of hits relating to one or two high-profile bearers of the name. In the second example, [Pankhurst] gives almost 19 million on Google, while [Pankhurst -Emmeline -Sylvia -Christabel] gives less than 2 per cent of that number.

Unfortunately, if you are searching for a surname which is also a place name, e.g. Kent or York, there is no simple way to exclude web pages with the place name, though on p. 327 I suggest a technique for restricting your hits to personal genealogy websites.

---

15   This hyphen is to be regarded as a substitute for the typographically correct minus sign, which your browser would almost certainly ignore and therefore not submit as part of your search.

Stop words

The reason for putting the Boolean operators AND/OR in upper case, incidentally, is that these are small words which search engines normally ignore, so-called 'stop words': [Waymark OR Wymark] finds 14 million hits on Google, [Waymark or Wymark] finds only 149 – the 'or' has been ignored and the alternative spellings treated as an AND search.

Other stop words include 'the' and 'of': if you search for [Alfred the Great] or [Isle of Man], you should find that the number of search results is very similar to those for [Alfred Great] or [Isle Man].

The counterpart of the – sign for exclusion, is the + sign, indicating that the term *must* be in the pages retrieved. Given that all the main search engines do this by default for all terms you type in, the only real use is to include stop words. For searching on names, places and occupations, this is not likely to be very useful – if you have stop words in a name, e.g. John of Gaunt, Robert the Bruce, Isle of Man, it is best to put treat the entire name as a phrase, as explained in the next section, in which case any stop words are not ignored.

Phrases and names

Another important issue when using a search engine is how to group words together into a phrase. If you just type in a forename and surname, for example, search engines will treat this as an AND search on the two components.

This *may* not matter, especially if you are looking for a site by name, as search engines tend to put near the top of their listings those hits which include all search terms in the page title. This is particularly the case with organizations and projects, so, for example, a Windows Live search on [Manorial Documents Register] produces around 29,000 hits, but the MDR area on the National Archives' site, which is the official home of the MDR, is at the top of the list (see Figure 19-5).

However, you can't count on this, and even with two-part place names, which you might expect a search engine to recognize, your results may include many irrelevant hits. On Live Search, for example:

- In a search for [genealogy Long Ditton] the third hit is the Genuki page for Ditton in Lancashire, which includes the phrase 'a very long time'.
- In a search for [genealogy South Norwood] the second hit is a South Carolina Genealogy Forum page which mentions a Richard Norwood.

The same will happen if you are looking for pages on a particular subject. If you are searching for words that are often found together and constitute a major topic in genealogy, you should expect your search results to be fairly

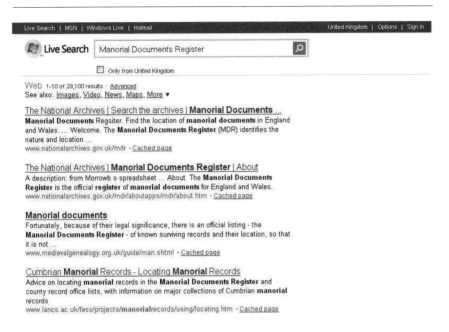

Figure 19-5 A search for [Manorial Documents Register] on Windows Live Search

accurate. For example, in a search for [poor law] on Live Search at least the first 100 results were, without exception, relevant. But for a less common phrase, results will be less satisfactory. In a search for [bounty migrants] (i.e. sponsored settlers to Australia), the first 20 hits on Live Search were entirely irrelevant.

The standard way of indicating that your words form a phrase is to surround them with inverted commas, e.g. ["South Norwood"] or ["John Smith"] or ["National Register of Archives"]. And the difference it can make is enormous: Google gives 4.3 million hits for ["John Smith"] against 41 million for [John Smith].

However, there is a downside: although you are getting more manageable and correct results, the phrase search will miss pages with "Smith, John", "John Richard Smith", so it is not an unmixed blessing. It will also inevitably miss "John, son of Richard and Mary Smith", but with present technology this is simply beyond the capabilities of search engines. Even so, with a reasonably unusual name, the phrase search can produce a list of hits short enough for each one to be checked – for example, a search for ["Cornelius McBride"] on Google produces only 89 hits, compared to half a million for [Cornelius McBride].

Of course, if your phrase is even slightly wrong, you may get no useful results at all – ["National Archives Register"] won't get you anywhere near the official page of the National Register of Archives, unless you're lucky and find other pages that also don't know its correct title, but do have a link to the official page.

Full Boolean algebra has a NEAR operator which largely solves these problems, but unfortunately it is not supported by any of the major search engines.

Refining your search

If you're looking for something very specific, you may find it immediately, as with the search in Figure 19-5. Otherwise, however, you shouldn't assume that your initial search will find what you want and produce a manageable list of results. If, for example, you are looking for individuals or families, or trying to find information on a particular genealogical topic, it is likely that you will have to look at quite a lot of the hits a search engine retrieves before finding what you are looking for. This makes it important to refine your search as much as possible.

The previous pages offer some advice on formulating your search, but however well you formulate it for the first run, you will often be able to refine it once you have looked at the initial results. Search engines provide a search box with your search terms at the top of each page of hits, so it is very straightforward to edit this and re-run the search.

Some search engines offer facilities to refine your search within the results you have already retrieved. In Google, clicking on the 'Search within results' link at the bottom of a results page takes you to another search page where you can specify a narrower search with additional words. However, this does not actually do anything clever – it just adds the new terms and re-runs your original search. If you know how to formulate searches, these facilities don't offer anything extra.

Search tips

Apart from taking care to formulate your query, there are a number of other things to bear in mind if your searching is going to be successful and not too time-consuming.

First, the better you know the particular search engine you are using, the better the results you will get. Look at the options it offers, and look at the Help or Tips pages. Although I have highlighted the main features of search engines, each has its idiosyncrasies. And while it is quite easy to find what a search engine will do, sometimes the only way to find out what it *will not* do is to see what is missing from the Help pages. It is also worth trying out some different types of query, just so you get a feel for how many results to expect and how they are sorted.

If you carry out searches on your particular surnames on a regular basis, it can be worth adding the URL of the results pages to your bookmarks

(Firefox) or favorites (Internet Explorer), making it easy to run the same query repeatedly.

This works because in most search engines the browser submits the search terms as an appendage to the URL, so, for example, when you search Google for [Grimsby trawlerman], the browser sends a URL which starts with <**http://www.google.co.uk/search?q=Grimsby+trawlerman...**>, which is then shown as the address of the first page of results. Bookmarking this page will allow you to retrieve the entire URL and then re-run the search.

There is one simple browser technique which will save you time when searching. Once you have got a list of search results that you want to look at, open each link you follow in a new window or tab so that the original list of search results remains open. (On Windows browsers a right mouse click over the link will bring up a menu with this option; on the Macintosh shift+click). Otherwise, each time you want to go back to your results the search engine will run the search all over again. Another useful trick for a long page of results is to save the page to your hard disk so that you can explore the hits at your leisure later.

Searching for files

Search engines can be used for finding other types of material online in addition to web pages. This material falls into two broad categories, which are generally dealt with in distinct ways.

First, there are files with textual material but which are in a proprietary document format rather than the HTML format used for web pages. All the main search engines index such material for a number of file formats, notably Adobe Acrobat (PDF) files, described in more detail on p. 52, and Microsoft Word files. This is important because many bodies put longer-term official information online in PDF format.

The content of such files is usually included automatically in the search engine's index, so you do not need to specify a particular file type when searching. However you will be able to choose 'file type' on the advanced search page of most search engines.

Multimedia files are generally handled differently, and the tendency is to have a separate search facility for each format. As you can see in Figure 19-1, Yahoo Search has separate tabs for images and video (audio is available from the 'more' link), while Google offers the images, groups (i.e. newsgroups, see p. 302), news, and maps tabs at the top of the home page.

Searching for photographs

Of the various multimedia file types, those of most interest to genealogists will be the graphics files of scanned or digital photographs. An overview

Figure 19-6 Search results in Google Images

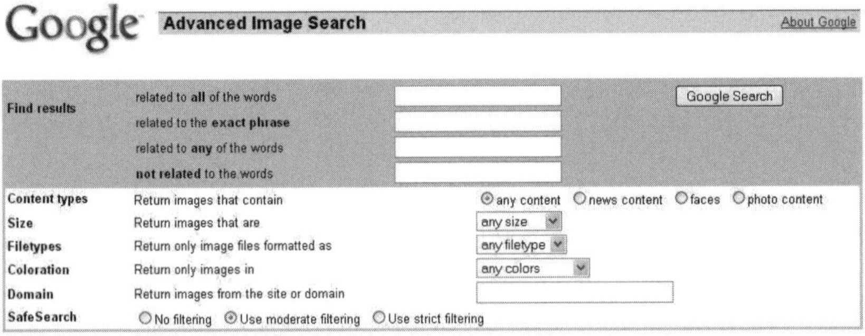

Figure 19-7 Google's Advanced Image Search

of the sorts of photographs you can expect to find online is given in Chapter 17.

When searching for images, you can't simply use the standard facilities of the search engines, since these look for text. Although any search results *will* include pages with images on them, particularly where there are relevant captions, this will probably not be obvious from the list of search engine results. This might be a way to find sites or pages that are devoted to photographs or postcards, but it will be a time-consuming way to find individual photographs.

Google has an excellent image search facility at <**images.google.com**>. The search results pages show thumbnail versions of the images which match your search criteria – clicking on an image takes you to a two-panel page with the image at the top and the page it comes from below. See Figure 19-6, the results of a search for [Chatham dockyard].

Mostly you will just get a normal search box, but if there is an advanced image search this should allow you to be more precise about the sorts of image you want, such as that from Google shown in Figure 19-7.

The Technical Advisory Services for Images has a very comprehensive review of image search facilities, including both general and specialist search engines, at <**www.tasi.ac.uk/resources/searchengines.html**>.

▌ Sites and domains

Although search engines are mainly used for searching the whole web, they can also be used to search individual websites. Since most major sites have their own search engine, the value of this may not be immediately obvious. But there are two advantages: you don't have to get to grips with a new search engine every time you visit a new site, and the big search engines often have much more sophisticated search facilities than those on individual sites, particular smaller ones. Using a general search engine, you can use the advanced search options to do more complex searches, specify a date range for pages retrieved, look for particular filetypes, etc. However, the external search results may not be as complete or as up-to-date as those from the internal search engine of a well-managed site.

Most search engines allow you to specify a site as one of the advanced search options – look on the advanced search page for a field labelled with the words 'site' or 'domain'. Just as with the OR search, you will see that if you know how to formulate it, you can carry out this type of search without going via the advanced search page, by using a special keyword in the basic search. The keyword varies from one search engine to another: in most it's the keyword **site**, followed by a colon, and then the site to be searched, e.g.

["tithe maps" site:www.nationalarchives.gov.uk]

In fact, you do not need to specify a complete site, but can restrict your search to a 'domain'. For example, a search with [site:nationalarchives.gov. uk] will include all National Archives sites, not just the main one. You can specify even less: [site:gov.uk] will conduct a search on pages from *any* UK government website, including those of local authorities. So the following search would be a good way of finding out which local record offices have projects to digitize tithe maps:

["tithe maps" project site:gov.uk]

Even if you want a specific county, it will often be quicker to type, say:

["tithe maps" project Staffordshire site:gov.uk]

than to find the site for Staffordshire's local authority or CRO, visit it, and then use its own search facility to find the tithe maps project.

However, there are some sites which can't be searched in this way: Genuki and WorldGenWeb are *distributed* services, which means that material is spread among many different servers. A search on [site:genuki. org.uk] will find only material which is on Genuki's main server and miss much of the county material which is in fact held elsewhere. Genuki, has its own search (see p. 331), which solves this problem.

▌Limitations

It is important to bear in mind some of the limitations of search engines. The most significant is that no search engine indexes anything like the whole of the web. A 1999 study conducted found that no search engine covered more than 16 per cent of the Web.[16] Although this study is several years old, there has not been any revolutions in search engine technology which suggest these results are not still broadly valid. Even a threefold improvement since 1999 would leave half the web missing from the best search engines. For this reason, when you cannot find something with a search engine, it does not mean it is not there.

Also, do not expect all results to be relevant. Even a fairly precisely formulated query may get some irrelevant results. A particular problem will be pages with long lists of names and places – these will inevitably produce some unwanted matches. For example, a surname interest list which contains an Atkinson from Lancashire and a Chapman from Devon would be listed among the results for a search on [Chapman Lancashire]. Particularly if you do not include terms like [genealogy] or ["family history"], or something that occurs more frequently on genealogy sites than elsewhere – ["monumental inscriptions"] or ["parish register"], for example – you will get many irrelevant results. And, of course, searching for a fairly common surname may retrieve numerous genealogical pages that are nothing to do with your own line.

There are ways to cut down on irrelevant results if you are looking for a

16   Steve Lawrence and C. Lee Giles, 'Accessibility of information on the web', *Nature*, 8 July 1999, pp. 107–109 (online at <**www.ist.psu.edu/faculty_pages/giles/publications/ Nature-99.pdf**>).

particular family. The more precise your geographical information the better: if you know your Chapman family came from Exeter, search not for [Chapman Devon] but for [Chapman Exeter Devon]. (Keep [Devon] in – you do not want Exeter College, HMS Exeter, Exeter in New Hampshire, etc.) If you search on both surnames of a married couple, even if they are individually quite common, you are much more likely to get relevant results, for example [Chapman Atkinson Exeter Devon genealogy]. If you use full names, all the better – even ["John Smith" "Ann Williams"] finds only 5,000 pages on Google; if you add [Yorkshire], it comes down to 974! You will still tend to retrieve a few surname listing pages, but there is little that can be done about that.

Finally, the web is full of spelling errors. For example, Google finds over 12,000 pages which mention a supposed county of 'Yorskhire'. In this sort of case, Google and Windows Live Search spot that you probably meant Yorkshire and offer to re-run the search; Yahoo automatically assumes you did misspell and includes results for both forms, though there is an option to show results for either spelling alone. The search engines often seem able to spot obvious misspellings for even quite small places, but you can't assume they will be as successful with surnames.

The 'invisible web'

Another problem in finding material on the internet, particularly records relating to individuals, is that much of it is simply not available in perma-nent web pages, which are readily accessible and can be indexed by search engines. This is what is called the 'invisible web', 'hidden web' or 'deep web'. and it includes:

- data held in databases, which can only be retrieved by completing a search form
- pages which cannot be seen without some sort of registration or login
- sites which deliberately exclude search engines

The only way to find the information is to go to the site and complete the registration procedure or fill in the search fields. Such material, which will include most of that covered in Chapters 4 to 6, cannot normally be retrieved by search engines. The same is true for much of the material covered in Chapter 14.

However, *some* such material does seem to be visible. For example, Google searches include some of the data at FamilySearch (see p. 101), as you can see by searching on [site:familysearch.org IGI *name*] or [site:family search.org "1881 census" *name*]. But since it is not remotely comprehensive – it finds only 73 of the several thousand Atkinson entries in the IGI, for example – it is not a substitute for visiting the site itself. In general, you should not count on this. Search engines will certainly not include data from commercial sites, since these require a login.

▌ Choosing a search engine

Which is the best search engine depends on a number of factors. The overriding factor is what you are looking for. There are several different aims you might have when using search engines. You might be trying to locate a particular site that you know must exist – you only need one result and you will recognize it when you see it. This is usually a search for a particular organization's website, or some particular resource that you've heard of but can't remember the location of.

Alternatively, you may be trying to find any site which might have information on a particular surname, or even a particular ancestor. The difference between this and the previous search is that there is no way of telling in advance what your search will turn up, and probably the search results will include a certain number, perhaps even a lot, of irrelevant sites. Another difference is that in the first case, you almost certainly have some idea of what the site might be called.

With this in mind, there are three main criteria to consider when deciding which search engine to use:

- the size of the index
- the way in which results are ranked
- the range of search options available

Size

The first of these is the most fundamental. Other things being equal, the search engine with the larger index is more likely to have what you are looking for. However, while this will be very important in looking for pedigree-related information, it will be largely irrelevant if you are looking for something like the Society of Genealogists' website, which you would expect *all* search engines to have in their indexes.

Since search engines are constantly striving to improve their performance and coverage, there can be no guarantee that what is the most comprehensive search engine at the time of writing will still hold that position when you are reading this.

But more to the point, it's hard to be sure exactly how large search engine indexes are at any one time. Some make explicit claims, which are impossible to verify; others don't provide any indication. To give you some idea, Table 19-2 shows the number of hits for some typical genealogical searches on the four main search engines in October 2008. All the figures should be

	[genealogy]	[genealogy Oxfordshire]	[genealogy Oxfordshire Brize Norton]
Google	73.4m	227,000	1,320
Yahoo	117m	631,000	1,190
Ask	320,000	24,000	175
Windows Live Search	85m	120,000	322

Table 19-2 Hits for [genealogy] on a range of search engines (October 2008)

treated with considerable caution (not to mention scepticism) as there is no way to verify their accuracy – indeed you can get quite different figures just by changing the order of your search terms. However, the figures for the narrowest of the searches, which are likely to be the most accurate, support the widespread view that Google and Yahoo have the largest indexes, well ahead of the other two.

Ranking

Unless you get only a handful of hits, one of the issues which will determine the usefulness of search results will be whether the most relevant ones are listed first. In fact poor ranking effectively invalidates the virtues of a large index – a page which is ranked 5,000 out of 700,000 might as well not be included in the results at all because you're never going to look at it.

It's difficult to be specific about how search engines rank their results (since these are valuable commercial secrets) but broadly speaking they assess relevance based on:

- the frequency of your search terms in the pages retrieved
- the presence of these words in high-profile positions such as the page title, headings, etc.

Google explicitly uses a popularity rating, giving higher priority to pages which many others are linked to, though probably other search engines do this, too. This is good if what you want are recommendations – which is the best site on military genealogy, say. But if you are searching for surnames and pedigrees, which are probably on personal websites, it may be positively unhelpful, as these will automatically rank lower than well-connected commercial sites which happen to have the same surname on them. Almost any surname search will tend to list the major genealogy sites high up, especially those with pages for individual surnames or surname message boards. Unfortunately, in spite of past experiments in this area, none of the major search engines currently offers any way of controlling how results are ranked.

For personal genealogy pages, the only way I have found of doing this is to include the phrase ["surname list"] in the search terms. The basis for this is that many of the software packages used to create a website from a genealogy database (see Chapter 20) will create a page with this as a title or heading. The results will also include, of course, some non-personal sites such as the county surname lists mentioned on p. 209, but the phrase does not seem to be common on non-genealogy sites, and is less likely to be encountered on commercial genealogy sites.

Overlap

However, there is an argument that choosing the 'best' search engine is not enough. It's not just that no individual search engine indexes more than half the web. The fact is that each search engine includes in its index some pages which may not be in another search engine's index at all. And there is a very useful tool which illustrates the size of the problem, the Ranking utility at <**ranking.thumbshots.com**>. This allows you to compare the top 100 hits for a search on any two search engines, and if you try it with something reasonably rare you get a clear indication of the limited coverage.

Figure 19-8 shows the results for the phrase ["bounty migrants" Australia] in Google and Yahoo. Although the two search engines have similar

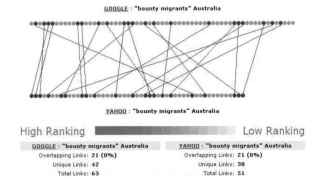

Figure 19-8 Thumbshots: searches for ["bounty migrants" Australia]

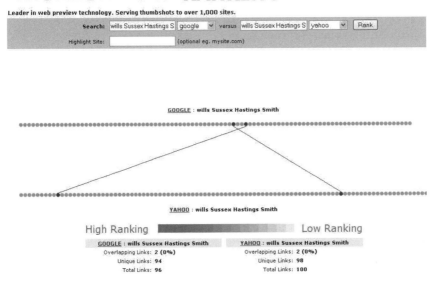

Figure 19-9 Thumbshots: searches for [wills Sussex Hastings Smith]

numbers of results, two thirds of these are not found by the other search engine. Of course, there are cases where this won't matter: if you're looking for the site of an organization, for example. But if you're searching, as here, for historical information, or for a particular ancestor by name, you could be missing useful material if you only use one search engine.

What you're missing can be even more startling if you do a search for more specific information. Figure 19-9 compares the results for [wills Sussex Hastings Smith] on Google and Yahoo: only two of the first 100 results are common to the two search engines!

The moral is obvious: in a comprehensive web search for individual ancestors and matching surname interests, you cannot afford to use only one search engine, no matter how large its index may be.

Using multiple search engines

One technique for overcoming the fact that no search engine indexes the whole of the web is to carry out the same search on several different search engines. The easiest way to do this is to add a range of other search engines to your browser's built-in search facility: in Internet Explorer 8, click on the down arrow to the right of the search box and select 'Find More Providers'; in Firefox, click on the down arrow to the left of the search box and select 'Manage Search Engines'. Once you have done this you can quickly carry out a search on several different search engines in sequence.

Even more labour-saving are meta-search engines. In these you enter your search only once and it is then automatically submitted to a range of search engines. One of the most popular is DogPile <**www.dogpile.com**>, which automatically submits a query to a number of search engines and directories. Another well-known meta-search engine is MetaCrawler at <**www.metacrawler.com**>.

It might seem that these types of search facility make visiting the individual search engines redundant, and they might well do so for certain types of search. But there are important limitations. While you can do an AND search or a phrase search by this method, anything more complex is going to fall down because of the different facilities offered by the different engines. Also, it is important to recognize that, for almost all searches, meta-search engines give *fewer* results than the individual search engines do – for example, MetaCrawler gives only 27 results for [wills Sussex Hastings Smith]. This is because meta-search engines select the first few results from each search engine, typically the first ten. In fact, a meta-search engine may retrieve no results at all from a search engine which is slow to respond and is timed out.

For these reasons, meta-search engines are not appropriate for all types of search. They are best when you are looking for a particular site, or want to find the most popular sites devoted to a particular subject. But they are ill-suited to locating pages devoted to particular pedigrees or surnames.

A similar tool for searching is a 'searchbot', sometimes also called an 'intelligent agent' or a 'desktop search tool'. Rather than a website which you must go to in order to carry out a search, a searchbot is a piece of software that runs on your own computer, allowing you to formulate searches offline and then go online to do the search. Searchbots work like meta-search engines – they submit a query to many different search engines – and have the same strengths and weaknesses. The advantage of a searchbot, though, is that the full results are then stored to your hard disk, and you can examine them at your leisure without re-running the search. It will also store the details of each search, making it easy to repeat.

There are dozens of searchbots, available as shareware or freeware from software archives such as Tucows (see <**www.tucows.com/Windows/ Internet/Searchbots/**> for Windows searchbots).

Genealogy search tools

The search tools discussed so far have been general-purpose tools, but there are also many special-purpose tools. Some of these are discussed elsewhere in the text: there is a whole range of search engines dedicated to locating living people, by geographical location or email address (see p. 233), and image search tools are discussed earlier in this chapter. Other useful dedicated tools are gazetteers, which allow you to locate places (see p. 237). Chapter 12 covers online catalogues to material which is itself not online. All of these are likely to be better for their particular purpose than the general search engines.

Unfortunately, there seems to be no comprehensive search engine specializing in genealogy, though there have been a number of short-lived attempts. In part no doubt, this is because of the difficulty of compiling a well-defined list of genealogy sites to index. Cyndi's List has a 'Search Engines' page at <**www.cyndislist.com/search.htm#Genealogy**>, but many of the sites listed are in fact directories and others are limited to searching online pedigrees (these are covered in Chapter 14).

Although restricted in scope, the Genuki Search at <**www.genuki.org. uk/search/**> is probably the most useful dedicated search engine for British and Irish family history. Although it confines itself to 'institutional' websites with material relevant to the British Isles, its index in fact includes many of the most important non-commercial genealogy sites:

- Genuki itself
- The National Archives
- the Society of Genealogists
- the Federation of Family History Societies
- the Guild of One-Name Studies
- the family history societies listed by Genuki (see p. 20)
- most county surname interest lists (see p. 209)

A new genealogy search site due to be launched in March 2009 is Geneally at <**www.geneally.com**>. At the time of writing the site is accessible in 'beta' mode, so it is not possible to evaluate it properly, but it certainly looks potentially useful.

Further information

Because of the importance of searching to serious use of the internet there are many sites with guides to search engines and search techniques. Note, however, that there have been many changes in individual search engines over the last three years and older materials will often be inaccurate when discussing the specifics of particular search engines. Most previously independent search engines now use Google or Yahoo's indexes for their results. At the end of 2006, Windows Live Search replaced Microsoft's older MSN Search.

There are useful comparative tables of some of the main search engine features in Infopeople's 'Search Tools Chart' at <**www.infopeople.org/ search/chart.html**> and on Search Engine Showdown at <**searchengine** showdown.com/features/>, which has links to reviews of each. For evaluation of the different search engines, see the links on the 'Evaluation Of Internet Searching And Search Engines' page at <**www.umanitoba.ca/ libraries/units/engineering/evaluate.html**>. Search Engine Showdown at <**www.searchengineshowdown.com**> has a lot of information about search engines, as does Search Engine Watch at <**www.searchenginewatch.com**>.

Among the many online tutorials, the University of California at Berkeley's 'Finding Information on the Internet' at <**www.lib.berkeley.edu/ TeachingLib/Guides/Internet/FindInfo.html**>, and BrightPlanet's very comprehensive 'Guide to Effective Searching of the Internet' at <**www. brightplanet.com/images/stories/pdf/searchenginetutorial.pdf**> are particularly recommended. Rice University has a concise guide to 'Internet Searching Strategies' at <**library.rice.edu/services/digital_media_center/ online_guides/using-electronic-resources /internet-searching-strategies**>.

There is a guide to searching specifically for genealogy sites and pages in 'Finding your ancestors on the Internet' at <**genealogy.about.com/library/ weekly/aa041700a.htm**>. The 'Search Engines' page on Cyndi's List at <**www.cyndislist.com/search.htm**> has many links to resources relating to search techniques, though a good number of these now have quite out-of-date information.

While there are any number of books about searching the web, there is, so far as I am aware, only one current book on the subject specifically for genealogists: Daniel M. Lynch's *Google Your Family Tree* (FamilyLink.com, 2008) covers the whole range of Google's facilities and services from a family history perspective, and three of its 14 chapters are devoted to getting the best out of the search engine.

20

PUBLISHING YOUR FAMILY HISTORY ONLINE

So far we have been concentrating on using the internet to retrieve information and contact others who share your interests. But you can also take a more active role in publicizing your own interests and publishing the results of your research for others to find.

Two ways of doing this have already been touched upon. You can post a message with details of your surname interests to a suitable mailing list (see Chapter 18). Although your message may be read by only a relatively small number of readers (compared to the total number of people online, that is), it will be archived, providing a permanent record. Also, you can submit your surname interests to the surname lists for the counties your ancestors lived in (Chapter 14). This will be easier for others to find than material in mailing list archives, since anyone with ancestors from a county is likely to check that archive.

Both of these methods are quick and easy, but they have the limitation that they offer quite basic information, which may not be enough for someone else to spot a link with your family, particularly with more common surnames. The alternative is to publish your family history on the web.

Publishing options

There are two ways of putting your family history online: you can submit your family tree to a pedigree database such as those discussed in Chapter 14, or you can create your own website. In fact, these are not mutually exclusive, and there are good reasons for doing both, as each approach has its own merits.

Pedigree databases

There are obvious advantages in submitting your family tree to one of the pedigree databases:

- It is a very quick way of getting your tree online.
- The fact that these sites have many visitors and are obvious places to search for contacts means that you are getting your material to a large audience.

But there are some disadvantages to note:

- The material is held in a database, which means it can only be found by going to the site and using the built-in search facilities. It will not be found by anyone using a general web search engine such as those discussed in Chapter 19.
- You can only submit material that is actually held in your genealogy database, and you will not be able to include any other documentary or photographic material relating to your family history.
- Depending on which pedigree database you use, you may be giving up some rights, and your control over the material may be limited (see p. 233).

As long as you check the terms and conditions of any site you use for this purpose, these disadvantages shouldn't discourage you from submitting your pedigree to a database. They simply mean that you might want to consider having your own website as well.

A personal website

Creating your own website may sound like much more work, but there are a number of reasons why it can be better than simply uploading your family tree to a database:

- You can put a family tree on your own site almost as easily as you can submit it to a database.
- You can include any other textual material you have collected which may be of interest: transcriptions of original documents, extracts from parish registers or General Register Office indexes for your chosen names.
- You can include images, whether they are scanned from old photographs in your collection or pictures you have taken of places where your ancestors lived.
- If you submit the address of your site to search engines, all the individuals in your tree and all the other information on your site will be indexed by them, so they can be found by the techniques discussed in Chapter 19. People will not need to be familiar with a particular pedigree database site.
- There will be no issues of rights or the ability to edit or remove material – it will be entirely under your control.

The great thing about a personal website is that it is not like publishing your family history in book form: you do not have to do all these things at once. You can start with a small amount of material – a family tree, or even just a list of your surname interests, perhaps – and add to it as and when you like.

But there are a couple of issues to be aware of if you are going to create your own site:

- If you set it up in free web space provided by your ISP you will have to move the whole site if you subsequently switch to another provider. Search engines and everyone who has linked to your site will have to be informed.
- If your site is going to provide more than a basic family tree, you will need to learn how to create web pages.

Both of these issues are tackled later in this chapter.

It is worth pointing out that apart from the major online databases, much of the genealogical material on the web is the result of the efforts of individuals making it available on personal sites. If you have any genealogical information that may be of interest to others, in addition to your personal pedigree, you should consider making it available online.

Whichever of these options you choose, you should avoid publishing information about living people, a topic that is discussed in more detail on p. 223.

Family trees for the web

Probably the most important thing to put on the web is your family tree. This will make it possible for other genealogists to discover shared interests and ancestors, and get in touch with you.

Whether you are going to submit your family tree to a pedigree database or create your own site, you will need to extract the data from your genealogy database software in a format ready for the web. (If you are not yet using a genealogy database to keep a record of your ancestors and what you have discovered about them, look at 'Software' on p. 371.) The alternative would be to type up the data from scratch, which would be both time-consuming and prone to error.

GEDCOM

GEDCOM, which stands for GEnealogical Data COMmunication, is a standard file format for exchanging family trees between one computer and another, or one computer program and another. It was developed in the 1980s by the LDS Church as a format for users of Personal Ancestral File (see p. 372) to make submissions to Ancestral File (see p. 216). It has subsequently been adopted and supported by all major genealogy software producers to enable users to transfer data into or out of their programs. It can also be used to download records from the various LDS databases at <**www.familysearch.org**> (see p. 101) in a format that allows them to be imported into a genealogy program. Although designed by the LDS Church for its own use, it has become the *de facto* standard for exchanging genealogical data electronically.

The reason you need to know about GEDCOM is that all the pedigree databases expect you to submit your family tree in the form of a GEDCOM file. Also, provided your genealogy software can save your pedigree information in GEDCOM format, there are many programs which can automatically create a set of web pages from that file. On the PC, GEDCOM files have the file extension *.ged*.

You do not need to know the technical details of GEDCOM in order to publish your family tree on the web, but Cyndi's List has a page devoted to GEDCOM resources at <**www.cyndislist.com/gedcom.htm**> with links to explanatory material and technical specifications. Dick Eastman has a straightforward explanation of what GEDCOM is at <**www.eogn. com/archives/news0219.htm**>. For the technically inclined, the GEDCOM specification is at <**homepages.rootsweb.ancestry.com/~pmcbride/ gedcom/55gctoc.htm**>.

Whatever genealogy software you are using for your family tree, you should be able to find an option to export data to a GEDCOM file. Typically, this option will be found under **Export** on the **File** menu but, if not, the manual or the online help for your program should contain information on GEDCOM export.

Genealogy databases

All recent versions of the main genealogy database programs have facilities to create a set of web pages, including the following:

- Ancestral Quest
- Family Historian
- Family Matters
- Family Origins
- Generations
- Kinship Archivist
- Legacy Family Tree
- Personal Ancestral File
- Relatively Yours
- Reunion (Macintosh)

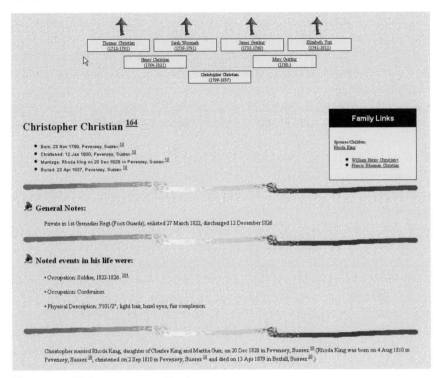

Figure 20-1 Web page created by Legacy

- RootsMagic
- The Master Genealogist
- Ultimate Family Tree
- Win-Family

If you have one of these programs, it will be the most straightforward tool to use for turning your pedigree online into a set of web pages.[17]

The programs vary in what they actually produce for a website, but at the very least all will give you:

- a surname index
- an index of individuals
- a series of linked pages with either family groups or details of individuals

You should have a choice between an ancestor tree, a descendant tree, or a

17   I have excluded Family Tree Maker from this listing, as it cannot create a standalone website.

full pedigree, and there are many options as to which individuals, and what information about them, to include.

By way of example, Figure 20-1 shows a page created by Legacy 7.0. This is a web version of a standard descendancy report. Whereas in a printed pedigree you have to turn manually to other pages, here the highlighted names are links which will take you straight to the entries for children. The small superscript numbers link to descriptions of the sources.

Family websites

Another possibility, halfway between a pedigree database and creating your own website, is to use one of the subscription services which act as online genealogy databases. These differ from the pedigree databases in that they provide more sophisticated facilities, such as sharing material with your family while excluding it from general view. They may also have a facility to enter data directly rather than submitting a GEDCOM file, though it's unlikely this would be a useful facility for anyone but the casual family historian. Among the sites which provide this sort of facility are:

- TribalPages at <**www.tribalpages.com**>, which allows you to set up a free website with certain limitations (no more than 50 photos), or you can subscribe $19 or $29 a year for a 'standard' or premium' site with greater facilities. With TribalPages you can choose to have your site password protected, which means you can restrict access to chosen members of your family.
- MyTrees.com at <**www.kindredkonnections.com**>, which offers a basic service free of charge and a subscription service at $15 for one month and $100 for a year. Details of living people are normally hidden but can be made accessible to family members.

Other services of this type are listed on the 'Genealogy Home Page Construction Kit' on Cyndi's List at <**www.cyndislist.com/construc.htm**>.

If you just want to share your family tree with your immediate (known) family, these may provide a better solution than trying to password protect an individual website. But they are less well suited to disseminating your pedigree to the wider world.

▌Web publishing basics

If you are just going to upload a GEDCOM file to a pedigree database, you do not need to know anything else about web publishing. But if you are going to create your own website you will need to familiarize yourself with what is involved in the process. While it is increasingly possible to create a website without in-depth technical knowledge, it is still essential to have *some* understanding of what is involved. There is not space here to deal with the topic in detail, but this and the following sections cover the basics and there are suggested sources of further information at the end of this chapter.

What is a website?

A website is simply a collection of individual files stored on a web server, which is a computer with (usually) a permanent connection to the web and the capacity to deal with lots of requests for web pages from all over the internet. While larger companies have their own dedicated computers to act as web servers, smaller organizations and home users simply get a portion of the file space on the server belonging to their Internet Service Provider (this is called web hosting).

When you create a website, you first create all the pages on your own computer, then you upload the files to your space on the web server.

Assuming you already have internet access, what you need in order to create a website is:

- web space
- software for creating web pages
- software for uploading the pages to your web space

If you are going to have photographs or scanned images of documents on your site, you will also need graphics editing software.

One important aspect of web publishing is that it can be done with any computer and a wide range of software. You do not need a specially powerful computer, and you almost certainly have web publishing software on your computer already even if you don't realize it (see p. 343). You will probably be able to use your browser for uploading pages, though there is dedicated freeware and shareware software which will make the process easier.

The other thing you need for a website is time. Even though basic web publishing is not difficult, you will need to learn how it works and you will want to experiment before unleashing your site on the public. You will also need to give some thought to exactly what material you are going to publish, and how best to organize it so that your visitors can find the information they are looking for – just as you would for a book, in fact.

Web space

In order to have a website you need to have space on a web server for the files which make up your website. If you are paying your Internet Service Provider for your connection to the internet, you will almost certainly find that your subscription includes this facility at no extra cost. It is usual for ISPs to give their customers at least 50Mb of space. Unless you are intending to include many high-quality graphics or a *very* large amount of primary data online this should be more than enough space for a personal genealogy site. It is even quite a respectable amount for a family history society.

While the free ISPs do not always give subscribers free web space, quite a number of them do. If yours does not, there are a number of companies that offer web space entirely free of charge regardless of who your ISP is. FortuneCity <**www.fortunecity.co.uk**>, for example, offers 100Mb of web space, while Tripod <**www.tripod.lycos.co.uk**> offers 1024Mb. A good place for genealogy sites is RootsWeb <**www.rootsweb.ancestry.com**> with its 'Freepages', free unlimited web space. Details will be found at <**accounts. rootsweb.ancestry.com**>. Other companies can be found by searching Yahoo for the phrase 'free web space', or consult the Free Webspace directory at <**www.free-webhosts.com**>.

The disadvantage of such services is that they will normally include advertising on your pages, either as a banner ad at the top of a page or as adverts in a separate pop-up window (that's how they can afford to host your site free of charge). There may also be some restrictions on what you can put on your site, though this is unlikely to be of concern to genealogists creating personal sites. The only significant limitation I've encountered is that RootsWeb does not let you upload GEDCOM files – they insist you submit them to their WorldConnect site instead (see p. 216).

The web address of your site will depend on who is providing your web space and what sort of account you have with them. There are two main standard formats for URLs of personal websites:

- <**site name/username**>, i.e. the folder 'username' on the shared site 'sitename'
- <**username.sitename**>, i.e. a domain name unique to 'username'

If you are planning a substantial website with material of general interest rather than simply your own pedigree, or if you are going to set up a site for an organization or genealogy project, it is useful to have a permanent address rather than one that is dependent on your current ISP or web space provider.

- Register your own domain name (see the Nominet site at <**www.nic.uk**> for information).
- Use a 'redirection service' such as V3 <**www.v3.com**>. This allocates a permanent free web address of the format <**go.to/user-id/**>, which re- directs people to your actual web space, wherever it currently may be.

Having your own domain name is the ideal solution, but the registration and hosting will require some modest annual expenditure, and you will need to master one or two technical issues. There is a straightforward guide to setting up your own domain in Dick Eastman's newsletters for 25 September and 2 October 2002, archived at <**www.eogn.com/archives/news0238.htm**> and <**www.eogn.com/archives/news0239.htm**>.

What is a web page?

When viewed on a web browser, web pages look like a form of desktop publishing and you might think that you need very complex and expensive software to produce a website. In fact the opposite is true: web pages are in principle very simple. Each page is simply a text file with the text that is to appear on the page along with instructions to the browser on how to display the text. The images that appear on a page are not strictly part of it, they are separate files. The page contains instructions telling the browser where to download them from. (This is why you can often see the individual images being downloaded after the text of a page has already appeared in the browser window.) In a similar way, all the links on a web page are created by including instructions to the browser on what page to load when the user clicks on the links. (You can easily get a general idea of how this all works if you load a web page, ideally a fairly simple one, into your browser and use the **View Source** option in Firefox or Internet Explorer, on the **View** menu in both browsers.)

This means that a web page is not a completed and fixed design like the final output of a desktop publishing program on the printed page. It is a set of instructions which the browser carries out. And the reader has a certain amount of control over how the browser does this, telling it not to load images, what font or colour scheme to use, what size the text should be and, most obviously, controlling the size and shape of the browser window it all has to fit into. The reason for this flexibility is that those who view a web page will be using a wide variety of different computer equipment, with a range of screen sizes and resolutions and no guarantee that particular fonts will be available. Also, readers will be using a range of different web browsers. The web page designer has to create a page that will look good, or at least be readable for all these users.

Figure 20-2 shows the text for a very simple web page. Figure 20-3 shows what this page looks like when displayed in a browser.

In Figure 20-2, the angled brackets mark the 'tags' which act as instructions to the browser, so the tag < IMG...> tells the browser to insert an image at this point. The tags are collectively referred to as 'markup', because they instruct the browser what to do with the text in the same way that in traditional publishing an editor marks up a manuscript for typesetting. All the

```
<HTML>

<HEAD>

<TITLE>This appears at the top of the browser window</TITLE>

</HEAD>

<BODY>

<H1>Here's the main heading</H1>

<P>Here's a very brief paragraph of text with <STRONG>bold</STRONG> and <EM>
italics</EM>.</P>

<P><IMG SRC="tree.gif">Here's another paragraph with an image at the start
of it.</P>

<P>Here's a link to the
<A HREF="http://www.nationalarchives.gov.uk/">National Archives</A> web
site.</P>

</BODY>

</HTML>
```

Figure 20-2 The text file for a simple web page

text that is not inside angled brackets appears on the page, but the tags themselves do not. Many of the tags work in pairs, for example the tags <EM>...</EM> tell the browser to find a way to emphasize the enclosed text, which is usually done with italics. Links to other websites and other pages on your own site are created by putting the tag <A HREF="site-or-file-name">...</A> round the hotspot, i.e. the text you want the reader to click on, with the web address or file name between the inverted commas ('A' stands for 'Anchor').

You can get a good idea of how this works by saving a copy of the page shown in Figure 20-3 from <**www.spub.co.uk/tgi4/dummypage.html**> and then editing it in Notepad or another text editor to see what happens if you move or delete tags. (Do not try it with a word processor!)

Figure 20-3 The page in Figure 20-2 viewed in a browser

The set of tags that can be used to create web pages is specified in a standard called Hypertext Markup Language (HTML). The standard is controlled by the World Wide Web Consortium (W3C) <**www.w3.org**> on the basis of extensive consultation with those who have an interest in the technology of the web. HTML has been through several versions since its inception in 1991, and the latest is version 4, which came into use at the beginning of 1998, though a new HTML 5 is under discussion.

Software

In order to create your website you will need suitable software, and there is quite a range of possibilities. Which is best depends on what software you have already got, what your website is to contain, and how serious you are about your site. One thing to remember is that no matter what software you use, the output is always a plain text file. It is not a file in a proprietary format belonging to a single manufacturer, which is what makes exchanging files between different word processors so problematic. This means you can use a variety of software programs to edit a single page.

Another important point is that you almost certainly do not need to buy additional software – you may well already have some web publishing tools installed on your computer, and if not there are free programs which will provide all the facilities you need.

There are three basic approaches to creating web pages:

- You can create them 'by hand', i.e. by typing in the tags yourself using a text editor.
- You can use a program which works like a word processor but automatically converts the page layout into the appropriate text and tags.
- You can use a program which automatically generates pages from a set of data.

The following sections look at the sorts of software that can be used to create web pages.

Editors

In the early days of the web there was no special-purpose software designed for creating sites, and commercial software had no facilities for turning material into web pages. The only way to create a site was with a text editor, typing in both the text of a page and the HTML tags. The surprising thing is that, in spite of the many pieces of software that are now able to create web pages, text editors are still in use among professional web authors. The reason is that these give you complete control and do not make decisions for you. The disadvantage, of course, is that you will need to know what the relevant tags are and how to use them. But even if you mainly use another program to create your web pages, a text editor can still be useful. This is particularly the case where you have been using a program that is not designed specifically for web authoring, but has the facility to save files in HTML format as an add-on. All such programs have *some* failings in their web page output. If you need to correct these, it is easiest to use a text editor.

Although you can use a very basic text editor like the Windows Notepad, you will find it is hard work to create web pages with something so primitive, and it is better to use a more sophisticated editor. Some, like TextPad or NoteTab (downloadable from **<www.textpad.com>** and **<www.notetab. com>** respectively), even though designed as general-purpose text editors, offer a number of features to make web authoring easier. TextPad, for example, allows you to have many documents open at once, and has a comprehensive search and replace function covering all open documents. It has a 'clip library' of the main HTML tags – just clicking on an entry in the library adds the tags to your page (see Figure 20-4).

Word processors

All the main word processors have the ability to create web pages. This is particularly useful if you already have material typed up, because you will be able to turn it into web pages very easily – there should be a **Save as HTML** or **Save as Web Pages** option on the **File** menu. But note that this will not create a web page for each *page* of your word-processed document,

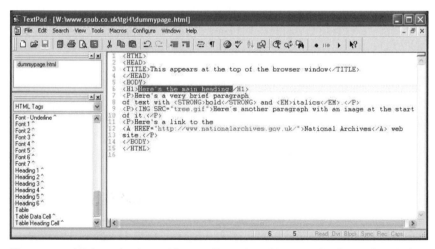

Figure 20-4 Web authoring with an editor: the <H1> tags in the main window were inserted **around** the text simply by selecting the text and then clicking on Heading 1 in the left-hand panel

it will turn each *document* into a single web page. Once you have saved a page (and thereby given it a file name) you will able to make links to it from other pages.

You might think that with this sort of facility there is no real need for other web authoring software but, unfortunately, word processors are not always particularly good at producing web pages that will read well on the wide variety of set-ups internet users have. In particular, they often try to reproduce precisely every nuance of the word-processed document, particularly the page layout, which may have no relevance for a web browser. This can lead to very cumbersome web pages that may download slowly and display poorly. However, for text-only pages with a straightforward layout, this is a very quick way to get material on to the web.

OpenOffice.org is a freeware office suite (with word-processing, spreadsheet, etc.) available for Window, Macintosh OS-X and Linux. Its word-processing component, Writer, can be used as a web editor with WYSIWYG ('what you see is what you get') and text-editing views. If you create a new HTML document from scratch, it produces good web pages, but pages created from existing word-processed documents are less good. Unfortunately, the OpenOffice Writer cannot be downloaded separately, you have to download the whole suite (from <**www.openoffice.org**>), which is over 100Mb in size. If you have a modem dialup connection this will be impracticable, but you may be able to find a copy on a computer magazine CD.

Desktop publishing

If you have desktop publishing software such as QuarkXPress or Microsoft Publisher, you might think these would be useful for creating websites, since they offer much more sophisticated page layout. Unfortunately, web pages created by such programs are often poor for readers, since they try to reproduce *exactly* what would appear on a printed page. This is quite misguided: on the web, the page designer has no control over the size and shape of the browser window, the absolute sizes of fonts, etc. Pages created by programs like these can be full of problems for readers that a novice web author is unlikely to be able to deal with, even if the hassle were worthwhile.

Dedicated web authoring software

A better all-round option is a piece of dedicated web authoring software. This will provide *only* the layout facilities that are available in HTML. Many such packages offer both a design/layout mode, which looks like a word processor, and a text editing mode which allows you to work directly with tags. For the last few years, the most highly regarded commercial program has consistently been Adobe Dreamweaver (see Figure 20-5). Microsoft has

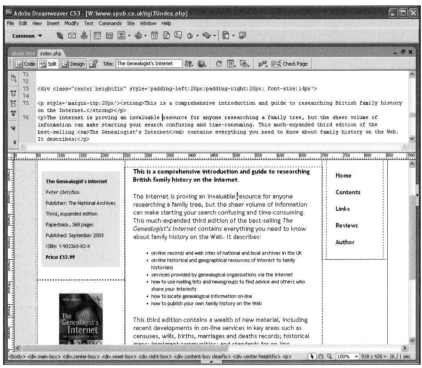

Figure 20-5 Editing the website for the third edition of this book in Dreamweaver CS3

recently replaced its popular FrontPage web authoring software with Expression Web. Unfortunately, both of these are priced for professional users, and it would be difficult to justify the expense for a small personal website, though there are very substantial discounts for educational users.

If you are only going to create a fairly simple site, you do not need to pay for a commercial web authoring package, as there are a number of free options:

- **EvrSoft's FirstPage** can be downloaded free from <**www.evrsoft.com**>. It is particularly good for those new to web authoring, as long as you don't mind working with tags, as it has Easy, Normal, Expert and Hardcore modes, with more and more complex features available as you progress. Although there is no WYSIWYG editing, there is a preview window which can show you immediately the effect of any changes you make to the page (see Figure 20-6).[18]

---

18 Your anti-virus software may object to one of the sample files installed by FirstPage, but the file *does not contain a virus*. You can delete the file to get rid of the warnings without affecting the operation of FirstPage.

- **Nvu** can be downloaded from <**www.nvu.com**>. It is available for Macintosh OS-X and Linux as well as Windows.

Trial versions of web authoring packages are frequently to be found on the cover CD-ROMs of computer magazines, and dozens of other shareware packages are available for free downloading. The best place to look is Tucows, which has a wide selection of web authoring software for Windows and Macintosh under 'Development & Web Authoring' at <**www.tucows. com/Windows/DevelopmentWebAuthoring/**> and <**www.tucows.com/ Macintosh/DevelopmentWebAuthoring/**> respectively. Look particularly at the pages for 'HTML Editors' and 'Visual and WYSIWYG editors'.

Online software

Some free web space providers have online tools for creating websites directly on the site without having to upload it from your own computer. Obviously, this will not help you convert your family tree for online viewing, but it is a quick way to get a website up and running. Some of the providers offering this facility are:

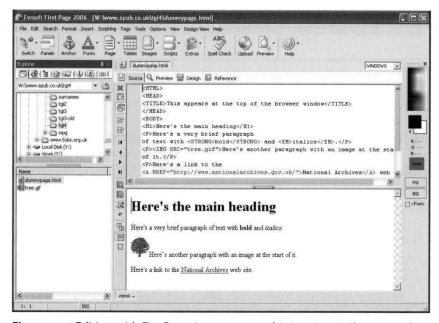

Figure 20-6 Editing with FirstPage. In some ways this is quite similar to an editor like TextPad, but note the preview panel which shows what the page looks like as well as the actual HTML below, and the colour palette at the right

- Freeservers <www.freeservers.com>
- Tripod <www.tripod.lycos.co.uk>
- Yahoo! GeoCities <**geocities.yahoo.com**>

Adobe Acrobat

All the software mentioned so far creates pages in HTML. But in fact browsers can cope with files in other formats, either by starting up the relevant application or by using a 'plug-in', an add-on component to display a particular file type.

Adobe Acrobat is a program that can turn any page designed for printing into a document for the web. It does this not by creating a page in HTML, but by using a proprietary file format ('PDF', which stands for 'portable document format'). A free reader is available, which can be used as a plug-in by any browser, allowing PDF files to be displayed in the browser window when they are encountered. (If you have not already got it installed, the Adobe Acrobat reader can be downloaded free of charge from <**www. adobe.com**>.)

This is not a complete answer to creating a genealogy website – a site consisting solely of PDF files would be very cumbersome, since the files are much larger than plain HTML files and would download slowly. But it is a good way to make existing material that you already have in word-processor files quickly available. It is particularly good for longish documents which people will want to save to disk or print out rather than read on screen. (Web pages do not always print well.) For example, if you want to put online one of the longer reports that your genealogy database can create, turning this into a PDF file would be a good way to do it. Figure 20-7 shows an Ahnentafel report from Personal Ancestral File turned into a PDF file – you can view the whole file at <**www.spub.co.uk/tgi4/eak. pdf**>. This can also be a good solution for putting trees online.

Macintosh OS-X has built-in facilities for creating PDF files, but for Windows you need additional software. Adobe's own software for creating PDF files is a commercial product costing over £250, an expense it would be hard to justify for a personal website (though you may find older versions in online auctions for much less). But there are a number of shareware and freeware programs available which can be used to create PDF files. Though they lack the more sophisticated document management features of Adobe Acrobat itself, they will be perfectly adequate for turning word-processor documents into web pages, or creating PDF files from your genealogy software. You can find a list and downloads at <**www.tucows. com/Windows/DesignTools/PDFTools/**>. OpenOffice (see p. 345) can import a wide range of documents and then save them in PDF format. Dick Eastman's newsletters have had a number of articles on free PDF

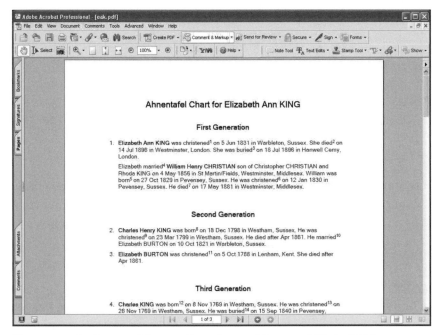

Figure 20-7 An Ahnentafel report from Personal Ancestral File in PDF format

creation tools in recent years – search the archive from the home page at
<blog.eogn.com> for 'PDF create'.

Databases and spreadsheets

If you store some of your genealogical information in a spreadsheet or
database, there are several ways of putting the data on a website.

First, most recent database and spreadsheet software can create web
pages directly (probably via a **File | Export** menu or a **File | Save As** menu
option). By way of example, Figure 20-8 shows the first few entries from a
database of Sussex parish register entries for the surname Christian as a
web page exported from Microsoft Excel.

If this option is not available, there is a reliable fall-back: plain text. Your
database or spreadsheet will undoubtedly have a **Save as text** function, and
all browsers can display plain text files. This will not look as good as the
example above, but if someone finds an ancestor in your list, that will be
the last thing they will be worried about.

You can even take this text file and embed it in a proper web page. There
is a special pair of tags, <PRE>... </PRE> (for *pre*formatted) which, when
put round formatted text like this, will preserve all the line breaks and the
multiple spaces, thus maintaining the original format.

Year	Month	Day	Place	Event	Surname	Forenames	Kin
1561	9	28	East Grinstead	C	Christian	William	s. Robert
1577	10	6	East Grinstead	M	Christian	Margaret	widow + Thomas Lullingden
1583	12	28	Lindfield	C	Christian	Jone	d. Rowland
1584	4	26	Lindfield	B	Christian	George	s. Rowland
1586	4	18	Lindfield	C	Christian	Jane	d. Rowland
1589	9	8	East Grinstead	M	Christian	Alice	+ William Goodyer
1595	2	1	East Grinstead	M	Christian	Agnes	+ Charles Adamson
1596	2	26	Pevensey	B	Christian	Joane	wife of Martin
1602	3	6	Waldron	C	Christian	Abraham	s. Martin
1602	6	19	Lindfield	B	Christian		child of Rowland
1606	2	6	Lindfield	M	Christian	Rowland	+ Joan Chantler
1606	12	26	Catsfield	C	Christian	Sara	d. Martin
1611	4	14	Pevensey	C	Christian	Marie	d. of Martine & _
1613	9	10	Lindfield	B	Christian	Rowland	
1613	11	10	Lindfield	B	Christian	Jone	widow
1615	8	10	Pevensey	B	Christian	Martin	
1615	10	19	Hellingly	M	Christian	Elizabeth	+ Steven Bankes
1615	11	13	East Grinstead	M	Christian	Robert	+ Mary Dyvol
1616	8	26	Pevensey	M	Christian	Darothie	+Thomas Harneden
1621	6	11	Pevensey	M	Christian	John	+Jhoane Hencoate

Figure 20-8 A web page exported from Microsoft Excel

Dynamic websites

In an ideal world, all of this would be unnecessary. You would simply upload the database file to your website and people could use their browser to search it, just as you do on your desktop. But the genealogy databases discussed above all produce static web pages. If you make any changes to your family tree, you will need to recreate the web pages from scratch and upload the whole lot to your site again.

A more satisfactory approach is to have a 'dynamic' website. When a visitor clicks on a link within your site, they are not taken to a fixed page, but instead a piece of software looks up the relevant data in a database and extracts the appropriate records to create a web page on the fly. This may be just a plain GEDCOM file or it may be a separate database created from a GEDCOM file, but either way you can easily update the family tree, by uploading a single new file, without having to upload perhaps hundreds of revised pages.

There are two basic ways to access data held in a file:

- When someone visits your site, an applet is downloaded, i.e. a small software application which runs from within your browser. This gets the relevant data from the site and turns it into the page displayed on the screen.
- When someone visits your site, the page is not simply delivered to the user as it is but runs a 'script' behind the scenes which incorporates the relevant data from a database or GEDCOM into the page displayed to the reader.

The differences might seem marginal, but are in fact very significant. The disadvantage of the first technique is that it will only work if the Java language is installed on the computer, and there may be other compatibility issues in the longer term. It seems that this approach may have a limited future: both the best known Java genealogy programs (JavaGED and WebGED Progenitor) are no longer available, though you may still come across sites that use them.

The disadvantage of the 'scripting' approach is that, while it doesn't make any special demands on the browser, which just gets a perfectly normal web page, special software has to be installed on the web server to make sense of the script. The most likely software requirement is for a scripting language called PHP, often used in combination with MySQL databases. This is not something you can simply install in your own web space on your own initiative, but it is standard practice in a commercial web hosting environment, and is increasingly widespread in the web space from consumer ISPs and free web space. For example, Tripod (see p. 339) offers PHP and MySQL, and the Free Webspace site has a 'power search' at <**www. free-webhosts.com/power-search.php**> which can be used to find hosting services with specific scripting and database facilities.

If PHP is available on the web server hosting your site, there are a number of tools you could look at:

- **PhpGedView** is an application which can be downloaded free from <**phpgedview.sourceforge.net**>. It has a wide range of charts and the useful ability to create PDF versions of reports. Individual users can be given access to particular areas of a site. A 'portal' page allows visitors to keep track of their own particular ancestors on the site.
- The Next Generation of Genealogy Sitebuilding (TNG), downloadable from <**lythgoes.net/genealogy/software.php**>, requires PHP and access to a MySQL database. It has a range of reports and the facility to design your own, and can link photos and documents to individuals in your tree. In fact you can have any number of distinct trees, and you can give each registered user access to branches that may not be visible to general visitors. TNG must be purchased – it is not freeware or shareware. Figure 20-9 shows a pedigree display from my own genealogy site at <**www. petex.org.uk**>, which uses TNG.
- **phpmyfamily**, which has a home page at <**www.phpmyfamily.net**>, requires MySQL and is primarily designed to allow family members to collaborate on a family tree. Facilities seem to be more limited than in the previous two applications.
- **Ancestor Forest** at <**ancestorforest.com/software/**> provides a basic tree and an individual report.

In such programs, you typically upload all the program files to your website, and then upload the data file for them to work with. You won't need to design any pages as such, though you will be able to customize them in various ways if you wish.

While these PHP projects don't require you to be a programmer, you will need to follow instructions about configuring the software for your own site, and will need to have (or develop) some understanding of how files are stored and made accessible on a website. For that reason, these are probably not appropriate tools for the reluctant or timid computer user.

Website design

Although there is a great deal of material, both in print and online, about website design, for someone publishing family history on the Web a few basic principles should suffice. What is important is to work out what the overall structure of your site will be (which other pages is each page going to link to?), and to do so *before* you start creating actual pages. There are also a few technical matters, such as file-naming conventions and file formats for graphics (see below).

There is no single right way to design a website. It depends on what it contains and who it is aimed at. For a personal genealogy site, your main visitors will be other genealogists looking for information on individuals

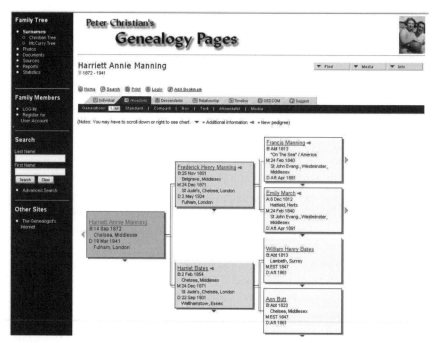

Figure 20-9 A pedigree display from TNG

and surnames that might be part of their own ancestry. If you have expertise in a particular area of genealogy, or have collected useful material on a particular topic, people may come looking for general background information. Your main job, then, is to make sure visitors to your site can see whether you have anything useful to them and can access it easily. While it is better, of course, if your site looks good, you should not be worrying about state-of-the-art graphic design, special effects, animation, background music, hit counters, or any of the other things that amateur web authors seem to find irresistible, but which irritate or distract readers and make pages slower to download.

Filenames

It is usual to give files for web pages names ending in *.html*. If you call a file *index.html* or *index.htm* it will be loaded by default, i.e. if the URL you have entered in your browser does not specify a particular file. For example, when you go to Genuki's home page at <**www.genuki.org.uk**> you get exactly the same page as when you enter <**www.genuki.org.uk/index. html**> – in the first instance, the server delivers *index.html* because you have not asked for any specific file. (The filenames *default.html* or *default. htm* are used instead on some servers, such as that of the National Archives – try <**www.nationalarchives.gov.uk/default.htm**>). This means your home page should normally be called *index.html* and be placed in the main folder in your web space.

On almost all web servers filenames are case sensitive: *index.html*, *Index. html* and *INDEX.HTML* are different files. To save confusion stick to lower case. If you are using software which automatically generates filenames rather than prompting you for filenames (GEDCOM converters and genealogy databases, for example), look for an option to force filenames to lower case.

Graphics

Web browsers can display graphics in three of the many graphics formats: GIF, JPEG and PNG, of which the last is not widely used. For colour photographs you need to use JPEG as it allows graphics with up to 16.7 million colours and is therefore capable of displaying subtle variations in tone. (JPEG files have the file extension .jpg on the PC.) The GIF format, which allows a maximum of 256 colours, is poor for colour photographs but good for black and white photographs, as well as for navigation buttons, logos, maps and the like, which have simple colour schemes. You can compare the strengths and weaknesses of these two formats by looking at the examples at <**www.spub.co.uk/wpg/figures/figure10.html**>.

If you are going to use graphics extensively, you will need a basic graphics editing program such as Photoshop Elements or PaintShop Pro. If you just need to crop images and convert them to GIF or JPEG format, there are freeware or inexpensive shareware tools that will do the job – look under 'Image Tools' at Tucows <**www.tucows.com/Windows/DesignTools/Image/ ImageEditors/**> or try the cover CDs of computer magazines.

Each graphic is kept as an individual file on the web server, and any page which uses it has a tag which contains the file name. If you have down-loaded *dummypage.html* to your own computer, it will not display the tree unless you also download the file *tree.gif* into the same folder, so that when the browser attempts to interpret the tag <IMG SRC="tree.gif"> it can find the file.

You can use the same graphic on many different pages, so if you have a graphic such as a logo which appears on every page on your site, you only need to put one copy of the file on the server.

Adding your family tree

If you are designing your own site you will need to know how to include the pages showing the family tree you have created from your genealogy database software. Whatever software you use for your genealogy, it will almost certainly create a new folder on your hard disk and put all the created files in it, perhaps in a number of sub-folders.

You need to upload this new folder and all the files it contains on to your website (see 'Uploading your website', below), retaining the filenames and folder structure. If you change filenames or move files you will find that some parts of the tree do not link correctly.

From your home page you will need a link to the index file in the family tree folder. So suppose you have called the folder *johnson* because it contains your Johnson family tree, you would have a link

```
<A HREF="johnson/">Johnson family tree</A>
```

on your home page. If you find this does not work, you may need to specify the exact filename of the index file (this should be fairly obvious if you look at the filenames in the family tree folder), for example:

```
<A HREF="johnson/default.htm">Johnson family
tree</A>
```

When you are creating a web tree with your genealogy software, it is always worth checking for an option to make filenames lower case. There are other reasons for giving the exact filename, discussed on p. 348.

Design tips

The web is, of course, a good source of advice about the design of web pages. Here are some of the most important points:

- Have a home page which tells visitors what they will find on the site and provides links to the main areas of your site.
- Give each page a helpful title and heading, so that if someone bookmarks it, or comes to it directly via a link from another site (perhaps a search engine), they can immediately see what the page is about.
- Conversely, make sure that every page has a link back to the home page or some other higher level page, so that if someone comes to your site from a search engine they can get to other pages.
- Don't make your pages too long, and don't include large or unnecessary graphics, as this will only increase the time it takes your pages to download, and potential visitors will be put off.
- Don't use unusual colour schemes. They are unusual for a good reason – they make text unreadable.
- Don't put light text on a dark background on a page with significant information – this can make it impossible to print out from some browsers.
- Put your email address on the site so that people can contact you.

For further advice, look at the 'Design Tips' area of Usable Web at <usableweb.com>.

Uploading your website

Once you have created a set of pages on your own computer, you need to go online and upload them to your web space. The standard way of doing this is to use a program called an FTP client. FTP stands for File Transfer Protocol, which is a long-established method for transferring files on the internet. There are many free and shareware FTP programs available from software archives like Tucows at <**www.tucows.com/Windows/IS-IT/ NetworkAdministrationProtocols/FTPFileTransferProtocol/**>. CuteFTP and WS-FTP are among the most popular for PC users.

Before you connect to the internet to upload, you will want to set up an entry for your website in your FTP client's list of sites. You need to enter:

- The address of the site. If you are not certain what it is, your ISP/web space provider will be able to tell you, and their help pages will probably provide detailed instructions for uploading files.
- Your username and password for that site.

Once you are logged in, you can transfer files by drag-and-drop. Finally, start your browser and type in the URL of your site to check it.

Web browsers can also be used to transfer files – see the online help in your browser for details of how to do this – and some hosting sites provide their own browser-based uploading facility.

▌ Publicity

Once you have created and uploaded your web pages, you will need to publicize the existence of your site. One simple way to do this is to put its URL in the signature attached to your email messages. Apart from that, there are a number of possible approaches.

Search engines

Making sure your site is known to the main search engines (see Chapter 19) is probably the most effective way to publicize your website. Since search engines index pages automatically, they have no way of knowing what the most important aspects of your site and your individual pages are unless you help them by organizing the material on each page. Among the things search engines look for when estimating the relevance of a page to a search done by a user are:

- words appearing in the page title and between heading tags
- the initial section of text
- words which appear frequently in the page

In addition, there are special tags you can add to a page to provide a brief description of the page and the site. These are <META> tags, which are placed in the <HEAD> section of the page. They will not be visible to someone viewing your page, but they are used by search engines.

```
<META NAME="description" CONTENT="The last will
and testament of Zebediah Poot, died 1687,
Wombourn, Staffordshire, England">
```

When a search engine lists this page in the results of a search, it will normally list its title (i.e. the text between the <TITLE> tags) and your description. If there is no description, it will take the first couple of lines of text from the <BODY> of the page.

You may see reference to a 'keywords' <META> tag, but this is now of limited usefulness as it seems that search engines no longer make use of it in indexing.

Don't expect submission to a search engine to produce a flood of visitors to your site within hours. It can take quite some time for the search engine to visit a new site and index it.

Mailing lists and forums

A good way to draw immediate attention to a new site is to post a message to appropriate mailing lists and discussion forums (see Chapter 18). You might think it is a good idea to post to every one you possibly can, to get maximum publicity, but there is little point in posting details of a Yorkshire website to a Cornish list. Choose the county lists relevant to the material you are putting on the web, and any special interest lists. It will be worth notifying the GENBRIT mailing list (see p. 308) with an indication of the main surnames and localities covered.

If there is a mailing list relating to some social group your ancestors belonged to it will be worth notifying that list, so if you have information on coalmining ancestors on your site, for example, it will be worth posting to the COALMINERS list (see Chapter 9).

Cyndi's List

Another useful approach is to submit details of your site to Cyndi's List using the online form at <**www.cyndislist.com/whatsnew.htm**>. This may or may not get your site a listing on the relevant category page on Cyndi's List, but it will still have undoubted benefits. First, all submissions to this page are included in the Cyndi's List mailing list (details of which are at <**lists.rootsweb.ancestry.com/index/other/Newsletters/CyndisList. html**>), which goes out to a large number of subscribers. This, in turn, will get a link to your site into the RootsWeb archive at <**archiver.rootsweb. ancestry.com/th/index/CyndisList/**>, and your site will be permanently listed in the 'What's New' pages on Cyndi's List at <**www.cyndislist.com/ whatsnew.htm**>. While it may take some time for your site to be indexed by search engines based on your direct submission, both of these locations are likely to be visited by search engines much more quickly, and the links to your site should be followed automatically.

Requesting links

You can request other people to link to your pages, but you need to be realistic about expecting links from other personal sites. People will generally do this only if there is some connection in subject matter between your site and theirs, and if you are prepared to create a link to their site in return. Do not expect major institutions like the National Archives or the SoG to link to a site with purely personal material, just because you have made a link to theirs.

To be honest, if your site contains only personal pedigree information, it is probably not worth bothering to request links from other personal sites, as this will probably not bring any significant number of visitors, certainly compared to the other options discussed so far. However, if your site has material relating to a particular subject, it will be well worth contacting the maintainers of specialist websites relating to that subject, such as those discussed in Chapters 8–11.

If you have transcriptions of original source material of broader interest than extracts for individual surnames you should contact Genuki, who aim to provide links to all UK source material online.

Preserving your family history

While the web is seen as a way of publishing your family history, in one important respect it is not like publishing it in print. A printed family history donated to a genealogy library will be preserved for ever, while your account with your web space provider is doomed to expire when you do, unless you can persuade your heirs otherwise.

But since a website is just a collection of files, there is no reason why all the information cannot be preserved, even if not online. If you copy all the files that constitute your site onto writeable CDs, these can be sent to relatives and deposited in archives just like printed material. The advantage of distributing your material in this way is that people do not need special software – a particular word processor or the same genealogy database as you – in order to view the files, and everyone with a computer has access to a web browser. HTML is a universal, non-proprietary standard which uses plain-text files, and is therefore much more future-proof than the file formats used by most current software.

If you are intending to do this you should make sure that every link gives a specific filename, as mentioned in 'Filenames' on p. 353. A web server knows to deliver a file called *index.html* if a link doesn't specify a filename; a standalone computer doesn't.

Note that you won't be able to do this if your site is dynamic, as you won't be able run the relevant software from a CD.

The problem of the long-term preservation of genealogy websites is discussed in Chapter 22.

Help and advice

While you should be able to get help from your ISP or other web host for problems relating to uploading, you are unlikely to be able to get any help from them with the business of creating your website, though they may have online tutorial material. However, there are countless sources of information online about creating a website online. If you are looking for material specifically aimed at genealogists, there are three main places to look. Genealogy Web Creations at <**www.genealogy-web-creations.com**> has a comprehensive set of pages devoted to all aspects of website design for family historians. An excellent overview of specifically genealogical web publishing with links to relevant software and tutorial materials is Cyndi's

'Genealogy Home Page Construction Kit' at <www.cyndislist.com/construc.htm>. Dick Eastman's newsletter (see p. 366) has had a number of articles about creating a website for your genealogy over the last few years, and it is well worth browsing or searching the archive from the home page at <blog.eogn.com>.

The GENCMP mailing list is a good place to look for recommendations and help in putting your pedigree online – see <lists.rootsweb.ancestry.com/index/other/Newsgroup_Gateways/GENCMP.html> for details. British-Genealogy has a 'Web pages design' discussion forum at <www.british-genealogy.com/forums/forumdisplay.php?f=226>.

In print

If you want a tutorial in print, a search on any online bookshop for 'HTML' or 'web publishing' will list the hundreds of general books on the subject, though it's probably best to browse in a physical bookshop to make sure you choose a book at the right technical level. I know of only three books devoted specifically to publishing genealogical information on the web:

- Cyndi Howells, *Planting Your Family Tree Online: How to Create Your Own Family History Website* (Rutledge Hill Press, 2004)
- Peter Christian, *Web Publishing for Genealogy*, 2nd edn (David Hawgood, 1999). There is also a US edition published by the Genealogical Publishing Co. (2000). The website for the book at <www.spub.co.uk/wpg/> includes the complete text
- Richard S. Wilson, *Publishing Your Family History on the Internet* (Writers Digest Books, 1999) <www.compuology.com/book2.htm>

Of these, Cyndi Howells' book is the only one which is reasonably up-to-date (insofar as such a thing is possible with online material). My own book, now out of print, doesn't cover the most recent developments, but does have the advantage of being available free online, and the general process of creating a website has not changed significantly. Note that the plausible sounding *Creating Family Web Sites for Dummies* by Janine C. Warner (John Wiley and Sons, 2005) is not aimed at genealogists and does not cover putting family trees online.

The family history magazines available on the news-stand often have articles on some aspect genealogical web publishing.

21

THE WORLD OF FAMILY HISTORY

Previous chapters have looked at ways of using the internet in direct connection with your own pedigree. This chapter looks at the 'non-virtual' world of family history which exists offline, and how you can use the internet to find out about it.

Societies and organizations

National bodies

There are a number of national genealogical bodies, all of which have websites:

- Society of Genealogists (SoG) <**www.sog.org.uk**>
- Institute of Heraldic and Genealogical Studies (IHGS) <**www.ihgs. ac.uk**>

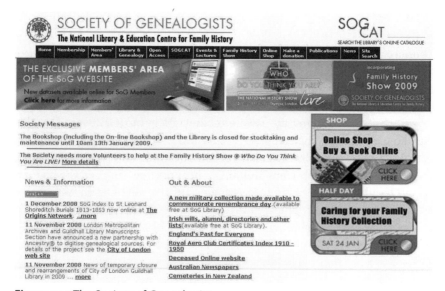

Figure 21-1 The Society of Genealogists

- Federation of Family History Societies (FFHS) <**www.ffhs.org.uk**>
- Guild of One-Name Studies (GOONS) <**www.one-name.org**>
- Scottish Genealogy Society <**www.scotsgenealogy.com**>
- Scottish Association of Family History Societies (SAFHS) <**www.safhs. org.uk**>
- Association of Family History Societies of Wales <**www.fhswales.info**>
- Genealogical Society of Ireland <**www.familyhistory.ie**>

Family history societies

There are around 200 local family history societies in the UK and Ireland, the overwhelming majority of which have websites. Most of these societies are members of one or more of the three national federations/associations listed above (which are themselves umbrella organizations, not family history societies in their own right). The FFHS includes many member societies from Wales and Ireland, and most English societies are Federation members.

The definitive starting point for finding FHS websites is Genuki's 'Family History and Genealogy Societies' page at <**www.genuki.org.uk/Societies/**>. This lists the national organizations and has links to separate pages for the constituent nations of the British Isles, where details of local societies are to be found.

The individual FHS websites vary greatly in what they offer, but all will have contact details and usually a list of publications. Most do not have their own online shops, but over 60 of them have an online 'stand' at GENfair, the FFHS online shop, at <**www.genfair.com**> – see p. 373, below.

▌ Events

There is a wide range of genealogical meetings, lectures, conferences and fairs in the UK, from the individual meetings of family history societies to major national events such as the SoG's annual Family History Show. One of the easiest ways to find out about such events is via the web.

The major source for the whole of the UK is the Geneva page (the Genuki Calendar of GENealogical EVents and Activities) at <**geneva.weald. org.uk**>, run by Malcolm Austen on behalf of Genuki and the FFHS (Figure 21-2). This lists events from the SoG's programme, any family history society events submitted, as well as the regional family history fairs regularly held around the country, though it does not generally include society events open only to members. Many societies have lectures on internet-related topics, details of which can be found on their websites. The SoG offers a substantial programme of IT-related events, many of which cover the use of the internet for genealogy. Details will be found on the Society's website at <**www.sog.org.uk/events/calendar.shtml**>.

Welcome to GENEVA

An online calendar of GENealogical EVents and Activities

This calendar is being run jointly on behalf of GENUKI and the Federation of Family History Societies. Event organisers are encouraged to check this calendar when picking a date to avoid clashes with other events in the same area. They are also encouraged to submit an entry for this calendar as soon as a date has been booked so that other organisers know about it and can try to avoid it.

*Please note that this calendar depends on **your** Family History Society submitting its events as well as you reading it. If your society's events are not listed, please complain to **them** rather than to me. If the calendar does not link to any further details, please **don't** ask me for further information - because I don't have any.* At the end of this page you'll find some other groups' event lists and how to submit events to GENEVA.

The venue area codes are (mostly) the usual Chapman County Codes extended to the rest of the world as per the GRD usage. Where it seems more helpful, London postcode prefixes and other variants may be used.

Be notified of page updates: [enter email] [OK] it's private ChangeDetection

2009	2009	2009

Skip to: Feb Mar Apr May Jun Jul Aug Sep Oct Nov Dec 2010

January	10-18	Fort Lauderdale, FL, USA	Irish Genealogy at Sea
January	14	SoG, LND	Surname Origins: Putting your name on the Map
January	17	Sherborne, SOM	Winter Workshop - On The Parish/In The Workhouse
January	16-20	Auckland, NZ	12th Australasian Congress on Genealogy & Heraldry
January	17	Barking, ESS	Family History Fair
January	17	SoG, LND	Scottish Records before 1707
January	17	SoG, LND	Upstairs - Downstairs: Domestic Service
January	19	ONLINE	Become a Better Genealogist: Research in England & Wales
January	20	Brixham, DEV	Start to Become a Family History Detective (weekly, Mon 1-3pm)
January	20	NLINE, ONLINE	Military Men & Women: Records of Britain's Armed Forces 1750 - 1920
January	21	SoG, LND	Tracing London Dockland Ancestors

Figure 21-2 Geneva

The National Archives' programme of events, many of which are of interest to genealogists, can be found online at <**www.nationalarchives. gov.uk/events/calendar.htm**>.

The annual Who Do You Think You Are? Live show at Olympia, which includes the Society of Genealogists' Family History Show and the National History Show, has a website at <**www.whodoyouthinkyouarelive.co.uk**>. The new Family History Event at the Barbican on 3 May 2009 has a website at <**www.thefhevent.com**>. Family History Fairs has been running local fairs around the country for many years and their website at <**www.family historyfairs.org**> gives locations and details for forthcoming events. Dates of all these shows are included in Geneva.

▍Courses

If you are interested in getting tuition in genealogical skills, the web is an ideal place to look for courses. The SoG offers a number of half- and one-day courses, listed on their events calendar at <**www.sog.org.uk/events/ calendar.shtml**>. For more intensive study, the IHGS has a complete syllabus of genealogy courses, each leading to a formal qualification – details of the qualifications and courses are linked from <**www.ihgs.ac.uk/ courses/**>.

The website for your local authority should have details of adult education in your area. For Greater London and over 30 other counties and metropolitan areas, Floodlight provides listings of what is on offer in the region. The London Floodlight is at <**london.floodlight.co.uk**> and there are links to all the others at the foot of the home page. Family history courses are listed under 'History'. Once you are looking at the family history courses on one Floodlight site, there are links to 'Family History courses in other areas' at the bottom of the right-hand column.

It is also worth checking the website of your local universities or colleges, whose Continuing Education departments may have suitable offerings in family or local history. Indeed, if you are looking for more advanced courses, the University of Strathclyde offers two postgraduate qualifications, details at <**www.strath.ac.uk/genealogy/**>.

While there has been an explosion in online courses in the last few years, this has still to make much of an impact on the world of family history, in the UK at least. The reason is that running online courses requires a considerable technical and administrative infrastructure, which genealogy organizations themselves are not really in a position to provide.

However, many universities are developing the possibilities of online courses, and so far there are two which include family history in their range of subjects:

- The University of Central Lancashire has an Institute of Local and Family History offering online courses, details of which will be found at <**www. uclan.ac.uk/facs/class/humanities/family/OnlineCourses/Courses Intro.html**>.
- The University of Dundee offers a Certificate in Family and Local History by distance learning, the prospectus for which will be found at <**www. dundee.ac.uk/cais/certificate/FLH-Main.pdf**>.

Pharos at <**www.pharostutors.com**> is a commercial company which runs online family history courses. There are over 40 different courses, which mostly focus on specific areas of genealogical research (e.g. the census, wills, Scottish research) rather than on general genealogical skills. All the tutors are well-known experts in their field. At the time of writing, the home page mentions a free 'Learning Genealogy Online' course under the heading 'Courses coming soon', though there are no further details as yet.

Local History magazine has a list of local history course providers at </**www.local-history.co.uk/Courses/**>.

▌ Magazines and journals

Many genealogical print publications have a related website, with at least a list of contents for the current issue and in some cases material from back issues.

The most comprehensive online listing is the 'Magazines, Journals,

Columns & Newsletters' page on Cyndi's List at <**www.cyndislist.com/ magazine.htm**>. Subtitled 'Print & Electronic Publications for Genealogy', this page provides links to websites for many print magazines, though many of course will be of interest only to those with North American ancestry. The Open Directory (see p. 27) has a small list of magazine websites at <**www.dmoz.org/Society/Genealogy/Magazines_and_ E-zines/**>.

The sites for the main genealogical monthlies available on the newsstand are:

- *Ancestors* <**www.ancestorsmagazine.co.uk**>
- *Family History Monthly* <**www.familyhistorymonthly.com**>
- *Family Tree Magazine* and *Practical Family History* <**www.family-tree. co.uk**>
- *Your Family Tree* <**www.futurenet.com/yourfamilytree/**>
- *Who Do You Think You Are?* <**www.bbcwhodoyouthinkyouare.com**>

The IHGS has a website for its magazine *Family History* at <**www.family-history.org**>. The SoG's website has a partial subject and name index to the *Genealogists' Magazine* at <**www.sog.org.uk/genmag/genmag.shtml**> and there is a project in hand to place a number of articles online.

In November 2008, ScotlandsPeople launched *Discover My Past Scotland*,

Figure 21-3 Discover My Past Scotland

a 40-page electronic magazine devoted to Scottish family history at <**www. discovermypast.co.uk**>. The magazine opens in a special viewer (Figure 21-3). You can subscribe to a single issue or take out a subscription for three, six, or twelve months. A six-page preview is available on the site.

In the past, there have been a number of magazines devoted specifically to the use of computers in genealogy, but now that almost every genealogist is online, these have largely disappeared. A US magazine *Internet Genealogy* was launched in 2006 and is published bi-monthly both in print and on the web. A free issue is available on the website at <**internet-genealogy.com**>, as are links and 'Net Notes' from past issues.

History and local history magazines are also likely to have material of interest to family historians, and the web makes it easy to check which past issues cover subjects of interest to you. The bimonthly magazine *Local History* has a website at <**www.local-history.co.uk**> with an index to the contents of past issues back to 1984 at <**www.local-history.co.uk/Issues/**>, as well as the usual listing for the latest issue. The site also provides links to other local history resources on the web, and a useful listing of local history societies at <**www.local-history.co.uk/Groups/**>. The *BBC History Magazine* has a main website at <**www.bbchistorymagazine.com**> with details of back issues and a growing series of podcasts. (There is one podcast per month covering three topics from the printed magazine.)

History in Focus is an online history magazine at <**www.history.ac.uk/ ihr/Focus/**> (note the upper-case *F* in the URL) published once or twice a year by the University of London's Institute of Historical Research. It takes a thematic approach to history, with each issue designed to 'provide an introduction to the chosen topic and to help stimulate interest and debate – the series will concentrate on highlighting books, reviews, websites and conferences that relate to the theme'. Although the material derives from recent academic research, and genealogists are not the target readership, many issues contain items relating to social history that are likely to interest the family historian, and the website reviews for each topic are particularly useful. Recent issues have been devoted to subjects such as slavery and migration.

If you have an Ancestry subscription (see p. 44) or can access Ancestry from the National Archives or a library, you will be able to make use of PERSI, the *Periodical Source Index*, at <**www.ancestry.com/search/rectype/ periodicals/persi/main.htm**>. This is a database containing 'a comprehensive subject index to genealogy and local history periodicals written in English and French (Canada) since 1800'. Although the majority of the periodicals covered are from North America, the index also seems to include many UK family history society magazines.

For websites relating to non-genealogical publications, see the section on 'Newspapers' on p. 184.

News

Email newsletters

As well as print publications there are, of course, purely online publications for genealogists. Links to these will be found on Cyndi's List at <**www. cyndislist.com/magazine.htm**>. The majority are US-based, so are not of relevance to UK genealogists where they deal with genealogical records, but they often have useful material on general genealogical topics, including the use of the internet.

Probably the best known of these US publications is Dick Eastman's Online Genealogy Newsletter, which originated on the Genealogy Forum in CompuServe, long before CompuServe was part of the internet. It is particularly strong on coverage of genealogy software and CD-ROMs, genealogical developments on the internet, new websites and more. Dick has many contacts in the UK, and regularly includes items of genealogy news from Britain.

There are two versions of the newsletter. The Standard Edition is available free of charge and you can receive articles by email or read them online at <**blog.eogn.com**>. The Plus Edition is only available by paying a subscription of $5.95 for three months or $19.95 for a year. It contains all the articles in the Standard Edition with the addition of one or two extra items each week. For the Standard Edition you can sign up to receive an email when it is published; the Plus Edition is emailed to you. Even if you don't want to subscribe to the Plus Edition, you can purchase individual articles of interest for $2. There is also a discussion board where you can discuss individual articles and general IT topics.

All issues back to the very first in January 1996 can be searched by keyword from <**blog.eogn.com**>, while there is also a browsable archive of newsletters up to October 2002 at <**www.ancestry.com/library/view/ columns/eastman/eastman.asp**>.

There are a few specialist mailing lists which are used to disseminate news. As mentioned on p. 295, John Fuller's NEW-GENLIST mailing list will keep you up to date with new genealogy mailing lists, while NEW-GEN-URL allows people to publicize new genealogy websites. Subscription details for all these lists will be found at <**www.rootsweb.ancestry.com/ ~jfuller/gen_mail_computing.html**>. The CyndisList mailing list announces additions to Cyndi's List (see <**www.cyndislist.com/maillist.htm**>).

Many of the major organizations and data services mentioned in this book have electronic newsletters designed to keep you informed of developments – the National Archives, the FFHS, ScotlandsPeople and Origins, to name just a few. There will normally be a link to information about such newsletters on the home page of a site. There are links to some of the best known on the Genuki mailing lists page at <**www.genuki.org.uk/indexes/ MailingLists.html**>.

Blogs

Until fairly recently, setting up a newsletter, whether it was sent by email or published on the web, required a certain amount of technical expertise, but this has completely changed with the rise of blogging. In one sense, this is nothing new – a blog (short for 'web log') is just a form of online newsletter. Dick Eastman's original email newsletter was recast as a blog in 2005 without any great upheaval, the blog format allowing it to be updated daily rather than weekly as before. But one of the things that has made blogging popular is the arrival of sites which making setting up and maintaining a blog very straightforward, without any need to find web space and learn how to create a website from scratch. Blogs also allow visitors to leave comments on each posting. Although reading someone's daily ramblings about how they're getting on with their genealogical research is of limited interest, the blog format is ideal for publishing snippets of information or opinion, and is an ideal way to keep up with new developments in the world of family history.

The most comprehensive listing of genealogy blogs is probably the Genealogy Blog Finder at <**blogfinder.genealogue.com**>, which tracks over 1,200 genealogy blogs. This listing includes many personal blogs, that are only likely to be of interest to a small number people, such as the 90 or so single surname blogs. A more concise list, concentrating on the major blogs, is the 'Blogs for Genealogy' page on Cyndi's List at <**www.cyndislist. com/blogs.htm**>. Google has a dedicated Blog Search at <**blogsearch. google.com**>, which finds over 200,000 blogs with 'genealogy' in the title.

A feature on many blogs is a set of links, typically in the right-hand column of the page, to other blogs the author thinks you may be interested in, and this can be a good way to explore the 'blogosphere'.

Among the blogs from major organizations and companies are:

- the Ancestry.com blog at <**blogs.ancestry.com/ancestry/**>
- the FamilySearch Labs blog at <**labs.familysearch.org/blog/**>, which reports on new developments at FamilySearch
- Cyndi's List at <**cyndislist.blogspot.com**>, a blog version of the newsletter mentioned above

Of course, these only report matters related to the particular site or organization. More general blogs include:

- Simon Fowler's *Ancestors Magazine* blog at <**www.ancestorsmagazine. co.uk/?page=blog**>
- Scottish Genealogy News and Events (SGNE), maintained by Chris Paton at <**scottishancestry.blogspot.com**>
- Irish Family History at <**www.irishfamilyhistory.ie/blog/**>
- Anglo-Celtic Connections at <**anglo-celtic-connections.blogspot.com**> covers British-Canadian issues and is written by John D. Reid
- Kimberly's Genealogy Blog at <**genealogy.about.com**>, written by Kimberley Powell

But there are also blogs devoted to very particular topics, for example:

- The Genetic Genealogist at <**www.thegeneticgenealogist.com**> covers news and issues the genealogical use of DNA testing

Figure 21-4 Scottish Genealogy News and Events

- Hugh Watkins Exploring Ancestry blog at <**ancestry.blogspot.com**> (already mentioned on p. 45) looks at Ancestry.com from the point-of-view of a UK user.
- Kylie Veale's blog at <**www.veale.com.au/phd/html/journal.html**> records the progress of her PhD research into online genealogy.

For more extensive discussion of blogging for genealogists, see Dick Eastman's piece 'Blogs explained' at <**blog.eogn.com/eastmans_online_genealogy/2005/11/blogs_explained.html**>. Blogger.com at <**www.blogger. com**> is probably the best-known site for starting your own blog.

One of the problems of blogs, in comparison with email newsletters, is that you have to check the site regularly for new entries. But most blogs (and indeed many other news sites) provide a 'news feed', which means that you are alerted when a new entry is posted. Your browser may have the facility to use these news feeds – for example, Firefox's 'live bookmarks' – as does some email software, such as Microsoft Outlook 2007 (see Figure 21-5). Otherwise you can download a piece of free software called a 'news reader' or 'news aggregator' to do this for you. Alternatively, if you have an account with Google or Yahoo, your Google or Yahoo home page can be set to display the titles of the latest entries from the blogs you are interested in.

There are too many options to cover in detail, but the Wikipedia article on 'Web feed' at <**en.wikipedia.org/wiki/Web_feed**> provides a starting point for more detailed information, and the BBC news site has an article on 'News feeds from the BBC' at <**news.bbc.co.uk/1/hi/help/3223484.stm**>,

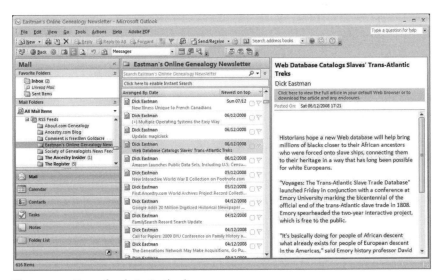

Figure 21-5 News feeds in Outlook 2007

which explains how to receive the feeds from their site, and this is equally applicable to blogs. The orange-and-white icon shown in Figure 21-6 is a commonly used symbol for a news feed (and you will often see the abbreviation RSS, which, strictly, applies to only one type of feed, but is often used generically for news feeds).

 Figure 21-6 RSS news feed icon

One problem with personal blogs is that people often start them full of enthusiasm but let them fall into neglect after a few months. It is not uncommon to come across a genealogy blog that has had no new entries for a year. Of course there may still be useful information in the existing entries.

Podcasting

A podcast is the internet equivalent of a radio or television broadcast, a digital sound or video file that is made available for live listing or viewing via the web. A podcast is 'streamed', that is delivered from the site via your web browser in real time, and you do not need to download it to your computer and then open it in a particular software application. Assuming your equipment is not too long in the tooth, you should be able to listen to or view podcasts without installing any software or reconfiguring your computer. However, if you have a dialup connection you may find practical difficulties in playing the podcasts because they really require broadband speeds.

Podcasts are ideal for making lectures available to those unable to attend an event in person. The most significant collection of podcasts relating to British genealogy and history, by far, is that of the National Archives, with over 70 lectures available from its podcast home page at <**www.national archives.gov.uk/rss/podcasts.xml**>.

Roots Television at <**www.rootstelevision.com**> is an online television channel devoted to family history. The topic coverage is quite extensive, including tutorials, both short and long, on a variety of subjects, and interviews with significant figures in the world of genealogy. The most recent pieces are listed on the home page, but the 'Browse Videos' field opens a drop-down list with a list of subject headings. The company is American but the 'British Roots' and 'Irish Roots' headings link to recordings specifically about British Isles genealogy, while the 'Conferences' heading includes UK events like the Who Do You Think You Are? Live show (see Figure 21-7). The 'How To' section contains the tutorial material.

Figure 21-7 Roots Television: Dick Eastman's coverage of the 2008 'Who Do You Think You Are?' Live show

YouTube at <www.youtube.com> is *the* site for amateur video publishing, but it is also used by professionals. For example, the US *Family Tree Magazine* has a number of videos available on the site from its YouTube home page at <www.youtube.com/user/familytreemagazine>, including, for example, a brief guide to Google Books (see p. 175). Lecturer Robert Raglan has a range of five-minute genealogy lessons available at <www.youtube.com/user/5minutegenealogy>. Mike O'Laughlin has 15 videos relating to Irish genealogy at <www.youtube.com/user/Mickthebridge>.

There is a brief article about podcasting for genealogists by George C. Morgan at <www.ancestry.com/learn/library/article.aspx?article=11140> and the Podcast category page on Wikipedia at <en.wikipedia.org/wiki/Category:Podcasting> has links to articles on specific aspects. There is a brief listing of relevant sites on the 'Podcasts for Genealogy' page on Cyndi's List at <www.cyndislist.com/podcasts.htm>.

Software

The web is an excellent source of information about genealogical software, since all the major software companies and many individual software authors, have websites providing details of their products. Genealogy share-ware can be downloaded from the sites, and even for normal commercial products there will often be a trial or demo version available for download.

There are a number of genealogy software listings online, but many are no longer actively maintained and contain out-of-date information. Depending on how long it is since it was last updated, an old site may still have useful information, like the GenealogySoftwareNews blog at <**www.genealogysoftwarenews.com**>, which may still be worth referring to, even though at the time of writing nothing had been added to the site since March 2008.

The best starting point for genealogy software is the 'Software and Computers' page on Cyndi's List at <**www.cyndislist.com/software.htm**>. This lists over 100 pedigree database programs (though not all of them are for English speakers) as well as a range of other software tools for special purposes such as charting or mapping. There are links to the websites of all the major genealogy software companies. Probably the best way to keep up with genealogy software news is Dick Eastman's newsletter (see above), which regularly includes news of recent releases and often provides fairly detailed reviews.

If you are just starting to use a computer for genealogy, it is probably worth downloading one of the two major freeware genealogy database programs for Windows:

- Personal Ancestral File (currently at version 5.2), often referred to as PAF, is a program developed by the LDS Church for its own members and made available for free download. It can be downloaded from the FamilySearch site at <**www.familysearch.org**> – there is a 'Download PAF' link on the home page. A manual can also be downloaded.
- Legacy (currently version 7.0) has been made available as freeware by the Millennia Corporation, and this can be downloaded from <**www.legacyfamilytree.com**>. This is the Standard Edition, which can be upgraded online to the Deluxe Edition for $29.95.

There are a number of resources for users of handheld computers. Cyndi's List has a 'PDAs & Handhelds' page at <**www.cyndislist.com/pda.htm**>. Beau Sharborough used to provide an annual 'roundup' of information about PDAs for genealogists, but the latest of these is for 2004 at <**www.rootsworks.com/pda2005/**>. However, the Utah Valley PAF Users Group blog has an article by Beau from 2007 which gives a more recent overview of the field at <**blog.uvpafug.org/2008/01/your-genealogy-in-your-pocket-pdas-by.html**>.

For normal commercial software, some of the online shops discussed in the next section offer a selection, while specialist suppliers have a wider range and can offer more detailed advice. If you are new to genealogy software, you are strongly recommended to use a specialist supplier who can offer advice, rather than simply selecting something off the shelf at your local computer store. Most genealogical software companies also have online ordering facilities, and if you can survive without a printed manual, you can often download the software after making a credit card payment.

The best-known retailers of genealogy software in the UK are S&N Genealogy at <**www.genealogysupplies.com**> and TWR Computing at <**www.twrcomputing.co.uk**>. Both offer a wide range of products and their websites offer considerable help in choosing the right software for your budget and requirements.

Online shops

Apart from the general online booksellers such as Amazon at <**www. amazon.co.uk**>, there are a number of online shops for genealogy books, data on CD-ROM, and software. Almost all use secure online ordering, though some are just online lists and orders must be sent by email or post.

The FFHS's online shop GENfair is at <**www.genfair.co.uk**> and sells not only the Federation's own publications, both books and data, but also books from many other publishers. As mentioned on p. 361, the site also includes many 'stands' where the publications of local family history societies can be bought.

Parish Chest at <**www.parishchest.com**> offers products from around 40 different suppliers, each of whom has a separate page on the site listing their products. Also, from the index pages relating to individual topics (e. g. military records, directories) you can select a particular county to find all suppliers with products of that category for the county. A search facility lets you search for products by name.

The IHGS has an online shop at <**www.ihgs.ac.uk/shop/**>. In addition to buying books and software online, you can also use the site to book places on the Institute's courses.

The Archive CD Books Project for the UK, which built up a very substantial collection of historical books scanned onto CD-ROM, closed down at the end of 2007 on the retirement of its founder, Rod Neep. The CDs from this project are no longer for sale, though you will find them in genealogical libraries and they occasionally come up in online auctions sites (see below). However, the Archive CD Books Projects for Australia, Ireland, the Netherlands, the USA and Canada are still in operation, and links to their sites will be found from <**www.rod-neep.co.uk**>.

The National Archives has an online bookshop at <**www.national archives.gov.uk/bookshop/**>, from which you can buy this book at a discount if this isn't your own copy. The Society of Genealogists has an online shop at <**www.sog.org.uk/acatalog/**>. This offers the complete range of the Society's own publications and a selection of books from other publishers. You can also use it to book places on the Society's lectures and courses or to renew your membership.

Dick Eastman runs RootsBooks at <**www.rootsbooks.com**>, an online shop with a UK branch at <**www.rootsbooks.co.uk**>. Here, there is a page for each part of the UK and for each English county, as well as pages for individual subject areas such as software and heraldry. The site uses Amazon's payment system and it's stock list is based on Amazon's, though prices seem to be slightly lower.

The Internet Genealogical Bookshop run by Stuart Raymond has a website at <**www.samjraymond.btinternet.co.uk/igb.htm**>. However, this is not an online store – books must be ordered by email and paid for on receipt of invoice.

Many other bookshops are listed on Cyndi's List at <**www.cyndislist. com/books.htm**>. For a list of genealogy bookshops in the UK, North America and Australasia, consult Margaret Olson's 'Links to Genealogy Booksellers' at <**homepages.rootsweb.ancestry.com/~socgen/Bookmjo. html**>, though many of the UK entries were out of date when I checked it in December 2008, and the page had not been updated since 2006.

If you are searching for second-hand books you will find many book-sellers online. Yahoo UK has a substantial list at <**uk.dir.yahoo.com/ Regional/Countries/United_Kingdom/Business_and_Economy/Shopping_ and_Services/Books/Bookstores/Antique__Rare__and_Used/**>. If you live outside the British Isles, you should find an equivalent page on your local version of Yahoo. There are also sites, such as UKBookworld at <**ukbook-world.com**> or Abebooks at <**www.abebooks.co.uk**>, that will search the catalogues of many individual booksellers.

John Townsend has a large stock of second-hand genealogy books with an online catalogue but offline ordering and payment at <**www. johntownsend.demon.co.uk**>.

The online auction site eBay at <**www.ebay.co.uk**> has a wide selection of genealogy items for sale, mainly books and CD-ROMs. These can be found under **Books, Comics & Magazines> Non-Fiction Books> Genealogy/ FamilyHistory**, though searching on 'Genealogy' may be quicker.

The newsgroup soc.genealogy.marketplace carries postings by those selling genealogical products or individuals trying to find a taker for second-hand material. It is most readily consulted on Google Groups at <**groups.google.com/group/soc.genealogy.marketplace/topics**>.

Secure purchasing

Concern is often expressed about the security of online payments, and many people are wary of making online purchases by credit card, but although there are certainly some dangers, the reservations are out of all proportion to the actual risks. In fact, online transactions are much more secure than ordering over the phone or allowing a waiter to take a card out of your sight. As long as your browser is using a secure connection, which means that anything you type in is encrypted before being sent across the internet to the supplier, your card details will be infinitely more secure than most of the ways you already use your card.

Probably the least likely avenue of credit card fraud is someone hacking into your internet connection. The 'Fraud the Facts 2008' leaflet on the CardWatch site (follow the 'All publications' link from <**www.cardwatch. org.uk/publications.asp**>) states that the commonest type of card fraud 'involves the theft of genuine card details in the real world that are then used to make a purchase over the internet, by phone, or by mail order'.

The Home Office's Crime Reduction site has tips for 'Shopping and banking safely online' at <**www.crimereduction.homeoffice.gov.uk/ fraud/fraud08.htm**>. The Department of Trade and Industry also offers advice about secure online shopping in its Consumer Direct site at <**www. consumerdirect.gov.uk/before_you_buy/online-shopping/**>. There is a list of the most important security tips at <**www.consumerdirect.gov.uk/ before_ you_buy/online-shopping/tips**>.

Of course, even if you are careful, you cannot be sure that a supplier will be – there have been enough reports of account or card details being inadvertently published online. The real danger is not interception of your details in an online transaction, but that a supplier will subsequently store your card details unencrypted on a computer which is then stolen, hacked into or, of course, left on a train. But this is just as likely to happen with telephone orders.

Although individual credit card purchases are the most common way of paying for goods and services over the internet, there is an alternative method you may come across. Web-based payment systems like PayPal at <**www.paypal.com**> and WorldPay at <**www.worldpay.co.uk**> work by giving you an account from which you can then make online payments. All your financial transactions are with the payment system itself, which pays other sites on your behalf, so you are only giving your financial details to a single organization. This sort of system is particularly good for traders who may not qualify to accept credit card payments, and is much used by online auction systems such as eBay, where the participants are private individuals rather than businesses and would not be permitted to accept credit card payments.

Service online

In fact a more significant problem with online suppliers is getting hold of them to deal with problems relating to your order or the product you have bought, particularly if the website gives no phone number or postal address. However, online traders based in the UK are bound by the same consumer protection legislation as any other trader.

Before the advent of the internet, purchasing anything abroad from the comfort of the UK was far from straightforward. Online shopping has made this much easier and, of course, those who live outside the UK can now easily order materials from British genealogy suppliers. Some practical difficulties remain: returning wrong or faulty products is not made easier by the internet, though of course it is no more difficult than with traditional catalogue-based home shopping.

Also, you are less likely to be familiar with the reputations of overseas traders, which could be a source of concern in areas where UK consumer legislation does not apply – an impressive website does not guarantee quality of service, let alone financial viability. However, one of the strengths of the internet is that it is a good word-of-mouth medium, and it is very unlikely that there could be an unreliable company whose misdeeds have escaped being reported in the genealogy mailing lists or discussion forums. These are therefore good places to look for reports from other customers on their experiences with companies, or to place a query yourself. For software, the GENCMP-L mailing list (gatewayed with the soc.genealogy. computing newsgroup) is full of comments, positive and negative, on software products and the companies that supply them, and a search of the archives at <archiver.rootsweb.ancestry.com/th/index/GENCMP/> should give you some idea of a product or a company's reputation (though don't forget that older comments may no longer be relevant, since suppliers obviously try to remedy problems that give rise to bad publicity). For UK genealogy companies, look at the archives of the GENBRIT mailing list at <archiver.rootsweb.ancestry.com/th/index/GENBRIT/>, which is gatewayed with the soc.genealogy.britain newsgroup, for past comments on genealogy suppliers, or post a query yourself.

Professional researchers

There are many reasons, even with the internet, why you might want to employ a professional genealogist to undertake research for you: if you cannot get to the repository where original records are held, whether for reasons of time or distance; or if the records themselves are difficult for the non-specialist to use or interpret.

The SoG has a leaflet 'Employing a professional researcher: a practical guide' on its website at <www.sog.org.uk/leaflets/researcher.pdf>, while Cyndi's List has a page on 'Professional Researchers, Volunteers & Other Research Services' at <www.cyndislist.com/profess.htm>. Michael John Neill has an interesting and detailed article on his own experience with a professional researcher at <**www.rootdig.com/professional/**>.

The Association of Genealogists and Researchers in Archives (AGRA) is the professional body for genealogical researchers in the British Isles, with a website at <**www.agra.org.uk**>. This provides a list of members, and an index to this by specialism, whether geographical or subject-based. Many but not all of the Association's members can be contacted by email. The Association's code of practice is also available on the site. Even if you don't employ an AGRA member to do your research, the code of practice is helpful in showing what standards to expect from *any* professional researcher.

The National Archives' website also has a database of Independent Researchers who are prepared to undertake commissions for research in records at the National Archives. The database is accessible from <**www. nationalarchives.gov.uk/irlist/**> and must be searched by subject heading, chosen from a drop-down list. The resulting list does not seem to be in any particular order.

For Scotland, the Association of Scottish Genealogists and Record Agents (ASGRA) is the professional association for researchers, and its site at <**www.asgra.co.uk**> has details of members and their specialisms.

The Association of Professional Genealogists in Ireland has a website at <**www.apgi.ie**> with a list of members. Individual researchers for Ireland can be found on the National Archives of Ireland website at <**www. nationalarchives.ie/genealogy/researchers.html**>.

Membership of one of the professional organizations guarantees that a researcher has reached a high level of skill in genealogy. A similar guarantee is provided by possession of a formal qualification in genealogy, of which those of the IHGS are the best known – the Higher Certificate, Diploma and Licentiate being regarded as professional-level qualifications (see p. 362). The IHGS has a list of those who have passed its professional qualifications at <**www.ihgs.ac.uk/aboutus/graduates.php**>.

Lookup services

If all you need is someone to check a particular reference for you, employing a professional researcher will be overkill. The internet makes it easy to find someone with access to particular printed publications, or records on CD-ROM, who will do a simple lookup for you. So-called 'lookup exchanges' give a list of publications and the email address of someone prepared to do searches in each. There is, unfortunately, no central listing of these, but most are county-based and there are links to the relevant exchanges from the individual Genuki county pages. The county forums on RootsChat at <**www.rootschat.com**> have places for posting lookup offers and requests.

Lookups are done entirely on a voluntary basis, so requests should be as specific as possible, and you may need to use a specific subject line in your message – see the details at the top of each page before sending a request. And, of course, be reasonable in what you expect someone to do for you in their own time.

One particular thing to bear in mind is that getting someone to do a lookup for you on one of the commercial data services is almost certainly asking them to break the terms and conditions of their subscription. Since most data services offer an inexpensive pay-per-view option, are available free of charge in a number of libraries and archives, and in some cases offer a free trial, asking for lookups on these services on a mailing list may be interpreted as a sign of fecklessness.

22

ISSUES FOR ONLINE GENEALOGISTS

While online genealogy is essentially about finding and making use of information, it is important to be aware of some general issues involved in using internet resources and in using the web as a publishing medium. Also important are the limitations in what is and is not likely to be on the internet. The aim of this chapter is to discuss some of these issues.

Good practice

Needless to say, technophobes, Luddites and other folk of a backward-looking disposition are happy to accuse the internet of dumbing down the noble art of genealogy – anything so easy surely cannot be sound research.

Loath as I am to agree with technophobes, there is actually some truth in this. Though the medium itself can hardly be blamed for its misuse, the internet does give scope to a sort of 'trainspotting' attitude to genealogy, where it is just a matter of filling out your family tree with plausible and preferably interesting ancestors, with little regard for accuracy or traditional standards of proof. Because more can (apparently) be done without consulting original records, it becomes easy to overlook the fact that a family tree constructed solely from online sources, unchecked against *any* original records, is sure to contain many inaccuracies even if it is not entirely unsound. This is far from new, of course; today's is hardly the first generation where some are concerned for their family tree to be impressive rather than accurate. The internet just makes it easier both to construct and to disseminate pedigrees of doubtful accuracy.

But genealogy is a form of historical research, and you cannot really do it successfully without developing some understanding of the records from which a family history is constructed, and the principles for drawing reliable conclusions from them. Some of the tutorial materials mentioned in Chapter 2 address these issues, but the most coherent set of principles and standards available online are those developed by the US National Genealogical Society, which can be found at <**www.ngsgenealogy.org/comstandards.cfm**>:

- Standards for Sound Genealogical Research
- Standards for Using Records, Repositories, and Libraries
- Standards for Use of Technology in Genealogical Research
- Standards for Sharing Information with Others
- Guidelines for Publishing Web Pages on the Internet

The first of these is essential reading for anyone new to genealogy. The third is important enough in the context of this book to bear reproducing in full – see the box opposite.

Using online information

The nature of the primary data online has an important implication for how you use information found on the internet: you need to be very cautious about inferences drawn from it. For a start, *all* transcriptions of any size contain errors – the only question is how many.

Where information comes from parish registers, for example, you need to be cautious about identifying an individual ancestor from a single record in an online database. The fact that you have found a baptism with the right name, at about the right date and in about the right place, does not mean you have found an ancestor. How do you know this child did not die two weeks later; how do you know there is not a very similar baptism in a neighbouring parish whose records are not online; how do you know there is not an error in the transcription? As more records are put online with images accompanying transcriptions or indexes, the last question may become less important, but no future internet development will allow you to ignore the other questions.

Unfortunately, the very ease of the internet can sometimes make beginners think that constructing a pedigree is easier than it is. It is not enough to find a plausible-looking baptism online. You have to be able to demonstrate that this must be (not just 'could be') the same individual who marries 20 years later or who is the parent of a particular child. The internet does not do this for you. The only thing it can do is provide *some* of the material you need for that proof, and even then you will have to be more careful with online material than you would be with original records.

In particular, negative inferences (for example so and so wasn't born later than such and such a date) can be very important in constructing a family tree, but the original material on the internet will rarely allow you to make such inferences. Not even where a particular set of records has been put online in its entirety could you start to be confident in drawing a negative inference. For example, there is no simple conclusion to be drawn if you fail to find an ancestor in a particular census. He or she could have no longer been alive, or was living abroad, or is in the census but has been

Standards for Use of Technology in Genealogical Research Recommended by the National Genealogical Society

Mindful that computers are tools, genealogists take full responsibility for their work, and therefore they –

- learn the capabilities and limits of their equipment and software, and use them only when they are the most appropriate tools for a purpose.
- refuse to let computer software automatically embellish their work.
- treat compiled information from on-line sources or digital databases like that from other published sources, useful primarily as a guide to locating original records, but not as evidence for a conclusion or assertion.
- accept digital images or enhancements of an original record as a satisfactory substitute for the original only when there is reasonable assurance that the image accurately reproduces the unaltered original.
- cite sources for data obtained on-line or from digital media with the same care that is appropriate for sources on paper and other traditional media, and enter data into a digital database only when its source can remain associated with it.
- always cite the sources for information or data posted on-line or sent to others, naming the author of a digital file as its immediate source, while crediting original sources cited within the file.
- preserve the integrity of their own databases by evaluating the reliability of downloaded data before incorporating it into their own files.
- provide, whenever they alter data received in digital form, a description of the change that will accompany the altered data whenever it is shared with others.
- actively oppose the proliferation of error, rumor and fraud by personally verifying or correcting information, or noting it as unverified, before passing it on to others.
- treat people on-line as courteously and civilly as they would treat them face-to-face, not separated by networks and anonymity.
- accept that technology has not changed the principles of genealogical research, only some of the procedures.

mistranscribed in the index, or was in the census until the relevant enumera-tion book went missing. Of course, such problems relate to all indexes, not just those online, but you can never be *more* confident about online records.

Also, you need to be very cautious about drawing conclusions based not on primary sources but on compiled pedigrees put online by other genea-logists. Some of these represent careful genealogical work and come with detailed documentation of sources; others may just have a name and possible birth year, perhaps supplied from memory by an ageing relative – insufficient detail to be of great value, with no guarantee of accuracy, and impossible to verify. At best you can regard such materials as helpful pointers to someone who might have useful information, or to sources you have not yet examined yourself. It would be very unwise simply to incorporate the information in your own pedigree simply because it appears to refer to an individual you have already identified as an ancestor.

Copyright

The internet makes it very easy to disseminate information, but just because you *can* disseminate material it does not mean that you *should*. Both websites and email messages are treated by the law as publications. If you circulate or republish material you did not create, you may be infringing someone's copyright by doing so. Of course, genealogical facts themselves are not subject to copyright, but a modern transcription of an original record will be, and a compilation of facts in a database is also protected, though for more limited duration.

This means you should not put on your own website, upload to a data-base or post to a mailing list:

- material you have extracted from online or CD-ROM databases
- material scanned from books that are still in copyright
- genealogical data you have received from others (unless they give their permission, of course)

There is a exemption of 'fair use' which allows some copying, but this is only for purposes of criticism or private study, not for republishing or passing on to others. Extracting a single record from a CD-ROM and emailing it to an individual is probably OK, but posting the same informa-tion to a mailing list, which means it will be permanently archived, is not. Note that some companies include licence conditions with CD-ROMs stating that you must not supply the information to third parties. Whether or not such a strict condition would stand up in court – a similar ban on lookups in a reference book would seem to be ridiculous – the supply of genealogy data on CD-ROM would be threatened by significant levels of copyright infringement.

A number of people have been shocked to find their own genealogical databases submitted to an online pedigree database without their knowledge. Mark Howells covers these issues very thoroughly in 'Share and Beware – Sharing Genealogy in the Information Age' at <**www.oz.net/~ markhow/writing/share.htm**>. Barbara A. Brown discusses the dissemination of 'dishonest research' in 'Restoring Ethics to Genealogy' at <**www.iigs. org/newsletter/9904news/ethics.htm.en**>. Steve's Genealogy Blog has a posting about 'Ethics in Publishing Family Histories' at <**stephendanko. com/blog/2007/07/31/ethics-in-publishing-family-histories/**>.

The current Crown Copyright rules, however, mean that you can include extracts from unpublished copyright material held by the National Archives as long as the source is acknowledged. The National Archives' 'Copyright' leaflet at <**www.nationalarchives.gov.uk/legal/pdf/copyright_full.pdf**> explains which of their holdings are and are not covered by Crown Copyright, and the Government's 'Crown Copyright in the Information Age' <**www.opsi.gov.uk/advice/crown-copyright/crown-copyright-in-the-information-age.pdf**> gives general guidance about Crown Copyright.[19]

David Hawgood's 'Copyright for Family Historians' at <**www.genuki. org.uk/org/Copyright.html**> offers some informal guidance tailored for genealogists, while for more general and definitive information, there is the official website of the UK Intellectual Property Office at <**www.ipo. gov.uk**>.

Privacy

Another important issue is privacy. Contrary to a widespread belief, the UK's Data Protection legislation does not prohibit the publication of private information about an individual – if this *were* the case, then, rather obviously, certain newspapers would no longer be commercially viable. The Human Rights Act enshrines in law a right to private life, but it's difficult to see how this could be used to censor information derived from official, publicly-available sources. Of course, if your online family tree says your still-living Uncle Arthur is a drunkard and he disagrees, that's another matter. The real problem with publishing information about living family members is many people will regard it as discourteous at the very least. Your Uncle Arthur will probably not sue for libel, but he might

---

19 Digital images of historical documents are regarded as copyright-free in some jurisdictions, including the USA and Germany. For this reason many such images are available, quite legally, on sites like Wikipedia.

stop talking to you or not leave you the family photographs.

In any case, even if it's just a matter of births, marriages and deaths, it's difficult to see any need to publish this information about the living in order to further genealogical research, which would be the only other justification. Conversely, though, in the absence of any legal protection, it's not clear that you have any legal recourse if someone publishes information about your immediate family online, though if they have used a pedigree database such as those discussed in Chapter 14, you should be able to get the service to take action. Where there's a need to use the web to share information within a family, there are many sites that will allow you to restrict who can see what information.

Myra Vanderpool Gormley discusses these issues briefly in 'Exposing Our Families To The Internet' at <**www.ancestry.com/columns/myra/ Shaking_Family_Tree06-19-97.htm**>. The privacy policies of some of the pedigree databases and tools for removing living people from genealogy databases are discussed on p. 233.

The objection to publishing information about living family members was always that they might take umbrage. But there is nowadays a more serious objection. Many commercial services use questions about someone's past as a security check. If you can amass enough information about someone, you can impersonate them online. In principle, an online tree might put someone at risk of identity theft. But in fact you probably don't list the names of your cousin's first school, pet hamster, favourite book etc. in an online tree. Any company still using the mother's maiden name as a security check should be avoided as incompetent.

Indeed it is the information that is already available, often made so by the individual concerned, that is the real threat. In these days of blogging, Facebook and Flickr, much about people's lives is publicly available in a way which goes well beyond the secrets revealed by a family tree.

On the other hand, it seems that a concern with privacy might be a threat to reasonable publication of genealogical data. In its original proposals for digitization of the civil registration service (see p. 71), the GRO argued that certain items of data should be withheld, including occupations, addresses and causes of death. While no one would argue that someone's privacy should be threatened just because genealogist's 'need' access to certain type of information, there has to be a *very* good case for suppressing information on the documents that are the foundations of citizenship. Given that details of marriages, for example, are published in advance specifically to permit public scrutiny, why on earth would anyone consider that the details on the eventual certificate give rise to privacy concerns? Considering how often we see reports of credit card details accidentally exposed on websites, highly confidential personal information absent-mindedly left in taxis, or sent, unsecured, by post, it seems absurd to be worrying about twenty-year-old addresses and the privacy of the dead.

There is a mailing list, LEGAL-ENGWLS, for the discussion of 'legal aspects of genealogical research in England and Wales including copyright, database rights, data protection, and privacy' – details at <**lists.rootsweb. ancestry.com/index/intl/UK/LEGAL-ENGWLS.html**>.

Quality concerns

While the increasing amount and range of genealogical material online, both free and commercial, can only be a good thing, it does not mean that these datasets are without their problems.

In particular there is the question of the accuracy of the indexing. Of course, anyone who indexes the 30 million records or so in a census is not going to do so without a level of error, but the question is: what is an acceptable level of error? What can digitizers reasonably be expected to do, without incurring insupportable extra costs, to minimize the level of error?

With so many massive datasets, where it's impossible to check every entry, one of the problems is that it's extremely difficult to come to firm conclusions about which site has the best-quality data and which has the most (and most serious) errors. Also, because of differences in the search facilities, it's not always possible to make direct comparisons, and it is therefore not even a straightforward matter to develop diagnostic tests as a basis for some sort of independent benchmarking

But with civil registration indexes and all the censuses available at more than one site, one hopes that competition, not to mention pride in their own products, will keep the data services striving for a good reputation. On the other hand, perhaps this is an optimistic view: as there are so many reasons why one might fail to locate an ancestor in a census, only some of which can be put down to errors in transcription or indexing, it may be they can afford to be cavalier about quality.

On the other hand, the number of competing commercial data services perhaps makes the fact of errors less important. Genealogists just have to accept that the alternative to having better-quality data at a significantly higher price is that occasionally you will need to use more than one site when looking for a particular record. The real problem *then* comes from the data monopolies such as we have seen to date in ScotlandsPeople and might be seeing in the proposed GRO digitization project, which permit us no alternative index.

Finding material

Information is not much use if you cannot find it. Search engines are able to capture only a fraction of the material on the web. Of course, it is impossible to foresee technological advances, but there is no sign at the moment that the coverage of search engines will improve significantly. Websites of individual genealogists, in particular, will probably become harder to find. In addition, the increasing amount of data held in online databases is not discoverable by search engines, and it becomes more important than ever for gateways and directories (or even books!) to direct people to the sources of online data.

The quality of indexing provided by search engines is limited by the poor facilities currently available for marking up text in HTML with semantic information. Search engines cannot tell that Kent is a surname in 'Clark Kent' but a place name in 'Maidstone, Kent'. This is because web authors have no way of indicating this in HTML markup. As so many British surnames are the names of places or occupations, this is a significant problem for UK genealogists.

The situation could improve when a more sophisticated markup language, XML, starts to be used widely on the web – this allows information to be tagged descriptively, and will enable the development of a special markup language for genealogical information. Such a development (and its retrospective application to material already published on the web) is some way off and will require considerable work, though the LDS Church has made a start by proposing an XML successor to GEDCOM (see the GEDCOM FAQ at <**www.familysearch.org/Eng/Home/FAQ/faq_gedcom. asp**>). But the benefits of such an approach are already apparent in a project like the Old Bailey Proceedings (see p. 125), which can distinguish between the names of the accused, the victim, and witnesses.

Another problem is the increasing number of sites with surname resources, making it impossible to check *everywhere* for others who share your interests. Mercifully, the number of pedigree databases (see Chapter 14) remains manageable for the present, but the number of sites, particularly message boards, with surname-related material makes exhaustive searching impossible.

However, on a more positive note, it's clear that, with so much work being done on making archival catalogues available, it will become easier than ever to track down original documents in record offices and other repositories, and genealogists in general will start to make much more use of records that in the past only the expert might have been able to take advantage of.

▌ Longevity

To anyone who has not grown up with the web, there is one deeply troubling aspect of internet resources: their tendency to disappear. We are used to the idea that once information is published in book form, it may become hard to find, but it doesn't generally disappear, particularly if it is important or useful, in less than a century or two. But the fact is that important internet resources are constantly at risk.

Large digitized datasets are not really threatened, because they have a commercial value which protects them from oblivion, but there are two types of valuable resource which are particularly vulnerable: publicly-funded and volunteer projects.

In the first of these cases, even if the initial funding does envisage some provision for long-term hosting and maintenance, it will not be open-ended. Also, there can be no guarantee that some new broom will not cancel funding already promised, deciding that the money can be better used for some new project. (Unfortunately, there is often more kudos in getting a new project off the ground than in maintaining an old one.)

An obvious example, is Familia (p. 204), whose initial funding was pulled in 2001. Eight years on, it is still available online, but neither the information (which is meant to be current) nor the links are being maintained. It has had two different hosts since 2001 (currently the Museums, Libraries and Archives Council), but it is understandable that they have not wanted to use more of their own limited funds for maintaining rather than just hosting Familia.

You can get a good idea of the problems faced by even the most successful projects from the following message posted on A Vision of Britain in December 2008 by the project's director, Humphrey Southall:

> A Vision of Britain through Time launched in October 2004, and for the first three years running costs were paid by the British Library. We managed to save up a little money in that period and we earned a bit more by licensing data, so we were able to keep it going for a fourth year, until September 2008.
>
> The site is still running in December 2008 through a new grant from the Joint Information Systems Committee, the IT arm of the Higher Education Funding Council. This grant is to build an extended version of the site to launch in the spring of 2009, but we are also using it to pay Edinburgh University, who host the site for us.
>
> That will keep us going only until the end of March 2009, and from then on we have to pay our way. This means the site is going to look a little different, but it is still far from commercial: the only use to which money

generated from the site will be put is keeping it going. The JISC grant will be funding a new web server for us, but we really need to start saving for the next new server which will be needed around 2012/13. However, the immediate problem is simply covering a five-figure annual hosting bill.

...

It is very frustrating that there seems to be no route at all by which a resource created by individual initiative can apply for public money to keep it running, no matter how uncommercial the original motive, how useful the content, how popular the end result.

Some of the most valuable genealogical resources on the web are the results of a single individual or a small group devoting massive amounts of time to them. Of course, these don't have the large-scale funding issues of A Vision of Britain, but they too are at risk: inevitably, the individuals concerned will at some point be forced by circumstances to give up their efforts, even if it is only the ultimate circumstance of their death. Unless arrangements for succession have already been put in place, all the material and any domain name for the project will become the responsibility of the next of kin, who, apart from having more pressing concerns, may not know what to do or who to contact to secure its future, or have the technical skills to manage a transition.

It's true that the Waybackmachine at <**www.archive.org**> can often provide a partial back-stop, but that is not a satisfactory basis for preserving valuable resources. The British Library has a digital archiving project, but that is solely for resources of their choosing. Of course, any archiving is better than nothing, but just copying files is quite inadequate for many modern sites, which use a variety of techniques to generate pages dynamically, rather than delivering static pages, and which may require the web server to be appropriately configured.

As far as I can see, this set of problems has received scant attention from the genealogical world, which is otherwise so concerned and so careful about the preservation of materials and information.

▎ Outlook

The changes in the practice of family history that have been brought about by the internet are extraordinary and on the whole very positive. However, it's important to keep a sense of perspective, and to recognize that none of this has made any difference to the fundamentals of family history research: consulting records and sharing information. Nor is there any prospect of basing a family tree solely on digitized records – just consider how long it's taking to get civil registration records online!

The internet is not going to 'automate' family history or modify its principles and methods. Nor does it need to – there is nothing wrong with the traditional methods of genealogy. The fact that many historical records are easier than ever to access doesn't make them any easier to interpret. Indeed, it may make them harder to interpret, if a search delivers an individual piece of information to you shorn of its context.

What the internet has revolutionized is not the process of genealogy, but the ease with which some of the research can be carried out.

The key aspects of this are:

- the increasing amounts of data available online
- the number of people with shared interests who have internet access

Although microfilm and microfiche are not going to disappear in the immediate future, any more than books are, the internet is now the publishing medium of choice for all large genealogical data projects, whether official, commercial or volunteer-run. Where public records or public funding are concerned, the web, because of its low cost and universal access, is the default publishing medium as a matter of principle.

Both the number of internet users and the amount of data available have now reached a critical mass, with the result that the genealogist without internet access is in a minority and at a relative disadvantage in access to data and contact with other genealogists.

Of course you can still research your family tree without using the internet – just about – but why would you choose to?

INTERNET GLOSSARY

Adobe Acrobat	A file format, popular for documents which need to be made available online with fixed formatting. Files have the extension .pdf, and so the term 'PDF file' is often used. See p. 52.
blog	An online personal journal (short for 'web log').
cookie	A piece of information stored on your hard disk by a website in order to identify you and your preferences each time you use the site.
database	1) A collection of individual items of information ('records') which can be retrieved selectively via a search facility. 2) A software program for managing data records (short for 'database management system').
directory	1) A collection of links to internet resources, arranged in a hierarchy of subject headings. 2) On some operating systems, a hierarchical folder containing individual computer files.
DjVu	A graphics file format used by some of the commercial data services, pronounced as *déjà vu* (see p. 56).
domain name	The part of an internet address which is formally registered and owned, and which forms the latter part of a server or host name, e.g. *bbc.co.uk* is the domain name, while <**news. bbc.co.uk**> and <**www.bbc.co.uk**> are individual servers within that domain.
download	To transfer a file from another computer to your own computer.
FAQ	Frequently Asked Questions, a document listing common questions in a particular area, along with their answers.
flame	A rude or abusive message.
freeware	Software which can be downloaded and used free of charge (see also *shareware*).

FTP	File Transfer Protocol, a method of transferring files across the internet (see p. 355).
gateway	1) A subject-specific *directory*. 2) A link which allows messages to pass between two different systems, e.g. newsgroups and mailing lists.
GIF	A graphics file format, mainly used on the web for graphic design elements, less suitable for colour photographs.
hit	A matching item retrieved in response to a search.
host	A computer connected to the internet which allows other internet users access to material stored on its hard disk.
hosting	Providing space on a *host* for someone's web pages.
HTML	HyperText Markup Language, in which web pages are written.
ISP	Internet Service Provider.
JPEG	A graphics file format, mainly used for photographs.
lurking	Reading the messages in a discussion forum, but not contributing yourself.
mailing list	A discussion forum which uses email.
message board	A web page which allows users to read and post messages, often also called a 'forum'.
meta-search engine	A site which automatically submits a search to a number of different *search engines*.
netiquette	The informal, consensual rules of online communication.
newsgroup	Open discussion forums held on an internet-wide network of 'news servers'.
plug-in	A piece of software used by a web browser to display files it cannot handle on its own.
podcast	An audio recording made accessible via the web (sometimes also used for video).
portal	A collection of internet resources for a particular audience – see the discussion on p. 15.
robot	A piece of software which trawls the internet looking for new resources, used by search engines to create their indexes.
search engine	Commonly, a website which has a searchable index of web pages, though more accurately *any* piece of software which searches an index.

searchbot	A piece of software which searches the web for you (a contraction of 'search robot').
server	A computer, usually with a permanent internet connection, which responds to requests for data from other computers on the internet. There are different types of server according to the service offered, e.g. mail server, web server, list server.
shareware	Software which can be downloaded free of charge, but requires payment for registration after a trial period (see also *freeware*).
spam	Unsolicited messages sent to multiple recipients.
streaming	Making an audio or video recording play in real time via a web browser rather than requiring a separate download.
subscribe	To join a mailing list.
URL	Uniform Resource Locator, a standard way of referring to internet resources so that each resource has a unique name. In the case of a web page, the URL is the same as the web address.
validation	A method of identifying gross data-entry errors in a database, checking that an item of data falls within an acceptable range of values.
World Wide Web	A collection of linked pages of information retrievable via the internet.
XML	eXtensible Markup Language, a more sophisticated and flexible markup language than *HTML*, likely to be increasingly used for websites.

All these terms are defined and explained on Wikipedia at <**en.wikipedia. org**>.

There are many internet glossaries online, including:

- the Internet Language Dictionary at <**www.netlingo.com/inframes. cfm**>
- Foldoc (the Free On-Line Dictionary of Computing) at <**foldoc.org**>

For glossaries of genealogy terms see p. 13.

BIBLIOGRAPHY

Anthony Adolph, *Collins Tracing Your Family Tree* (Collins, 2008)

Nick Barrett, *Who Do You Think You Are? Encyclopedia of Genealogy* (Harper, 2008)

Amanda Bevan, *Tracing Your Ancestors in the National Archives: the Website and Beyond*, 7th edn (The National Archives, 2006)

Peter Christian, *Web Publishing for Genealogy*, 2nd edn (David Hawgood, 1999) – full text online at <**www.spub.co.uk/wpg/**>

Peter Christian and David Annal, *Census: The Expert Guide* (The National Archives, 2008)

John Grenham, *Tracing your Irish Ancestors* (Gill & Macmillan, 2006)

Mark Herber, *Ancestral Trails,* 2nd edn (The History Press, 2005)

Cyndi Howells, *Cyndi's List*, 2nd edn (Rutledge Hill, 2004)

Cyndi Howells, *Planting Your Family Tree Online* (Thomas Nelson, 2004)

Daniel M. Lynch, *Google Your Family Tree* (FamilyLink.com, 2008)

Virginia Shea, *Netiquette* (Albion Books, 1996) – full text online at <**www. albion.com/netiquette/book/**>

Richard S. Wilson, *Publishing Your Family History on the Internet* (Betterway Books, 1999)

INDEX

192.com 233, 247

A Church Near You 100
A Vision of Britain through
  Time 81, 238–39, 387
abbreviations 13–14
  Latin 274
ABCgenealogy 258
About.com 11, 13, 267, 270
abroad, researching from 11, 18
Access to Archives (A2A) 124,
  140, 193, 202
acronyms 13, 14
ActiveX 55
addresses 232
administrative units 12, 238,
  239 see also counties
Adobe Acrobat 52–54, 321,
  348–49
Adolph, Anthony 6, 393
adoption 60, 234–36
Africa 24
alumni records 135
Amazon 359
America see also Canada,
  USA
  Central 24
  migration 162–64
  South 25, 164
Ancestor Forest 351
Ancestors magazine 364, 368
Ancestorsonboard 161
Ancestral File 101, 216, 336,
  349
Ancestral Quest 336
Ancestry 29, 34, 35, 38, 44–45,
  54, 57, 67–68, 84, 85–86, 98,
  108, 119, 122, 136, 138, 147, 149,
  162, 163, 183, 190, 191, 214, 217,
  225, 226, 305, 365, 367
  image quality 93
  index quality 95
Ancestry Insider 45
AncestryIreland 50, 110
AND search 313, 330
Anglo-American Legal
  Tradition 123

Anglo-Indian ancestry 169–71
Annal, David xv, 393
announcements 301
anti-virus software 346
Apple Macintosh 55, 345
applets 273, 350
apprentices 130
Archaeology UK 238
Archive CD Books 373
archives 1, **192–208**, 386 see
  also county record offices
  Australian 166
  depositing in 358
  guides to 193–94
  images 279
  Jewish 172
  national 196–202
  New Zealand 166
  overseas 208
  photo archives 287
Archives & Museum of Black
  Heritage 169
Archives Hub 205
Archives Network Wales 194
ARCHON Directory 112, 193,
  203, 205
armed forces 142–57
  photographs 286
  army 148–51
  India 170, 286
Asia 24
Asian ancestry 168, 169–71
Ask (search engine) 312
Association of Family History
  Societies of Wales 361
Association of Genealogists
  and Researchers in Archives
  (AGRA) 377
Association of Professional
  Genealogists in Ireland 377
Association of Scottish
  Genealogists and Record
  Agents (ASGRA) 377
auctions 374
Austen, Malcolm 306, 361
Australia 25, 79, 164–66, 202,
  236

Avotaynu 171, 172
A–Z (London) 254

Baedeker 250
Bangladesh 169–71
Baptist Historical Society 112
Barnett, Len 146
Barrett, Nick 6, 393
Bartholomew, John 257
Bartrum, Dr Peter 228
batch numbers 103–4, 104
battles 143–44, 147
BBC 8, 166, 174, 229, 261
BBC History Magazine 365
Behind the Name 267, 270
Berners-Lee, Tim 229
Bevan, Amanda 393
biblical genealogies 229
bibliography 260, 393
biography 178, 231–32
  naval 147
  Welsh 203
Black and Asian Londoners
  Project 168
Black and Asian Studies
  Association 169
Black British ancestry 166–69
  black communities 125
  black history 168
blogs 5, 45, 89, **367–71**, 372,
  384
BMDindex 48, 65–66
Bolles Collection 231
bookmarks 23, 102, 245, 320,
  355, 369
  public xiv, 131
books 6, 175–79
  digitized **175–78**, 230, 267
  online bookshops 2, 373–76
  reference 178–79
  second-hand 374
Boolean logic 314, 319
Booth, Charles 255
Borthwick Institute 42, 117
bottom-posting 307
Boundary Commission 249,
  252, 257

Bounty, HMS 229
Boyd's London Burials 108
Boyd's Marriage Index 108
BrightPlanet 314, 332
Brightsolid xiv, 38, 46, 88
Bringing Civil Registration into the 21st Century 74
Britains Small Wars 143
British Association for Adoption and Fostering 235
British Association for Cemeteries in South Asia 114
British Association for Local History 263
British Cartographic Society 257
British Columbia 79
British History Online 249, 261
British Library 168, 169, 184–87, 202, 205, 245, 250, 258
   catalogue 182, 184–87, 310
   digital archiving 388
   India Office Collections 16, 168, 169–71, 202
   Map Library 237
British Vital Records Index 106
British-Genealogy 81, 99, 114, 144, 173, 179, 263, 304, 359
broadband xi
Brown, Barbara A. 383
BT 232
buildings, historic 279
bulletin boards 4, 303–6
Burke's Peerage and Gentry 227–28, 231

calendars 272–73
Canada 24, 164, 236, 368
cap badges 151
Capital Punishment UK 126
Caribbean 9, 24, 166–69
Cary, John 250
CASBAH 169
case sensitivity 353
catalogues 192, 386
   Family History Library 206–8
   library 204
   National Archives 198–99
   National Archives of Scotland 200
   Public Record Office of Northern Ireland 200–201
   Society of Genealogists (SoG) 208
Catholic Archives Society 111
Catholic Encyclopaedia 273
Catholic History 111

CD-ROM, data on 38, 82, 102, 109, 179, 216, 223, 268, 307, 366, 377, 382
cemeteries 113–14
   military 154, 156
census 7, 28, **80–98**, 385
   1881 81, 84, 148, 268
   1891 240
   1901 xiv, 29, 30, 34, 50, 53, 84, 85, 87, 148
   1911 30, 46, 80, 84, **88–91**
   1911 (Ireland) 53, 96–97
   1911 (Scotland) 43
   1921 129
   1926 (Ireland) 96
   Canada 98
   commercial sites 84–95
   indexes 81–84
   indexes, local 83–84
   Ireland 95–98, 124
   overseas 98
   Scotland 86, 87
   searching 93
   ships 148
   site comparison 91–95
   substitutes (Ireland) 97
   USA 98
Census Finder 83, 97
Census Links 98
Chancery records 199
Channel 4 156, 172
Channel Islands 77
Chapman County Codes 213, 244
Charting the Nation 256
Chartist Ancestors 141
Chater, Kathy 166
Cheshire Wills 117
CheshireBMD 68
child migration 234–36
children in care 265
Chinese immigration 126
Christian, Peter 359, 393
Church Database (Genuki) 100
churches
   Anglican 100–101
   Church of Ireland 201
   Genuki Church Database 240
   nonconformist 111–13
   photographs 113, 284
   Presbyterian Church 201
   Roman Catholic Church 110–11
civil registration 2, 7, 28, 60–79
   certificate exchanges 77
   digitization 30, 71–72
   indexes 45, 61–70, 203, 385
   Ireland 74–77

ordering certificates 60, 61, 73, 75
   overseas 78–79, 78
   Scotland 42, 72–74, 78
Civil Registration. Vital Change 71
clans 229
clergy 138–40
Clergy of the Church of England Database 139
climate history 263
coinage 276
collaboration 2
Collage (Guildhall Library) 253, 281
College of Arms 230
Collins, Elaine xv
colonies 25, 158–74, 281
colour depth 93
Commonwealth War Graves Commission 153
company records 140–41, 157
CompuServe 4, 366
Consumer Direct 375
consumer protection 376
convicts 164, 165, 202
cookies 58
COPAC 202, 205
copyright 175, 177, 223, 307, 334, 382–83
Cornucopia 194
Council of Irish Genealogical Organisations 74, 96
counties 12, 37, 239, 242–44, 242–44
   indexing 37
county record offices xii, 1, 17, 117, 121, 193, 195, 203, 262, 281
courses 362–63
Court Service 116
credit cards 39
   security 374–75
Crew List Index Project (CLIP) 148
crime 125–27, 265
Crown Copyright 383
Curious Fox 263
currency 277–78
currency converters 278
customer service 375
Customs and Excise xii, 276
CuteFTP 355
Cyndi's List xv, 2, 4, 11, 14, **21–23**, 26, 79, 98, 111, 113, 120, 125, 130, 131, 138, 143, 158, 161, 162, 164, 171, 172, 173, 184, 208, 211, 215, 224, 226, 227, 231, 236, 237, 244, 267, 276, 279, 285, 287, 332, 336, 338, 357, 359, 364, 366, 367, 371, 372, 374, 376

Dance, Philip 269
Darwin, Charles 222
Data Protection 383
data services xiii, 28, **39–50**,
 378, 385 *and passim*
 choosing 57
data validation 34
data, quality of 385
databases 350, 382, 386
 accuracy 234
dates 272–73
DeadFred 287
Death Duty Registers 118
Debt of Honour Register
 153–54
Department of Health 236
Department of Trade and
 Industry 375
desktop publishing 345
dictionaries 14, 392
 biography 178, 231–32
 Irish 275
 Latin 273–74
 measures 276
 medical 276
 occupations 128–29
 surnames 266–69
 Welsh 274
*Dictionary of National
 Biography* 178, 231, 232
*Dictionary of Occupational
 Terms* 128
Digital Library of Historical
 Directories xiv, 179–80
digitization **28–30**, 99, 115,
 179, 203, 385
Directgov 17, 203
directories 179–84
 telephone 183, 232
 trade 131
 web 15, 26–27, 169, 310, 311,
 386
Discover My Past Scotland 364
discussion forums 4, 12, 213,
 293–309
 starting 308
 web-based 303–6
DjVu image format 56
DNA surname projects 225
DNA testing 1, 224–26, 368
document services 50–52
DocumentsOnline 39, **51**, 53,
 117, 123, 142, 146, 149, 151, 152
DogPile 330
domain names 340
Domesday Book 123
DOVE 37, 72
Dreamweaver 345

E179 database 120, 199
East India Company 114, 170

Eastenders 229
Easter, dates of 273
Eastman, Dick 13, 259, 369,
 371, 374
Eastman's Online Genealogy
 Newsletter xv, 219, 336, 341,
 348, 359, 366, 367, 372
eBay 374
eCATNI 200
electoral registers 232–33
Electric Scotland 265
email 382
 addresses 211, 233–34, 297
 filtering 301
 formatting 299–300
 signature 297
 software 299–300
Emery, Dr Ashton 13
emigration 11, 158–74
 Scottish 202
Encyclopedia Britannica 179
Encyclopedia of Genealogy 13
Eneclann 124
England Tombstone Project
 114
English Heritage 280
English Surnames Survey 122
Enquire 12
Equity Pleadings 199
e-shopping 373–76
Etchells, Guy 88, 113, 275
ethics 382–85
ethnic groups 27, 158–74
Europe 24
 migration 171
events 361
Exploring Ancestry 369
Expression Web 346

Facebook 5, 234, 384
Familia 182, 204, 387
Families In British India
 Society 150
Family Historian (software)
 336
Family History 364
Family History Archives 177
Family History Centers 82,
 104, 146, 167, **205–8**, 208
Family History Event 362
Family History Fairs 362
Family History Library 9,
 206–8
family history magazines 359
Family History Monthly 364
family history organisations
 360
family history societies 4, 19,
 20, 27, 106, 109, 214–15, 253,
 361, 373
 Anglo-Scottish Family

History Society 109
Catholic Family History
 Society 111
Dyfed Family History
 Society 113
Families in British India
 Society 170
Family History Society of
 Cheshire 69
Genealogical Society of
 Ireland 74, 361
Jewish Genealogical Society
 of Great Britain 171
North West Kent Family
 History Society 242
Quaker Family History
 Society 112
Railway Ancestors Family
 History Society 134
Romany & Traveller Family
 History Society 173
Scottish Genealogy Society
 361
Shropshire FHS 215
Sussex Family History
 Group 215
family history, preserving 358
Family Matters 336
Family Origins 336
Family Records Centre 72
Family Tree magazine 364
Family Tree magazine (US)
 371
Family Tree Maker 337
FamilyHistoryOnline xiv, 29,
 83
FamilyRecords 7, 16, 60, 80,
 111, 116, 235
Familyrelatives **49**, 56, 57, 66,
 84, 109, 122, 136, 147, 149, 183
 census 87
FamilySearch 4, 9, 13, 38, 75,
 79, 84, 101–6, 110, 116, 177,
 205–8, 216, 223, 268, 325, 336,
 367, 372
 census 82
 Indexing Project 32, 104–6,
 107
 Record Search Pilot xiv, 54,
 104–6
famous people 229
FAQ 12, 18, 59, 306–7, 307
favorites 321
Federation of Family History
 Societies (FFHS) xiv, 8, 29,
 72, 81, 83, 108, 331, 360, 361,
 366, 373
Feet of Fines 123
FHS Online **83**
Fianna 96, 97, 110, 111, 112
FidoNet 4

filenames 353
finding information 386
Findmypast xiv, xv, 29, 38, 42,
46–47, 56, 57, 59, 64–65, 78,
82, 84, 85, 88, 108, 135, 138,
146, 149, 161, 170, 233, 268
census 85
image quality 93
index quality 95
Firefox 321, 369
First Fleet 164
FirstPage 346
Fisher, Jim 12, 243
Flash 59
Flash file format 56
Fleet Air Arm 144
Flickr 289, 384
Floodlight 362
foreign languages 13, 25
see also dictionaries
forenames 270
transcription of 35
FortuneCity 340
Fowler, Simon xv, 368
Francis Frith Collection 284
Free Webspace directory 340
FreeBMD 2, 31, 32, 38, 45, 61,
62–64, 271
FreeCEN 82
Freedom of Information Act
88
Freeholders' Records (Ireland)
201
FreeReg 106
Freeservers 348
freeware 348
French Protestant Church of
London 174
Friends Reunited 219, 234
From-Ireland 76, 124
FTP 355
Fuller, John xiv, 77, 100, 172,
213, 236, 244, 294, 295, 366

Gale 187
gaols 126
gateways 310, **311**, 386
archives 193–94, 208
genealogy 21–26
historical 260
map history 258
subject gateways 15
Gazetteer of British Place
Names 238, 243
gazetteers 237–44
historical 238–41
overseas 244
Gazettes-Online 152, 188–89
GEDCOM 102, 215, 218, 220,
224, **335–36**, 340, 350, 386
GEDCOM Index 218

GENBRIT 12, 306, 308, 376
GenCircles 217, 223, 224
GENCMP mailing list 359
gender errors 34
GenDocs 8, 14, 81, 112, 113,
254, 265
Genealogical Research
Directory 209
Genealogical Society of Utah 81
Genealogists' Magazine 364
genealogy
getting started 2, 6–14
good practice 379–80
methods 1, 388
off-line 2
standards 379–80
Genealogy Gateway, The 26
Genealogy Home Page
Construction Kit 338
Genealogy Links 26
Genealogy Resources on the
Internet 294, 297
Genealogy.com 14, 305
GenealogyPro 13
GeneaNet 218
General Register Office (GRO)
16, 29, 60, 61, 234, 243, 384
General Register Office
(Northern Ireland) 74, 75
General Register Office for
Scotland (GROS) 16, 29, 42,
72, 109, 234, 268, 270
Generations 336
Genes Reunited xiv, 38, 50, 53,
57, 84, 85, 87, 219–21, 221, 223,
224
image quality 93
genetics 224–26
Geneva 361
GeneWeb 218
GENfair 361, 373
GenForum 214, 305
Genmaps 249, 253
GenServ 219, 223
Genuki xii, 4, 7, 11, 12, 16, 17,
18–21, 23, 25, 61, 71, 72, 81,
84, 100, 104, 110, 114, 122, 124,
125, 130, 143, 145, 148, 158,
180, 181, 184, 203, 206, 210,
215, 225, 226, 228, 243, 244,
247, 253, 258, 262, 273, 294,
295, 302, 358, 361, 377
Church Database 240
gazetteers 239
Search 331
GenWeb 24–25, 79, 110, 158,
167
GeoCities 348
Geograph 291
Georgian Newspaper Project
190

Get-a-map 237, 245
Getty Thesaurus of
Geographic Names On-Line
244
Gibbs, Steven 273, 276
GIF image format 353
Giles, C. Lee 324
Glasgow City Archives 282
Global Gazette, The 104, 148
glossaries 13, 14, 228, 277, 392
Google 15, 312, 316, 317, 318,
319, 327
Advanced Search 314
Books 175, 231, 267, 371
Earth 247, 259
Groups 12, 303, 374
Image search 323
Maps 245, 247, 258, 291
Gormley, Myra Vanderpool
384
government 1, 16, 17, 31, 71,
193, 203
Australia 165
local 17, 203, 242, 243
Republic of Ireland 17, 74
websites 323
graphics 353
Grenham, John 11, 393
Griffith's Valuation 42, 97, 124
Grogan, Margaret 76
Groome, Frances 241
Guardian 9, 188
Guild of One-Name Studies
211, 267, 331, 361
Guildhall Library 138, 253, 281
Gypsies 125, 173–4

Hall, Jay 148
Hampshire 251
handheld computers 372
handwriting 271–72
Hawgood, David 383
hearth tax 120, 122
help, getting 12–13
heraldry 230–31
Ireland 203
Heraldry Society 231
Heraldry Society of Scotland
231
Herber, Mark 6, 393
Heritage Lottery Fund 28, 31,
179, 193, 261, 283
Hidden Lives 265
Historic Parishes of England &
Wales 252
Historical Directories 135
History in Focus 9, 365
Histpop 81
holocaust 172
homosexuality 125
hospitals 199, 265

hotspots 342
House of Commons 228, 277
Howells, Cyndi 21, 359, 393,
　See also Cyndi's List
Howells, Mark 14, 383
HTML 300, 343–49, 345, 358,
　386
　tags 341, 343, 356
Huguenot Society of Great
　Britain & Ireland 173
Huguenots 111, 126, 173–74
Human Rights Act 383

I Found It! 26
IGI 75, 102, 104, 204, 205, 222,
　223, 325
image archives 279
Image Partners 270
images 32–38, 44, 334
　file formats 44, 63, 353
　format 52–56
　quality 93–94
　resolution 93
　searching for 321–23
　viewers 52–56
Images of Empire 281
Images of England 279
Images Online (British
　Library) 250
Immigrant Ships Transcribers
　Guild 161
immigration 25, 158–74
Imperial War Museum 156
indexes 32–38, 380
indexing
　problems 33–38
　quality 94–95
India 78, 169–71
India Office 202
Information Commissioner
　88
Institute of Heraldic and
　Genealogical Studies (IHGS)
　109, 360, 362, 364, 377
　bookshop 373
Institute of Historical
　Research 131, 139, 173, 261,
　365
insurance records 124
Intellectual Property Office
　383
intelligent agents 330
International Society of
　Genetic Genealogy (ISoGG)
　225
Internet Archive 136, 176, 254,
　267, 269, 285
Internet Explorer 59, 320, 341
Internet Genealogical
　Bookshop 374
internet genealogy 1

history 3–5
　timeline 5
Internet Genealogy 365
Internet Library of Early
　Journals 189
Intute 26, 145, 260
invisible web 325
Ionian Islands 78
Ireland 9, 11, 17, 41, 57, 111,
　200, 202, 235
　census 95–98
　civil registration 74–77
　gazetteers 241
　government 17, 74
　heraldry 230
　land ownership 122
　maps 257
　Nonconformity 112
　parish registers 109–10
　property records 124
　public libraries 204
　seamen 147
　wills 119
Ireland CMC Genealogy
　Record Project 77
IrelandGenWeb 110
Irish Ancestors 11, 17, 110, 119,
　242
Irish Famine 163
Irish Genealogy Toolkit 11
Irish immgration 125
Irish language 274
Irish Origins 124
Irish Times 188
Irish War Memorials Project
　156
Irvine, Sherry 112, 119
Isle of Man 77
ISPs 308, 335, 339, 340

Jaunay, Graham 210
Java 55, 58, 351
JavaGED 351
JavaScript 58
Jewish 125, 171–73
Jewish Chronicle 188
Jewish Historical Society of
　England 171
Jewish Telegraph 172
JewishGen 172
journals 363–65
JPG image format 54, 353

Kent 174, 251
Kidon Media-link 184
Kinship Archivist 336

Lambeth Palace Library 138
land ownership 122–23
land tax 120
Latin 270, 273–74, 275

Lawrence, Steve 324
Lay Subsidy 122
LDS Church 9, 101, 146, 205,
　216, 223, 335, 372, 386
Legacy (software) 336, 338,
　372
legal profession 137
legal terms 275–76
Leitrim-Roscommon
　Genealogy 97, 124
Lewis, Samuel 250
libraries 1, 169, 192, 232, 281
　see also British Library
　Bodleian Library 205
　Cambridge University
　　Library 205
　Catholic Central Library 111
　Dr Williams's Library 112,
　　113
　Family History Library 21,
　　104, 208
　Guildhall Library 118, 124
　Huguenot Library 173
　Ireland 17
　John Rylands University
　　Library 112
　national 202–3, 258
　National Library of Australia
　　244
　National Library of Ireland
　　124, 203, 230, 258
　National Library of Scotland
　　158, 191, 202, 205, 256, 258
　National Library of Wales
　　16, 121, 127, 202, 205, 250,
　　258, 281
　overseas 208
　picture libraries 284
　Priaulx Library 77
　public 91, 178, 182, 187,
　　203–4
　Quaker 112
　Trades Union Congress
　　Library Collections 141
　Trinity College, Dublin 205
　university 195, 204–5
　University of Edinburgh 256
　Waterford County Library
　　76
　Wellcome Institute 138
Library and Archives Canada
　96, 236
Library Ireland 178, 242
links 342
Linux 345
list servers 293, 296, 298
listserv 296
Live Search 312, 314, 327
Liverpool Museums 170
livery companies 131, 282
Lloyd's Register of British and

Foreign Shipping 148
Local Heritage Initiative 262
local history 261–64
  societies 263
Local History Magazine 261,
  263, 363, 365
locating people 232–36
London 112, 114, 117, 125, 130,
  131, 168, 171, 243, 281
  cemeteries 113
  maps 253–55
London & North Western
  Railway Society 134
London Ancestor, The 249,
  252, 257
London Gazette 143
London Metropolitan
  Archives 168, 281
London School of Economics
  (LSE) 255
longevity of online resources
  387–88
Look4them 236
lookups 191, 377–78
Lord Lyon King of Arms 230
LostCousins 221, 222
lurking 309
Lynch , Daniel M. 332

magazines 363–65
  on-line 366–67
MAGIC (Multi-Agency
  Geographic Information for
  the Countryside) 245, 252
mailing lists 4, 12, 20, 100, 114,
  127, 133, 138, 139, 144, 145, 151,
  160, 162, 166, 167, 171, 172,
  173, 174, 191, 213, 226, 229,
  230, 244, 263, 264, 267, 286,
  288, 293–302, 357, 366, 367,
  376, 385
  archives 234, 295–96, 309,
    333
  county 19, 308
  digests 299
  joining 296–98
Manis, Cliff 219
Manorial Documents Register
  199
Manorial Society of Great
  Britain 276
Map My Ancestors 259
Map of London Poverty 255
mapping
  interactive 258–59
maps 245–58
  collections 257
  counties 243
  dealers 250
  finding 258
  historical 248–57

Ireland 257
local collections 251–52
London 253–55
parishes 252–53
satellite 247
Scotland 255–56
Scottish clans 230
tithe 121
MapYourAncestors 258
MARINERS mailing list 145
markup 341
Master Genealogist, The 337
Mayflower 163, 229
measurements 276
Measuring Worth 277
medals 152–53, 153
medical profession 137–38
medical terms 276
Medieval English Genealogy
  123, 261, 273
medieval terms 277
Medway CityArk 107
merchant navy 144–48
message boards 214, 263,
  303–6
MetaCrawler 330
meta-search engines 329–30
Methodist Archives and
  Research Centre 112
Michael (Multicultural
  Inventory of Cultural
  Heritage in Europe) 194
microfiche 389
microfilm 1, 5, 81, 110, 146, 167,
  207, 208, 389
Microsoft Excel 349
Microsoft Outlook 369
Microsoft Publisher 345
Microsoft Word 321
Middle East 24
migration 158–74, 234–36
Migrations Museum Network
  159
military 286
Ministry of Defence 142
missing persons 236
missionaries 139
Mitchell Library, Glasgow 282
Mitchell, Brian 111
Mitosearch 226
Modern British Surnames 269
Modern Records Centre
  (University of Warwick) 130
money, value of 277–78
monumental inscriptions
  113–14
Morgan, George C. 371
MOTCO 255
Moving Here 11, 158
Multimap 245, 247, 263
multimedia files 321

Mundus 139
Murphy, Sean 75
museums 264
  Archives & Museum of
    Black Heritage 169
  immigration 159
  Imperial War Museum 143
  maritime 145
  Museum of London 281
  National Army Museum 151
  National Maritime Museum
    145
  overseas 208
  RAF 152
MyHeritage 218
MySQL 351
MyTrees Online 338

names 266–70
  searching for 318
NameX 268
naming patterns 270
National Archives 7, 16, 29, 31,
  38, 45, 51, 80, 88, 91, 142,
  196–99, 331, 366, 370, 383
  and passim
  bookshop 373
  catalogue 81, 113, 149,
    198–99
  events 362
  research guides **196**
National Archives and
  Records Administration
  (USA) 162–64
National Archives of Australia
  165, 236
National Archives of Canada
  164
National Archives of Ireland
  17, 96, 98, 109–10, 164, **202**,
  241, 377
National Archives of Scotland
  16, 42, 120, 126, 199–200
National Archivist xiv
National Burial Index 108
National Farm Surveys of
  England and Wales 123
National Genealogical Society
  (USA) 379–80, 379–80
National Institute of Standards
  and Technology (USA) 289
National Monuments Record
  279, 281
National Register of Archives
  112, 140, 193, 195
National Register of Archives
  (NRA) 202
national service 143
National Trust Names 268
Nations' Memorybank 291
naturalization 159

Nature 324
naval records 145–48
Neep, Rod 99, 179
Nelson, Horatio 147
netiquette 306–7
New South Wales 79
New Zealand 164–66
Newgate Calendar 126
news feeds 369
newsgroups 4, 213, 302–3, 357, 374
  charters 306
  history 4
newsletters 302, 366–67
newspapers 184–91
Newspapers Digitisation Project 186
Newsplan 187
Next Generation of Genealogy Sitebuilding 351
nobility 226–29
Nominet 340
North East Midland Photographic Record 283
NortheastBMD 70
NorthernIrelandGenWeb 110
Notepad 344
NoteTab 344
Nvu 347

obituaries 191
occupations 128–34
Ofcom xi
Office for National Statistics (ONS) 270, 278
Ogre, The 123
O'Laughlin, Mike 371
Old Bailey Proceedings 32, 125, 160, 386
OLD-ENGLISH mailing list 271, 275
Old-maps 248, 263
Olive ActivePaper Archive 185
Olive Tree Genealogy 129, 173
Olson, Margaret J. 4, 374
OneGreatFamily 219
one-name studies 3, 209, 211
Online Names Directories 210
Online Parish Clerks 262
Open Content Alliance 176
Open Directory 27, 159, 169, 173
Open Library 176
OpenOffice.org 345
OpenStreetMap 247
optical character recognition 34, 66
OR search 314
Ordnance Survey 201, 202, 237, 245, 248, 257
  Ireland 241

Original Record, The 51
Origins 34, 35, 38, 41–42, 42, 55, 57, 82, 84, 85, 108, 117, 118, 119, 130, 146, 265, 268, 366
  census 86
  image quality 93
orphanages 265
Otherdays xiv
Oxford English Dictionary 128, 178

PaintShop Pro 353
Pakistan 169–71
palaeography 7, 271–72
Pallot's Indexes 108
Parish Chest 373
Parish Finder 240
parish registers 7, 28, 99–114, 208
  Ireland 109–10
  Scotland 109
Parker, James 231
Parliament 168
passenger lists 42, 161–62, 163, 165
PastPix 284
PastScape 281
Pathways to the Past 146
Paton, Chris 368
paying for records 30
payment systems 38–39, 375
PayPal 375
pay-per-view 38, 39, 42, 43, 46, 58, 73
PDAs 372
Pedigree Resource File 101, 216
pedigrees 2, 215–24, 226–29, 334, 335–38, 354, 382
  databases 215–24, 333, 336, 386
peerage 226–29
PERSI (Periodical Source Index) 365
Personal Ancestral File 224, 335, 336, 348, 372
Pharos 363
photographers 281, 285–86
photographs 151, 155, 279–92, 334
  aerial 247
  dating 9
  dating and restoration 287–89
  digital 289
  portraits 286–87
  relevance 324
  searching for 321–23
  sharing 289–92
  ships 148
PhotoLondon 281, 285
Photoshop Elements 353

PHP 351
PhpGedView 351
phpmyfamily 351
Picture The Past 283
Pictures in Print 251
Picturesheffield 282
plug-ins 59, 251
PNG image format 353
podcasting 370–71
Poll Tax 122
population 81
Port gateway 145
portals 15, 310, **311**
PortCities 160, 167, 262
postcards 285
Powell, Kimberley 61, 368
Powys Heritage Online 262, 265
Prerogative Court of Canterbury 117
prisoners 126, 286
prisons 125–27, 127, 265
privacy 60, 220, 223, 383–85
Probate Service 116
professions 134–40
Project Gutenberg 177
property records 120–24, 121–22, 275
Public Record Office of Northern Ireland (PRONI) 16, 96, 98, 110, 119, 120, 124, **200–201**, 242

QinetiQ xiv, 29, 80
Quakers 163
QuarkXPress 345
queries, genealogical 12, 18, 21, 25, 306
QuickTime 59

Raglan, Robert 371
Randell, Brian 18, 181, 253
Raymond, Stuart 374
record offices 283
redirection service 340
regiments 78, 149
Register Offices 70–71
Registrar General (Ireland) 74
registration districts 70–71, 239
  Ireland 75
  Scotland 72
regnal years 272
relationships 14
Relatively Yours 336
relevance 324
researchers, professional 376–77
Retail Price Index 278
Returns of Owners of Land 122–23

Reunion 336
Roger Vaughan Picture
   Library 286, 288
Roll of Honour 157
Roman numerals 276
Romani people 173
Roots Surname List (RSL) 212
Roots Television 225, 370
RootsChat 304, 377
RootsForum 4
ROOTS-L 4, 212, 293
RootsMagic 337
RootsUK 38, 48, 53, 57, 84, 85,
   86
RootsWeb 4, 14, 62, 134, 173,
   191, 212–13, 213, 214, 216, 223,
   226, 230, 293, 295, 297, 300,
   305, 308, 340
   User-Submitted Databases
   110
Roque, John 253
Rossbret 127, 265
Royal Air Force 151–52
Royal College of Nursing 132
royal family 227
Royal Historical Society 260
Royal Institute of Chartered
   Surveyors 132
Royal Marines 144
Royal Navy 144–48
royalty 226–29
RSS 370
RTF file format 300

S&N Genealogy Supplies 47,
   84, 373
saints' days 272
Sanders, Bob 146, 147
satellite maps 247
scanning 288, 382
schools 265
   photographs 286
Scotland 9, 11, 42–44,
   199–200, 261
   archives 194
   blogs 368
   civil registration 72–74
   clans 229
   crime and punishment 126
   forenames 270
   gazetteers 241
   heraldry 230
   maps 255–56
   Nonconformity 112
   parish registers 109
   photographs 284
   social history 265
   wills 118
Scotland BDM Exchange 78
Scotland Online 42, 88
ScotlandsPeople 11, 28, 29, 38,

39, 42–44, 51, 54, 57, 59, 73,
   82, 84, 85, 87, 107, 109, 118,
   230, 364, 366, 385
   image quality 93
Scots Abroad 158
Scots at War 143, 150
Scots language 274
Scotsman 188
Scottish Archive Network
   (SCAN) 11, 194, 200, 271,
   276, 278
Scottish Association of Family
   History Societies 109, 361
Scottish Emigration Database
   161
Scottish Military Historical
   Society 151
Scottish National Death and
   Burial Index 109
Scottish Strays Marriage Index
   109
ScottishDocuments 42
seamen 144–48
Search Engine Showdown 331
Search Engine Watch 332
search engines 12, 15, 181, 234,
   310–32, 334, 356, 386
   choosing 326–29
   evaluation 331
   genealogy 330
   index size 326
   meta-search 329–30
   quality of indexing 386
   ranking 327–28
searchbots 330
searching 310–32
   domains 323–24
   files 321
   limitations 324–25
   photographs 321–23
   techniques 313–21
   tutorials 331–32
secure payments 374–75
security, online 384
shareware 348, 371
Shea, Virginia 306, 393
Sheffield Local Studies Library
   282
ships 148, 161
Shockwave 59
shops, online 38, 39, 58, 361,
   373–74
Siemens 72
slave trade 167, 168
Snow, John 254
social history 264–66
social networking 5, 234
   photo sharing 289–92
Society of Genealogists (SoG)
   xi, 8, 12, 41, 42, 57, 72, 91, 132,
   135, 209, 230, 331, 360, 361,

362, 364, 373, 376
   events 361
   library 208
   surnames 212
software
   archives 330, 355
   databases 349
   desktop publishing 345
   genealogy 335, 366, 371–73
   searchbots 330
   spreadsheets 349
   text editors 343–44
   web publishing 343–49
Soundex 268
South Africa 78
Southall, Humphrey 387
Spartacus Educational 111, 265
Speed, John 250
spelling errors 325
staff records 140–41
Stanford, Edward 255
Stanier, Alan 278
Statistical Accounts of Scotland
   261
Stepping Stones xiv
Stockdill, Roy 7
stop words 318
Stow, W. 254
Stratford-Devai, Fawne 104,
   146, 148
Streetmap 245
streets 245, 254
Stringer, Phil 18
StudyAncestors 9
subscription services 38
Sun Fire Office 124
surname interests 3, 167, 172,
   173, 209–15, 331, 386
surname lists 19, 20, 210–11,
   333
surnames 23, 266–69
   matching 268
   variants 267
Sussex 251
Sussex Record Society 122

TalkingScot 81, 305
tax records 199
taxation records 277
Technical Advisory Services
   for Images 323
telephone directories 232
telephone numbers 232
terminology 275–77
   genealogy 13–14
   heraldry 231
   legal 275–76
   measurements 276
   medical 276
   medieval 277
   occupations 128–29

Scottish 274
trade 129
Territorial Army 149
text editors 343–44
text files 349
TextPad 344
The Genealogist xiv, 36, 47, 53,
57, 65, 78, 84, 85, 108, 112, 147,
149, 182
census 86
image quality 93
index quality 95
Thesaurus of British Surnames
268
Thumbshots 328
TIFF image format 54
Times, The 188, 190
Tippey, David 179
tithe records 120, 121
Tithe Survey of England and
Wales 121
titles 228
top-posting 307
towns 242
Townsend, John 374
trade unions 141
Trafalgar 147
transcriptions 1, 32–38, 334
accuracy of 33, 95, 380
copyright of 383
transportation 164, 202
TribalPages 338
Tripod 340, 348
Tucows 330, 347, 355
tutorials
genealogy 6–12
searching 331–32
TWR Computing 373

UK BDM Exchange 77
UK Church directory 100
UK Genealogy 123
UKBMD 68–70
Ulster Covenant and
Declaration 201
Ulster Historical Foundation
50, 110
Ultimate Family Tree 337
UNESCO Archives Portal 208
uniforms 151
universities 135, 363 see also
libraries
Aberystwyth 228
Cambridge 136

Central Lancashire 363
Dundee 363
Glasgow 74, 157
Leicester 179, 271, 276
London 205
Open University 129, 288
Oxford 136
Portsmouth 121, 251
Trinity College, Dublin 136
UCLA 254
Warwick 130
UntoldLondon 160
URLs xi–xii, 321, 340
USA 11, 25, 79, 162–64

Veale, Kylie 369
Victoria County History 261
Victorian Web 264
ViewFinder 280
Vital Records Index 102
volunteer projects 113

Wales 9
seamen 148
Wales on the Web 203
War Graves Photographic
Project 155
war memorials 156–57
wars 143–44
Watkins, Hugh 369
Waybackmachine 150, 277, 388
web
history of 3–5
size of 310
Web 2.0 5
web browsers 341, 353
compatibility 59
problems 57–59
web hosting 339, 351
web pages
definition 341–43
uploading 355
web publishing 333–59
software 343–49
Web Publishing for Genealogy
359
web servers 58, 339, 353
web space 339–41
WebGED Progenitor 351
websites
definition 339
design 352–55
dynamic 350–52
family 338

links 357
personal 23, 215, 284, **333–59**
publicising 356–58, 366
stability of xii
Wellcome Institute 138
Welsh
in Patagonia 164
Welsh Genealogies 228
Welsh language 274
West Sussex Record Office
282
Westminster City Archives
281
Who Do You Think You Are?
8, 364
Who Do You Think You Are?
Live 362, 370
Wikimedia Commons 291
Wikipedia 11, 136, 144, 150,
153, 174, 179, 228, 229, 230,
244, 267, 291, 307, 369, 392
WikiTree 218
wills 32, 116–20
Ireland 119, 201
Scotland 118
Wilson, Richard S. 359, 393
Wiltshire Wills 118
Win-Family 337
word processors 344
workhouses 83, 265
World Families Network 225
World Tree 217
World Vital Records 50
World Wide Web Consortium
(W3C) 343
WorldConnect 216, 340
WorldPay 375
Wright, Andrew 271
WS-FTP 355
WYSIWYG 345

XML 386

Yahoo 23, **26–27**, 233, 312,
340, 374
GeoCities 348
Groups 229, 264, 288, 294,
296, 297, 298, 300, 304, 308
Search 312, 314, 316, 327
Ybase 226
York 117
Your Family Tree 288, 364
Your Maps Online 250
YouTube 5, 371